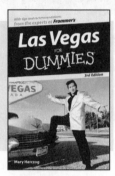
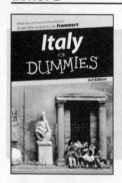

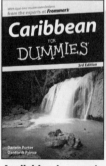
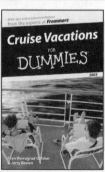

Washington D.C. For Dummies, 3rd Edition

The Metrorail System

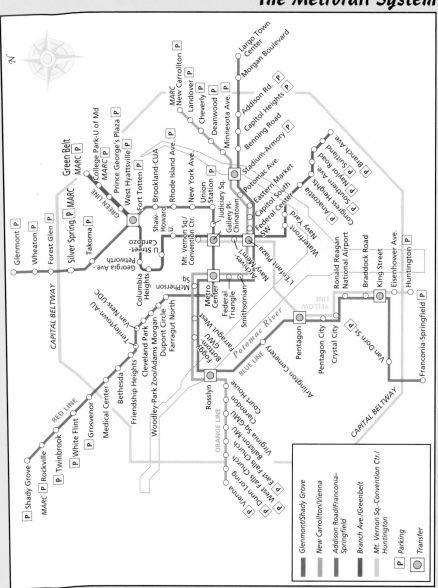

Metro Stops for Washington, D.C.'s Top Attractions

Attraction	Metro Stop
Air and Space Museum	L'Enfant Plaza
Arena Stage	Waterfront
Arlington Cemetery	Arlington Cemetery
Bureau of Engraving & Printing	Smithsonian
Capitol Building	Capitol South
Capitol Children's Museum	Union Station
Convention Center (Old)	Metro Center
Convention Center (New)	Mount Vernon Sq-7th
Corcoran Gallery	Farragut West
Discovery Theatre	Smithsonian
Federal Bureau of Investigation	Archives
Ford's Theatre	Metro Center
Freer Gallery	Smithsonian
Hirshhorn Museum	L'Enfant Plaza
Holocaust Museum	Smithsonian
House Where Lincoln Died	Metro Center
Iwo Jima Memorial	Arlington Cemetery
Kennedy Center	Foggy Bottom-GWU
Korean War Memorial	Foggy Bottom-GWU
Library of Congress	Capitol South
Lincoln Memorial	Foggy Bottom-GWU
Mazza Gallerie/Chevy Chase Pavillion/Chevy Chase	Friendship Heights
MCI Center	Gallery Pl-Chinatown
Nat'l Aquarium	Federal Triangle
Nat'l Archives	Archives-Navy Mem'l
Nat'l Gallery of Art	Archives-Navy Mem'l
Nat'l Geographic Society	Farragut North
Nat'l Museum of African Art	Smithsonian
Nat'l Museum of Natural History	Smithsonian
Nat'l Museum of Women in Arts	Metro Center
Nat'l Postal Museum	Union Station
Nat'l Theater	Metro Center
Nat'l Zoo	Cleveland Park
Pavillion at the Old Post Office	Federal Triangle
Pentagon	Pentagon
Phillips Gallery	Dupont Circle
Ronald Reagan Nat'l Airport	Nat'l Airport
Renwick Gallery	Farragut West
Sackler Gallery	Smithsonian
Shakespeare Theater	Archives Navy Mem'l
Shops at Union Station	Union Station
Smithsonian Castle	Smithsonian
Supreme Court	Capitol South
Textile Museum	Dupont Circle
Vietnam Veterans Memorial	Foggy Bottom-GWU
Warner Theater	Metro Center
Washington Monument	Smithsonian
White House	McPherson Square
White House Visitor Center	Federal Triangle
Woodrow Wilson House	Dupont Circle

Legend:
- RED LINE
- ORANGE LINE
- BLUE LINE
- GREEN LINE
- YELLOW LINE

Washington, D.C.
FOR
DUMMIES®
3RD EDITION

by Tom Price

WILEY

Wiley Publishing, Inc.

Washington, D.C. For Dummies, 3rd Edition

Published by
Wiley Publishing, Inc.
111 River St.
Hoboken, NJ 07030-5774
www.wiley.com

For general information on our other products and services, please contact our Customer Care Department within the U.S. at 800-762-2974, outside the U.S. at 317-572-3993, or fax 317-572-4002.

For technical support, please visit www.wiley.com/techsupport.

Wiley also publishes its books in a variety of electronic formats. Some content that appears in print may not be available in electronic books.

Library of Congress Control Number: 2005923234

ISBN-13: 978-0-7645-7671-3

ISBN-10: 0-7645-7671-2

Manufactured in the United States of America

10 9 8 7 6 5 4 3 2 1

3B/QT/QV/QV/IN

WILEY

About the Author

Tom Price has lived in and written about Washington for more than two decades. As a political journalist and a parent of a college-aged Washington native, Tom knows the ins and outs of both official Washington and the kid-friendly landscape. From 1982 through 1995, Tom was a correspondent in the Cox Newspapers Washington Bureau. Since then, he has been a freelance writer whose work has appeared in books, magazines, and newspapers and on Internet sites. He is the author of *Washington, D.C. For Dummies,* 2nd Edition and *Frommer's Irreverent Guide to Washington, D.C.,* 5th Edition. With his wife, Susan Crites Price, Tom is coauthor of *The Working Parents Help Book: Practical Advice for Dealing with the Day-to-Day Challenges of Kids and Careers,* which won a Parents' Choice Award, was a Scholastic Book Club selection, and has been featured by "Today" and "Oprah." Previously, Tom, a Pittsburgh native, reported for newspapers in Pennsylvania and Ohio.

Dedication

For Susan and Julie, who make me happy and proud.

Author's Acknowledgments

First, I want to thank Elise Ford, an accomplished travel writer who brought me to Frommer's in the first place and has provided invaluable guidance ever since. I also want to thank my editors, Kathleen Warnock and Stephen Bassman; my mother, Anna Mae Price; my daughter Julie, who helped in the research; and, of course, Susan, who is always my best and most important editor.

Publisher's Acknowledgments

We're proud of this book; please send us your comments through our Dummies online registration form located at www.dummies.com/register/.

Some of the people who helped bring this book to market include the following:

Editorial

Editors: Stephen Bassman, Development Editor; Kelly Ewing, Project Editor

Cartographer: Roberta Stockwell

Editorial Manager: Michelle Hacker

Editorial Supervisor: Carmen Krikorian

Senior Photo Editor: Richard Fox

Front cover photo: Lincoln Memorial, © Shaun Egan, Getty Images.

Back cover photos: Washington Monument, © Joseph Sohm; Visions of America/Corbis

Cartoons: Rich Tennant www.the5thwave.com

Composition Services

Project Coordinator: Michael Kruzil

Layout and Graphics: Joyce Haughey, Stephanie D. Jumper, Lynsey Osborn, Heather Ryan, Melanee Prendergast, Julie Trippetti

Proofreaders: David Faust, Leeann Harney, Jessica Kramer, Joe Niesen, TECHBOOKS Production Services

Indexer: TECHBOOKS Production Services

Publishing and Editorial for Consumer Dummies

Diane Graves Steele, Vice President and Publisher, Consumer Dummies

Joyce Pepple, Acquisitions Director, Consumer Dummies

Kristin A. Cocks, Product Development Director, Consumer Dummies

Michael Spring, Vice President and Publisher, Travel

Kelly Regan, Editorial Director, Travel

Publishing for Technology Dummies

Andy Cummings, Vice President and Publisher, Dummies Technology/General User

Composition Services

Gerry Fahey, Vice President of Production Services

Debbie Stailey, Director of Composition Services

Contents at a Glance

Maps at a Glance

Table of Contents

Introduction

• •

*W*hen you visit Washington, D.C., you're visiting the capital of the world — a city with more power than any other on the planet, and one filled with world-class tourist attractions as well.

It wasn't always this way. Almost nothing stood on the sites of the White House, Capitol, and other current U.S. government buildings when George Washington selected the spot to become the new nation's capital city in 1791, primarily because of its central location between the already quarrelling North and South. As recently as the 1960s, critics described Washington as a cultural backwater, a sleepy Southern town, a place without decent restaurants where the sidewalks were rolled up at dusk.

Washington has long had its shrines to freedom and its halls of government — the Washington Monument, Lincoln Memorial, Library of Congress, and the other government companions to the White House and Capitol. But the city now also has many fine restaurants and hotels, museums, galleries, and performing arts organizations.

Along with New York, Washington was a target of the terrorist attacks of September 11, 2001. American Airlines Flight 77 was flown into the Pentagon, across the Potomac River from D.C. in Northern Virginia. United Airlines Flight 93, which crashed in rural Pennsylvania, was believed to have been destined for the White House or the Capitol. As I write this book, tours of the Pentagon are given only to select groups, security has been ratcheted up everywhere, and ugly concrete barriers block traffic and mar beautiful views throughout the city. But, like New Yorkers, Washingtonians have been determined to resume normal activities, which include playing host to many visitors. There is little that you could have done here on September 10, 2001, that you can't do today.

I've loved Washington since long before I moved here. For a journalist who focuses on politics and government, there's no better place to be. Having lived in D.C. for more than 20 years now, I've come to know it as deeply as I love it. I'm thrilled to be able to share that knowledge with you.

About This Book

You probably picked this book because you're too busy to wade through a sea of information or you aren't interested in spending weeks planning a five-day trip. Perhaps you're a first-time visitor to Washington, D.C.,

---

Dummies Post-it® Flags

As you're reading this book, you'll find information that you'll want to reference as you plan or enjoy your trip — whether it be a new hotel, a must-see attraction, or a must-try walking tour. Mark these pages with the handy Post-it® Flags included in this book to help make your trip planning easier!

---

and you don't know where to begin. Or maybe you're frustrated by all the detail in conventional guidebooks. (You know what I mean: You want to find out when a museum opens, and the author tells you how to *build* one.) Armed with *Washington, D.C. For Dummies,* 3rd Edition, you'll feel like a capital insider in no time.

Think of this as a reference book. You can read it from cover to cover if you like (I'll be flattered!), but more likely you'll want to dip into the chapters or sections that are the most interesting or important to you at a particular moment. The Table of Contents and Index allow you to find what you need when you need it — hotels, restaurants, sights, stores, nightspots, and more.

This book doesn't overwhelm you with choices, but it does give you enough information to pick what's best for you. When money is involved, you'll find options at various price levels.

Please note that travel information is subject to change at any time — and this is especially true of prices. I therefore suggest that you write or call ahead for confirmation when making your travel plans. The authors, editors, and publisher cannot be held responsible for the experiences of readers while traveling. Your safety is important to us, however, so we encourage you to stay alert and be aware of your surroundings. Keep a close eye on cameras, purses, and wallets, all favorite targets of thieves and pickpockets.

I've offered lots of D.C. travel tips to visiting friends and family over the last two decades, and that's exactly what I'm offering you. When you've finished your visit and are heading back home, I expect you'll have acquired some of the affection that I feel for this town and that you'll want to come back.

Conventions Used in This Book

To help you get information quickly, I use some abbreviations and symbols throughout this book. Washington, D.C., is referred to as "Washington," "D.C.," or "the District." (Its formal name is "Washington, District of Columbia.")

Hotels and restaurants are listed alphabetically, with prices and evaluations.

Credit cards accepted are listed this way:

> AE: American Express
>
> DC: Diners Club
>
> DISC: Discover
>
> MC: MasterCard
>
> V: Visa

The dollar signs that accompany the hotel and restaurant reviews give you a sense of their price ranges, as shown in the following table. For a hotel, the dollar signs represent the average of the lowest and highest undiscounted rate for a double-occupancy room for one night during high season. For each restaurant, I've averaged the highest and lowest prices for an appetizer or salad, main course, and dessert at dinner per person, not including taxes and tips.

Cost	*Hotel*	*Restaurant (Main Courses)*
$	Less than $125	Less than $15
$$	$125–$200	$15–$25
$$$	$201–$300	$26–$40
$$$$	$301–$400	$41–$50
$$$$$	More than $400	More than $50

In the individual reviews, I give more specific information about costs. I can't, of course, tell you about special discounts that hotels and restaurants often offer. And prices, as you know, are subject to change, so it's a good idea to call ahead to confirm hours and prices and to ask about special offers and discounts when you make your reservations.

You'll find two kinds of listings in the hotel section — first, reviews of the best in each price range and then a listing of some runners-up. Don't be shy about picking from the second list if you're unable to get a room at one of the best. The runners-up also are fine places to spend the night.

For hotels, restaurants, and attractions that are plotted on a map, a page reference is provided in the listing information. If a hotel, restaurant or attraction is outside the city limits or in an out-of-the-way area, it may not be mapped.

Foolish Assumptions

I've written this book for both the frequent flier and the inexperienced traveler. The assumptions I've made about both (and, truthfully, I hope they're not foolish!) are that:

✔ You may be an inexperienced traveler who is trying to determine whether or not to visit Washington, or you may be looking for help in deciding when and how to make the trip.

✔ You may be an experienced traveler, but you don't want to spend much time planning your trip, or you don't have much time to spend in the city once you arrive. You want expert advice on how to get the most out of your time and how to enjoy a hassle-free visit.

✔ You're not looking for a book that provides every piece of information available about Washington sights, or one that lists every hotel and restaurant in the city. Instead, you want a book that focuses on the best places to eat and sleep in all price ranges, and the best ways to enjoy your days here.

If you fit any of these criteria, *Washington, D.C. For Dummies,* 3rd Edition is the book you're looking for.

How This Book Is Organized

The Table of Contents at a Glance and complete Table of Contents at the front of this book are useful tools for finding information quickly. At the back of the book is an Appendix, which lists helpful service information and phone numbers, and the index, the most useful tool for navigating the book. The heart of *Washington, D.C. For Dummies,* 3rd Edition, is divided into six parts. Within each part are chapters that delve into specifics. Each chapter is written so that you don't have to read what comes before or after it. When necessary, I refer you to other sections of the book for more information.

Part I: Introducing Washington, D.C.

Here's an overview of Washington and a taste of what you can expect to encounter when you visit. I've compiled a brief list of the best of everything D.C. has to offer, as well as information about the weather, seasons, and special events, to help you decide when you'd like to visit.

Part II: Planning Your Trip to Washington, D.C.

What do things cost in Washington? What's the best way to get here? This part is where I tell you what you need to know to plan your visit successfully. I also include information for travelers with special needs or interests, such as families with kids, people with disabilities, seniors, and gay and lesbian visitors.

Part III: Settling into Washington, D.C.

Okay, here's where I really get into the good stuff. Meet D.C.'s best hotels and restaurants in all price categories. Find out how to get around and how to get along. Come with me through the city's most interesting neighborhoods. Discover the wonders of the underground Metrorail system.

Part IV: Exploring Washington, D.C.

The sights, of course, are why you're coming. In Part IV, I tell you what you want to know about the top sights (and some particularly interesting lesser known attractions), and give you the skinny on tours and shopping. I toss in some itineraries at no extra charge (you're welcome), as well as suggestions for excursions nearby.

Part V: Living It Up After Dark: D.C. Nightlife

This part is where you find out what's going on after the museums close and the government goes to sleep for the night. Washingtonians may be known as workaholics who think "party" must be preceded by "Republican" or "Democrat." But D.C. has a vibrant after-dark scene, from country, rock, and jazz clubs to world-class symphony, dance, opera, and theater.

Part VI: The Part of Tens

Not, as famous as the FBI's Ten Most Wanted list, perhaps, but the *For Dummies* Part of Tens nevertheless is full of cool information. In this part, you find the best places to view the city's breathtaking skyline, as well as places that are worth driving to see — the only time driving is worthwhile in D.C., I may add.

Appendix

At the back of the book is your Quick Concierge, a compendium of handy information you may need while visiting Washington. In it, I include phone numbers and addresses for area hospitals and pharmacies, tips for finding ATMs, information on where to take a broken camera or which radio station plays your music, and other useful tips. Check out this Appendix when searching for answers to the little questions that may come up as you travel.

Icons Used in This Book

You find the following icons (little pictures) scattered throughout the margins of this guide. They call your attention to particular kinds of information.

Cut your costs with these money-saving suggestions or alerts to great deals.

 Best of the Best highlights the best the destination has to offer in all categories — hotels, restaurants, attractions, activities, shopping, and nightlife.

 The Capitol Dome highlights events and attractions that are unique to D.C.

 This worried fellow warns of tourist traps, rip-offs, hazards, activities that aren't worth your time, and other pitfalls.

 These icons call your attention to hotels, restaurants, and attractions that are especially good for children.

 This icon draws your attention to details or plans that you should take care of before you leave home.

 This bull's-eye alerts you to facts, hints, and insider information that can help you make the best use of your time.

Where to Go from Here

Now that you know what to expect from this book, you can start to plan your visit — or, if you're already in D.C., you can decide what to do right now. See and do all you can. And have fun. Your tax dollars help to pay for much of what you'll encounter here, so you may as well get your money's worth.

Part I

Introducing Washington, D.C.

The 5th Wave   By Rich Tennant

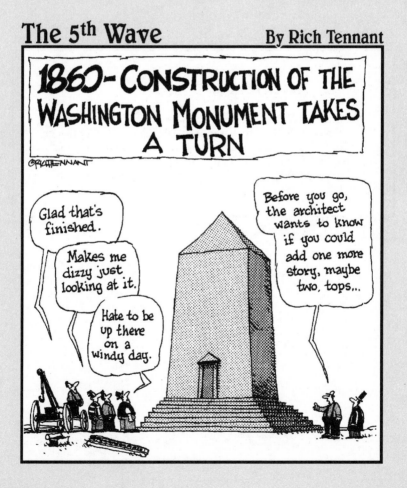

In this part . . .

In this part, I take a look at D.C. in a nutshell. You get a quick tour of the top attractions, places to eat, and places to stay. I also include some historical information, which is a big part of D.C.'s lure, and I tell you about the seasons and provide a calendar of annual events to help you decide when you'd like to visit.

Chapter 1

Discovering the Best of Washington, D.C.

. . . .

In This Chapter

▶ Discovering the best restaurants and hotels
▶ Enjoying the best attractions
▶ Taking advantage of the best free shows
▶ Finding the best stuff for kids

. . . .

*W*ashington, D.C. is much more than just the home of the United States government. D.C. offers hotel choices that range from the ultra-ritzy to the ultra-cheap; restaurants that feature many of the world's ethnic cuisines; and rich cultural, historical, scientific, and educational museums and monuments.

One of Washington's best selling points is that many of these top attractions are free. Unlike in London, Paris, Rome, or other major capitals, you don't have to open your wallet before you can open the doors to most of the popular museums, galleries, and other sights. You don't even have to open doors to enjoy another pleasant sight — Washington's impressive landscape.

The car-free National Mall — lawns, gardens, ponds, and walkways — stretches from the Lincoln Memorial to the Capitol and is bordered by many of the Smithsonian's facilities. The cherry trees along the tidal basin are spectacular in the spring.

Whether you're interested in touring the brick and cobblestone streets of Georgetown or enjoying the Latin-influenced nightlife in Adams-Morgan, this chapter points you to the best Washington, D.C. has to offer.

 You can find the details on each location or activity later in this guide. Throughout the book, look for the "Best of the Best" icon to highlight our picks.

The Best Hotels

For more information on the hotels listed, see Chapter 9.

- ✔ **Best power palaces:** If you've got money, connections or both — or just want to act like you do — try staying at one of these spots where lobbyists and government officials hang their hats, or just hang out. You can't beat the location of the opulent **Willard Inter-Continental**, which can keep both the White House and D.C.'s city hall in its sights. That's why the powerful and those who seek to influence them have been staying on this site since the middle of the 19th century. Across Lafayette Square from the White House, the **Hay-Adams** is another favorite among the rich and the politically connected. Less expensive, but close to the Congressional action, the **Capitol Hill Suites** counts U.S. representatives among its long-term residents. Short-term tourist guests get dining privileges at the Republican Party's nearby Capitol Hill Club.

- ✔ **Best guest houses and charming hotels:** Amidst all of Washington's wealth and pretensions, some accommodations become distinct by daring to be true to themselves. The **D.C. Guest House** is a 19th-century mansion, recently renovated to the eclectic personal tastes of its owners, who lavish warm attention on their guests. Also eclectic — and eccentric — and not so recently refurbished, the **Tabard Inn** exudes character and charm in three adjacent town houses on a tree-lined street near Dupont Circle. Exuding upscale character and charm, **The Jefferson** is quiet and elegant and keeps its guests coming back for its personalized service.

- ✔ **Best suites:** Suites with cooking facilities — and sometimes separate sleeping quarters — are wonderful for families looking to save money on meals and to enjoy a little privacy. You get lots of choices at **Georgetown Suites**, from a one-room studio to more luxurious townhouse and penthouse accommodations. **One Washington Circle** also offers a variety of floor plans, from "guest quarters" with sleeping and sitting areas in one large room to "grande staterooms" with separate bedroom, dining area, living area, and bath and a half. Most have kitchens and balconies. Business travelers and families are attracted to **The River Inn** because of spacious studios, large one-bedroom suites, and occasional super-duper deals that drop the $300-plus rack rates to less than a C note.

- ✔ **Best hotels with international appeal:** Because it stands not far from the State Department, World Bank, Kennedy Center, and George Washington University, the **State Plaza** attracts diplomats and other international travelers bound for those diplomatic, artistic and educational venues. The location of Irish-owned **Jurys Normandy Inn** — near diplomatic facilities in the exclusive Kalorama neighborhood — makes it a popular spot for diplomats and other international visitors as well. The French own the **Sofitel Lafayette Square** and are quite proud of serving up *art de vivre* — "the art of French living" — in the hotel's restaurant food, bar drinks, gift shop gifts, room decor, and even the staff's uniforms.

✔ **Best budget digs:** Youthful idealists in Washington on a shoestring and other budget-minded visitors find **Hostelling International** to be a simple but adequate place to spend the night for rock-bottom prices in dormitory-style rooms. For families and cost-conscious touring groups, the centrally located **Hotel Harrington** provides large rooms and suites starting at $95. The low-cost **Red Roof Inn** chain operates an urban version of its roadside motels near the MCI Center, Convention Center, Chinatown, and many attractions of the fast-growing Penn Quarter entertainment and arts neighborhood.

The Best Restaurants

For more information on the restaurants listed here, see Chapter 10.

✔ **Best power palaces:** So you want to watch James Carville and Mary Matalin duke it out over dinner? Grab a table at the **Palm,** where famous faces feast on steak and lobster. Several influential lobbyists own the **Caucus Room,** and others dine there. Senators and Supreme Court justices hang out at **The Monocle,** while other senators and lobbyists breakfast, lunch, and dinner at **La Colline** — unless they're boycotting everything French.

✔ **Best for big spenders:** Pretend you're a member of Congress, for whom (other people's) money is no object, and sample the best Washington food that lots of money can buy. Entrees start above $30 and the tasting menu is $100 at **Le Paradou,** an exquisite contemporary French restaurant that opened in mid-2004. Also exquisite and French (or "French/Californian," as chef Chef Michel Richard terms it) is **Michel Richard's Citronelle,** where fixed-price meals range from $80 to $125 and a seat at the chef's table starts at $250. Chef Roberto Donna's private dining room at **Galileo,** which he calls **Laboratorio,** charges $110 to $125 for the spectacular Italian food and another $70 if you'd like perfectly matched wines.

✔ **Best for fighting the deficit:** In all-American tradition, **Luna Grill & Diner,** offers old-fashioned Blue Plate Specials and New Age Green Plate Specials for vegetarians. **Booeymonger,** a local deli chain, is open from breakfast to late in the city, till not quite so late in the suburbs. Another local chain, **Firehook Bakery,** offers inventive sandwiches on its own breads and pours D.C.'s best coffee, locally roasted Quartermaine.

✔ **Best for debating foreign policy:** It's dreadfully undiplomatic to pick out a handful of best international restaurants from the zillions that do business in this very international town. But, here goes: **Montmartre** really tastes and feels like France, as does **Cafe La Ruche,** for a lot fewer francs. **City Lights of China** offers good Chinese food in attractive surroundings, while the surroundings at **Eat First** are as plain as its name.

✔ **Best for international fare:** You get real Neapolitan pizza at **Pizzeria Paradiso** and **2Amys.** To nibble your way through small plates of various nationalities, try the **Venetian Room** for Italian *sputino,* **Zaytinya** for Mediterranean *meze,* **Jaleo** for Spanish tapas, and **Andale** for Mexican *antojitos.* And, for a fun night out with a group, go sit on the floor and eat with your fingers at Moroccan **Marrakesh.**

✔ **Best for romancing your No. 1 constituent:** At **Coeur de Lion,** you and your sweet can sink into plush seats, gaze into each other's candlelit eyes, be lulled by soft jazz from the adjacent Blue Bar Thursday, Friday, or Saturday night, and finish your meal with the Chocolate Ménage au Trois dessert. In cold weather, reserve the table nearest the fire in **Sea Catch**'s front dining room, where the walls are made of stone and wood paneling and floor-to-ceiling windows overlook the C&O Canal. Fireside tables also beckon in **1789 Restaurant,** which occupies a 19th-century, Federalist-style home in Georgetown. The **Venetian Room,** with its dark, plush decor, is another prime spot for romance.

✔ **Best for pre-voters:** Kids as well as grownups cast ballots for **2Amys** and **Pizzeria Paradiso.** Not only is the food kid-friendly, but these places are cheerful and noisy. The Tex-Mex **Austin Grill**s also are gaily noisy, and — downtown and in the suburbs — gaily decorated. The **Old Ebbitt Grill** draws White House staff and pleases adult palates. But the large menu also includes much of interest to children — burgers and finger-food appetizers, for example. And kids' wandering attention can be directed to the hunting trophies and other odd stuff that's scattered throughout this large restaurant/pub.

The Best Attractions

For more information on the attractions listed here, see Chapter 11.

✔ **Best memorial:** For me, the **Thomas Jefferson Memorial** wins hands-down because of its idyllic setting on the Tidal Basin, its gorgeous views of cherry trees and other Washington landmarks, its suggestion of Tom's home of Monticello, and the inspiring words engraved around the rotunda. It also helps that Jefferson is my favorite Founding Father. The **Abraham Lincoln Memorial** is a close runner-up, however, for similar reasons. The view from the top of the memorial's steps is a breathtaking sweep of the entire National Mall to the Capitol dome, Lincoln's words are engraved on the walls, and this was the site of many historical events, including Martin Luther King, Jr.'s "I Have a Dream" speech.

✔ **Best place for saying "it's about time they built this":** The **National Museum of the American Indian** and the **World War II Memorial** both opened in mid-2004, and both generated controversy. Critics charge that the new museum relies too much on Indian myth and not enough on hard science, and disagreements continue to rage over the monument's size, design, and location on the once-sacrosanct parkland between the Lincoln Memorial and the Washington Monument. (Perhaps the critical scrutiny explains why they didn't build these much needed tributes sooner.) On a less solemn note, it's also about time they built the **Robert F. Kennedy Stadium,** where Major League Baseball is scheduled to resume play in 2005, some 33 years after the national pastime deserted the nation's capital.

✔ **Best places for culture:** The **National Gallery of Art** is one of the world's great art museums, and it keeps getting better. In fall 2004, for example, the gallery set up a permanent display space for photography for the first time. If you prefer art that moves, you'll find world-class performances at the **John F. Kennedy Center for the Performing Arts,** which is home for the National Symphony, Washington Opera, Washington Ballet, Washington Performing Arts Society, and many traveling shows, both classical and popular. See Chapter 15 for more information.

✔ **Best spot to be emotionally moved:** Somewhere there may be someone who was untouched by a visit to the **U.S. Holocaust Memorial Museum,** but I have yet to meet him. More than a reminder of Nazi atrocities, this museum also conducts memorable programs about genocide. At **Arlington National Cemetery,** the endless rows of plain white grave markers tug at your heart, silently proclaiming the sacrifice of America's military men and women. Many famous Americans have more elaborate memorials here, including presidents Kennedy and Taft. Emotions at the **Vietnam Veterans Memorial** flow from the controversial nature of that war and the constant presence of veterans and friends and relatives of the dead, who search out specific names on the black granite wall. The simplicity of young Chinese-American architect Maya Lin's design became a prototype for many later memorials erected around the country.

✓ **Best government building:** The surroundings are a mess now because of construction of an underground visitor center and ugly, stop-gap security barricades, but the **Capitol** remains Washington's preeminent building. The dome is the number-one symbol of American democracy. And the interior is a fascinating mix of the American democratic spirit and ornate old European decoration.

The Best Free Shows

For more information on the performing arts events listed, see Chapter 15.

✓ **Best free classical music:** For the best music ever written, performed by a world-class orchestra, for free, under the stars, you just can't top the **National Symphony**'s free summer concerts at the Carter Barron Amphitheater in Rock Creek Park and on the Capitol's West Lawn.

✓ **Best free play:** You can equal the National Symphony's excellence (see preceding entry) with the best plays ever written, performed by a world-class troupe, for free, under the stars. That would be the **Shakespeare Theatre**'s free summer performances, also at Carter Barron.

✓ **Best free military music:** The Army, Navy, Marine Corps, and Air Force bands present **military concerts,** — where else? — at Carter Barron and outside the Capitol.

✓ **Best free who-knows-what:** In the **Kennedy Center**'s Grand Foyer, the Millennium Stage presents free performances every single day at 6 p.m. Performers range from storytellers to headliners such as Bobby McFerrin or the Pointer Sisters, although most are not well known.

The Best Stuff for Kids

For more information on the attractions listed, see Chapter 11.

✓ **Best animals:** With 2,700 animals on 163 acres of land, the **National Zoological Park** — better known as the National Zoo — can keep kids hopping till they run out of juice. In June 2004, the zoo added Kid's Farm, aimed at children ages 3 to 8, where kids can pet farm animals and help with grooming.

✓ **Best things to touch that you wouldn't think you'd want to touch:** Children squeal with delight and parents feel a bit squeamish at the **National Museum of Natural History**'s insect zoo. Pet a tarantula. Hold a giant hissing cockroach. Crawl around in a model termite mound.

✔ **Best printed products:** You wouldn't think the **National Postal Museum** would be a big hit with the small set. But the little museum's interactive exhibits have made it a children's favorite. Kids also like to tour the **Bureau of Engraving and Printing,** where stamps, currency, government bonds, and White House invitations are made. Part of the reason is the jovial tour guides, whose red ties are decorated with images of dollars.

✔ **Best for history and dessert:** The **National Museum of American History** has hands-on history and science rooms where kids can pretend to be a telegraph operator, cotton picker, or high-wheel bicycle rider. The museum also boasts an old-fashioned ice-cream parlor that really sells ice cream.

✔ **Best flying objects:** Because kids love things that go zoom, the **National Air and Space Museum** is must-see D.C. for families. Luckily for parents, big folks find this place fascinating as well.

Chapter 2

Digging Deeper into Washington, D.C.

*W*ashington, D.C. is a city where knowledge is power, so it helps to arrive knowing some background information (even if you don't intend to run for office). You should know who Pierre L'Enfant is and where Lincoln was assassinated. And if you expect to carry on conversations with local politicos, you should know the different between "pork" and "POTUS."

History 101: The Main Events

It all began, of course, with dinosaurs, then saber tooth tigers, and then human beings who eventually came to be called, because of European ignorance, American Indians. But what is now called Washington didn't really start its journey to becoming the capital of the United States until those Europeans started exploring what they thought of as the New World. Capt. John Smith, of Pocahontas fame, poked around the Potomac River near Washington in 1608, and another group of early European immigrants began to settle along the Anacostia River here in 1622.

Midway through the next century, the river port of George Towne (now Georgetown) was founded, named for King George of England, not the father of the still-unfounded United States. (An Old Stone House built there in 1765 has survived to become modern Washington's oldest building, on bustling M Street.) With George Towne, Maryland, and

Alexandria, Virginia, developing as river ports, the colonies didn't look to this area for anything related to government until the end of the Revolutionary War, when the Continental Congress began casting about for the best place to locate the new nation's capital.

In 1790, the new U.S. Congress, in one of many North-South compromises, authorized President Washington to select a site on the Potomac River, in the northern reaches of the Southern states. Washington, a surveyor by trade, picked the confluence of the Potomac and the Anacostia, a few miles up stream from his home at Mount Vernon, and hired French engineer Pierre L'Enfant to design the city. The District of Columbia, named for Christopher Columbus, was a perfect diamond, 10 miles on each side, straddling the Potomac River, with 69 of its square miles donated by Maryland and the remaining 31 by Virginia. (Virginia reclaimed its land in 1846, making the Potomac Washington's southwestern border.

The federal government finally moved to D.C. in 1800, with the Capitol and the Executive Mansion still unfinished. Fifteen years later, those seminal structures of American democracy had to be rebuilt, after being burned by the British in 1814 during the so-called War of 1812. The refurbishers painted the president's house white, and it's been called the White House ever since.

In the succeeding centuries, Washington has grown with the government it houses and changed with the nation that government leads. During the Civil War, president Lincoln ringed the capital city with forts and insisted on completing the Capitol's dome. As the government expanded to fight the depression, the New Deal's Works Progress Administration hired the unemployed to build the new bureaucracies' headquarters. The Pentagon, the world's largest office building, sprang to life during World War II. Magnificent Union Station was opened during the heyday of railroad travel in 1907, National Airport when commercial aviation was coming into its own in 1941, and Metrorail in 1976 when the Washington region's leaders realized they needed a subway system to move their booming population off the ever-more-congested highways and streets. In this new era of terrorism, on September 11, 2001, hijackers crashed American Airlines Flight 77 into a section of the Pentagon, which was rebuilt and reopened in a year. (See the "Years to remember: A D.C. timeline" sidebar in this section.)

Many visitors don't know this fact, but we D.C. residents don't enjoy the full benefits of U.S. citizenship because we don't live in a state. We have no voting representation in Congress, and Congress can override the actions of our elected mayor and council. We are subject to all the obligations of citizenship, however, including federal taxes and the draft. That's why the slogan on our license plates reads "Taxation Without Representation."

Years to remember: A D.C. timeline

A lot can happen to a city over the course of 400 years. Here are just a few noteworthy events.

1608: Capt. John Smith explores the Potomac River.

1622: Europeans begin to settle along the Anacostia River.

1751: George Towne is founded.

1765: Olde Stone House, now Washington's oldest building, is erected in George Towne.

1790: Confluence of Potomac and Anacostia rivers selected as site for U.S. capital.

1800: Federal government moves to District of Columbia.

1814: British burn Capitol and Executive Mansion during War of 1812.

1817: Restored Executive Mansion painted white, dubbed the White House.

1846: Land south of Potomac returned to Virginia.

1861–65: Washington ringed with forts during Civil War.

1865: Capitol Dome completed. Lincoln assassinated in Ford's Theatre.

1907: Union Station opens.

1941: National Airport opens.

1943: Pentagon completed.

1976: First Metrorail stations open.

2001: Pentagon hit in September 11 terrorist attacks.

2002: Damaged Pentagon section reopens.

2005: New Congress takes office, with Washington residents still on the outside looking in.

Architectural Basics

Washington architecture is a hodge-podge that just gets hodgier and podgier as time runs on. Even though the city's street plan largely follows architect L'Enfant's original diamondlike approach, the buildings that line the streets have been constructed willy-nilly according to the whims of the owners and the tastes of the time.

Much like a medieval cathedral, the **Capitol** — D.C.'s most prominent building — grew over the decades, and each section reflects not only the vision of an architect but the on-site alterations of construction managers as well. The Capitol Dome, perhaps the best-recognized symbol of American self-government, wasn't added until 1865. The West Front terraces were built between 1884 and 1892 and the East Front extension from 1958 to 1962. Now, the East Lawn is a mess, as an underground visitor center is constructed.

You can find a real cathedral, the **Washington National Cathedral,** in the residential Upper Northwest area. (See Chapter 8 for a description of the neighborhood.) Under construction from 1907 to 1990, it was built the old-fashioned way, "stone-on-stone," with no structural steel for support.

The **White House,** designed by Irish architect James Hoban, was modeled after an Irish country home. Columned porticos on the North and South fronts were added later. The **Old Executive Office Building** next door, sporting 900 Doric columns, is a surreal wedding cake in a style dubbed Second Empire. **Arlington House** in Arlington National Cemetery, once the home of Robert E. Lee, is a classic plantation house, built by slaves in Greek Revival style. It's made of brick, covered by cement, which was scored and painted to look like marble and sandstone. **Union Station** is a marvelous Beaux Arts structure, built for the thriving railroad business at the beginning of the 20th century and restored as a bustling transportation, shopping, eating, and entertainment center at the end.

Many government buildings and monuments pay tribute to ancient Rome and Greece, with architects and committees again imposing their own twists on the classical recipes. On a smaller, domestic scale, the residential streets of Georgetown and Capitol Hill are lined with 19th-century town houses and mansions.

The Restaurant Scene

Washington doesn't really have a distinct cuisine, and that's not necessarily a bad thing. Because every community in America is represented in Congress, nearly every cuisine in America makes its way to at least one eating establishment here. The same is true for the cuisines of the world, because nearly every nation sends diplomats, journalists and business people to monitor and try to influence the U.S. government.

To the extent that any dishes can be called local, they've probably been borrowed from Maryland's nearby shore. If they're in season and the waiter assures you that they're good, order up a crab-cake dinner or sandwich. Or engage in the labor-intensive celebration of digging the meat out of hard-shell crabs, an activity usually conducted on paper-covered tables and accompanied by generous quantities of beer. Soft-shell crabs, the same animal caught when it's between hard shells, are easier to eat.

The exception to the borrowed-cuisine rule is the half-smoke — a mild sausage usually served on a hotdog bun. You'll find half-smokes at nearly every sidewalk food cart and in many short-order eateries. The only thing special about this sausage is that it doesn't seem to be sold under that name anyplace else.

For a more detailed look at D.C. food and restaurants, see Chapter 10.

The Local Lingo

What Washington lacks in unique food, it more than makes up for in unique language — the jargon of politics and government. You'll hear it spoken not only when you tour the halls of Congress but when you eavesdrop on conversations in a restaurant, along the sidewalk, or on a Metrorail train.

If you're fluent in this jargon, then you know that a lawmaker doesn't propose a piece of legislation; he *drops a bill.* The heads of the powerful House subcommittees that control spending bills are not chairmen; they're the *college of cardinals.* A *gaggle* is not a gathering of geese but a gathering of reporters around a news source. You could write a book about this stuff. In fact, several people already have. Check out *Hatchet Jobs & Hardball: American Political Slang,* by Grant Barrett (Oxford University Press).

Here are a few definitions of words or phrases you may hear and wonder about as you wander about D.C.

- ✔ **Advance man:** A political operative who prepares an event before the candidate arrives.

- ✔ **Background:** Interviewer-interviewee agreement by which the information imparted can be reported but the source's identity must be kept confidential.

- ✔ **Carpetbagger:** Politician who moves into a new community to seek power.

- ✔ **Dark horse:** Candidate who probably can't win.

- ✔ **Eleventh Commandment:** GOP tradition — often honored in the breach — that Republicans should not speak ill of other Republicans.

- ✔ **Fat cat:** Someone with lots of money.

- ✔ **Gentle lady:** What the gentlemen of the House call their female colleagues because, for some reason, just plain "lady" doesn't suffice.

- ✔ **Gerrymander:** To draw odd-shaped legislative districts in order to benefit the party in power.

- ✔ **Hack:** A low-ranking party worker who does what he's told.

- ✔ **Junket:** A government official's all-expenses-paid trip that has questionable value to government.

- ✔ **Lame duck:** Government official who has been defeated or can't run for re-election.

- ✔ **Off the record:** Information that can't be published.

- ✔ **The other body:** What the House calls the Senate and the Senate calls the house.

- ✔ **Pork:** Legislated benefits for a small group rather than for the national interest.

- ✔ **POTUS:** In acronym-obsessed Washington, the President of the United States.

- ✔ **Red tape:** Bureaucratic rules that slow down action.

- ✔ **SCOTUS:** The Supreme Court of the United States.

- ✔ **Smoke-filled room:** Where politicians cut deals without public scrutiny, and where today smoking probably isn't allowed.

- ✔ **Think tank:** Organization that conducts research and analysis.

- ✔ **Veep:** The vice president.

- ✔ **Waffle:** Not taking a clear stand.

Recommended Television Shows, Movies, and Books

The best fictional treatment of Washington going right now is **"The West Wing"** television show on NBC (with reruns on Bravo). By employing political insiders as consultants — including Bill Clinton Press Secretary Dee Dee Myers — "The West Wing" does a pretty darn good job of accurately portraying life in the **White House.** The program is popular with Washingtonians and has spawned a parlor game of watching for plot twists that probably rise above reality. (My wife Susan hates it when I do that during the show!) Because Martin Sheen's President Jed Bartlet is a liberal Democrat, some liberals I know like to call him "the real president" or "my president" and wish that Sheen — a longtime liberal political activist — would run for real elected office.

Sticking with accurate representation of reality, the best Washington movie to tell it like it is **All the President's Men,** starring Robert Redford and Dustin Hoffman as then-young *The Washington Post* reporters Bob Woodward and Carl Bernstein, who broke the Watergate scandal. This wonderful flick somehow manages to be entertaining while showing how reporters really go about their (often tedious) jobs. A spectacular overhead shot of Woodstein (as the pair was nicknamed) doing research in the **Library of Congress'** Main Reading Room marvelously evokes two little guys tackling an enormous challenge. My favorite slice of dialogue occurs when a big-shot politician issues the quintessentially Washingtonian threat that if Woodward publishes certain information, "our relationship will be over." Woodward ponders for a moment and then replies, "We don't have a relationship."

You can find many good books about Washington and the game of politics, starting with the real Woodward and Bernstein's *All the President's Men* (Simon & Schuster), upon which the movie was based. Their boss, Washington Post Co. publisher, president, and chair Katherine Graham, collected and annotated more than 100 pieces about Washington that were published posthumously as *Katharine Graham's Washington* (Vintage) in 2002. The annotations record the Washington of her lifetime, from 1917 to preterrorist 2001, and showcase (sometimes surprisingly) the words of John Dos Passos, Russell Baker, David Brinkley, Will Rogers, James Thurber, Simone de Beauvoir, and many more people. Theodore H. White's *The Making of the President 1960* (Buccaneer) chronicles the inside workings of the Kennedy-Nixon campaign race and changed political reporting forever. In *The Boys on the Bus* (Random House), Timothy Crouse reveals how the campaign press corps gets its inside stories. Woodward again — this time with co-author Scott Armstrong — exposed the inside workings of the Supreme Court in *The Brethren* (Island).

Not all Washington books are nonfiction — or particularly serious. This town has spawned quite a few good mystery writers. Margaret Truman, President Harry's daughter, writes the **"Capital Crime Series,"** with (so far) more than a dozen murder-mysteries set in various Washington locations: *Murder in the White House* (Fawcett), *Murder in Georgetown* (Fawcett), *Murder at the Library of Congress* (Fawcett), *Murder at Ford's Theatre* (Ballantine), *Murder on Capitol Hill* (Fawcett), *Murder in the Supreme Court* (Fawcett). . . You get the bloody picture. Elliott Roosevelt, son of President Harry's predecessor, wrote such a successful murder-mystery series that, since his 1990 death, his publisher (St. Martin's Minotaur) keeps issuing **"Elliott Roosevelt Mysteries"** written by other (still living) authors. The detective-hero is Elliott's mother, First Lady Eleanor Roosevelt, and the murders often take place in a very violent White House. While alive, Elliott penned such titles as *The White House Pantry Murder* (St. Martin's), *Murder in the Oval Office* (Avon), and *Murder in the Rose Garden* (St. Martin's).

For hard-boiled private eye action set in Washington mean streets not often traversed by politicians or tourists, check out George Pelecanos' works, such as *Right as Rain* or *Hell to Pay* (both published by Warner).

Chapter 3

Deciding When to Go

● ●

In This Chapter

▶ Joining (or avoiding) the crowds

▶ Understanding D.C.'s weather

▶ Choosing a season to visit

▶ Exploring Washington's annual events

● ●

A lthough by most standards Washington remains a busy town throughout the year, some seasons are busier than others. Deciding when to visit may affect what you see, how much you pay, and how many people you'll battle at the museums and other attractions.

Discovering the Secret of the Seasons

You can't choose a bad time to visit Washington if your primary goal is to see the sights and you're not concerned about the crowds or the weather. You can tour the museums, monuments, and government buildings any season. Cultural, entertainment, and sports activities are always going on. And the stores are glad to sell to you whenever you walk in with money.

Overall, the best times to visit D.C. are spring and fall — April through mid-June and September through mid-November. Temperature and humidity tend to be moderate. The flowers are on display in the spring. The weather in the fall can be close to ideal. Congress is likely to be at work, and cultural and entertainment activities are running full force.

Unfortunately, spring also brings crowds. I've always believed that all Americans should visit Washington at least once. But when I was a reporter trying to get from one Capitol Hill building to another on a tight schedule, I used to quietly grumble as I picked my way through gangs of middle-school students blocking sidewalks as they milled about waiting for their tour buses to arrive.

In terms of expense, visiting in the spring means that you find fewer lodging bargains, especially during the work week when business travelers fill the hotels. In addition, events like the Cherry Blossom Festival are so popular that hotels and restaurants can charge top prices.

You can find more bargains in hotter summer months, as hotels try to fill the rooms that empty during Congressional vacations by offering money-saving package deals. You can also enjoy a great deal of free, outdoor entertainment in the summer.

If you're anxious to see government in action, keep in mind that Congress tries to take lengthy recesses in August and near year's end. Another strike against August is that it can feel like an equatorial rainforest — excruciating heat, even more excruciating humidity, and frequent, vicious thunderstorms. The first year we lived in Washington, after moving from the Midwest, my wife and I wilted when August hit. We both arranged spur-of-the-moment vacations and just started driving north. The National Weather Service says July is hotter and has more rain, but August always feels worse.

Washington does get a real winter most years, usually with snow and some periods of extreme cold in January and February, even though for many years the city government seemed not to understand the concept of snow and how to plow it. On the other hand, Washington looks gorgeous after a snowfall, especially when the congressional Christmas tree is on display at the foot of Capitol Hill. And D.C.'s latest administration has been doing a much better job of clearing the streets when the snow falls.

That said, why don't you slip Vivaldi into your CD player and consider the pros and cons of Washington's four seasons.

Spring: Blooming beautiful in D.C.

Spring is a popular time for D.C. visits because:

- ✔ The days are clear and comfortable, and Washington is at its most lush and beautiful.

- ✔ Gardens in and around the Mall and monuments (around the entire city, for that matter) bloom with tulips, daffodils, cherry blossoms, dogwoods, and azaleas.

However, keep in mind the following springtime pitfalls:

- ✔ Washington's weather always is fickle. Scattered among the gorgeous spring days are an occasional preview of summer's heat, humidity, and thunderstorms, along with a sporadic period that feels a bit too cool. Wear layers of clothing and bring rain gear.

- ✔ Tourists, especially busloads of schoolchildren, pour in like a monsoon. Expect crowds, longer lines, and more traffic.

Summer: Having fun in the D.C. sun

Summer is another popular time to visit because:

- ✔ The kids are out of school.

- ✔ Many hotels offer money-saving packages.

- ✔ Many museums offer extended hours.

- ✔ Free events, such as outdoor concerts, are plentiful.

On the other hand:

- ✔ Summer means *major* heat, folks. And humidity. The 3 Hs — heat, humidity, and haze — make frequent appearances until well after Labor Day. (See Table 3-1 for month-by-month averages of D.C.'s temperature and rainfall.)

- ✔ The influx of summer vacationers can mean longer-than-usual lines at attractions and cold-drink vendors.

- ✔ Some theaters are dark (or at least darker) in July and August. If you're hoping to see a production by one of Washington's theater companies, check to make sure that it has summer offerings.

Table 3-1 Washington, D.C.'s Average Temperatures (°F/°C) & Rainfall (in inches)

	Jan	Feb	Mar	Apr	May	June	July	Aug	Sep	Oct	Nov	Dec
Avg. High	44/7	46/8	54/12	66/19	76/25	83/29	87/31	85/30	79/26	68/20	57/14	46/8
Avg. Low	30/-1	29/-1	36/2	46/8	57/14	65/19	69/20	68/20	61/16	50/10	39/4	32/0
Rainfall	3.21	2.63	3.6	2.71	3.82	3.13	3.66	3.44	3.79	3.22	3.03	3.05

(Source: U.S. National Weather Service.)

Fall: Harvest good times in Washington

If you don't have to worry about school schedules, fall probably is the best time to travel to D.C.:

- ✔ The weather is as good as it gets. Heat and humidity drop as the calendar wears on.

- ✔ Lines are shorter; crowds are smaller.

- ✔ Entertainment and cultural opportunities abound.

But watch out for:

✔ Congress reconvenes, and the convention scene heats up, putting more demands on hotels and restaurants, particularly during the work week.

✔ Traffic can be worse than in summer. (But you're too smart to drive around Washington anyway, aren't you?)

Winter: A great place to celebrate the holidays

Winter brings visions of softly falling snowflakes and holiday cheer, although the snow often holds off until the holidays are over. Advantages of a winter visit include

✔ You don't need to worry about heat and humidity.

✔ Lines at museums and other attractions are short or nonexistent.

✔ Colorful, often free, holiday events are plentiful from December into January.

✔ Airlines and tour operators offer good deals.

✔ When snow surrounds the monuments, you get picture-postcard views of the Capitol, the White House, and other photogenic buildings.

✔ Congress and the White House set up their competing Christmas trees. (The congressional tree is better!)

Winter does have its downsides, however:

✔ While its average temperatures look good on paper, Washington is always visited by some extremes. A damp, windy, 40-degree day on the Mall can feel colder than zero in Alaska. And D.C. does get real cold and windy winter weather — subzero temperatures and even the occasional blizzard — if only for short spells.

✔ You have fewer opportunities to take advantage of outdoor activities.

Washington's Calendar of Capital Events

D.C.'s date book is jam-packed with special events. Some holidays cele-brated throughout the country are extra-special here (Independence Day, for example). I list available dates and times (note that D.C. is in the Eastern Standard Time Zone), but please double-check specifics before planning your vacation around an event; they're subject to change. See the Friday "Weekend" section of *The Washington Post* for comprehensive, up-to-date listings.

Because the easiest way to get around D.C. is by Metrorail — the local subway — the event listings include the Metrorail stops closest to them. The site listings in Part IV give detailed directions. Unless otherwise noted, the events are free.

January

Martin Luther King, Jr.'s Birthday, Lincoln Memorial (☎ 202-619-7222; www.nps.gov/linc; Metro: Foggy Bottom-George Washington University), is celebrated in word and music on the third Monday in January at the Lincoln Memorial, site of the great civil rights leader's "I have a dream" speech.

Inauguration Day, U.S. Capitol (Metro: McPherson Square, Federal Triangle, Archives-Navy Memorial, Federal Center Southwest, Capitol South, Union Station) occurs at noon on January 20 every fourth year, the day the president is sworn in at the Capitol. A **parade** along Pennsylvania Avenue from the Capitol to the White House follows the swearing in. You need political contacts to get a seat on the Capitol lawn or on the parade route bleachers. (A friend with an office window or balcony that overlooks the route is good, too.) Otherwise, head for that long stretch between Congress's and the president's workplaces that morning — the earlier, the better. The next presidential inauguration is January 20, 2009.

January is Washington's coldest month, so the inauguration can be a bone-chilling event. Be prepared! I remember wading through the snow to cover my first inaugural, Jimmy Carter's in 1977. It was so bitterly cold for Ronald Reagan's inaugural in 1985 that the outdoor events were cancelled.

February

During **Black History Month,** African Americans' struggles and achievements are celebrated in numerous ways throughout the city. Museums, libraries, and other sites feature readings, speeches, musical performances, and other events. Check these Web sites: National Park Service (www.nps.gov/ncro/PublicAffairs/Calendar.htm), Smithsonian Institution (www.si.edu/events), and the Washington Convention and Tourism Corp. (www.washington.org).

On February 12 at noon at the Lincoln Memorial, a wreath-laying, band music, and a dramatic reading of the Gettysburg Address mark **Abraham Lincoln's Birthday,** Lincoln Memorial (☎ 202-619-7222; www.nps.gov/linc; Metro: Foggy Bottom-George Washington University).

March

As with Black History Month, many Washington institutions commemorate the achievements of women during **Women's History Month,** various locations. You can find information on the Internet from the National

Park Service at www.nps.gov/ncro/PublicAffairs/Calendar.htm, the Smithsonian Institution at www.si.edu/events, and the Washington Convention and Tourism Corp. at www.washington.org.

March–April

At the **Smithsonian Kite Festival,** Washington Monument grounds (☎ 202-357-3030; http://kitefestival.org; Metro: Smithsonian), you can compete, watch the experts, or just find a place to fly your own kite. The Smithsonian Associates and the National Air and Space Museum sponsor this carefree Washington tradition, usually in late March or early April, in conjunction with the Cherry Blossom Festival.

Daily events bloom all over town during the **National Cherry Blossom Festival,** various locations (www.nationalcherryblossomfestival. org.), which runs from late March into early April each year. The official highlight is the **parade** at the end of the festivities. But the real stars are the cherry blossoms, especially those around the Tidal Basin, and they make their appearances whenever they darn well please. The National Park Service provides updates on the likely timing of the blooms at www. nps.gov/nacc/cherry. The blooms provide a great backdrop and canopy for a picnic at the Tidal Basin or on the Washington Monument Grounds.

Since 1878, presidents have invited children to roll eggs on the White House lawn the Monday after Easter, which is April 17 in 2006, and April 9, 2007. We took our daughter to the **White House Easter Egg Roll** (☎ 202-456-7041; www.whitehouse.gov; Metro: McPherson Square) during the Clinton and Bush I administrations and have the wooden eggs with the mass-produced presidential signatures to prove it! Modern presidents have added entertainment — inside and outside the White House grounds — to occupy the youngsters during the inevitable waits in line. Free tickets timed for entrance are distributed first-come, first-served at the Ellipse Visitor Pavilion on the southwest corner of 15th and E streets NW. One person can get up to five tickets. Most tickets are distributed beginning at 7:30 a.m. Saturday, with some additional tickets made available beginning at 7:30 a.m. Monday. Children of all ages can attend, as long as at least one child is 7 or younger and no more than two adults are in the group.

Note: Rules for Egg Roll admission are subject to change from year to year, so be sure to check before your visit. Outdoor events also can be affected by bad weather.

April

For four days in mid-April, more than 100 artisans from around the country, selected from more than 1,000 entrants, display their expertise at basketry, ceramics, decorative fiber, furniture, glass, jewelry, leather,

metal, mixed media, paper, wearable art, and wood during the
Smithsonian Craft Show, National Building Museum, 401 F St. NW
(☎ **202-357-4000;** www.smithsoniancraftshow.org; Metro: Judiciary
Square). The Smithsonian calls this "the nation's most prestigious juried
exhibition and sale of contemporary American crafts." Admission is $15
for adults, $12 for seniors, and free for children 12 and younger.

May

What better place to mark **Memorial Day** than Washington, D.C., the site
of so many memorials? Ceremonies abound at monuments to American
heroes of the past. One of the most moving begins with a **wreath-laying**
at 11 a.m. at the Tomb of the Unknowns in Arlington National Cemetery,
where members of the Army's 3rd Infantry, the Old Guard, place flags at
more than 260,000 graves just prior to the weekend (☎ **703-607-8052;**
www.arlingtoncemetery.org). Usually, the president or another high-
ranking government official participates.

One of the most pleasant places to be on Memorial Day weekend is on
a blanket or a folding chair on the Capitol's West Lawn as the National
Symphony Orchestra presents its **Memorial Day Concert** at 8 p.m. on
Sunday (☎ **202-467-4600;** www.kennedy-center.org/nso; Metro:
Capitol South, Union Station, Federal Center Southwest). The rain date
is Memorial Day itself, but the concert is rarely postponed unless the
weather is truly terrible. With the performers enclosed in a band shell
and a national audience looking on via PBS, the concert isn't resched-
uled lightly. This event is eclectic, with classical, popular, and patriotic
music performed by the orchestra and glamorous guest stars.

 You can catch the **dress rehearsal** at 7:30 p.m. the day before the
National Symphony's Memorial Day and Independence Day concerts
at the Capitol.

June

Traditional music, crafts, and ethnic foods from the United States and
around the world fill the Mall with enticing sounds, sights, and scents
from late June through early July during the **Smithsonian Festival of
American Folklife** (☎ 202-275-1150; www.folklife.si.edu/center/
festival.html; Metro: Smithsonian). One of Washington's premier outdoor events, the festival typically highlights one or two states and foreign countries.

July

The nation's capital does it up big for the nation's **Independence Day
Celebration.** Highlights include the **parade** along Constitution Avenue
starting a little before noon, the National Symphony Orchestra **concert**
(again with big-name guests) on the Capitol's West Lawn at 8 p.m., and

the **fireworks** launched from around the Lincoln Memorial Reflecting Pool shortly after 9 p.m. Oh, and the Smithsonian folklife festival (see preceding entry) is in full swing! Expect big crowds, especially at the Capitol for the concert. Popular spots for viewing the fireworks include the Mall, the Jefferson Memorial, the Ellipse behind the White House, the Marine Corps (Iwo Jima) Memorial, and areas along the Virginia side of the Potomac River that can be reached from George Washington Memorial Parkway parking lots.

Since the 2001 terrorist attacks, July 4 visitors to the Mall have had to pass through security checkpoints. You can't have alcoholic beverages, glass bottles, fireworks, or grills on the Mall or other surrounding federal land, including the banks of the Potomac and Anacostia rivers.

Here's another place the locals go to watch the fireworks: the Key Bridge, which crosses the Potomac River between Georgetown and Arlington. Get there early to grab a railing-side spot. There's no seating, and you can stand on the sidewalks only (not in the traffic lanes).

To avoid the July 4 crowds, you can catch the same show (sans fireworks) by attending the Capitol concert **dress rehearsal** at 7:30 p.m. July 3.

August

On an August evening each year, the U.S. Army Band performs Tchaikovsky's rousing **1812 Overture** (Sylvan Theater at the Washington Monument, ☎ 202-685-2851; www.mdw.army.mil; Metro: Smithsonian), accompanied by cannon fire from the Presidential Salute Gun Battery of The Old Guard (the 3rd Infantry Regiment). Call or check the Web site for the exact date.

September

Washingtonians mark the end of summer by toting blankets and folding chairs to the Capitol Lawn and listening to the National Symphony Orchestra perform its **Labor Day Concert** (☎ 202-467-4600; www.kennedy-center.org/nso; Metro: Capitol South, Union Station, Federal Center Southwest) with some guest celebrities. The concert starts at 8 p.m. on the Sunday of Labor Day weekend.

During the **Kennedy Center Open House,** Kennedy Center (☎ 800-444-1324 or 202-467-4600; www.kennedy-center.org; Metro: Foggy Bottom-George Washington University), the hall and grounds of the performing arts center showcase performances in music, theater, and dance, along with special activities for kids. This event is popular, so be prepared to encounter lines for the inside events.

October

One evening in October, **Arlington House** (Arlington National Cemetery; Metro: Arlington Cemetery), where Robert E. Lee once lived, is lighted by candles. Staff and volunteers dress in period clothing and discuss Lee's life while 19th-century music plays. Call ☎ **703-235-1530** or visit www.nps.gov/arho for date, time, and free tickets.

The famous **Marine Corps Marathon** (☎ **800-786-8762;** www.marine marathon.com) is so popular that you have to enter a lottery to have a chance of being one of the 16,000 runners on the last Sunday of October. Nicknamed the Marathon of the Monuments, the race starts near the Iwo Jima statue at the edge of Arlington Cemetery and winds through Georgetown and D.C., passing such landmarks as the Capitol, Union Station, Jefferson Memorial, Lincoln Memorial, Pentagon, and the Smithsonian museums before returning to the starting point. You don't have to be a world-class runner to participate. Many highly fit amateurs rise to this challenge — my former next-door neighbors, for example. If you want to run, register by phone or online. If you're not a runner, stake out a spot along the route and watch.

November

During the **Veterans' Day Ceremony** at Arlington National Cemetery (☎ **703-607-8052;** www.arlingtoncemetery.org; Metro: Arlington Cemetery), the president or another high-ranking government official lays a wreath at the Tomb of the Unknowns at 11 a.m. November 11.

December

In early December, a member of the First Family throws a switch to light the large Christmas tree in the Ellipse. The **White House Christmas Tree Lighting** (☎ **202-208-1631;** www.pageantofpeace.org; Metro: Federal Triangle) ceremony kicks off the Pageant of Peace, which continues most of the month. Features include a Yule Log, a circle of smaller trees — each decorated on the theme of a state, territory, or the District of Columbia — and musical performances from 6 to 8:30 p.m. most nights. You have to apply early to get a free ticket for a seat for the tree lighting. In 2003, all tickets were snapped up in less than 45 minutes by people standing in line at the Ellipse Visitor Pavilion. Some had been there for nine hours!

Keep in mind that it gets bitterly cold in Washington in the winter from time to time. If it's cold when you visit, bundle up good, or you may spend all your time at the pageant huddled beside the burning Yule Log.

During the **Kennedy Center Holiday Celebrations,** Kennedy Center (☎ **800-444-1324** or 202-467-4600; www.kennedy-center.org; Metro: Foggy Bottom-George Washington University), the performing arts center hosts holiday-themed events throughout the month, including dancing in the Grand Foyer on New Year's Eve.

Part II
Planning Your Trip to Washington, D.C.

The 5th Wave   By Rich Tennant

"It's creepin' me out too, but you're the one who wanted a hotel room close to the Lincoln Memorial."

In this part . . .

*T*his part helps you get serious about planning your visit. Here you find the nitty-gritty about options — and costs — for your trip. I compile some tips for keeping your possessions safe — and what to do if you lose something. Then I give advice for folks with special interests: families, seniors, travelers with disabilities, and gay and lesbian visitors to D.C.

Chapter 4

Managing Your Money

. . . .

In This Chapter

▶ Planning your budget
▶ Cutting costs — but not the fun
▶ Handling money
▶ Dealing with a lost or stolen wallet

. . . .

*W*hen I was a newspaper reporter, a joke around the Washington bureau was that the only guy on staff who thought D.C. living costs were reasonable was the guy who transferred from Tokyo! Washington is not a cheap place to live, especially when it comes to housing. But, believe it or not, the District can be a reasonably priced place to visit. Many attractions and events are free, and you can take cheap public transportation to most places. You also can use this book to find good deals.

Planning Your Budget

No matter how clever a traveler you are — unless you're staying with friends who feed you and schlep you around town — you can't avoid opening you wallet to eat here, sleep here, get here, get around here, and enjoy some of Washington's entertainment options.

Transportation

D.C. offers many forms of local transportation. Some are easier on your pocketbook — and stress level — than others.

The most expensive — and nerve-shattering — is **driving yourself.** If you drive to D.C., park your car when you get here and don't touch it until you leave. Even then, you may be charged $20 or more each night for parking at your hotel. (For a list of other typical city costs, see Table 4-1.) No one in his or her right mind drives while sightseeing here. The streets are too crowded. There's not enough street parking. Garage parking fees reach the stratosphere. All the circles, squares, and meandering

avenues make for mind-numbing traffic patterns. Washington is full
of important people — or people who think they're important — and
they drive as though the function of all other vehicles is to get out of
their way.

Table 4-1   What Things Cost in Washington, D.C.

Item	Cost
Taxi from Reagan National Airport to downtown	$10
Metrorail from National to Metro Center: Rush hour (5:30–9:30 a.m. and 3–7 p.m. weekdays)	$1.65; normal hours $1.35
Taxi from Dulles Airport to downtown	$50
SuperShuttle van service from Dulles to downtown	$22 first passenger, $10 each additional
Express Metrobus from Dulles to L'Enfant Plaza	$3
SuperShuttle from Baltimore-Washington International Airport to downtown	$31 for first passenger, 11 each additional
Taxi from BWI	$50
Pay telephone call (local)	50¢
Metro	$1.35–1.85 most trips within D.C.
Taxi	$5.50 (within same zone)
Admission to all Smithsonian museums	Free

The good news is that **cabs** are relatively cheap, the **Metrorail** subway
system is one of the best in the world, and the **Metrobuses** can take you
just about any place you want to go.

Metrorail (☎ 202-962-1234; wmata.com) is the first choice for moving
around town, because it's fast, clean, comfortable, and reasonably
priced. You can find stations near most major attractions. It starts running at 5 a.m. Monday through Friday, 7 a.m. on weekends, and closes
at midnight Sunday through Thursday and 3 a.m. Friday and Saturday.
Fares, based on distance traveled, range from $1.35 to $2.35 per trip,
except during weekday rush hours and after 2 a.m. Friday and Saturday;
then, the range is $1.35 to $3.90. When you travel among the main attractions from Capitol Hill to Dupont Circle and Foggy Bottom, you pay just

$1.35 at any time. Up to two children ages 4 and younger ride free with a paying adult. If you travel during peak morning and evening commute time, expect standing-room-only, packed-like-sardines crowds on the trains.

Metrobuses (☎ 202-962-1234; wmata.com) run all the time, but less frequently in the wee hours and on weekends. The fare is just $1.25 no matter where you go, unless you stumble onto one of the few express buses that cost $3.

Taxis cost less than in most big cities, but the bizarre fair structure can baffle longtime residents as well as first-time tourists. D.C. taxis don't have meters. Instead, the city is divided into zones, and you're charged according to the zones you travel through. You see a map — with north NOT at the top! — posted in the back seat of the taxi. A cab ride to a destination within the same zone costs $5.50 Add $2.10 for crossing into the next zone, $1.90 for the zone after that, and so on. Then add $1.50 for each passenger who accompanies you, 50 cents for each bag the driver lifts into the trunk, $1 during rush hour (7 to 9 a.m. and 4 to 6:30 p.m.), and $2 if you summon a cab by telephone instead of hailing it on the street. One child under 6 rides free with a paying adult. The zone-based fare doubles if a snow emergency is declared. If you take a D.C. cab into the suburbs (to an airport, for example), you're charged by the mile as the cabby reads it on his odometer. The good news for tourists is that Zone 1 contains many major attractions, including the Capitol, White House, and Smithsonian museums on the Mall. The bad news is that humidity, air pressure, and phases of the moon can alter the fare calculations — or, at least, it seems that way. The fare downtown from National Airport is about $10. It's about $50 from Dulles and about $65 from Baltimore-Washington International.

To find out a fare before you ride, call the D.C. Taxicab Commission at ☎ 202-645-6018, or check out the D.C. government's cool fare calculator at citizenatlas.dc.gov/atlasapps/taxifare.aspx.

Another option is to sit back and relax on **Tourmobile** (☎ **202-554-5100, 888-868-7707;** www.tourmobile.com), an open-sided tram that makes more than 20 stops near top tourist sites daily except December 25 and January 1. The Tourmobile is a great way to get an overview of the top attractions and is especially attractive to families, the elderly, travelers with disabilities, and the weary of all ages. For $20 ($10 for children 3 through 11, free for younger kids), you can get off and reboard as many times as you want between 9:30 a.m. and 3:30 p.m. and ride until 4:30 p.m. A two-day pass is $30 (adults) or $15 (children). You can buy tickets from the driver or at Tourmobile ticket booths.

The final good news for travelers watching their wallets is that D.C. is pedestrian friendly. Because many of the top sights are close to each other, **walking** often is the best way to travel between them. Just watch for those self-obsessed Washington drivers.

Lodging

You can spend as little as $20 a night for a bed in dormitory-like rooms at **Hostelling International** (☎ **202-737-2333;** hiwashingtondc.org) or pay $4,200 for a night in the **Willard Intercontinental**'s Presidential Suite (☎ **202-628-9100**). In between those extremes, you'll find it just about impossible to obtain undiscounted, high-season rates below $125. Without landing a special deal, you'll have to view anything less than $200 as a modest price. But deals abound. If you make like Sherlock Holmes, you may be able to sleuth your way to a room for less than $100 at a no-frills hotel or a B&B. (See Chapter 9 for hotel listings.)

If you have a flexible schedule, you can save by visiting D.C. when things are slow and hotels slash prices to fill rooms. That would be Thanksgiving through New Year's, July, August, and weekends year round.

You also can save by putting a little extra effort into your hotel search. Check a couple online travel agencies, such as **Expedia.com** and **Travelocity.com**. If a hotel has a toll-free phone number, call it and the local number as well. Check the hotel's Internet site, too. After a reservation clerk quotes you a price, ask whether he's got anything better. Then ask again. It's amazing how often you'll find different prices with each query. Also be sure to mention your membership in AAA, AARP, frequent-flier programs, hotel frequent-sleeper programs, and any other corporate rewards programs. Government employees often qualify for discounts.

Dining

As with lodging, you can spend whatever you want to dine in D.C. One Italian chef, the highly regarded Roberto Donna, illustrates this fact. In **Laboratorio**, Donna's private dining room with open kitchen at his restaurant **Galileo** (☎ **202-331-0880;** www.robertodonna.com), you'll pay $125 for a weekend dinner, or $195 with perfectly matched wines.

Food bargains are scattered throughout the city. Not surprisingly, many Asian and Mexican/Southwestern restaurants offer tasty meals at modest prices. D.C. is experiencing a boom in restaurants that serve little dishes in the $5 to $10 range — Spanish *tapas,* Mediterranean *meze,* Latin American *antojitos,* Italian *sputino.* And the District has some home-grown diners, delis, and bakeries that serve inexpensive salads, sandwiches, and soups — even blue plate specials — for less than $10.

You also can save while sampling expensive restaurants by opting for early-bird specials, post-theater menus, and fixed-price deals, as well as eating your main meal at lunch when prices are lower. (See Chapter 10 for restaurant listings.)

Sightseeing

Seeing the sights is Washington's best bargain. You can walk into almost all of D.C.'s top attractions for free. Try that in New York, London, or Paris! (See Chapter 11 for attractions listings.)

Shopping

Washington's no New York, London, or Paris when it comes to shopping. And, in this case, the comparison's not in D.C.'s favor. Once again, you can spend at any level. Major department stores and other national chain shops are scattered around town. But the most interesting shopping is that which is unique to Washington or at least special to Washingtonians.

Most museums and galleries have shops built upon their exhibits — astronaut ice cream at the **Air and Space Museum** (☎ 202-357-2700; www.nasm.si.edu), prints of the **National Gallery's** paintings (☎ 202-737-4215; www.nga.gov), and the annual White House Christmas ornament at the **White House Visitor Center** (☎ 202-208-1631; www.nps.gov/whho/welcome.htm). Washingtonians tend to be avid readers, so you can choose from many bookstores, including niche stores devoted to gay/lesbian, feminist, African-American, and New Age literature.

Quaint and rowdy **Georgetown** is stuffed with quaint and rowdy shops that sell antiques, art, vintage comic books, movie posters, biker boots, and exotic clothing. **Union Station** (☎ 202-289-1908; www.unionstationdc.com) contains a multilevel shopping mall with chain stores and small shops specializing in American and international crafts. Washingtonians frequent **Adams-Morgan,** the city's most ethnically diverse neighborhood, imports, unusual clothing, and secondhand goods.

For flea market action, head for Capitol Hill's Victorian-era **Eastern Market** (☎ 202-544-0083; www.easternmarket.net) on Sunday. For a miniature version of Beverly Hills' Rodeo Drive, explore Wisconsin Avenue where it crosses the D.C.-Maryland border in the **Friendship Heights** neighborhood. If your vacations must include a discount mall visit, drive 30 miles south on I-95 (yuck!) to enormous **Potomac Mills** (☎ 800-826-4557, 703-490-5948; www.potomacmills.com).

Nightlife

If you want to catch a big show, concert, or major dance performance, you'll pay $20 to $80 for most seats. If your budget won't stretch that far, Washington — the land of the freebee — will come to your rescue.

The Kennedy Center's **Millennium Stage** (☎ 202-467-4600, 800-444-1324; www.kennedy-center.org/programs/millennium) serves up free entertainment nightly throughout the year. The **National Symphony Orchestra** (☎ 202-467-4600 and 800-444-1324; www.kennedy-center.org/nso) and **military bands** play free outdoor concerts at several sites throughout the summer. The **Shakespeare Theater** (☎ 202-547-1122; www.shakespearetheatre.org) performs outdoors for about a week each summer.

Most Washington bars and nightclubs don't impose cover charges, although you may be unpleasantly surprised at what they charge for beverages.

TicketPlace (☎ 202-842-5387; www.ticketplace.org) sells tickets at a discount for same-day performances and on Saturday for Sunday and Monday shows. You can call for recorded information around the clock. The TicketPlace box office, at 407 7th St. NW between D and E streets, is open Tuesday through Friday from 11 a.m. to 6 p.m. and Saturday from 10 a.m. to 5 p.m. You can also purchase tickets online Tuesday through Friday from noon to 4 p.m. Some tickets are only available online and not at the box office, however. After service charges are added, the box office sells tickets for 62 percent of face value. Online sales are 67 percent of face value. To receive daily notices of TicketPlace's online offerings, send your e-mail address to TicketPlace@cultural-alliance.org.

Cutting Costs — But Not the Fun

To conserve your cash, follow these tips:

- ✔ **Visit in the off-season.** In Washington, that means Thanksgiving through New Year's, July, August, and weekends year round. That's because Congress tries to be away at those times, so fewer business travelers are in town.

- ✔ **Travel midweek.** You sometimes can find cheaper flights on Tuesday, Wednesday, and Thursday. When you ask about airfares, see whether you can get a cheaper rate by flying on a different day. For more tips on getting a good fare, see Chapter 5.

- ✔ **Package it.** You sometimes can save money by booking a package that includes airfare, hotel, sightseeing, restaurant perks, and maybe even ground transportation. For particulars, call a travel agent or visit an online travel agency (see Chapter 5).

- ✔ **Rent a kitchen.** Dining out three times a day adds up, even if you take all your meals at hamburger joints and pizza parlors. Book a hotel room or suite with a kitchen, and you can make breakfasts and late-night snacks for a lot less than you'd pay at restaurants. A refrigerator and microwave are particularly handy when you're traveling with kids.

✔ **Opt for kids-stay-free hotels.** You can save money at hotels that let kids stay free in their parents' room. Ask whether two double beds or a sofa bed or rollaway is available.

✔ **BYOM (bring your own munchies).** Toss pre-purchased snacks into your backpack each day. They're cheaper than buying them in vending machines or from tourist-area stands. Easy access to appropriate munchies helps keep the younger tourists contented.

✔ **Bring a water bottle for each member of your party.** Refill the bottles from water fountains as you trek around town. This way, you avoid paying for pricey sodas or bottled H_2O. And having water on hand makes it easy for you to stay hydrated — an important health concern in hot weather.

✔ **Take Metrorail or hoof it.** You can get around D.C. on the cheap by utilizing the subway and your feet. If you're planning to take at least five Metrorail (☎ 202/962-1234; wmata.com) trips in a day, purchase an all-day fare card for $6.50, and you can get on and off the subway as many times as you like after 9:30 a.m. on weekdays and all day on weekends and holidays. A seven-day short-trip pass costs $22 and is valid all the time, although you must pay a rush-hour surcharge for longer trips. When you're not taking the subway, walk. Or hop the 30-series buses for trips along all of Wisconsin Avenue, most of Pennsylvania Avenue, and M Street in eastern Georgetown.

✔ **Always ask for discount rates.** Membership in AAA, frequent-flier plans, trade unions, AARP, or other groups may qualify you for savings on car rentals, plane tickets, hotel rooms, and even meals. Ask about everything; you may be pleasantly surprised.

✔ **Try expensive restaurants at lunch instead of dinner.** Lunch tabs are usually a fraction of what dinner would cost at a top restaurant, and the menu often boasts many of the same specialties.

✔ **Skip the souvenirs.** Your photographs and your memories may be the best mementos of your trip. If you're concerned about money, you can do without the FBI T-shirts, Washington Monument key chains, and other trinkets.

Handling Money

You're the best judge of how much cash you feel comfortable carrying or what alternative form of currency is your favorite. That's not going to change much on your vacation. True, you'll probably be moving around more and incurring more expenses than usual (unless you happen to eat out every meal when you're at home), and you may let your mind slip into vacation gear and not be as vigilant about watching your wallet. But, those factors aside, the only type of payment that won't be quite as available to you away from home is your personal checkbook.

Using ATMs and carrying cash

The easiest and best way to get cash away from home is from an ATM (automated teller machine). The **Cirrus** (☎ **800-424-7787;** www. mastercard.com) and **PLUS** (☎ **800-843-7587;** www.visa.com) networks span the globe; look at the back of your bank card to see which network you're on and then call or check online for ATM locations at your destination. Make sure that you know your personal identification number (PIN) before you leave home and don't forget to find out your daily withdrawal limit before you depart. Also keep in mind that many banks impose a fee every time your card is used at a different bank's ATM, and that fee can be higher for international transactions (up to $5 or more) than for domestic ones (where they're rarely more than $1.50). On top of this charge, the bank from which you withdraw cash may add its own fee. To compare banks' ATM fees within the United States, use www.bankrate.com. For international withdrawal fees, ask your bank. You can find 24-hour ATMs on nearly every street in D.C., it seems, as well as in hotel lobbies, many public buildings, and some restaurants.

Charging ahead with credit cards

Credit cards are a safe way to carry money: They also provide a convenient record of all your expenses, and they generally offer relatively good exchange rates. You also can withdraw cash advances from your credit cards at banks or ATMs, provided you know your PIN. If you've forgotten yours, or didn't even know you had one, call the phone number on the back of your credit card and ask the bank to send it to you. It usually takes five to seven business days, though some banks will provide the number over the phone if you tell them your mother's maiden name or some other personal information.

 Some credit-card companies recommend that you notify them of any impending trip abroad so that they don't become suspicious when the card is used numerous times in a foreign destination and block your charges. Even if you don't call your credit-card company in advance, you can always call the card's toll-free emergency number if a charge is refused — a good reason to carry the phone number with you. But perhaps the most important lesson here is to carry more than one card with you on your trip; a card may not work for any number of reasons, so having a backup is the smart way to go.

Toting traveler's checks

These days, traveler's checks are less necessary because most cities have 24-hour ATMs that allow you to withdraw small amounts of cash as needed. However, keep in mind that you'll likely be charged an ATM withdrawal fee if the bank is not your own, so if you're withdrawing money every day, you may be better off with traveler's checks — provided that you don't mind showing identification every time you want to cash one.

You can get traveler's checks at almost any bank. **American Express** offers denominations of $20, $50, $100, $500, and (for cardholders only) $1,000. You pay a service charge ranging from 1 to 4 percent. You can also get American Express traveler's checks over the phone by calling ☎ 800-221-7282; Amex gold and platinum cardholders who use this number are exempt from the 1-percent fee.

Visa offers traveler's checks at Citibank locations nationwide, as well as at several other banks. The service charge ranges between 1.5 and 2 percent; checks come in denominations of $20, $50, $100, $500, and $1,000. Call ☎ 800-732-1322 for information. AAA members can obtain Visa checks without a fee at most AAA offices or by calling ☎ 866-339-3378. **MasterCard** also offers traveler's checks. Call ☎ 800-223-9920 for a location near you.

If you choose to carry traveler's checks, be sure to keep a record of their serial numbers separate from your checks in the event that they're stolen or lost. You can get a refund faster if you know the numbers.

Dealing with a Lost or Stolen Wallet

Be sure to contact all your credit-card companies the minute you discover that your wallet has been lost or stolen and file a report at the nearest police precinct. Your credit-card company or insurer may require a police report number or record of the loss. Most credit-card companies have an emergency toll-free number to call if your card is lost or stolen; they may be able to wire you a cash advance immediately or deliver an emergency credit card in a day or two. Call the following emergency numbers in the United States:

- ✔ **American Express** ☎ 800-221-7282 (for cardholders and traveler's check holders)
- ✔ **MasterCard** ☎ 800-307-7309 or 636-722-7111
- ✔ **Visa** ☎ 800-847-2911 or 410-581-9994

For other credit cards, call the toll-free number directory at ☎ 800-555-1212.

If you need emergency cash over the weekend when all banks and American Express offices are closed, you can have money wired to you via **Western Union** (☎ 800-325-6000; www.westernunion.com).

Identity theft and fraud are potential complications of losing your wallet, especially if you've lost your driver's license along with your cash and credit cards. Notify the major credit-reporting bureaus immediately; placing a fraud alert on your records may protect you against liability for criminal activity. The three major U.S. credit-reporting agencies are **Equifax** (☎ 800-766-0008; www.equifax.com), **Experian** (☎ 888-397-3742; www.experian.com), and **TransUnion** (☎ 800-680-7289; www.transunion.com). Finally, if you've lost all forms of photo ID, call your airline and explain the situation; it may allow you to board the plane if you have a copy of your passport or birth certificate and a copy of the police report you've filed.

Taxing Matters

The D.C. general sales tax is 5.75 percent, restaurant tax 10 percent, and hotel tax 14.5 percent. Maryland's sales and restaurant taxes are 5 percent. An additional 1- to 10-percent lodging and amusement tax may be imposed by localities. Virginia's general sales tax is 4.5 percent, with local options for taxes on lodging, restaurants and admissions to events.

Chapter 5

Getting to Washington, D.C.

. . . .

In This Chapter

▶ Figuring out how to get here
▶ Comparing Washington's airports and train station
▶ Finding the best fares
▶ Considering a package tour

. . . .

*O*ne of Washington's assets is an abundance of ways to get here. D.C. has terrific train service between here and New York. If train travel is your thing, you can find service up and down the East Coast, with less appealing routes to and from the west. Metropolitan Washington also has three major airports, all served by major airlines. And, of course, the city is connected to the Interstate Highway System — though driving into town is no fun, and driving around town is even worse.

Flying to Washington, D.C.

The city's three major airports compete with each other and encourage price competition among the airlines. Each has distinct advantages and disadvantages for the traveler.

 Consider hiring a limo — a real limo, not a van service that calls itself a limo — if you fly into Dulles or BWI. The price is surprisingly close to a cab, particularly on the trip from D.C. to the airport. (You're charged more money when you're picked up at the airport, because the driver meets you inside the terminal.) My wife and I have used **Airport Car Service** (☎ **301-656-9100**) several times and have been quite happy with the results. It's $59 from downtown D.C. to Dulles, $69 from Dulles to D.C., $69 from D.C. to BWI, and $79 from BWI to D.C. — plus tip. There's nothing like lounging in the back of a Lincoln Town Car during that long ride.

 If you take the SuperShuttle van from any airport, ask whether a discount is associated with your hotel.

D.C. Metropolitan Area

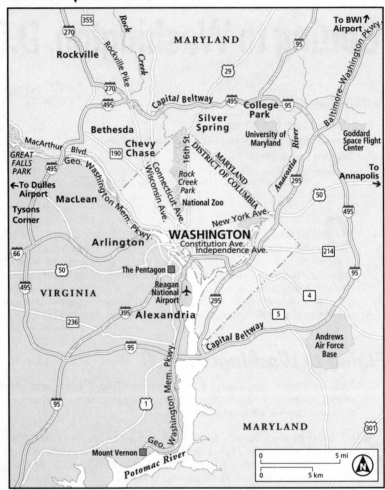

Finding out which airlines fly there

Ronald Reagan Washington National Airport (☎ 703-417-8000; www.metwashairports.com/national), known to locals simply as "National," is the most convenient. **Washington-Dulles International Airport** (☎ 703-572-2700; www.metwashairports.com/dulles), known, naturally, as "Dulles," is 25 miles west of downtown in what used to be the Virginia countryside. **Baltimore-Washington International Airport** (☎ 800-435-9294; www.bwiairport.com) is 30 miles northeast of D.C. and 8 miles from Baltimore and is known by its acronym, "BWI."

Ronald Reagan Washington National Airport

Republican members of Congress who didn't think enough things had been named for the 40th president bestowed this rather lengthy name on the airport. (It's located in Arlington, Virginia, and is managed by a regional authority.) The locals, for the most part, still call it National.

Nomenclature aside, National is a marvelous airport. The original terminal, opened in 1941 on the eve of America's entry into World War II, is a historic structure that is being restored and will stay in use. The new terminal, opened in 1997, is a striking, modern architectural triumph, with picture-window views across the Potomac River to Washington's landmarks. The views from planes arriving from the north and west are spectacular as well, especially after dark, as you can clearly see Washington's most familiar buildings and monuments from the approaching aircraft. The new terminal was designed by renowned architect Cesar Pelli and has original art incorporated throughout it.

The food options at National are unusually palatable for an airport, including a number of spots operated by local eateries and a few sit-down restaurants, such as Legal Sea Foods and T.G.I. Friday's. If you find yourself in need of last-minute gifts or souvenirs, you can chose from a large selection of shops, including stores run by Smithsonian Institution museums, the National Geographic Society, and the National Zoo.

The airport is compact and easy to get around. With all the security added in the wake of September 11, 2001, National is probably the safest airport to fly into or out of in the world. And you can't beat the convenience.

You pay $1.35 ($1.55 in rush hour) for a 12-minute ride on Metrorail's Yellow Line from National to the Archives-Navy Memorial Station about halfway between the White House and the Capitol. The trip to Metro Center takes 18 minutes and costs an extra dime in rush hour because you have to change trains or take a long loop on the Blue Line. A taxi to downtown costs about $10 (before tip) and takes about 20 minutes (depending, of course, on Washington's notorious traffic).

 National's downside includes the fact that it *is* "national." If you want to fly here nonstop from outside the United States, Canada, Bermuda, or the Caribbean, you have to touch down at Dulles or BWI. The airport also has fewer long-distance flights within the United States. Noise restrictions limit traffic late at night and early in the morning. And, because it's so close to the city, the airport has a high demand for its flights, so you find fewer bargains at National than at Dulles or BWI. "Fewer" doesn't mean "none," however. If you book early and follow the tips listed in the section "Getting the best deals on airfares," later in this chapter, you can find good prices at National as well.

The following national and international airlines serve National Airport: Air Canada, Air Tran, Alaska, America West, American, ATA, Chautauqua, Colgan Air, Continental, Delta, Frontier, Midwest, Northwest, Spirit, United, and US Airways. The airport also is served by these regional carriers: Allegheny, American Eagle, Atlantic Coast, Atlantic Southeast, Comair, Continental Express, Delta Express, Express Jet, Mesa, Piedmont, PSA, Trans States, and US Airways Express, (See the Quick Concierge at the back of this book for complete listings of phone numbers and Web sites.)

Washington-Dulles International Airport

Like Reagan Airport, Dulles also sports impressive architecture: the soaring main terminal. Designed by highly regarded architect Eero Saarinen, it opened to many *oohs* and *ahs* in 1962. The airport's main attractions today are its international and long-haul domestic service and its sometimes-better fares than you can find at National. At Dulles, you can even catch a flight on Aeroflot . . . should you happen to *want* to catch a flight on Aeroflot.

Dulles' main disadvantage is location — of the airport itself within metropolitan Washington and of the facilities within the airport. The cab ride to D.C. takes about 45 minutes in favorable traffic and costs about $50.

The **SuperShuttle** (☎ **202-296-6662, 800-258-3826;** www.super shuttle.com) van charges $22 for the first passenger and $10 for each companion.

Travel within the airport is a bit of a challenge as well. Dulles has grown and grown. As new terminals were added, airport architects didn't bother to connect them. Not many of Dulles' gates are at the main terminal. As a result, for most travelers, entering the terminal is just the beginning of their airport journey. If you land at Dulles, you'll probably de-plane at one of the so-called "midfield" terminals. You then make your way to a loading zone where you board a monstrous bus (euphemistically called a "mobile lounge"). You then de-bus at the main terminal. Some of these contraptions take passengers directly to and from the planes.

One time I flew out of Dulles, I hopped onto the wrong mobile lounge, which took me to the wrong midfield terminal, which left me puzzling for a bit over why I didn't see any signs to my gate. When I figured out what I had done, I had to take another mobile lounge back to the main terminal and then another back to the right midfield terminal. Fortunately, because I had arrived at the airport early, I still caught my flight. This escapade is one of many reasons I always leave myself a lot of extra time when I set out for an airport — and even more when the airport is Dulles.

The cheapest trip from Dulles to D.C. is by the 5A express Metrobus, which drops you at L'Enfant Plaza, a couple blocks south of the National Mall, which has a Metrorail station, or at the Rosslyn Metrorail station in Virginia, across the river from Georgetown. The ride costs $3. It departs Dulles approximately hourly from about 6:30 a.m. to 11:30 p.m. every day.

National and international airlines serving Dulles Airport are: Aeroflot, Air Canada, Air France, AirTran, Alaska, Alitalia, All Nippon, American, America West, Austrian, British Midland, British Airways, BWIA West Indies Airways, Continental, Delta, Ethiopian, Frontier, Independence Air, JetBlue, KLM Royal Dutch, Korean Air, Lloyd Aereo Bolivaiano, Lufthansa, Northwest, SAS-Scandinavian, Saudi Arabian, TACA International, TED, United, US Airways, Virgin Atlantic. These regional carriers serve Dulles: American Connection, American Eagle, Continental Express, Delta Connection/Comair, Northwest Express, United Express/Mesa, United Express/Air Wisconsin, US Airways Express, Colgan Air, Mesa. PSA, Air Midwest. (See the Quick Concierge at the back of this book for complete listings of phone numbers and Web sites.)

Baltimore-Washington International Airport

BWI's prime attraction is price. It's served by discount carrier Southwest Airlines, which pushes down the prices of other carriers that fly to the same cities. Its distance from Washington means airlines have to try a little harder to attract D.C. clientele. That means that often — though not always — you can find cheaper airfares at BWI than at National.

BWI's disadvantage is, like Dulles', location. By cab, you're 45 minutes and $65 away from D.C., if the traffic flows smoothly. The **SuperShuttle** (☎ **703-416-6661, 800-258-3826;** www.supershuttle.com) or van service sets you back $31 for the first passenger and $11 for each companion. At least when you walk into BWI's terminal, though, you don't have to take a bus to your plane.

As at Dulles, Metrobus runs a $3 express from BWI — this one to the Greenbelt Metrorail station. The B30 bus leaves the airport every 40 minutes between 7 a.m. and 10:50 p.m. weekdays, 9:40 a.m. to 10:50 p.m. weekends.

On weekdays, you also can ride the **MARC train** (☎ **410-539-5000, 866-743-3682;** www.mtamaryland.com) from BWI to Union Station for $6. The interval between trains varies from 10 to 90 minutes, but usually is less than an hour. **Amtrak** (☎ **800-872-7245;** www.amtrak.com) runs trains frequently on the same route from before 7 a.m. until after midnight. Stay off the Metroliner and Acela Express, and you can ride for $13 — less if you qualify for a senior, AAA, or other discount.

BWI is served by these airlines: Aer Lingus, Air Canada Jazz, Air Jamaica, AirTran, American, America West, British Airways, Continental, Delta, Frontier, Hooters Air, Icelandair, Midwest, Northwest, Southwest, United, US Airways, and USA3000. (See the Quick Concierge at the back of this book for complete listings of phone numbers and Web sites.

Getting the best deal on airfares

Deregulation of the U.S. airline industry has brought a flood of discounted fares to the market. The problem is . . . a flood of different fares is on the market. How do you find the best one for you?

If money's no object, you may choose to fly first class or the less pricey but still premium business class. If money is an object, but you must buy a ticket on short notice, you can be stuck with a full-fare coach ticket. The high cost of full-fare coach — theoretically, the low-cost way to travel — can be shocking. Susan and I had to travel between D.C. and Chicago several times on business a few years ago. We were able to plan several weeks ahead on all but one occasion, and we were able to buy round-trip tickets for between $200 and $300 each. Once, however, our client summoned us on short notice, and each ticket cost more than $1,200 — on the client's tab, thank goodness.

If you want bargains, then you don't want plain-vanilla coach fares. You want . . . bargain fares. And you, or your travel agent, have to work a bit to find the best ones.

Checking many sources to save

Taking full advantage of the magic of computers, airlines now practice what is called *yield management.* Ticket prices are adjusted day-by-day — hour-by-hour, minute-by-minute — based on what the computer knows about the history of ticket-purchasing on a particular flight and how sales are going right now. The goal is to fill the plane and sell every ticket at the highest possible price. That means you're not going to get a bargain on a flight that's heading toward a sellout. But, because the airline wants to fill every seat — the seat's always there, and if no one's in it, it's not producing any income — you can find cut-rate fares on flights in danger of taking off without a full load.

The way for you to take advantage of this system is to check every possible source of information about ticket prices and to keep your travel plans as flexible as possible. That's because recent studies have shown that the cheapest ticket doesn't always show up in the same information source. To maximize your chances of finding it, you need to telephone the airlines, visit their Internet sites, check for newspaper ads, call a travel agent, and visit online travel agencies as well.

Finding bargains on the Internet

If contacting multiple sources is more hassle than you're willing to endure and you're comfortable on the Internet, checking several Web sites probably is your best bet. Visit a couple online travel agencies, such as **Travelocity** (travelocity.com), **Expedia** (expedia.com), and **Orbitz** (orbitz.com). (Canadian travelers should try www.expedia.ca and www.travelocity.ca; U.K. residents can go for expedia.co.uk and opodo.co.uk.) Check out mega-sites that compile comprehensive lists of specials, such as **Smarter Living** (smarterliving.com). For last-minute trips, **Site59** (www.site59.com) in the United States and **LastMinute** (www.lastminute.com) in Europe often have better deals than the major-label sites.

Finally, visit the Web sites of the airlines that the online agencies say have the lowest fares to see whether you can get them even lower. Check the sites of airlines that you know fly the route you want to travel. And, if you try to collect miles in a particular frequent-flier program, check that airline's Web site, too.

Start your search as early as possible, but check back at the last minute as well; prices can drop on flights that aren't selling well. At the airlines' and travel agencies' Web sites, you can register for e-mail notices that alert you to last-minute deals on routes you specify or on any routes in case you may find one tempting.

If you can be flexible about travel dates or time of day, you increase your chances of finding the best bargain. Be alert for packages that save money by combining airline, hotel, and other reservations in a single purchase.

Be aware that the cheapest tickets are likely to carry the stiffest restrictions — no refunds and high penalties for making changes in your itinerary.

If you're willing to give up some control over your flight details, use an *opaque fare service* like **Priceline** (www.priceline.com) or **Hotwire** (www.hotwire.com). Both offer rock-bottom prices in exchange for travel on a "mystery airline" at a mysterious time of day, often with a mysterious change of planes en route. The mystery airlines are all major, well-known carriers — and the possibility of being sent from Philadelphia to Chicago via Tampa is remote. But your chances of getting a 6 a.m. or 11 p.m. flight are pretty high. Hotwire tells you flight prices before you buy; Priceline usually has better deals than Hotwire, but you have to play their "name our price" game. *Note:* In 2004, Priceline added non-opaque service to its roster. You now have the option to pick exact flights, times, and airlines from a list of offers — or opt to bid on opaque fares as before.

Another online travel service is **SideStep** (www.sidestep.com). Although you have to download software to use the service, the advantage is that it searches low-cost airlines — such as Southwest — while other online travel agencies do not.

Some airlines offer discounts to older passengers. If you think you may qualify, be sure to ask. The discounts may not apply to the lowest fares, however, so it still pays to search. Southwest Airlines, in particular (which uses Baltimore-Washington International Airport as a hub), offers discounts on its already low fares.

Many airlines offer free tickets to children younger than two who don't occupy a seat. I urge you to think carefully about the implications of this arrangement before you take advantage of it. There's a reason that airplanes have seat belts and that the pilot urges you to keep your seat belt fastened when you're not standing in line at the potty. Things — including passengers — can get thrown around the cabin if the plane runs into turbulence, and sometimes the turbulence is unexpected. Picture your child flying out of your lap in that situation. The Federal Aviation Administration recommends that children who weigh less than 40 pounds ride in an approved child safety seat (car seat) that is properly belted into the airplane seat. Make sure that your safety seat is labeled "certified for use in motor vehicles and aircraft." To encourage this practice, some airlines offer discounted tickets for children younger than two.

To give your kids — and you! — a little more room on your flight, request seats behind the bulkhead. You'll have to store all your bags in the overhead bins, however, because you won't have a seat in front of you to place them under.

Getting to D.C. Without Leaving the Ground

You don't have to fly into Washington. D.C.'s railway station is a tourist attraction in its own right. The bus probably is the cheapest way to get here. And you can always drive, although dealing with your car once you arrive can be a major headache.

Riding the rails

Whenever I travel up the East Coast, as far as New York, I take the train. Rail tickets usually are cheaper than airfare, and the train is *soooo* much more pleasant. The seats are bigger and much more comfortable. You can walk about with ease. You can sit at a table in the club car and eat, or play cards, or have a cup of coffee or beer while spreading the newspaper out before you. You can work, if you're so inclined. You arrive at and depart D.C. right on Capitol Hill. Union Station — built at the beginning of the 20th century in the heyday of rail travel — is a marvelous place, with Metrorail and tour-bus stations inside and a taxi stand outside. The food court has a huge selection of places where you can buy great eats for the trip. Whenever the Price family goes to New York for an outing, the vacation starts as the train pulls out, and we picnic on food we bought at the station.

The trip between New York and Washington takes from about 2 hours and 45 minutes to 3 hours and 30 minutes, depending on which train you choose. The **Metroliner** and **Acela Express** are faster and more comfortable than the garden variety trains that make more stops along the way. In my experience, the premium service isn't worth the doubled price. The regular round-trip fare of about $150 jumps to about $300 on the express trains, even more if you want a first-class seat. Like the airlines, Amtrak (☎ 800-872-7245; www.amtrak.com) offers special deals. Except for weekday Acela and Metroliner service, up to two children aged 2 to 15 can ride for half price with a paying adult, and one younger child can ride free on an adult's lap. Students and veterans can buy discount cards that save 15 percent on most trains except the weekday Metroliners and Acelas.

In the Washington-New York corridor, train travel can be faster than flying. You can arrive minutes before the train departs the station. You travel from and to the heart of each city. It's a rare day when rain, fog, or snow disrupts the schedule. You can catch a train in the Boston-Washington corridor just about any time you want. Service from elsewhere is less frequent and not competitive with air travel in terms of time.

Taking a car

I live in D.C. Therefore, I drive in D.C. But you don't have to, and I advise you not to.

Driving *to* D.C. is another issue. For a family, it can be less expensive than air or rail travel, and some people just prefer to drive. The traffic on the region's highways is horrendous, especially at rush hour (which starts earlier and ends later with each passing day). But once you're in town, you can park your car and leave it alone until you're ready to go home. However, be aware that parking fees tend to be as horrendous as the traffic, often $20 or more per day. When you make your reservation, ask your hotel whether it offers parking and what it charges. Make sure that you're sitting down when you ask this question.

 If you're driving to Washington, you may save money by booking a suburban hotel that offers free parking and is near a Metrorail station. It may take you longer to get to your first sightseeing stop of the day. But Metro remains fast and cheap, even from the farthest suburb. From Shady Grove, at one end of the Red Line in suburban Maryland, for example, the 34-minute trip to Metro Center costs $3.90 in rush hour and $2.35 at other times. When you're researching hotels, ask how long it takes to walk to the Metro station, whether there's free shuttle service, or what it costs to take a cab and how easy it is to get one. You can park at some Metrorail stations, but competition for the spaces is heavy and starts before the rooster crows.

If you do drive to Washington, you encounter the **Capital Beltway** (I-495), which surrounds the city like a medieval moat — filled with raging drivers instead of raging sea monsters. Beware all who enter: There are speeders, chronic lane-changers, and vicious road-ragers . . . or one enormous parking lot. Surviving the Beltway is challenge number one. Challenge number two is to actually get into the city.

Assuming that you're traveling to Washington on the Interstate Highway System:

- ✔ If you arrive from the northwest, you'll be on I-270; follow the I-495 signs to Virginia. Immediately after crossing the American Legion Memorial Bridge into Virginia, take the George Washington Parkway east to I-66 east. That will take you across the Theodore Roosevelt Memorial Bridge into Washington on Constitution Avenue near the Lincoln Memorial

- ✔ From the west, I-66 is a straight shot onto Constitution Avenue.

- ✔ From the south, take I-95 to I-395 and then follow signs into Washington.

- ✔ From the northeast on I-95, there is no direct route into town. The easiest (using that term loosely) way probably is to stay on I-95 south after it merges with I-495, then take the Baltimore-Washington Parkway (Maryland Route 295) south to U.S. 50 west, which runs through the heart of D.C.

- ✔ From the east, you'll probably be on U.S. 50, which you can take into the middle of town.

Easily accessible on foot and by the Metrorail, Washington is your worst driving nightmare: confusing traffic circles, often poor signage, and streets that dead-end and then resume their course further along. That's not to mention scarce and expensive parking. Traffic is heavy from predawn to post-sunset. One wrong turn, and you may end up in Virginia. I had lived in Washington for years — I do mean years! — before I could consistently negotiate the drive from National Airport to my home in Upper Northwest without missing a turn and finding myself on a freeway to Virginia after I had entered the District.

 AAA (☎ **800-763-9900;** www.aaa.com) and some other automobile clubs offer free maps and driving directions to their members. If you're a member, give your club a call.

Riding the bus

For travelers on a tight budget, the bus probably is the cheapest way to reach D.C. from most cities in the Northeast. Bus fares typically cost less than half the price of regular train tickets. As I write this book, **Peter Pan**

Driving to D.C.

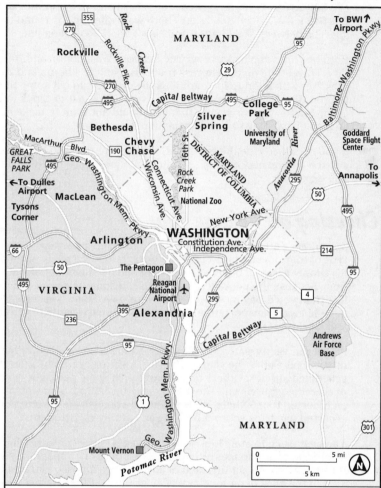

Driving into D.C.

If you drive to Washington, ask your hotel for directions.

In general:

• From the **Northwest**: Take **I-270**, follow **I-495** signs to Virginia, go east on **I-66**, which will take you onto Constitution Ave.

• From the **West**: Take **I-66** onto Constitution Ave.

• From the **South**: Take **I-95**, go north on **I-395**, then follow signs into Washington.

• From the **Northeast**: Take **I-95**, then go west on **U.S. 50**, which becomes New York Ave.

• From the **East**: Follow **U.S. 50** into town.

(☎ 800-237-8747; www.peterpanbus.com) and **Greyhound** (☎ 800-229-9424; www.greyhound.com) both were offering $31 round-trip specials between Washington and New York if booked on line.

Both bus lines run express service between Washington and New York City. Travel time on the express routes is listed at 4 hours and 20 minutes, but with good road conditions the drivers can cut some time off the run. The D.C. bus terminal, 1005 1st St. NE, is a four-block walk to the Union Station Metrorail stop that you would not want to make at night, so plan on cabbing to your destination if you arrive then.

 If you decide to ride the bus to D.C., make sure that you book express service, or you may end up spending a lot more time on the road than you expected.

Choosing a Package Tour

Sometimes you can save money buy purchasing a *package tour.* This type of tour doesn't mean that you have to follow a guide around town. It's simply a way of buying your airfare and accommodations at the same time. Because the packager buys in bulk, it sometimes can sell to you for less than you'd pay by shopping on your own. Some packages also include local transportation, meals, admission to events or attractions, and local tours.

Prices can vary greatly. Some packages offer a better class of hotel than others. Some offer the same hotels for lower prices. Some offer flights on scheduled airlines. Others book charters. In some packages, your choice of accommodations and travel days may be limited. Some let you choose an escorted tour. Others allow you to add on just a few excursions or escorted day trips without booking an entirely escorted tour.

The best place to start looking for packages is the travel section of your local Sunday newspaper or in the nearest major newspaper if your paper is too small to attract this kind of advertising. You also can find packages in the back of national travel magazines, at the Internet travel agency sites, and at the Internet sites of many airlines and hotel chains. The Internet sites often let you build a package by choosing among hotels, flight times, and other options. Car rentals are offered, too, but you really don't want a car in D.C. unless you plan to use it to leave town.

Liberty Travel (☎ 888-271-1584; www.libertytravel.com) is one of the biggest packagers in the Northeast. **American Express Vacations** (☎ 800-346-3607; travel.americanexpress.com/travel) is another good option. Their Web sites can direct you to the office nearest your home if you want to meet a travel agent face-to-face.

Among airlines that offer Washington packages are **American** (☎ **800-321-2121;** www.aavacations.com) and **US Airways** (☎ **800-422-3861;** www.usairwaysvacations.com), which, as long as it stays in business, is headquartered near National Airport.

If you've already picked your hotel, ask whether it offers land/air packages.

 If you're unsure about the pedigree of a smaller packager, check with the Better Business Bureau in the city where the company is based, or go online at www.bbb.org. If a packager won't tell you where it's based, find another packager.

Chapter 6

Catering to Special Travel Needs or Interests

. . . .

In This Chapter

▶ Making vacation fun for your kids
▶ Reaping the benefits of age (finally!)
▶ Dealing with disabilities
▶ Exploring gay-friendly D.C.

. . . .

*W*orried your kids are too young — or you're too old — to enjoy Washington? Need to find places with easy access for the disabled? Want to seek out gay-friendly activities and venues? This chapter is the right spot, because Washington is friendly to everyone.

Finding Family-Friendly Fun in D.C.

Washington is one of the most family-friendly destinations around. Those yellow school buses migrate here all year round for good reason: Class trips to Washington are rites of passage, like braces and pimples.

Many attractions have special sections and programs for children. Washington's abundant parkland offers countless places for kids to let off steam. Restaurants entice the young and restless with kids' menus or half-portions, booster seats and high chairs, crayons, coloring books, and other pacifiers. The best ones offer menus for children that range far beyond the traditional hotdogs, French fries, and peanut-butter-and-jelly sandwiches.

When you check hotels, ask about special rates for families and perks like free or lower-priced food for kids in hotel restaurants. When you want some time *without* the kids, many hotels can link you up with baby sitters. Ask the concierge.

When you're traveling with kids, a suite with kitchen facilities can be a great place to stay. With a refrigerator and microwave, you can eat breakfast before setting out on your adventures, and you can return for a midday snack and nap, which is a great way for the little ones to recharge. Separate sleeping areas — perhaps a bedroom and a living room with foldout sofas — let your kids enjoy their own space (and TV), while you relish some peace and privacy. Bring some snacks.

Many Washington attractions offer colorful, age-appropriate workbooks that enhance youngsters' visits. Some host family film sessions, workshops, and educational programs for children. In museums, ask at the information desk. Kid-friendly food is available at most museum restaurants as well. At National Park Service sites, ask about the Junior Ranger program.

The home page of every national park's Web site has a button labeled "kids" that takes you to information about kid-friendly places and activities. Washington's parks are listed at this Web site: data2.itc.nps. gov/parksearch/state.cfm?st=dc.

Hands-on exploring in D.C.

Children want to do more than look when they're on vacation. Here's a small sampling of the things kids can *do* in D.C.

- ✔ Use dry ice and their breath to do a laboratory bench investigation of carbon dioxide at the **National Museum of American History**'s Hands On Science Center.

- ✔ Pet a tarantula (well, kids think it's cool!) at the **National Museum of Natural History**'s insect zoo.

- ✔ Touch a moon rock and peer into John Glenn's Friendship 7 space capsule at the **National Air and Space Museum.**

- ✔ Attend a **family concert** at the Kennedy Center and touch the musical instruments during the "petting zoo" period.

- ✔ Ride the **carousel** on the National Mall.

And that list is just a teeny-tiny sampling.

Frolicking in wide, open spaces

Washington's parks offer an open invitation for your kids to behave like, well, kids. They can run around, ride the carousel, or fly a kite on the mammoth lawn known as the National Mall. If they'd prefer to frolic on water, your family can rent pedal boats under Mr. Jefferson's gaze on the Tidal Basin. Or you can take a hike in the middle of the Potomac River on Theodore Roosevelt Island. For more detailed information on the best activities for families, check out *Frommer's Washington, D.C. with Kids.*

Drafting a plan for your clan

To start your family vacation off right, let your kids get involved in the planning. They can start by writing to the **Washington, D.C., Convention and Tourism Corp.,** 901 7th Street NW, 4th Floor, Washington, DC

20001-3719, or going to the Web site www.washington.org for general information.

The computer-literate can find useful and interesting information at the Web sites listed throughout this book. In addition to the preceding park service site, check out

- ✔ Smithsonian Institution for children: smithsonianeducation. org/students

- ✔ White House Web site for kids: www.whitehouse.gov/kids

- ✔ National Zoo: natzoo.si.edu

Throughout this book, this Kid Friendly icon marks the best places and activities for children.

Making Age Work for You: Tips for Seniors

If you're a senior citizen, you're (finally!) eligible for some special benefits when you travel. *Senior citizen* can be defined as being a lot younger than many may expect — 50 years old for AARP membership, for example, and 55 for many discount programs.

Elderhostel (☎ 877-426-8056; www.elderhostel.org) includes Washington in its educational tours for travelers 55 and older (and a spouse or companion of any age). Nine D.C. programs, ranging from two to five nights, are being offered as I write this book. One two-night trip features visits to monuments and government buildings where such topics as federalism, interaction of the three government branches, and Washington's history are discussed. For recreation, there's a night at the theater preceded by a pre-theater dinner. A five-day program, focused on the United States and the Middle East, includes lectures by diplomats, visits to an embassy, international agency, or the State Department, and a stop at the Foreign Service Institute, where U.S. diplomats are trained. The activities are put together in connection with the American Foreign Service Association, the professional organization of U.S. diplomats.

Savings for the senior set

As you plan your trip, and after you arrive, always ask whether any restaurant, lodging, attraction, or form of transport has a senior rate. Carry identification that shows your age, and you may end up with significant savings over your younger counterparts.

You may want to check out the benefits of joining **AARP** (known as the American Association of Retired Persons prior to setting its focus on recruiting Baby Boomers *before* they reach retirement age). Various discounts are available to AARP members, and local chapters run programs — including tours — for members. Information is available at ☎ 888-687-2277 or at the AARP Web site at www.aarp.org.

American citizens and permanent residents who are at least 62 can buy a **Golden Age Passport,** which gives you lifetime free entrance to all properties managed by the **National Park Service** (☎ 888-467-2757; www. nps.gov/fees_passes.htm) — national parks, monuments, historic sites, recreation areas, and national wildlife refuges. At places that charge a per-vehicle fee, the passport admits all passengers. If the fee is per person, the passport admits you, your spouse, and your children. The passports are sold for $10 at park service facilities that charge an entrance fee. Besides free entry, the passport gets you a 50% discount on federal-use fees charged for such facilities as camping, swimming, parking, boat launching, and tours.

Most park service sites in Washington are free anyway. The pass does save you a few bucks at the Great Falls in Maryland and Virginia, which I recommend for a nearby excursion, and at the Frederick Douglass National Historic Site.

Here are some additional ways for you to save money just by revealing your birth date:

✔ Many hotel chains offer senior discounts. Always ask when making a reservation. You may have to register and pay a fee to join a seniors club.

✔ Although most U.S. airlines no longer routinely offer lower fares to older travelers, you still can find special deals for seniors. **American** (☎ 800-433-7300; www.aa.com) offers lower fares to 65-and-older travelers on some flights, for example, and **United** (☎ 800-720-1765; www.silverwingsplus.com) has created a "Silver Wings Plus" program for those who are at least 55. So, when you book your flight, it pays to ask.

✔ **Amtrak** (☎ 800-872-7245; www.amtrak.com) travelers aged 62 and older receive a 15 percent discount on most train tickets and 10 percent off the North America Rail Pass for 30 days worth of travel in the United States and Canada. The discount doesn't apply to weekday Metroliner and Acela Express service, to sleeper accommodations, or on the Auto Train between Washington's Northern Virginia suburbs and Florida.

✔ Seniors 65 and older can buy half-price Metrorail fare cards in the Metro Center Station ticket office (12th and F streets NW) and at many stores, including Safeway and Giant grocery stores. You also can ride buses for 50 cents. In both cases, you must provide some proof of your age (driver's license, birth certificate, or passport).

Asking about senior discounts pays off, even if you don't consider yourself to be a senior citizen. You don't necessarily have to be 65. Many establishments — restaurants, theaters, and museums — offer discounts at age 62, while some even begin as early as age 55.

More senior resources

For more information on senior traveling, check out these publications: the quarterly magazine *Travel 50 & Beyond* (www.travel50andbeyond.com), and the books *Travel Unlimited: Uncommon Adventures for the Mature Traveler* (Avalon); *101 Tips for Mature Travelers,* available from Grand Circle Travel (☎ **800-221-2610** or 617-350-7500; www.gct.com); *The 50+ Traveler's Guidebook* (St. Martin's Press); and *Unbelievably Good Deals and Great Adventures That You Absolutely Can't Get Unless You're Over 50* (McGraw-Hill), by Joann Rattner Heilman.

Traveling without Barriers: D.C. for the Disabled

Washington is a highly accessible city for disabled visitors, and all major transportation providers offer services to help the disabled traveler get here in the first place.

To scope things out, check out **Access-Able Travel Source** (☎ **303-232-2979;** www.access-able.com). The Web site lists travel agents who have experience serving individuals with disabilities and provides some information about accessibility to lodging, transportation, and attractions for major cities around the world, including D.C. It also provides leads for renting wheelchairs and other health-care equipment.

Getting to, and around, town

Tell your air, rail or bus carrier ahead of time if you need any assistance — both when you make your reservation and again when you check in at the airport or station. If you travel with a Seeing Eye dog or other service animal, ask about rules for taking it with you.

If you need special accommodations or assistance, **Amtrak** asks you to make your reservation by telephone (☎ **800-872-7245**) or at a ticket counter, rather than online. If the regular reservations clerk can't answer all your questions, ask to speak to a customer service agent. The railroad also operates text telephone service (TDD/TTY) from 5 a.m. to 1 a.m. Eastern time at ☎ **800-523-6590.** If you need accessible sleeping accommodations on an overnight train, Amtrak suggests you reserve at least 14 days before your trip. The railroad makes all bedrooms available to all passengers after that time.

Amtrak offers discounted fares to disabled passengers. You must purchase tickets by phone or at a ticket counter, and you must show documentation of your disability at the ticket counter and when boarding the train. Acceptable documentation includes a transit system disability ID card, a membership card from a disabilities organization, or a letter from a physician.

If you require the assistance of a personal care attendant and provide notice 24 hours in advance, Greyhound (☎ **800-752-4841;** www.greyhound.com) lets the attendant travel for half fare. If you're traveling alone and alert Greyhound 48 hours prior to your travel, the company can arrange assistance along your route.

The National Park Service offers a **Golden Access Passport** that is essentially the same as the **Golden Age Passport** described earlier in this chapter in the section "Savings for the senior set." The access passport is free to citizens or permanent residents who are visually impaired or permanently disabled, regardless of age. You can get one at a park service facility that charges a fee by showing proof of medically determined disability and eligibility for receiving benefits under federal law. In addition to the benefits conferred by the Golden Age Passport, the Golden Access Passport covers admission for a care assistant if you travel with one. You can get more information at ☎ **888-467-2757** or www.nps.gov/fees_passes.htm.

Visitors with disabilities find **Metrorail** an excellent way to get around D.C. Every station has elevators, as well as fare-card vending machines, entrance gates, and telephones, all built to accommodate wheelchairs. For the hearing-impaired, blinking lights along the edge of the track announce the arrival of trains, and (for everyone's convenience) newly installed announcement signs give information about the approaching train. A bumpy surface has been placed along platform edges to help the vision-impaired locate the edge. Elevator control panels and signs in the stations contain Braille. On the train, bells chime and announcements occur when the doors are about to open or close, and the driver announces each station. All **Metrobuses** kneel for easier access, and almost all have low floor ramp or a lift. The TTY number for Metro information is ☎ **202-638-3780.**

Metro gives passengers with disabilities the same discounts available to seniors, but they must possess valid proof of disability. If the individual doesn't already have a Medicare card, however, the discount probably isn't worth the paperwork for someone who's visiting for a few days or even a few weeks.

 Unfortunately, Metrorail's elevators are notorious for breaking down, a minor inconvenience for most passengers but a major problem for anyone with a disability. (Metro management was severely embarrassed a few years ago when a frustrated man in a wheelchair — who had encountered several out-of-service elevators — screamed an obscenity and was ticketed. Management quickly apologized, tore up the ticket, and gave the man complimentary passes.) When entering the Metrorail system, ask the attendant whether elevators are working at your destination. You can also call ☎ **202-962-1212** for information on elevator outages. When elevators are out, Metro provides shuttle buses to serve those stations. Ask the attendant where to catch them.

Tourmobile has trams that are accessible to passengers with disabilities. The company also has vans with wheelchair lifts. For information, call ☎ 888-868-7707 or 202-554-5100. **Bike the Sites,** in conjunction with **City Scooter Tours** (☎ 888-441-7575; www.cityscootertours.com), rents and offers guided tours of the Mall and Tidal Basin areas on sit-upon powered "mobility scooters."

Building accessibility

The **Smithsonian Institution**'s museums, as well as most other public museums and attractions, are accessible to individuals with disabilities. Many films aired in museum theaters offer narrated audiotapes for the vision-impaired. Most live theaters have infrared headsets for the vision- and hearing-impaired. Live productions often feature at least one signed performance during the run. Call the theater for specifics. Some older facilities are less accessible than the newer ones, but that's far from universal. The best bet is to call ahead to make sure that the facility can accommodate your needs.

The Smithsonian has published a free guide to accessibility at its facilities. You can obtain it — *Smithsonian Access: A Free Guide for Visitors* — by asking at museum information desks, calling ☎ **202-357-2700** (voice) or 202-357-1729 (TTY), or writing to Smithsonian Information, SI Building 153, Washington, D.C. 20560-0010. The guide is available in large print, audiocassette, Braille, and CD-ROM versions. You also can read it online at www.si.edu/opa/accessibility/access/index.htm. You can find additional information for Smithsonian visitors with disabilities at the Web site www.si.edu/visit/visitors_with_disabilities.htm.

You may find that some old properties, historic inns, and bed-and-breakfasts are inaccessible, but most major D.C. hotels and restaurants are accessible. Ask specifically when you make a reservation. If you book through a travel agency or tour group, be sure to make your needs known.

For more information

Organizations that offer assistance to disabled travelers include **MossRehab** (www.mossresourcenet.org), which provides a library of accessible-travel resources online; **SATH (Society for Accessible Travel and Hospitality)** (☎ 212-447-7284; www.sath.org; annual membership fees: $45 adults, $30 seniors and students), which offers a wealth of travel resources for all types of disabilities and informed recommendations on destinations, access guides, travel agents, tour operators, vehicle rentals, and companion services; and the **American Foundation for the Blind (AFB)** (☎ 800-232-5463; www.afb.org), a referral resource for the blind or visually impaired that includes that includes information on traveling with Seeing Eye dogs.

For other sources of information targeted to travelers with disabilities, visit the community Web site **iCan** (www.icanonline.net/channels/travel/index.cfm), which has destination guides and several regular columns on accessible travel. Also check out the quarterly magazine **Emerging Horizons** ($14.95 per year, $19.95 outside the U.S.; www. emerginghorizons.com); **Twin Peaks Press** (☎ 360-694-2462; http://disabilitybookshop.virtualave.net/blist84.htm), offering travel-related books for travelers with special needs; and *Open World Magazine,* published by SATH (subscription: $13 per year, $21 outside the U.S.).

Resources for Gay and Lesbian Travelers

Washington has a large and vibrant gay and lesbian community, so the city is a welcoming place for GLBT (gay, lesbian, bisexual, and transgender) visitors. Just ask our two gay City Council members, one of whom was a Republican until he turned independent to protest the GOP's "indifference, intolerance, and injustice." The center of gay life is Dupont Circle, but gay and lesbian Washingtonians are thoroughly integrated into neighborhoods throughout the city. Gay and lesbian tourists are likely to be made welcome wherever they decide to visit.

Gathering gay and lesbian information about Washington

The prime source of news for and about D.C.s gay community is the **Washington Blade** (www.washingtonblade.com), a weekly newspaper that's been hitting the streets here since 1969. It's filled with local, national, and international news, plus information about entertainment and community resources. It's widely available for free throughout the city.

Washington's premier gay and lesbian bookstore is **Lambda Rising,** at 1625 Connecticut Ave. NW (☎ 202-462-6969; www.lambdarising.com). The **Human Rights Campaign,** the nation's largest GLBT-rights political action organization, operates an Action Center and Store at 1629 Connecticut Ave. NW (☎ 202-232-8621).

The following travel guides are available at most travel bookstores and gay and lesbian bookstores, or you can order them from **Giovanni's Room** bookstore, 1145 Pine St., Philadelphia, PA 19107 (☎ 215-923-2960; www.giovannisroom.com): *Spartacus International Gay Guide* (Bruno Gmünder Verlag; www.spartacusworld.com/gayguide) and *Odysseus International Gay Travel Planner* (Odysseus). Both are good, annual English-language guidebooks focused on gay men. The *Damron* guides (www.damron.com), with separate annual books for gay men and lesbians, and *Gay Travel A to Z: The World of Gay & Lesbian Travel Options at Your Fingertips* by Marianne Ferrari (Ferrari International; Box 35575, Phoenix, AZ 85069) are good gay and lesbian guidebook series.

Out and About (☎ 800-929-2268 or 415-644-8044; www.outandabout.com) offers guidebooks and a newsletter ($20 per year for 10 issues) packed with solid information on the global gay and lesbian scene.

Getting to and staying in D.C. the gay-friendly way

Many travel agencies offer tours and itineraries specifically for gay and lesbian travelers. **The International Gay and Lesbian Travel Association (IGLTA)** (☎ **800-448-8550** or 954-776-2626; www.iglta.org) is the trade association for the industry and offers an online directory of gay-friendly travel businesses. **Above and Beyond Tours** (☎ **800-397-2681;** www. abovebeyondtours.com) is the exclusive gay and lesbian tour operator for United Airlines. **Now, Voyager** (☎ **800-255-6951;** www.nowvoyager. com) is a well-known San Francisco-based gay-owned and operated travel service.

The IGLTA lists the following D.C. hotels as gay-friendly.

✔ **Henley Park Hotel.** 926 Massachusetts Ave. NW. Mount Vernon Square Metro. ☎ **202-638-5200** (800-222-8474) www.henleypark. com. See Chapter 9.

✔ **Hotel Helix.** 1430 Rhode Island Ave. NW. Farragut North or McPherson Square Metro. (☎ **202-462-9001** or 866-508-0658; hotelhelix.com).

✔ **Hotel Madera.** 1310 New Hampshire Ave. Dupont Circle Metro. (☎ **202-296-7600** or 800-368-5691; hotelmadera.com). See Chapter 9.

✔ **Hotel Rouge.** 1315 16th St. NW. Dupont Circle Metro. (☎ **202-232-8000** or 800-738-1202; www.rougehotel.com). See Chapter 9.

✔ **Jurys Washington Hotel.** 1500 New Hampshire Ave. NW. Dupont Circle Metro. (☎ **202-483-6000** or 800-424-3729; www.jurys-washingtondc-hotels.com). See Chapter 9.

✔ **Morrison-Clark Historic Inn and Restaurant.** 1015 L St. NW. Mount Vernon Square Metro. (☎ **202-898-1200** or 800-332-7898; www. morrisonclark.com). See Chapter 9.

✔ **Sofitel Lafayette Square.** 806 15th St. NW. McPherson Square Metro. (☎ **202-730-8800** or 800-763-4835; www.sofitel.com). See Chapter 9.

✔ **Topaz Hotel.** 1733 N St. NW. Dupont Circle Metro. (☎ **202-393-3000** or 800-775-1202; www.topazhotel.com).

For really special accommodations, make a reservation at the **D.C. Guest House,** a newly renovated 1876 mansion. Gourmet breakfast is served in an elegant dining room. You'll feel like guests in a home because this place is lovingly restored and operated by four friends who spread their personal, eclectic tastes throughout the mansion. 1337 10th St. NW 20001. Mt. Vernon Square Metro. ☎ **202-332-2502.** www.dcguesthouse.com.

Chapter 7

Taking Care of the Remaining Details

"Are we there yet?" Well, not quite. But after I share with you a few more details, you'll be ready to stick your plans in your pocket and begin to enjoy D.C.

Renting a Car — Not!

I live in D.C. Therefore, I drive in D.C. But you don't have to, and I advise you not to. (See Chapter 5 for reasons why you don't want to get behind the wheel.) Ask all who live here. They'll tell you that, even with the grid system, getting from place to place can be confusing, and the cost of parking can take a large chunk out of your budget. Rely on shuttle, taxi, bus, or rail service from the airport or train station. Use Metrorail and your own two feet for sightseeing — or buses and taxis when necessary.

If you decide you really want or need to drive despite my warnings, see the next section.

Getting the best rental rate

If you insist on renting a car, keep in mind that car-rental rates vary widely. The price depends on many factors: the size of the car, the length of time you keep it, where and when you pick it up and drop it off, where you go in it, and a host of other factors. Asking the following key questions can save you big bucks:

✓ **Is the weekend rate lower than the weekday rate?** Ask whether the rate is the same for a Friday morning pickup as it is for one on Thursday night. If you keep the car five or more days, a weekly rate may be cheaper than the daily rate.

✓ **Are you charged a drop-off fee if you return the car to a location that's different from where you picked it up?** If, for example, you're leaving town from a different airport from the one you arrived at or you're driving to another city in a rental car, the company may tack on a hefty charge to leave it in a location other than the original pickup point.

✓ **Is the rate cheaper if you pick up the car at the airport instead of a location in town?** One location may be more practical than the other, so don't forget to factor convenience into your decision.

✓ **Do you get a special rate for being a member of AAA, AARP, frequent-flier programs, or other organizations?** Such memberships can entitle you to discounts ranging from 5 to 30 percent.

✓ **Can you have the discounted rate you saw advertised in the local newspaper?** Be sure to ask for that specific rate; otherwise, you may be charged the standard (higher) rate.

✓ **Is age an issue?** Many car-rental companies add on a fee for drivers under 25, while some don't rent to younger drivers at all.

Adding up the costs of renting a car

On top of the standard rental prices, you need to watch out for other charges that may be applied. The *Collision Damage Waiver (CDW)* absolves you of responsibility to pay for damage to the vehicle in exchange for a hefty daily fee. Check with your auto insurance agent and the credit-card company you use to rent the car. You're probably already covered.

Car-rental companies also may try to sell you *liability insurance* (to cover you if you harm others in an accident), *additional liability insurance* (to increase the coverage you already have), *personal accident insurance* (to cover injury to yourself or your passengers), and *personal effects insurance* (to cover possessions that you carry in the rental car). If you don't know whether you're already covered, check with your auto and homeowner's insurance agent(s). You may not need to purchase this extra coverage. If your own insurance doesn't cover you for rentals, however, or if you don't have auto insurance, definitely consider the additional coverage. Ask the car-rental agent to explain it to you thoroughly and make sure that you understand the explanation. Unless you're toting around the Hope diamond — and you don't want to leave that in your car trunk anyway — you probably can skip the personal effects insurance. But driving around without liability or personal accident coverage is never a good idea. Even if you're a good driver, other people may not be, and liability claims can be complicated.

Some rental-car companies also offer *refueling packages,* which means that you pay for an entire tank of gas up front and don't face extra charges if you fail to return the car with a full tank. This service may be convenient, but the best way to save money is to fill the tank yourself at a gas station just before you return to the rental lot. The refueling package makes sense only if you routinely run late and face penalty charges for returning the car without a full tank.

Frequent fliers can cheer themselves up with the knowledge that most car rentals are worth at least 500 miles in their frequent-flier accounts. Be sure to show your card.

Booking a rental car on the Internet

As with other aspects of planning your trip, using the Internet can make comparison-shopping and renting a car much easier. The major online travel agencies — such as **Travelocity** (www.travelocity.com), **Expedia** (www.expedia.com), **Orbitz** (www.orbitz.com), and **Smarter Living** (www.smarterliving.com) — have search engines that dig up discounted car-rental rates. Enter the size of the car you want, the pickup and return dates, and the city where you want to rent, and you'll be quoted prices. Pick the deal you want and make your reservation at the site. As with buying airline tickets, checking the car-rental companies' sites can pay off, too.

Travel and Medical Insurance: To Buy or Not to Buy?

Three primary kinds of travel insurance are available: *trip cancellation, lost luggage,* and *medical.* Trip cancellation insurance is a good idea for some people, but lost luggage and additional medical insurance don't make sense for most travelers. Be sure to explore your options and consider the following insurance advice before you leave home:

✔ **Trip cancellation insurance.** If you pay a large portion of expensive vacation costs up front, consider purchasing this type of insurance. When you buy a package tour, insurance comes in handy if the packager or tour company defaults, a member of your party becomes ill, or (heaven forbid!) you experience a death in the family and aren't able to go on vacation. You probably won't be reimbursed if you cancel your trip just because you change your mind. Reasons that qualify for reimbursement can range from sickness to natural disasters to the State Department declaring your destination unsafe for travel. Insurers usually don't cover general fear — as many travelers discovered when they tried to cancel trips in October 2001 because they were wary of flying.

Note: Many tour operators include insurance in the cost of the trip or can arrange insurance policies through a partnering provider, a convenient and often cost-effective way for the traveler to obtain insurance. Make sure that the tour company is a reputable one, however. In addition, some experts suggest that you avoid buying insurance from the tour or cruise company you're traveling with, saying it's better to buy from a "third-party" insurer than to put all your money in one place.

✔ **Lost luggage insurance.** Your homeowner's insurance should cover stolen luggage if your policy encompasses off-premises theft. Check your existing policies or ask your insurance agent before you buy any additional coverage. Airlines are responsible for up to $2,500 for checked luggage they lose on domestic flights. If you plan to check items more valuable than the standard liability — and if your valuables aren't covered by your homeowner's policy — get baggage insurance as part of your comprehensive travel-insurance package or buy "BagTrak" from **Travel Guard** (see listing later in this section). Don't buy insurance at the airport, as it's usually overpriced. Be sure to take any valuables or irreplaceable items with you in your carry-on luggage, as many valuables (including books, money, and electronics) aren't covered by airline policies.

If your luggage is lost, immediately file a lost-luggage claim at the airport, detailing the luggage contents. For most airlines, you must report delayed, damaged, or lost baggage within four hours of arrival. The airlines are required to deliver luggage, once found, directly to your house or destination free of charge.

✔ **Medical insurance.** If you get sick while on vacation, your existing health insurance should cover your expenses. But keep in mind that some HMOs may differ on the benefits they offer while you travel. You may want to review your policy or ask your agent before leaving home.

If you think you need additional insurance, make sure that you don't pay for more coverage than you need. You also should call around to find a good deal on insurance. Here are some reputable issuers of travel insurance:

- **Access America** (☎ 866-807-3982; www.accessamerica. com).

- **Travel Guard International** (☎ 800-826-4919; www. travel-guard.com).

- **Travel Insured International** (☎ 800-243-3174; www. travelinsured.com).

- **Travelex Insurance Services** (☎ 888-457-4602; www. travelex-insurance.com).

Protect yourself further by paying for the insurance with a credit card. By law, consumers can get their money back on goods and services not received if they report the loss within 60 days after the charge is listed on their credit card statement.

Staying Healthy When You Travel

If you suffer from a chronic illness, consult your doctor before your departure. For conditions like epilepsy, diabetes, or heart problems, wear a **MedicAlert Identification Tag** (☎ 888-633-4298; www.medic alert.org), which immediately alerts doctors to your condition and gives them access to your records through MedicAlert's 24-hour hotline.

Most health insurance policies cover you if you get sick away from home — but check, particularly if you're insured by an HMO. Always carry your insurance ID card in your purse or wallet.

Pack **prescription medications** in your carry-on luggage and carry prescription medications in their original containers. Also bring along copies of your prescriptions in case you lose your pills or run out. And don't forget sunglasses and an extra pair of contact lenses or prescription glasses.

CVS (www.cvs.com), Washington's major drugstore chain (with more than 40 D.C. locations), has three stores in the city with 24-hour pharmacies:

- ✔ Dupont Circle: 6 Dupont Circle NW. Dupont Circle Metro. ☎ **202-785-1466** (pharmacy), 202-785-1466 (main).

- ✔ Dupont Circle: 2200 M St. NW. Dupont Circle Metro. ☎ **202-296-9876** (pharmacy), 202-296-9877 (main).

- ✔ Upper Northwest: 4555 Wisconsin Ave. NW. ☎ **202-537-1587** (pharmacy), 202-537-1587 (main).

Rite Aid also dispenses prescriptions around the clock at 1815 Connecticut Ave. NW, 2½ blocks north of the Dupont Circle's Metro Q Street exit (☎ **202-332-1718**; www.riteaid.com).

If you need immediate medical attention, head for the **emergency room** at one of the following District hospitals. In a true emergency, call an ambulance. If it's not an emergency and you drive, call ahead for directions.

- ✔ **Children's National Medical Center,** 111 Michigan Ave. NW, Upper Northwest (☎ **202-884-5000**)

- ✔ **George Washington University Hospital,** 900 23rd St. NW, downtown (☎ **202-715-4911**)

- ✔ **Georgetown University Hospital,** 3800 Reservoir Rd. NW, Georgetown (☎ **202-444-2119**)

- **Sibley Hospital,** 5255 Longboro Rd. NW, Upper Northwest (☎ 202-537-4000)

- **Washington Hospital Center,** 110 Irving St. NW, Upper Northwest (☎ 202-877-7000)

Washington's hospitals also can **refer you to a physician** if you don't really need emergency room care. Try calling one of the following hospitals for a referral:

- **George Washington University Hospital** (☎ 888-449-3627)

- **Georgetown University Hospital** (☎ 202-342-2400)

- **Sibley Hospital** (☎ 202-537-4638)

- **Washington Hospital Center** (☎ 202-877-3627)

Avoiding "economy-class syndrome"

Deep vein thrombosis — or, as it's known in the world of flying, "economy-class syndrome" — is a blood clot that develops in a deep vein. It's a potentially deadly condition that can be caused by sitting in cramped conditions, such as an airplane cabin, for too long. During a flight (especially a long-haul flight), get up, walk around, and stretch your legs every 60 to 90 minutes to keep your blood flowing. Other preventative measures include frequent flexing of the legs while sitting, drinking lots of water, and avoiding alcohol and sleeping pills. If you have a history of deep vein thrombosis, heart disease, or other condition that puts you at high risk, some experts recommend wearing compression stockings or taking anticoagulants when you fly; always ask your physician about the best course for you. Symptoms of deep vein thrombosis include leg pain or swelling, or even shortness of breath.

Staying Connected by Cell Phone or E-mail

It used to be travelers wondered if their hotel room would have a phone and if they should use a pay phone anyway to save money. Now it seems everyone travels with a cell phone and an e-mail account, and the question becomes whether your cell phone works in a strange city and where you can find Internet access.

Using a cell phone across the United States

Just because your cell phone works at home doesn't mean it'll work elsewhere in the country (thanks to our nation's fragmented cell phone system). It's a good bet that your phone will work in Washington. But take a look at your wireless company's coverage map on its Web site before heading out. If you need to stay in touch at a destination where you know your phone won't work, you can **rent** a phone that does from **InTouch USA** (☎ 800-872-7626; www.intouchglobal.com) or at a rental-car location. But beware that you'll pay $1 a minute or more for airtime.

If you're not from the United States, you'll be happy to know that **GSM (Global System for Mobiles)** service is available in Washington. But, to be safe, you should ask your wireless provider whether your phone will work here.

Accessing the Internet away from home

Travelers have many ways to check the Internet and e-mail on the road. Using your own laptop or hand-held device gives you the most flexibility. A growing number of hotels offer Internet access in rooms or at a business center; ask about charges first, or you may be unpleasantly surprised at check-out time. Call your hotel in advance to see what your options are.

You also can take advantage of a growing number of cybercafes, where you can go online while you sip a beverage or nibble at lunch, often for a fee. At **Kramerbooks & Afterwards** (1517 Connecticut Ave. NW, just above Dupont Circle; ☎ **202-387-1400;** www.kramers.com), you can check e-mail free at the bar. You can search for other Washington cybercafes at www.cybercaptive.com and www.cybercafe.com.

All D.C. public libraries (☎ **202-727-0321;** www.dclibrary.org) offer free Internet access. The main library is the downtown **Martin Luther King Library** (901 G St. NW at 9th Street; ☎ **202-727-0321**). The **West End Branch** (☎ **202-724-8707**) is at 1101 24th St. NW at L Street. The **Georgetown Branch** (☎ **202-282-0220**) is at 3260 R St. NW at Wisconsin Avenue. On Capitol Hill, the **Southeast Branch** (☎ **202-698-3377**) is at 403 7th St. SE at D Street. Call for hours, which vary.

In a pinch, at all three D.C. area airports, you can get online at an **Internet kiosk.** These kiosks, which are also located in shopping malls, hotel lobbies, and tourist information offices around the world, give you basic Web access for a per-minute fee that's usually higher than cybercafe prices. The kiosks' clunkiness and high price mean that you should avoid them whenever possible.

To retrieve your e-mail, ask your **Internet Service Provider (ISP)** if it has a Web-based interface tied to your existing e-mail account. If your ISP doesn't have such an interface, you can use the free **mail2web** service (www.mail2web.com) to view and reply to your home e-mail. For more flexibility, you may want to open a free, Web-based e-mail account with **Yahoo! Mail** (http://mail.yahoo.com). Your home ISP may be able to forward your e-mail to the Web-based account automatically.

If you need to access files on your office computer, look into a service called **GoToMyPC** (www.gotomypc.com). The service provides a Web-based interface for you to access and manipulate a distant PC from anywhere — even a cybercafe — provided that your "target" PC is on and has an always-on connection to the Internet. The service offers top-quality security, but if you're worried about hackers, use your own laptop rather than a cybercafe computer to access the GoToMyPC system.

If you're bringing your own computer, the buzzword in computer access to familiarize yourself with is **Wi-Fi (wireless fidelity).** More and more hotels, cafes, and retailers are signing on as wireless "hotspots," where you can get high-speed connection without wires, networking hardware, or a phone line. You can get Wi-Fi connection one of several ways. Many laptops sold in the last year have built-in Wi-Fi capability (an 802.11b wireless Ethernet connection). Mac owners have their own networking technology, Apple AirPort. For those with older computers, you can plug an 802.11b/**Wi-Fi card** (around $50) into your laptop. You then sign up for wireless access service much as you do cell phone service, through a plan offered by one of several commercial companies that have made wireless service available in airports, hotel lobbies, and coffee shops. **T-Mobile Hotspot** (www.t-mobile.com/hotspot) serves up wireless connections at more than 1,000 Starbucks coffee shops nationwide. **Boingo** (www.boingo.com) and **Wayport** (www.wayport.com) have set up networks in airports and high-class hotel lobbies. IPass providers also give you access to a few hundred wireless hotel lobby setups. Best of all, you don't need to be staying at the swanky spot to use the hotel's network; just set yourself up on a nice couch in the lobby. The companies' pricing policies can be Byzantine, with a variety of monthly, per-connection, and per-minute plans. In general, you pay around $30 a month for limited access. As companies jump on the wireless bandwagon, prices are likely to get more competitive.

In addition, major Internet Service Providers (ISP) have **local access numbers** around the world, allowing you to go online by simply placing a local call. Check your ISP's Web site or call its toll-free number and ask how you can use your current account in Washington, and how much it will cost. If you're traveling outside the reach of your ISP, the global **iPass** network has dial-up numbers in Washington. You have to sign up with an iPass provider, who then tells you how to set up your computer. For a list of iPass providers, go to www.ipass.com and click Individuals Buy Now. One solid provider is **i2roam** (www.i2roam.com; ☎ **866-811-6209** or 920-235-0475). Bring a **connection kit** with power and phone adapters, a spare phone cord, and a spare Ethernet network cable — or find out whether your hotel supplies them to guests.

Keeping Up with Airline Security

With the federalization of airport security, procedures at U.S. airports are more stable and consistent than ever. Generally, you're fine if you arrive at the airport **1 hour** before a domestic flight and **2 hours** before an international flight; if you show up late, tell an airline employee, and she'll probably whisk you to the front of the line.

Bring a **current, government-issued photo ID,** such as a driver's license or passport. Keep your ID ready to show at check-in, the security checkpoint, and sometimes even the gate. (Children under 18 don't need government-issued photo IDs for domestic flights.)

In 2003, the Transportation Security Administration (TSA) phased out **gate check-in** at all U.S. airports. In addition, **E-tickets** have made paper tickets nearly obsolete. Passengers with E-tickets can beat the ticket-counter lines by using airport **electronic kiosks** or even **online check-in** from your home computer. Online check-in involves logging on to your airlines' Web site, accessing your reservation, and printing your boarding pass — airlines even offer you bonus miles when you do so! If you're using a kiosk at the airport, bring the credit card you used to book the ticket or your frequent-flier card. Print your boarding pass from the kiosk and simply proceed to the security checkpoint with your pass and a photo ID. If you're checking bags or looking to snag an exit-row seat, you'll be able to do so using most airline kiosks. Even the smaller airlines are employing the kiosk system, but always call your airline to make sure that these alternatives are available. **Curbside check-in** is also a good way to avoid lines, although a few airlines still ban curbside check-in; call before you go.

 Because of its location near so many important government facilities, **National Airport** has received more security scrutiny than any other airport in the United States. This special attention extends beyond the airport to airplanes in the air on their way to and from D.C. You're not allowed to get out of your seat when you're within 30 minutes of the runway — the penalty may be having the plane diverted to another airport and you being placed in very deep trouble. If you need to use the lavatory, don't wait till the last minute, or you may find yourself in line at sit-down time.

Security checkpoint lines are getting shorter than they were during 2001 and 2002, but some doozies remain. If you have trouble standing for long periods of time, tell an airline employee; the airline can provide a wheelchair. Speed up security by **not wearing metal objects,** such as big belt buckles. If you've got metallic body parts, a note from your doctor can prevent a long chat with the security screeners. Keep in mind that only **ticketed passengers** are allowed past security, except for folks escorting disabled passengers or children.

Federalization has stabilized **what you can carry on** and **what you can't.** The general rule is that sharp things are out, nail clippers are okay, and food and beverages must be passed through the X-ray machine — but that security screeners can't make you drink from your coffee cup. Bring food in your carryon rather than checking it, as explosive-detection machines used on checked luggage have been known to mistake food (especially chocolate, for some reason) for bombs. Travelers in the United States are allowed one carry-on bag, plus a "personal item," such as a purse, briefcase, or laptop bag. Carry-on hoarders can stuff all sorts of things into a laptop bag; as long as it has a laptop in it, it's still considered a personal item. The TSA has issued a list of restricted items; check its Web site (www.tsa.gov/public/index.jsp) for details.

Airport screeners may decide that your checked luggage needs to be searched by hand. You can now purchase luggage locks that allow screeners to open and relock a checked bag if hand-searching is necessary. Look for Travel Sentry certified locks at luggage or travel shops and Brookstone stores (you can buy them online at www.brookstone.com). Luggage inspectors can use a special code or key to open these locks, which are approved by the TSA. For more information on the locks, visit www.travelsentry.org. If you use something other than TSA-approved locks, your lock will be cut off your suitcase if a TSA agent needs to hand-search your luggage.

Part III
Settling into Washington, D.C.

"Six of Jennifer's goldfish died today, and, well, I just don't think it's worth the three of us keeping our reservations at Takara's Sushi Restaurant tonight."

In this part . . .

In this part, you get into the real details: Washington's best hotels (and a few runners-up), the best restaurants, and the best places to catch a quick snack or a drink with a capital view. Because you need to know how to get to all these great places, I also give you the lowdown on D.C.'s spectacular subway system, comprehensive network of bus routes, confusing taxi fares, and state-themed streets (on which you should never ever drive).

Chapter 8

Arriving and Getting Oriented

*Y*ou can get to Washington easily by train or plane and, in a sense, by automobile. Once you're here, a car is not the best bet for local transportation — D.C.'s world-class Metrorail system is. After you settle in, you'll discover that Washington's most interesting neighborhoods are fairly close to each other and easy to navigate. You may be surprised by the diversity.

Finding the Way to Your Hotel

The train takes you right to Capitol Hill, where Union Station is an easy cab or subway ride away from the hotels that are most attractive to tourists. National Airport is nearly as convenient, but you'll face a bit of a trek from Dulles or Baltimore-Washington International.

Signs for taxis and other ground transportation are posted in the airports' baggage claim areas, as well as outside the terminals. At National Airport and Union Station, you also see signs to on-site Metrorail stations.

From Ronald Reagan Washington National Airport

National is Washington's most convenient airport. It's close to town, is easy to get around, and has terrific transportation connections. It's also an attraction in its own right, thanks to the eye-popping terminal that opened in 1997.

Two **information desks** are located on the main concourse in the new terminal, and one is near the baggage claim area of the old terminal.

Washington, D.C. Airports

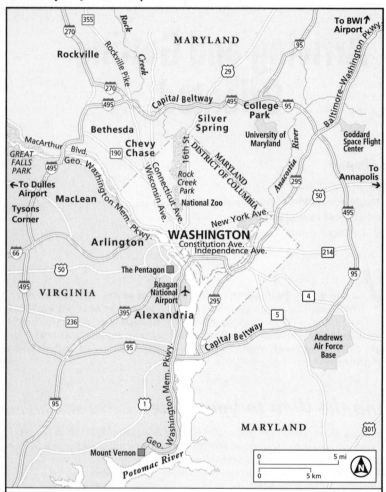

Getting into Town from the Airports

- **From Dulles International Airport:**
  Take the Dulles Airport access road (the only road out) to I-66 east through the Virginia suburbs and over the Theodore Roosevelt Bridge (still I-66), which lands you on Constitution Avenue and the western edge of the national Mall near the Lincoln Memorial.
- **From Baltimore Washington International Airport:**
  Take the airport access road to Highway 295 (Gladys Spellman Parkway; also known as the Baltimore-Washington Parkway) south to Route 50 west (New York Avenue).
- **From Reagan National Airport:**
  Take the George Washington Memorial Parkway north to the 14th Street Bridge, which dumps you onto...14th Street! Just follow the signs to Washington.

ATMs are on the main concourses in the old and new terminals and in the baggage claim area of the new terminal. A **currency exchange** service is at the north end of the new terminal's main concourse.

Before you leave home, find out whether your hotel offers complimentary shuttle service. If not, the cheapest and quickest way into town is **Metrorail.** You pay $1.35 ($1.55 in rush hour) for a 12-minute ride on Metrorail's Yellow Line from National to the Archives-Navy Memorial Station, which is about halfway between the White House and the Capitol. The trip to Metro Center takes about 18 minutes and costs an extra dime in rush hour because you have to change trains or take a long loop on the Blue Line. Rush-hour fares are charged on weekdays before 9:30 a.m. and from 3 to 7 p.m. You also pay the rush-hour surcharge when the trains run after 2 a.m. Usually trains run from 5 a.m. till midnight Monday through Thursday, 5 a.m. to 3 a.m. Friday, 7 a.m. to 3 a.m. Saturday, and 7 a.m. until midnight Sunday. Hours may vary on holidays and during special events.

A **taxi** to downtown costs about $10 (before tip) and takes about 20 minutes (depending, of course, on Washington's notorious traffic).

To avoid price gouging, ask for the fare before you get in a cab. D.C. cabs don't have meters. (The suburban cabs do.) Fares are calculated according to an arcane zone system, which is displayed on a nearly indecipherable map in the cab's back seat. To be safe, ask your hotel ahead of time to estimate the fare from the airport. Allow plenty of time to get to the airport for your return flight if you travel weekdays from 6 to 10 a.m. and 3 to 8 p.m. For more information on taxi fares, see Chapter 4.

From Dulles International Airport

Dulles is in suburban Virginia, about 26 miles from downtown D.C. To get into town, pick from the following:

✔ The **cab** ride to downtown Washington takes about 45 minutes in favorable traffic and costs about $50.

✔ The **SuperShuttle van** (☎ **202-296-6662** or 800-258-3826; www. supershuttle.com) charges $22 for the first passenger, $10 for each companion.

✔ The best bargain is the **5A express Metrobus,** which runs from Dulles to L'Enfant Plaza near the National Mall in D.C. or to Rosslyn, Virginia, just across the river from Georgetown. At both stops, you can enter the Metrorail system or hail a taxi. The bus costs $3. It departs Dulles approximately hourly from about 6:30 a.m. to 11:30 p.m. every day.

Dulles' **ATMs** are on the lower level of the main terminal and on concourses A, B, C, and D. **Currency exchange** services are located on both levels of the main terminal and on concourses B, C, and D. An **information counter** is on the lower level of the main terminal.

From Baltimore-Washington International Airport

BWI often has the least expensive airfares, especially on low-cost Southwest Airlines. But it's also the farthest away from the heart of D.C., so getting from the airport to your hotel takes longer and costs more money.

By **cab,** you're 45 minutes and $65 away from downtown Washington if the traffic flows smoothly. The **SuperShuttle van** (☎ 703-416-6661 or 800-258-3826; www.supershuttle.com) service charges $31 for the first passenger and $11 for each companion.

As at Dulles, **Metrobus** runs a $3 express from BWI — this one to the Greenbelt Metrorail station. The B30 bus leaves the airport every 40 minutes between 7 a.m. and 10:50 p.m. weekdays and 9:40 a.m. to 10:50 p.m. weekends.

On weekdays, you also can ride the **MARC train** (☎ 410-539-5000 or 866-743-3682; www.mtamaryland.com) from BWI to Union Station for $6. The interval between trains varies from 10 to 90 minutes, but usually is less than an hour. **Amtrak** (☎ 800-872-7245; www.amtrak.com) runs trains frequently on the same route from before 7 a.m. until after mid-night. Stay off the Metroliner and Acela Express, and you can ride Amtrak for $13 — less if you qualify for a senior, AAA, or other discount. A courtesy shuttle operates between BWI Airport and the nearby BWI Rail Station.

ATMs and **information** desks are scattered throughout the airport. **Currency exchange** services are available on the upper level by Pier C and on both levels of the International Pier.

From Union Station

Amtrak has great service in the Northeast Corridor. In my experience, it's the most efficient way to travel from New York to Washington and from points between. Trains arrive a few blocks from the U.S. Capitol at historic **Union Station,** a tourist attraction unto itself (see Chapter 11). You can make taxi and Metrorail connections here.

From the Union Station **Metrorail** station, you pay $1.35 to ride a few minutes to most hotels you'd be likely to stay at in central D.C. **Taxi** fares are more complicated. (See Chapter 4 for an explanation.) To get from Union Station to most of Washington's prime tourist area, you'll pay the cabbie $5.50 to $7.60, plus $1.50 for each additional passenger, plus possibly more add-ons — plus a tip.

An Amtrak **information** station is in the middle of the gates area and tourist information in the Main Hall.

Arriving by car

They say you shouldn't subject yourself to seeing the making of either law or sausage. To that, I will add driving in Washington. Driving *to* Washington isn't much fun, either — at least not when you get close to D.C.'s infamous Beltway. If you do drive on a weekday, try to schedule your arrival at the Beltway between 10 a.m. and 3 p.m. — or after 8 p.m. — to avoid the worst of the rush-hour insanity, which seems never to go away entirely.

When you make your hotel reservations, ask for directions. To help visualize the territory, see the "Driving to D.C." map on p. 55.

Once you get to your Washington destination, park your buggy and leave it parked until you leave. You'll be much happier if you get around town via Metrorail, Metrobus, taxi, or your own two feet.

If you drive to a hotel in town, be prepared to pay $20 or more to garage your car each day.

Figuring Out the Neighborhoods

Many first-time visitors are surprised to find that Washington is not all marble and memorials. Even in the most populated areas, you can find grass, trees, flowers, and a place to chill. You can discover much more in Washington than the White House, the Capitol, and the other familiar places featured on the nightly news. In fact, the District has several distinct and distinctive neighborhoods. You can explore their different facets during your visit and leave with a kaleidoscope of impressions. To get you started, here are thumbnail sketches (and a handy map) of D.C.'s major 'hoods.

Adams-Morgan

Vibrant and diverse — that's **Adams-Morgan,** whose crossroads are 18th Street and Columbia Road NW, north of Dupont Circle. This neighborhood's ethnic restaurants, boutiques, and jumping nightlife draw funseekers, especially in the evening and on weekends. Then, Adams-Morgan is packed, and parking is nearly impossible. The Dupont Circle and Woodley Park-Zoo Metrorail stations are a hike, but doable for the physically fit. After dark, however, take a taxi or the No. 98 Metrobus, which runs from the Woodley Park-Zoo Metrorail Station from about 6 p.m. to 3:15 a.m. weeknights, from 10 a.m. to 3:15 a.m. Saturdays, and from 6 p.m. to midnight Sundays. Be sure to exercise your street smarts.

Adams-Morgan is not a popular place for tourists to unpack their suitcases, because the area isn't convenient to the main tourist attractions — and there aren't any hotels in the neighborhood anyway.

Washington, D.C. Neighborhoods

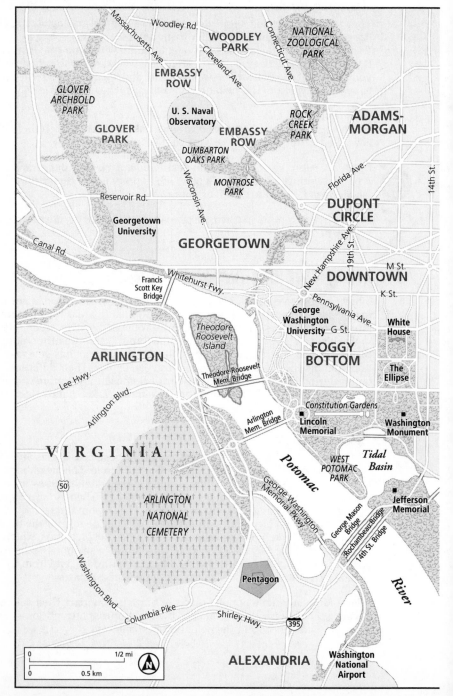

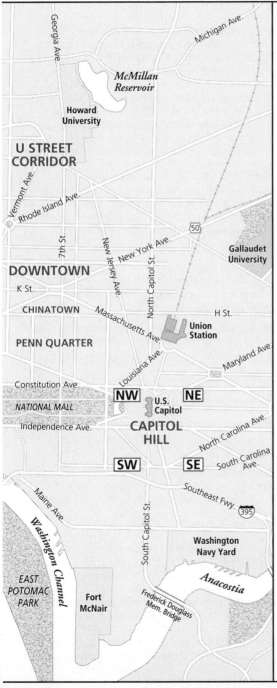

WHAT'S DOING WHERE?

- **ADAMS-MORGAN**
  This neighborhood is vibrant and diverse. Come here to enjoy ethnic restaurants, boutiques, and nightspots. The place really jumps in the evening and on weekends.

- **CAPITOL HILL**
  Congress dominates Capitol Hill, and the Supreme Court has its digs here, too. But the Hill also is a charming residential neighborhood, with a bustling old-fashioned market. And gorgeous old Union Station is filled with shops and eateries as well as gates to trains.

- **CHINATOWN**
  D.C.'s Chinatown is quite small, but it's got some very good restaurants and a large ornamental gateway.

- **DUPONT CIRCLE**
  Day or night, there's always something doing in Dupont Circle. Pop into the galleries, restaurants, and boutiques that abound here. Check out the nightspots or just watch the crazy world saunter by.

- **FOGGY BOTTOM/WEST END**
  As laid back as Dupont is lively, Foggy Bottom boasts quiet residential streets, George Washington University, the State Department, and the Kennedy Center.

- **GEORGETOWN**
  The oldest part of D.C., Georgetown encompasses exclusive residential streets, Georgetown University hangouts, lots of wildly diverse shops, many restaurants, lively nightspots, and an entertaining street scene.

- **NATIONAL MALL**
  The heart of official Washington, the Mall is lined with museums, dotted with memorials, and bordered by government headquarters buildings.

Capitol Hill

The Hill, as it is known around Washington, extends from the U.S. Capitol in three directions: north, south, and east. Two of the three branches of the federal government live here, as do a lot of people. In addition to housing the Congress and the Supreme Court, **Capitol Hill** is a charming residential neighborhood, with 19th-century houses, brick sidewalks, and tree-lined streets. You also find Union Station, the National Postal Museum, the Folger Shakespeare Library, the historic — and lively — Eastern Market, and quite a few restaurants, watering holes and mom-and-pop stores popular with the lawmakers, congressional staffers, lobbyists, and journalists who work, and sometimes live, here. The neighborhood brims with vitality and a persona uniquely its own.

Unfortunately, the area closest to the Capitol has become an eyesore and a travel nightmare because of construction projects and stop-gap security devices thrown up around government buildings. The Hill is another place to watch your step after dark, particularly beyond the Capitol grounds and the first few blocks of Pennsylvania Avenue SE.

The perks of staying on Capitol Hill are

- ✔ In addition to having easy access to the Hill's attractions, you can walk to the Mall or hop Metrorail to anywhere. The Hill is served by Red, Blue, and Orange Line stations.

- ✔ If you arrive and depart by train, your lodging is conveniently close to Union Station, which is a great place to eat and shop.

- ✔ This area is easier on your pocketbook than many other D.C. neighborhoods.

On the downside:

- ✔ Although the area has its *pocket parks* (small, welcome green spots in the midst of urban surroundings), it has less elbow room than other sections of the city.

- ✔ You won't encounter many problems in the immediate vicinity of the major hotels and attractions, but the farther you go from the Capitol, the less safe you'll be at night.

Downtown

Office buildings, shops, hotels, restaurants, galleries, nightspots and some government headquarters vie for space in this central area, which runs roughly from 6th to 22nd streets NW, north of Pennsylvania Avenue and south of the Dupont Circle neighborhood. Once as scintillating as white bread, the area now is a prime destination on evenings and week-ends thanks to redevelopment along Pennsylvania Avenue, the con-struction of the MCI Center sport/entertainment arena, the addition of high-quality restaurants and nightspots, the growth of art galleries, and the endurance of long-standing theaters. **Downtown** encompasses

Chinatown, the White House, and the Connecticut Avenue/K Street business-shopping-lobbying hub.

The advantages of staying downtown are

> ✔ You're within walking distance of major attractions, as well as all those nightspots, theaters, and shops.
>
> ✔ Many of the city's best restaurants are located here, as are a large number of inexpensive eateries frequented by downtown workers at lunch time.

On the other hand:

> ✔ You can pay a high price for the convenient location.
>
> ✔ Much — though not all — of the area loses its vitality when the office workers go home for the night.

Dupont Circle

One of Washington's liveliest neighborhoods all day long, the **Dupont Circle** area is an ideal spot for people watching. (Check out the street musicians and chess players in the heart of the circle itself.) Early in the morning, workers arrive at the embassies, businesses, think tanks, and other nonprofit organizations that set up their headquarters here. The area's many restaurants feed people from breakfast through dinner. The neighborhood is filled with art galleries and specialty shops. The night-spots keep hopping until well after midnight. Kramerbooks ("open early to late, seven days a week") offered food, drink, and live music long before that became de rigueur for all bookstores. Dupont Circle is the traditional hub of Washington's gay community, which parties in the neighborhood's gay-oriented night spots and shops — among many other places — at Lambda Rising bookstore and the Human Rights Campaign store.

On the upside:

> ✔ This area is hip, trendy, lively, colorful, more interesting, and less homogenized than most of the other neighborhoods in town.
>
> ✔ You're close to some of the city's best nightlife and dining.
>
> ✔ You can find reasonable prices here, too.

The drawbacks are

> ✔ You're further from major tourist attractions than you would be in several other areas.
>
> ✔ All that after-dark partying means the area can get very noisy at night.
>
> ✔ In a city full of traffic and parking horrors, this neighborhood can be particularly nightmarish.

Foggy Bottom/West End

Insiders call the State Department **"Foggy Bottom"** because that's the neighborhood in which its headquarters stand, and the name seems perfect for the obfuscating parlance that marks much diplomatic dialogue. George Washington University also occupies an ever-expanding portion of the neighborhood. That leaves an ever-shrinking piece of the pie to Foggy Bottom's charming residential streets of brick row houses, Lilliputian gardens, and mature trees. Here, you also find the Kennedy Center, the Watergate complex, and quite a few hotels. The neighborhood got its name, by the way, because much of it was low, swampy land that produced much fog and mist and later was an industrial area, then called "Funkstown," that was engulfed in smoke and smog.

Foggy Bottom encompasses the area west of the White House, east of Georgetown and south of Pennsylvania Avenue. **West End** refers to the small neighborhood surrounded by Foggy Bottom, downtown, Dupont Circle, and Georgetown. There you find office buildings and a few hotels and restaurants.

The pros:

✔ You're close to the White House, Kennedy Center, State Department, George Washington University, the infamous Watergate, and Georgetown.

✔ You can hop Metrorail or the 30-series Metrobuses for longer trips.

✔ A very pleasing European ambiance pervades the neighborhood.

✔ Foggy Bottom is quieter than other sections of town.

The only con is that the quiet also means that the area usually has less excitement than elsewhere.

Georgetown

One of Washington's best-known neighborhoods was established before the District of Columbia was a gleam in Pierre L'Enfant's eye. Fragments of a former era, when **Georgetown** was a bustling tobacco port, endure in the residential architecture and the cobblestone and brick streets off the main drags.

On Wisconsin Avenue and M Street, however, the mood is far from genteel, especially on weekends. A mix of shops, restaurants, and nightspots draws the young — and the young at heart — from D.C., the suburbs, local universities, and all over the world. Georgetown University, Dumbarton Oaks, the C&O Canal, the *"Exorcist* Steps" (featured in the movie), and some of the city's most exclusive residences contribute to Georgetown's enduring cache.

Georgetown has no Metrorail station, but 30-series Metrobuses run on Wisconsin and on M to Pennsylvania Avenue. You can hike in from the Foggy Bottom-GWU Metrorail Station. Georgetown Metro Connection shuttle buses run from the Foggy Bottom, Dupont Circle, and Rosslyn stations from 7 a.m. to midnight Monday through Thursday, 7 a.m. to 2 a.m. Friday, 8 a.m. to 2 a.m. on Saturday, and 8 a.m. to midnight Sunday. Fare's a buck — or 35 cents with a Metrorail transfer.

Staying in Georgetown is great because:

- ✔ Like Dupont Circle, Georgetown jumps a lot more than most of the rest of Washington.

- ✔ An abundance of shopping, dining, and nightlife is within walking distance.

- ✔ Walk just northwest of the central Wisconsin Avenue and M Street intersection, and you're in another college community — Georgetown University.

- ✔ Walk just northeast, and you enter Washington's most exclusive residential neighborhood, home to some of the richest, most powerful, and most famous people in the world.

On the other hand:

- ✔ If you seek tranquility, especially at night, stay elsewhere. The noise on weekends (when the student population comes out to party) can grow very loud.

- ✔ Georgetown has no Metrorail station, so you have to hail a cab, hop a bus, or hike to Foggy Bottom or (believe it or not) the Rosslyn Station in Virginia.

- ✔ Georgetown can get very crowded. Traffic is bad at all times and is particularly horrendous during rush hour, on weeknights, and throughout the weekends.

The National Mall

Washington's long, long lawn stretches from the Capitol to the Lincoln Memorial and is where you find many museums, monuments, and memorials. The **Mall** is lined by major Smithsonian Institutions and is across the street from major federal government offices. You encounter somber contemplation at places like the Vietnam War Memorial and joyful play on the grass and walkways (kite-flying, cycling, jogging, strolling, and squirrel-watching).

There's no point reviewing the pluses and minuses of staying on the Mall, because you can't.

Upper Northwest

The **Upper Northwest** area is essentially everything north and west of what I describe in the preceding sections. It's mostly nice residential neighborhoods, D.C.'s best public schools, some office buildings, and the restaurants, theaters, and retail establishments that serve them. Some hotels and tourist attractions, notably the Washington National Cathedral and the National Zoo, are here. I live in this neighborhood, but I take visitors elsewhere to sightsee. Where Wisconsin Avenue crosses into Maryland is an area that I refer to as Washington's Rodeo Drive — a number of exclusive stores (plus some discounters) for those who are inclined to expend substantial vacation bucks on shopping.

The good of staying here:

  ✔ Families appreciate the area's proximity to the National Zoo, a major child-pleaser, on Connecticut Avenue.

  ✔ You find Washington's answer to Beverly Hills' Rodeo Drive near the Friendship Heights Metrorail Station.

  ✔ Washington National Cathedral is on upper Wisconsin Avenue.

The only bad thing is that you'll be taking Metrorail, Metrobus, or a taxi to see most of the sights.

Gathering Information After You Arrive

If you need information after you arrive in Washington, head for one or more of these spots:

  ✔ **Washington, D.C., Visitor Information Center,** on the ground floor of the Ronald Reagan International Trade Center Building, 1300 Pennsylvania Ave. NW, at the Federal Triangle Metrorail Station (☎ **202-328-4748,** 866-324-7386; www.dcvisit.com). From March 15 through Labor Day, the center is open 8:30 a.m. to 5:30 p.m. weekdays and 9 a.m. to 4 p.m. Saturdays. The rest of the year, it's open 9 a.m. to 4:30 p.m. weekdays, closed weekends.

    This center is a full-service spot. Staff members can answer your questions, and you can pick up free brochures. You can buy Metro fare cards, theater tickets, and sightseeing tickets. You can use its computers to find out information about hotels, restaurants, and events and can even book a hotel reservation.

  ✔ **The White House Visitor Center,** in the Commerce Department Building, 15th and E streets NW, near the Federal Triangle Metrorail Station (☎ **202-208-1631;** www.nps.gov/whho/welcome.htm). At press time, White House tours are limited to groups of at least ten who get tickets from a member of Congress. But the National Park Service continues to operate this visitor center, which isn't in the White House.

It's open 7:30 a.m. to 4 p.m. every day except Thanksgiving, December 25, and January 1. You can find information here about other parts of Washington in addition to the White House. You can use restrooms, telephones, and water fountains and obtain first aid if you need it.

✔ **The Smithsonian Information Center,** in the "Castle," 1000 Jefferson Dr. SW, on the National Mall, near the Smithsonian Metrorail Station (☎ **202-633-1000;** TTY 202-357-1729; www. si.edu/visit/infocenter/start.htm; e-mail info@si.edu). Stop here for information about the Smithsonian and other attractions. Watch a 24-minute video for an overview of the institution. Peruse a model of the Mall to help you locate your first stop. Find attractions and Metro and Tourmobile stops using an electronic map.Pick up a free guide in any of seven languages.

This center also has information about events elsewhere in the city. Your kids can access information from the video-display monitors while you challenge the staff with your questions. If you're on overload, ask one of the volunteers for help in planning your itinerary. On your way out, you may want to pay your respects to British subject James Smithson, whose bequest gave birth to the institution. His crypt is just inside the Jefferson Drive entrance. The center is open 8:30 a.m. to 5:30 p.m. daily except December 25.

Getting Around Washington

Washington can be a challenge to navigate, particularly for a newcomer. But once you know the basics, you can negotiate the tourist areas with ease.

D.C. has streets, avenues, roads, drives, places, squares, circles — and probably some other arteries that have slipped my mind. The avenues, roads, drives, and places go every which way. Roadways run into physical barriers and disappear, only to reappear again several blocks away. Circles and squares pop up in your way and leave you searching for your route on the other side. But the street-naming system is based on a grid that extends throughout the city. If you understand how the street-naming system works, you can find almost any address and figure out where you are most of the time.

The key to the city: Getting from here to there

When D.C. was created from land ceded by Maryland and Virginia, it was a perfect square, ten miles on a side, with one corner pointing due north. In due course, Virginia was given back most of Southwest D.C. and a portion of Northwest, which is why the district now has an irregular shape defined by the Potomac River along its border with Virginia.

The street-naming system, based on the original square, has endured. The city is divided into quadrants, and all the streets are known by the quadrant they're in: Northwest (NW), Northeast (NE), Southeast (SE), and Southwest (SW).

Understanding the District's directions

The Capitol dome is the center of D.C. geography. Three streets — North Capitol, East Capitol, and South Capitol — run in those directions from the Capitol grounds. You won't find a West Capitol Street, but you can imagine it running due west from the Capitol down the center of the National Mall. These streets define the boundaries of the four quadrants.

All of Washington's numbered streets run north-south, counting from the Capitol. First Street NE is the first street east of North Capitol Street. First Street NW is the first street west of North Capitol Street. First Street SE is the first street east of South Capitol Street. Just to confuse things, here and there you encounter a Half Street, which is closer to Capitol Street than a portion of First Street.

Washington's east-west-running streets all have names that — in most cases — work through the alphabet as they get further north and south of East Capitol Street and the middle of the National Mall. The streets closest to East Capitol and the middle of the Mall are named for letters — A Street, B Street, and so on. As you continue north and south and the alphabet is exhausted, you run into streets with two-syllable names — Adams, Bryant, Channing, and so on. Then you hit three-syllable names (Allison, Buchanan).

Unfortunately, you find numerous exceptions to these rules. For some reason — or perhaps for no reason at all — no J, X, Y, or Z streets exist. Some streets break the alphabet and syllable rules. And the roadways that aren't streets — avenues, roads, drives, places — do whatever they feel like doing.

If you understand the basic street grid, you can find almost any address and figure out where you are most of the time. If you're looking for 450 H St. NW, you know it's in the Northwest quadrant of the city, eight streets north of the middle of National Mall, between Fourth and Fifth streets. If you're looking for 850 Fourth St. NE, you know it's in the Northeast quadrant, between H and I streets.

 You'll notice I said "almost." The numbered streets don't mess around. But some named streets defy the alphabet and syllable standards. And, because there is no J Street, the block between K and L is the 1000 block. I'm sorry. At least you'll be able to estimate locations within a few blocks. (And then you can ask directions!)

Movin' around on Metro

Washington's extensive public transportation system makes getting around the city a cinch. **Metrorail,** called Metro by locals, is the city's subway system. Rail stations open at 5 a.m. on weekdays and at 7 a.m. on weekends. Final trains leave stations around midnight Sunday through Thursday and around 3 a.m. Friday and Saturday. If you're traveling late at night, check the exact time of the last train leaving the station you'll be using. The schedule is posted at the kiosks in each station. You can reach Metro information at ☎ **202-637-7000** (TDD 202-638-3780) or online at www.wmata.com. Request a **Metro Visitor's Kit** by calling ☎ **888-638-7646** or 202-962-2733.

Finding Metrorail stations

To find a Metrorail station on Washington's streets, look for the brown pole topped by the letter M and the station name. You should see a *colored stripe* beneath the M to indicate the line or lines that stop there. The different Metrorail lines are named for colors — Red, Blue, Orange, Yellow, and Green. Trains are well marked, but sometimes trains from different lines (such as Blue and Orange) use the same tracks. If you're unsure, ask the station manager or another waiting passenger. If you find yourself on the wrong train, hop off and take a train back to the station where you made the mistake.

Metrorail's cars are air-conditioned, and the seats are upholstered. Stations are clean and well lighted. Though Metrorail is showing its age (not unlike most people), a major effort is underway to replace tired escalators, refurbish old trains, and bring new trains on line.

Trains run every few minutes during rush hour, less often at other times, least often late at night. I always carry reading material for when I'm sitting on the train and waiting at the station. Or you can use your transportation time to people-watch.

Paying your way on Metro

Getting around via Metrorail is relatively inexpensive. Fares are based on distance traveled and time of day. Off peak, the minimum fare is $1.35. You pay less than $2 for most places within D.C., even during rush hour (weekdays before 9:30 a.m. and from 3 to 7 p.m.) There's also a surcharge after 2 a.m. You can buy fare cards from vending machines inside the stations. The machines accept coins (from nickels to quarters) and bills (from $1 to $20). Some machines take credit cards. Bear in mind that the machines return up to only $5 in change — *in coins only* — so make sure that you use small bills when you buy a low-value fare card. Experiencing difficulty? Ask the station manager — or a nearby local — for help.

Washington, D.C. Metro Stops

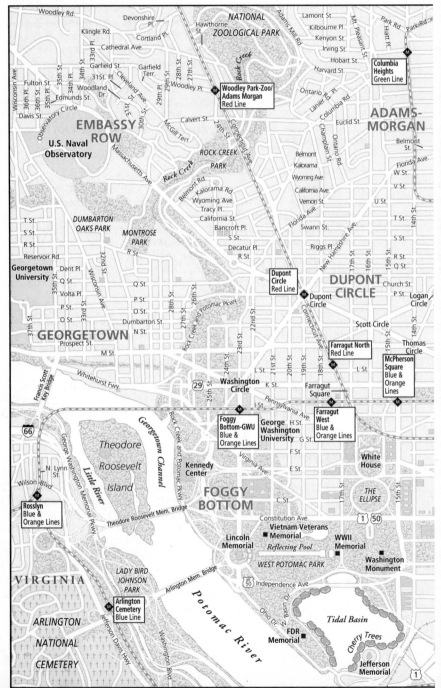

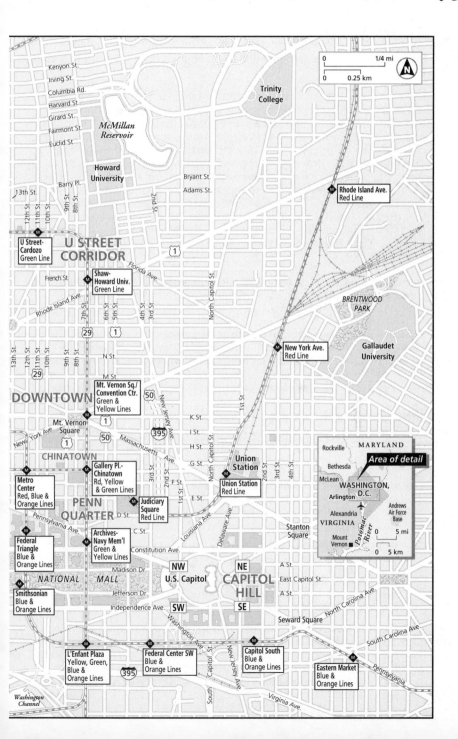

Estimate the amount of fare you need throughout your D.C. stay and buy one fare card per person with that amount on it. That way, you don't have to stop at a fare card vending machine each time you want to take a ride.

Each passenger needs a fare card. One or two children younger than five can ride free with a paying passenger. Disabled persons and seniors 65 and older can ride for half price with a special fare card, but they must possess valid proof of disability or age. For the senior discount, identification can be a driver's license or birth certificate. If the disabled person doesn't have a Medicare card, however, the discount probably isn't worth the paperwork for someone who's visiting for a few days or even a few weeks. A convenient place to purchase the half-price fare cards is the sales office inside the Metro Center Metrorail Station. You can get to it through the station's 12th and F streets entrance or by taking a train to the station. The sales office is open weekdays from 7:30 a.m. to 6:30 p.m. The cards also are sold at some stores, including Safeway and Giant groceries.

One-day rail passes cost $6.50 and allow unlimited rides for a single weekday after 9:30 a.m. or all day Saturday and Sunday. You can buy them at all Metrorail stations.

After you insert your fare card in the entrance gate, it's stamped and returned. Don't walk off without it (as many visitors do). You need to reinsert it in the exit gate at your destination, where the card is returned if value is left on it. If you underestimate the fare, you can add what's necessary at the *Addfare* machines found near the exit and entrance gates.

Hints for smooth riding on Metrorail

First-time passengers sometimes find the system intimidating. Follow these tips, and you should enjoy a smooth ride. (Should you start to hyperventilate, just ask a station attendant for help.)

- ✔ **Use the maps.** Wall-mounted maps and the lists of station-to-station fares are posted in Metrorail stations. Take your time in locating the station closest to your destination. When in doubt, ask the station manager.

- ✔ **Hold onto your fare card** when it's returned to you. Keep it handy for reinsertion at your destination.

- ✔ **Don't board the wrong train.** It sounds obvious, but the minute (or two) that you take to note the station stops, listed on columns inside the stations, is worth it.

- ✔ **Do not eat, drink, or smoke on Metro or in the stations.** *This rule is serious!* Washington's Metro is one of the cleanest subway systems in the world, and this rule is the reason for it. The police will fine — and even arrest — you for sipping a soft drink or nibbling on potato chips in a station or on a train. Keep your snacks in your backpacks.

✔ **Get a transfer ticket** if you're switching from Metrorail to Metrobus. You can get one from a machine where you enter the Metrorail system to start your trip, and it lets you transfer to a regular bus for 35 cents and to an express bus for $1.65. You can't get a bus-to-subway transfer.

✔ On the escalator, **stand to the right and walk on the left.** Blocking walkers by standing on the left is considered exceedingly rude. A columnist for *The Washington Post* staged a contest a few years ago to come up with a name for people who stand to the left. The winning entry: "Tourists."

Traveling by bus

Metrobuses run throughout Washington and its Maryland and Virginia suburbs. Metrorail is faster and more comfortable. But the subway doesn't go to as many places as the buses do. For tourists, the 30-series buses are quite useful.

All 30, 32, 34, 35, and 36 buses travel down Wisconsin Avenue from the D.C.-Maryland border to M Street in the heart of Georgetown. They then go through the heart of downtown and along part of the National Mall on their way to Capitol Hill.

To find Metrobus stops, look for the red, white, and blue signs with route numbers. You can request a free **map** of all Metrobus Routes in D.C. and Virginia, which is probably all you need to hit the major sights, by phoning ☎ **202-637-7000.** A map of the D.C. and Maryland routes is available, as well. You also can get the maps at Metrorail stations and Metro sales offices.

Bus fare is $1.25, except for some suburban express routes that cost $3. Bus-to-bus transfers are free; ask the driver of your first bus. Drivers don't make change, so you need to carry exact fare. Most buses run daily around the clock — frequently during rush hour, infrequently in the wee hours.

Up to two children younger than five ride free with a paying passenger. Seniors 65 and older and persons with disabilities can ride for 60 cents. Valid proof of age or disability must be presented when boarding. For seniors, a driver's license or birth certificate works. A disabled person needs a Medicare card or a special Metro ID that, for a visitor, probably is more trouble to get than it's worth.

Taxi! Cabbing it in D.C.

Hailing a cab in Washington usually is a snap, except for late at night. Stand on a main street, by a busy intersection, or in front of a hotel or large office building to better snag a taxi. When I need to order a cab, I call **Diamond** (☎ **202-387-6200,** 202-797-5916, 202-797-5915, or, for airport service, 202-387-2600). Diamond's not perfect, but I seem to get a

Taxicab Zones

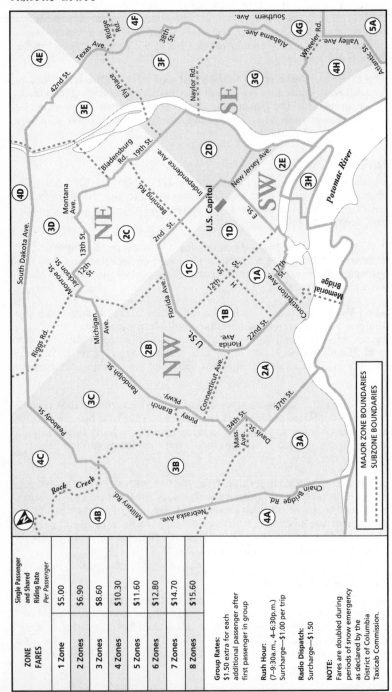

ZONE FARES	Single Passenger and Shared Riding Rate *Per Passenger*
1 Zone	$5.00
2 Zones	$6.90
3 Zones	$8.60
4 Zones	$10.30
5 Zones	$11.60
6 Zones	$12.80
7 Zones	$14.70
8 Zones	$15.60

Group Rates:
$1.50 extra for each additional passenger after first passenger in group

Rush Hour:
(7–9:30a.m., 4–6:30p.m.)
Surcharge—$1.00 per trip

Radio Dispatch:
Surcharge—$1.50

NOTE:
Fares are doubled during periods of snow emergency as declared by the District of Columbia Taxicab Commission.

— MAJOR ZONE BOUNDARIES
----- SUBZONE BOUNDARIES

higher percentage of well-maintained cabs with knowledgeable drivers with Diamond than with some other companies.

Strangers to D.C. may find the zone fare system baffling — as do the locals. But if you ride a Washington cab, you have to deal with it. For details, see Chapter 4.

Items left in a cab are supposed to be turned in to the D.C. Taxicab Commission (☎ **202-645-6018,** fax 202-889-3604; dctaxi.dc.gov/dctaxi). If you leave something in a cab, phone, fax or e-mail the commission with this information: your name, daytime telephone number, a brief description of the item (include model and phone number for cell phone), and the date it was lost. Also have the name, ID number, and vehicle license plate number of the cab, if you know it. If you have a receipt, enlarge it to double size and fax it. The commission's office hours are 8:30 a.m. to 4 p.m. Monday thru Friday, except holidays. You're supposed to be able to leave a recorded message, but when I called on a recent Tuesday evening, the voice mail box was full.

Taking a ride on Tourmobile

An excellent alternative mode of transportation for tourists is **Tourmobile** (☎ **202-554-5100,** 888-868-7707; www.tourmobile.com), the tram that stops by major tourist attractions and at points in Arlington Cemetery. The $20 fare ($9 for children 3 through 11 and free for younger kids) lets you ride all day with unlimited reboarding privileges. That means you can ride the full route, listening to the tour guide's narrative, and get a good overview of most of the big attractions. Then you can use the Tourmobile as a bus to go from place to place for the rest of the day. A two-day pass is $30 or $15.

Trams stop about every 20 minutes at the red, white, and blue Tourmobile signs from 9:30 a.m. until 4:30 p.m. daily except Dec. 25 and Jan. 1. Final reboarding is at 3:30 p.m. You can buy tickets from the driver or at Tourmobile ticket booths.

All Tourmobile trams are equipped with priority seating for individuals with disabilities and wheelchair storage space. Individuals with disabilities who can transfer from their wheelchairs and climb three steps can board any Tourmobile. Vehicles with lifts are dispatched when a request is made to a Tourmobile driver or at a ticket booth. You can schedule service by a lift-equipped vehicle in advance by calling ☎ **703-979-0690** between 8 a.m. and 5 p.m. daily except December 25 and January 1. Disabled riders can leave the tram at any stop and arrange a reboarding time with the driver.

Walking through Washington

Like Nancy Sinatra's boots, Washington is made for walking. In these health- and budget-conscious times, putting mileage on your feet instead of your wallet, fare card, or car makes sense. On foot, you discover things that you may otherwise miss, things that make a trip special. (When you get home, please write and tell me what they are.)

Try a Mall crawl, walking from museum to museum between the Capitol and the Washington Monument. The museums are air-conditioned; you can rest and rejuvenate in a restaurant or snack bar. Or stroll through the residential side streets of Foggy Bottom and/or Georgetown.

Keep your wits about you when you walk. That's not to say that D.C. isn't safe to walk around. It is, especially in the major tourist zones. It just pays to be prepared. Stride with a sense of purpose; dawdlers appear vulnerable, which is just what professional pickpockets look for. Be alert in crowds, where a bump from a pickpocket can easily be missed. Be aware of your surroundings. Stow wallets, cash, and credit cards in front pockets or a money pouch worn under your clothing. Wear your purse across one shoulder and over the chest — bandolier style.

The safe zones include the major tourist areas and Metro. At night, use the buddy system and stick to the main commercial blocks when in Adams-Morgan and Capitol Hill. If Metro's service has stopped for the night, and you're still out on the town, take a taxi. Know your destination before you set out. Hold your kids' hands on city streets and sidewalks, on all Metro escalators, and on Metro platforms. Lock your hotel room door, car doors, and trunk. Lock valuables in a safe deposit box (if not in your room, then at the front desk). Keep a close eye on your pocketbook, camera, and wallet. Hold onto your purse in a restaurant. Leave the family jewels at home; what you do bring, don't flash.

On Capitol Hill, you won't encounter many problems in the immediate vicinity of the major hotels and attractions, but the farther you go from the Capitol, the less safe you'll be at night.

Driving your car

I have yet to meet a person who enjoys driving in Washington. The traffic is oppressive and constantly getting worse. Washington also seems to be cursed by an ever-growing number of drivers who drive as if no one else is on the road. Street parking is at a premium. Garage parking will consume your family's lunch money.

If you plan on arriving by car, ask about parking rates at your hotel when you make a reservation. It may prevent your requiring treatment for shock when the final hotel tab is totaled up.

Chapter 9

Checking In at D.C.'s Best Hotels

*B*ecause so many different kinds of people come to Washington with regularity, the city has a wide variety of accommodations. The idealistic young and penniless come here, perhaps to protest, to volunteer for the many do-gooder groups in town, or just to see the sights. At the other extreme, high-rolling lawyers and lobbyists arrive with no worry about expense accounts because their clients will be picking up whatever tab is presented. The rest of the world, in the gigantic middle between those extremes, is looking for budget, moderate, or moderately luxurious accommodations. Fortunately, visitors can find them all.

Finding the Best Room at the Best Rate

Some folks call a hotel, ask for a rate, and pay it with no more questions asked. These are the same folks who go to an automobile dealer and pay sticker price. You, however, aren't going to mimic these people by paying the first price you're quoted, because you're going to use the tips that follow to find the best hotel room for your money.

Finding the best rates

If you walk in off the street and ask for a room for the night, you'll be told the hotel's maximum charge for that room — its *rack rate*. (During your next hotel stay, take a peek at the fire and/or emergency directions posted on the back of your door; the rack rates usually are posted on or near these notices.) If a hotel can get away with collecting its rack rate for a room, the management is very happy. But here's the scoop: Hardly anyone forks over the rack rate. The step you need to take to avoid being

Hotels in Washington, D. C.

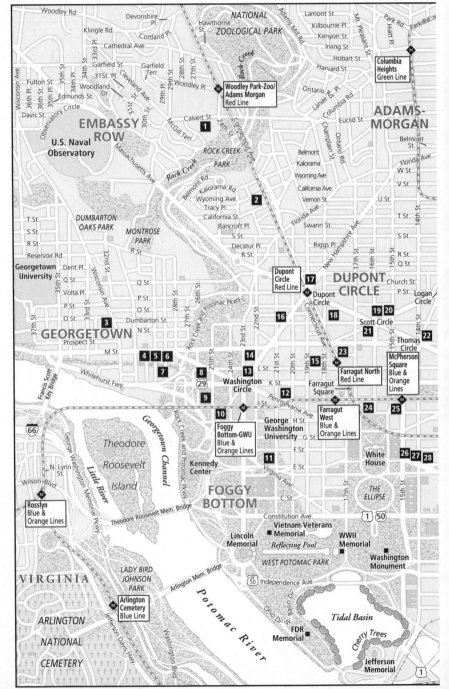

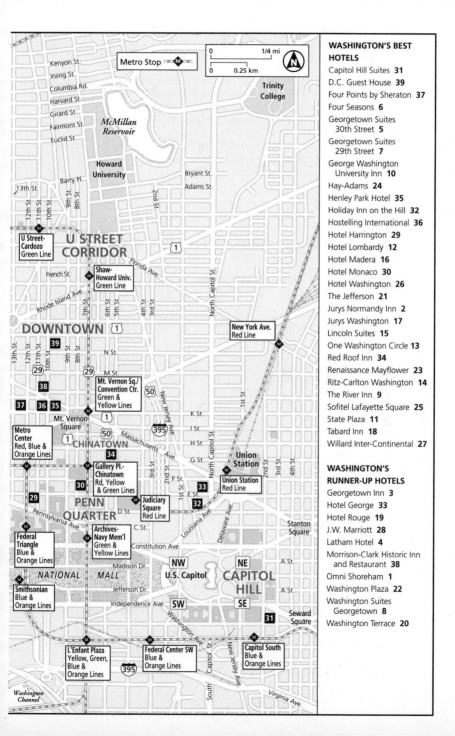

Metro Stop ━━●━ M

0   1/4 mi
0   0.25 km

Kenyon St.
Irving St.
Columbia Rd.
Harvard St.
Girard St.
Fairmont St.
Euclid St.

McMillan Reservoir

Trinity College

Howard University

Bryant St.
Adams St.

13th St.
12th St.
11th St.
10th St.
9th St.
8th St.
2nd St.

Barry Pl.

U Street-Cardozo Green Line

U STREET CORRIDOR

Florida Ave.

French St.

Shaw-Howard Univ. Green Line

Rhode Island Ave.

7th St.
6th St.
5th St.
4th St.
3rd St.

North Capitol St.

New York Ave. Red Line

DOWNTOWN

13th St.
12th St.
11th St.
10th St.
9th St.
8th St.

N St.

39
29
38
37 36 35

M St.

Mt. Vernon Sq./Convention Ctr. Green & Yellow Lines

50

New Jersey Ave.

1st St.

K St.

Mt. Vernon Square

Metro Center Red, Blue & Orange Lines

50
Massachusetts Ave.

I St.

395

H St.

CHINATOWN

34

Gallery Pl.-Chinatown Rd, Yellow & Green Lines

3rd St.
2nd St.
1st St.

G St.
F St.

Union Station

Union Station Red Line

3rd St.
4th St.

30

PENN QUARTER

Pennsylvania Ave.

29

Judiciary Square Red Line

33
32

D St.

Archives-Navy Mem'l Green & Yellow Lines

C St.

Louisiana Ave.

Delaware Ave.

Stanton Square

Federal Triangle Blue & Orange Lines

Constitution Ave.

NW

NE

A St.

NATIONAL MALL

Madison Dr.

U.S. Capitol

CAPITOL HILL

Smithsonian Blue & Orange Lines

Jefferson Dr.

SW

SE

A St.

Independence Ave.

31

Seward Square

Washington Ave.

L'Enfant Plaza Yellow, Green, Blue & Orange Lines

395

Federal Center SW Blue & Orange Lines

South Capitol St.

New Jersey Ave.

Capitol South Blue & Orange Lines

Washington Channel

Virginia Ave.

WASHINGTON'S BEST HOTELS
Capitol Hill Suites **31**
D.C. Guest House **39**
Four Points by Sheraton **37**
Four Seasons **6**
Georgetown Suites 30th Street **5**
Georgetown Suites 29th Street **7**
George Washington University Inn **10**
Hay-Adams **24**
Henley Park Hotel **35**
Holiday Inn on the Hill **32**
Hostelling International **36**
Hotel Harrington **29**
Hotel Lombardy **12**
Hotel Madera **16**
Hotel Monaco **30**
Hotel Washington **26**
The Jefferson **21**
Jurys Normandy Inn **2**
Jurys Washington **17**
Lincoln Suites **15**
One Washington Circle **13**
Red Roof Inn **34**
Renaissance Mayflower **23**
Ritz-Carlton Washington **14**
The River Inn **9**
Sofitel Lafayette Square **25**
State Plaza **11**
Tabard Inn **18**
Willard Inter-Continental **27**

WASHINGTON'S RUNNER-UP HOTELS
Georgetown Inn **3**
Hotel George **33**
Hotel Rouge **19**
J.W. Marriott **28**
Latham Hotel **4**
Morrison-Clark Historic Inn and Restaurant **38**
Omni Shoreham **1**
Washington Plaza **22**
Washington Suites Georgetown **8**
Washington Terrace **20**

charged the rack rate is surprisingly simple: Ask whether the hotel offers a cheaper or discounted rate. You almost always get a better price! Better yet, don't walk in off the street. Make reservations ahead of time.

Room rates change with the season, as occupancy rates rise and fall. If a hotel is close to full, it's less likely to extend discount rates; if a hotel is close to empty, it may be willing to negotiate. D.C. hotels are more likely to negotiate with you on weekends and during low season.

Room prices are subject to change without notice; therefore, the rates quoted in this book may be different from the actual rate you receive when you make your reservation.

Low season — low rates

The three best times of year to find deals on hotel rooms in D.C. are

- ✔ **Thanksgiving through New Year's.** Fewer travelers leave home and hearth.

- ✔ **July and August.** Congress is in recess, and the city is in siesta mode.

- ✔ **Weekends** throughout the year. Politicians (and all the folks who follow them) get outta town on the weekends, leaving space for everyone else.

Between Thanksgiving and early January, the pace here slows down. Many members of Congress take very long breaks from Washington. (The House calls them "district work periods." The Senate calls them "recesses." They're usually actually a bit of both.) And folks in the rest of the country are less likely to pack up for a Washington vacation during the year-end holidays. With fewer people in town, hotels cut their rates. (Someday "Thankmas" may become a national — extended — holiday.) During July and August, when the Senate and House office buildings are morguelike because the elected officials are away for their summer recess/work period, hotels woo visitors with lower charges. (For more on Washington's high and low seasons, see Chapter 2.) And on the weekends, the gang on the Hill heads home again, as do the visiting lobbyists, and hotel rates again take a dip.

High season — high prices

High season in Washington is

- ✔ **Mid-March through June.** Everyone wants to visit D.C. in the spring, and who can blame them? The city blossoms in the warm weather, but, alas, so do hotel prices.

- ✔ **September through mid-November.** Congress is back in session, and Capitol Hill is hopping in fall. The weather outside may be delightful, but it's a safe bet that hotel prices will be frightful.

In spring, the Cherry Blossom Festival, good weather, and school districts' spring breaks historically draw visitors to the city in huge numbers. The weather is usually mild into June, and that keeps the crowds coming. High season also occurs when Capitol is a beehive of activity, and those who want to influence Congress converge on the city's hotels.

Surfing the Web for hotel deals

You can use the Internet to gather information and make hotel reservations. In fact, because so many different deals are available, your best bet is to use both the telephone and the Internet when you search for the best prices. Check several online sources as well.

Major hotel chains — and many individual hotels — book rooms online the same way that airlines and Amtrak book transportation. (See the Quick Concierge for chains' Web addresses and phone numbers.)

Expedia offers a long list of special deals and "virtual tours" or photos of available rooms so that you can see what you're paying for (a feature that helps to counter claims that the best rooms are often held back from bargain booking Web sites). **Travelocity** posts unvarnished customer reviews and ranks its properties according to the AAA rating system. Also reliable are **Hotels.com** and **Quikbook.com**. An excellent free program, **TravelAxe** (www.travelaxe.net), can help you search multiple hotel sites at once, even ones you may never have heard of — and conveniently lists the total price of the room, including the taxes and service charges. Another booking site, **Travelweb** (www.travelweb), is partly owned by the hotels it represents (including the Hilton, Hyatt, and Starwood chains) and is therefore plugged directly into the hotels' reservations systems — unlike independent online agencies, which have to fax or e-mail reservation requests to the hotel. Be sure to **get a confirmation number** and **make a printout** of any online booking transaction, in case questions about your reservation arise when you check in.

In the opaque Web site category, **Priceline** and **Hotwire** are even better for hotels than for airfares; with both, you're allowed to pick the neighborhood and quality level of your hotel before offering up your money. On the down side, many hotels stick Priceline guests in their least desirable rooms. Be sure to go to the **BiddingforTravel** Web site (www.biddingfortravel.com) before bidding on a hotel room on Priceline; it features a fairly up-to-date list of hotels that Priceline uses in major cities. For both Priceline and Hotwire, you pay upfront, and the fee is nonrefundable. *Note:* Some hotels don't provide loyalty program credits or points or other frequent-stay amenities when you book a room through opaque online services.

Reserving the best room

The amount you spend to bed down eats a big chunk of your travel dollars. In all but the smallest accommodations, the rate you pay for a room depends on many factors — chief among them being how you make your reservation. Prices change, sometimes faster than room service can deliver coffee and a bagel.

Calling your friendly travel agent

A travel agent may be able to negotiate a better price with certain hotels than you can get by yourself. Often, the hotel gives the agent a discount in exchange for steering his or her business toward that hotel.

Your travel agent may suggest a package deal (with airfare) and/or traveling with a group. (See Chapter 5 for more on package tours.) Booking with a group can be the best way to get the best deal. Not only do you hand over the responsibility of planning the trip to someone else — the tour operator — you often get a better rate. Hotels, joyful at the prospect of booking 20 rooms instead of one or two, give tour operators a discount that's passed on to you.

Making your own hotel reservations

Hotel chains take telephone reservations through a central toll-free number and at the individual hotels. (See the Quick Concierge at the back of the book for toll-free numbers for the major chains.) Sometimes the toll-free number and the local numbers produce different rates. Your best bet is to call both, to see which reservations agent gives you a better deal.

Be sure to mention membership in AAA, AARP, frequent-flier programs, and any other corporate rewards programs, or whether you're a government employee, when you make your reservation. You never know when doing so can save you a few dollars off your room rate.

After you make your reservation, ask a few more questions. These inquiries can go a long way toward making sure that you secure the best room for the best price.

✔ **Always ask whether a corner room is available at the same price.** Sometimes a corner room has more space and more windows (with views). And the corner location may mean a quieter environment. If you're located at the end of the hall, you don't hear your neighbors passing your room or using the elevator all night.

✔ **Steer clear of construction zones.** Be sure to ask whether the hotel is renovating. If it is, request a room away from the renovation site. The noise and activity may be a bit more than you want to deal with on your vacation.

   ✔ **Request smoking or nonsmoking rooms.** Be sure to indicate your preference. Otherwise, you may get stuck with a room that doesn't meet your needs.

   ✔ **Inquire about the location of the restaurants, bars, and nightspots.** These areas of the hotel can be sources of irritating noise. On the other hand, if you want to be near the action, or if you have a disability that makes it difficult for you to get around, you may choose to be close to these amenities.

 Even if you secure a relatively quiet room, strange noises, loud TVs, and snoring partners can wreak havoc with your sleep. Carry earplugs when you travel.

Arriving Without a Reservation

Arriving in D.C. and *then* looking for a place to stay is not the preferred way to find a bargain — or a room of any kind, for that matter. If you do find yourself in this bind, call the major hotel chains and ask what they have available. (See the Quick Concierge at the back of this book for their phone numbers.) Or try some local reservation services, such as **Capitol Reservations** (☎ **202-452-1270,** 800-847-4832; www.hotelsdc.com) and **Washington, D.C. Accommodations** (☎ **202-289-2220,** 800-503-3330; www.dcaccommodations.com).

When it's open, the **Washington, D.C., Visitor Information Center** (Ronald Reagan International Trade Center Building, 1300 Pennsylvania Ave. NW; Federal Triangle Metro; ☎ **202-328-4748,** 866-324-7386; www.dcvisit.com), helps walk-ins book hotel rooms. From March 15 through Labor Day, it's open 8:30 a.m. to 5:30 p.m. weekdays and 9 a.m. to 4 p.m. Saturdays. The rest of the year, it's open 9 a.m. to 4:30 p.m. weekdays, closed weekends.

Washington's Best Hotels at All Prices

In this section, I get down to the really important stuff: D.C.'s best hotels at various price levels.

I provide reviews of these hotels and list them alphabetically. I also include two indexes to help you quickly find the hotels you want to consider. One index lists the hotels by price range, the other by neighborhood. And I show the hotels' locations on a map. In case these inns are booked, I offer a list of runners-up.

Table 9-1 also explains what the dollar-sign ratings in each listing mean. The price range reflects the average of the lowest and highest undiscounted rate for a double-occupancy room for one night during high season — the infamous rack rate. By exercising a little bit of diligence, you should never have to pay that much.

Table 9-1	Key to Hotel Dollar Signs	
Dollar Sign(s)	*Price Range*	*What to Expect*
$	Less than $125	In this category, you may share a dormlike room at a hostel; stay in an older, no-frills hotel; stay at a B&B (perhaps with a shared bathroom); or check into a plain, budget motel. Your room will be clean, but may or may not include a TV and phone. Don't expect room service or chocolates on the pillows.
$$	$125–$200	The rooms in this category may be smallish or in older buildings, but you can count on a TV (most likely with cable) and other amenities (coffee maker, soaps, shampoos). You can find some good bargains in housekeeping suites in this price range.
$$$	$201–$300	These rooms are in full-service hotels minus the most luxurious of amenities, or they're nice all-suite properties. Expect hair dryers, irons, coffee makers, on-site restaurants, health clubs (on- or off-site), and cable TV. You may even have access to room service.
$$$$	$301–$400	Now you're talking luxury. Besides a large, well-decorated room, you can count on a spacious bathroom with ample towels and a terry robe — as a loaner, so don't pack it as a souvenir. Expect a full range of amenities, multiple phones, a data port, minibars, on-site restaurant(s), a health club, and room service. The staff pays great attention to the hotel's appearance and to high-quality service.
$$$$$	More than $400	You pay for the prestigious name, location, service, and opulence. Expect round-the-clock concierge and room service, sumptuous lobbies and room furnishings (entertainment centers, heated towel racks, in-room safes), one or more restaurants for fine dining, a bar and/or lobby cocktail lounge, an on-site spa/health club, shuttle service, staff members who trip over themselves to serve you, and an evening turndown of your bedding with chocolates left at the bedside.

If you're traveling with kids, note the Kid Friendly icons. These hotels feature amenities that are especially attractive to families.

Capitol Hill Suites
$$$ **Capitol Hill**

You become an instant Capitol Hill insider when you bed down here. You're two blocks from the Capitol Grounds and across the street from the Library of Congress's Madison Building. You get dining privileges at the nearby Capitol Hill Club, the Republican Party social club that's next door to GOP National Committee headquarters. And you may bump into one of the lawmakers who take advantage of the hotel's long-term rates to make this their Washington home. All suites have kitchenettes. The junior suites are one-room efficiencies, with one queen bed and an armchair with ottoman or sofa bed. Superior suites have two queen beds, an alcove for the kitchenette, and a sitting area with an armchair and ottoman or a sofa bed. The one-bedroom suites have a king or queen bed and a separate living room with a sofa bed. Renovating the hotel in 2000, the operators tried to capture what they call the "traditional Capitol Hill" look. That means lots of navy blue and burgundy, leather, marble, and cherry wood. Room rate includes continental breakfast and use of a nearby health club. Valet parking is available. The Capitol South Metrorail Station is about a block away.

See map p. 102. 200 C St. SE (at 2nd Street). ☎ *800-424-9165* or 202-543-6000. Fax: 202-547-2608. www.capitolhillsuites.com. *Metro: Capitol South. From escalator exit, walk 1 block east on C Street to 2nd Street. From elevator exit, walk 1 block east on D Street and then 1 block north on C Street. Parking: $28 per night. Rack rates: $219–$239 double. Children under 18 stay free in parents' room. Rates include continental breakfast. AE, DC, DISC, MC, V.*

D.C. Guest House
$$$ **Downtown**

This 19th-century mansion is a wonderful find a bit off the beaten tourist track but just one block from the D.C. convention center. It's just what you're looking for in a bed-and-breakfast — a building with character, decorated according to the personalities of the owners, who provide attentive service because they really want their guests to enjoy their stay. The four owners have appointed the house with modern furnishings, original art, and African artifacts. The ambience ranges from country manor to urban chic. Guest rooms are large, warm, and comfortable. All rooms have working fireplaces, and most have private baths. You're served a gourmet breakfast in an elegant dining room. Almost unheard of in Washington, you can park your car for free about a block away. As one owner pointed out to me, that puts your car closer to your room here than it would be in the parking garage of many large hotels. The owners, by the way, really know how to shop in Washington. So, if shopping's your thing, ask them for suggestions.

See map p. 102. 1337 10th St. NW (between N and O streets). ☎ *202-332-2502. Fax 202-332-6013.* www.dcguesthouse.com. *Metro: Mt. Vernon Square. Walk 1 block* north on 7th Street to N, then left 3 blocks to 10th, and then right on 10th. Free park-ing. Rack rates $175–$250 double. Rates include breakfast. AE, DISC, MC, V.

Four Points by Sheraton
$$$ **Downtown**

This hotel has a room with a view, but it's not the room you'll be sleeping in. Rather, it's the heated indoor pool on the roof, one of many amenities that makes this place a good buy, especially if you can snag one of the $159-a-night deals. From the pool, you get a panoramic look at D.C., includ-ing the Capitol dome. Four Points offers concierge services, room service, valet parking, fitness center, business center, and an on-site restaurant. Each room has high-speed Internet access, two-line phones with dataports and voicemail, a coffee maker, and security safe designed to accommodate a laptop computer. You can ask for a microwave and minifridge. Rooms come with one queen bed, one king bed, or two double beds. Studio and one-bedroom suites with kitchenettes also are available. This hotel is a place where corner rooms are a bit bigger.

See map p. 102. 1201 K St. NW (at 12th Street). ☎ **888-481-7191** *or 202-289-7600. Fax 202-349-2215.* www.fourpointswashingtondc.com. *Metro: Metro Center. From G and 12th streets exit, walk 3 blocks north on 12th to K Street. Parking: $26 per night. Rack rates: $239–$259 double. Children younger than 18 stay free in parents' room. AE, DC, DISC, MC, V.*

Four Seasons
$$$$$ **Georgetown**

Where Foggy Bottom meets Georgetown, you find one of Washington's most celebrity-friendly (and kid-friendly) hotels. The rich and famous love this place because of its luxury and the staff's discretion and impeccable service. The concierge can rent you a tux, find you a toothbrush, or get you theater tickets. You can take high tea or sip a cocktail in the Garden Terrace. An indoor pool and a health club offer all imaginable amenities. If you want to work — *what?* — the hotel has every imaginable business service as well. George Washington never slept here, but Tom Hanks, Sheryl Crow, and Nicolas Cage have. The hotel also brags about its serv-ice to "VICs" (Very Important Children). Kids receive gifts and snacks at check-in. They can use the hotel's board games, videotapes, coloring books, kid-sized terry bathrobes, toddler slippers, and Teddy bears. Parents can request baby necessities, such as a crib, high chair, and bottle-warmer. Children's menus are offered for meals and at tea. The hotel can get you an experienced, bonded, and insured baby sitter.

See map p. 102. 2800 Pennsylvania Ave. NW (at 28th Street). ☎ **800-819-5053** *or 202-342-0444. Fax: 202-944-2076.* www.fourseasons.com. *Metro: Foggy Bottom-George Washington University. Walk 1 block north on 23rd Street to traffic circle, go left around circle to Pennsylvania Avenue, and then go left onto Pennsylvania for 4 blocks. Parking: $26 per night. Rack rates: $600 and up double. One child under 18 stays free in parents' room. AE, DC, MC, V.*

Georgetown Suites
$$ Georgetown

This Georgetown accommodation can be good for families because the suites with bedrooms allow for some privacy and the kitchens enable you to cook. I know cooking isn't what most vacationers put on their itineraries. But vacationing with kids can be much more pleasant when you can return to your lodgings for meals, snacks, and naps. Here, your options include a free continental breakfast. Your lodging choices include a one-room studio "suite" (queen-size bed and sitting area with loveseat), a "double double suite" (two double beds and a sitting area), or a one-bedroom suite (king bed and separate living room with pull-out queen-size sofa). A two-bedroom suite has two bathrooms, master bedroom with king bed, a second bedroom with full bed, and a living room with queen sofa-bed. All have a kitchen with refrigerator, coffee maker, microwave, and dishwasher. More luxurious townhouse and penthouse accommodations are available. The hotel has an exercise room, and you can obtain business services at the nearby Georgetown Business Center. The suites are in two buildings. The main building, at 1111 30th St. NW, is quieter. Additional perks: Local phone calls and high-speed Internet access are free.

See map p. 102. Main building: 1111 30th St. NW (just below M Street); second building: 1000 29th St. NW (at K Street). ☎ **800-348-7203** *or 202-298-7800. www.george townsuites.com. Metro: Foggy Bottom-George Washington University. Walk 1 block north on 23rd Street to traffic circle, go left around circle to Pennsylvania Ave., go left onto Pennsylvania for 5 or 6 blocks, and then turn left on 29th or 30th street. Or take Georgetown Connection Route 1 shuttle bus from Foggy Bottom-GWU Metrorail Station or a 30-series Metrobus. Parking: $18 per night. Rack rates for studios to one-bedroom suites: $155–$215; others higher. AE, DC, DISC, MC, V.*

George Washington University Inn
$$$$ Foggy Bottom

Located in a quiet, tree-lined residential section of Foggy Bottom, the George Washington University Inn is an ideal place to park your suitcase if you're visiting the university or sampling the performing arts at the Kennedy Center. The inn, which is owned by the university, is essentially on the GWU campus; it's about 3 long blocks from the Kennedy Center. The short walk to the Foggy Bottom-GWU Metrorail Station and to the 30-series Metrobus routes on Pennsylvania Avenue makes visiting the rest of the city easy, too. The 95 rooms (31 of which are one-bedroom suites) are relatively large, decorated in colonial Williamsburg style, and come with minirefrigerators, microwaves, and coffee makers. You get free access to a fitness facility 2 blocks away, and valet parking is available if you want it. You often can find deep discounts.

See map p. 102. 824 New Hampshire Ave. NW (between H and I streets). ☎ **800-426-4455** *or 202-337-6620. Fax: 202-298-7499. www.gwuinn.com. Metro: Foggy Bottom-George Washington University. Walk west on I Street, across 24th Street, and then left on New Hampshire. Parking: $21.50. Rack rates: $325–$365 double. Children younger than 12 stay free in parents' room. AE, DC, MC, V.*

Hay-Adams
$$$$$ Downtown

The Hay-Adams is such a Washington institution that its reopening after an $18-million renovation was front-page news in *The Washington Post's* business section. It's hard to imagine a better location for an upscale hotel — directly across picturesque Lafayette Square from the White House. Built in 1928, the Hay-Adams long has been a top choice of the rich, the powerful, and the simply famous. Sure, Warren Beatty, Annette Bening, and Meg Ryan have stayed here. But so have Charles Lindbergh, Amelia Earhart, and Sinclair Lewis. The prime attraction of the Hay-Adams always will be what it always has been — that location. Windows in the higher-level rooms on the south side look across Lafayette Square to the White House, with the Washington Monument in the distance. Now, all the amenities are 21st-century state-of-the art. Impressed by hotel rooms with two telephones? Every Hay-Adams room has *three* two-line phones, including a cordless phone. You also get voice mail, a high-speed Internet connection, a component audio system, 24-hour room service, business services, valet parking, and — of course — the concierge. Will you pay mightily for this luxury? Well . . . if you have to ask. . . .

See map p. 102. One Lafayette Square (at 16th and H streets NW). ☎ *800-853-6807 or 202-638-6600. Fax: 202-638-2716.* www.hayadams.com. *Metro: McPherson Square. From the Vermont Ave.-White House exit, walk south one block on Vermont, turn right on H, walk one more block, and cross 16th. Valet parking: $28. Rack rates: $385–$600 double. Children younger than 17 stay free in parents' room. AE, DC, DISC, MC, V.*

Henley Park Hotel
$$$ Downtown

I have a friend who always tries to stay here during his periodic, several-week business visits to Washington, because he appreciates the attentive service and the effort the staff makes to get to know regular guests. The rooms are small but comfortable and feature two-line speaker phones with voice mail and data ports, irons and ironing boards, terry cloth robes, coffee makers, 24-hour room service, and safes. Business travelers receive complimentary transportation to downtown locations from 7:30 to 10 a.m. weekdays . Guests also get free access to an off-site fitness center. The comfort and attentiveness spill over to the on-site Blue Bar, which offers live, mainstream jazz Thursday, Friday, and Saturday evenings, and to the Coeur de Lion restaurant, where maitre d' Ralph Fredericks carries attentive service to stratospheric heights. Rates less than $100 are sometimes available.

See map p. 102. 926 Massachusetts Ave. NW (between 9th and 10th streets). ☎ *202-638-5200 or 800-222-8474. Fax 202-638-6740.* www.henleypark.com. *Metro: Mount Vernon Square. Walk 2 blocks south on Seventh Street, then right across Mount Vernon Square, and right on Massachusetts. Valet parking: $22. Rack rates: $195–$255 double. Children stay free with parents in some rooms. AE, DC, DISC, MC, V.*

Holiday Inn on the Hill
$$$ Capitol Hill

This Holiday Inn enjoys a choice location, about 2 blocks from Union Station and the Capitol grounds, and within walking distance of many other attractions. A $10-million renovation completed in 2003 made this hotel more stylish and expensive. Staff wear designer uniforms, and the facilities are strikingly decorated. Standard rooms now come with one king bed and easy chair or sofa, or two queen beds with easy chair. Every guest room has free high-speed Internet access, the lobby, restaurant, and meeting rooms enjoy wi-fi wireless access points. A large rooftop pool, which enjoys a great view of the area, is open in summer. The always-open fitness center has treadmills, steppers, circuit trainer, free weights, and recumbent bicycles. Many of the hotel's employees have been here a long time, and that translates into staff and visitor satisfaction. Deep discounts are often available with reservations.

See map p. 102. 415 New Jersey Ave. NW (between D and E streets). ☎ 800-638-1116 or 202-638-1616. Fax: 202-638-0707. www.sixcontinentshotels.com/holiday-inn?_franchisee=WASCH. *Metro: Union Station. From the Union Station Shops/Massachusetts Avenue exit, cross Massachusetts, walk around the circle to Louisiana, turn right on Louisiana, right on D, and right on New Jersey. Parking: $24. Rack rates: $185–270 double. Children 18 and under stay free with their parents. AE, DC, DISC, MC, V.*

Hostelling International
$ Downtown

I promised you accommodations in all price ranges, and this one is the lowest price you're gonna get — at least anywhere you'll *want* to stay, unless you're visiting a friend with a spare bed or space on the floor. If you want candy, you better bring it with you because you don't get Godiva on your pillow here. And you can't watch TV in bed. Whaddaya expect at these prices? Basic basic describes this 270-bed facility. It is, however, clean and comfortable, with dorm-style rooms (all air-conditioned), and it's just 3 blocks from Metro Center. The rooms, some co-ed, sleep 4 to 12 guests. Bathrooms are down the hall. But you get free continental breakfast, high-speed internet access, and use of a theatre-style TV room with 60-inch screen, kitchen, dinning room, luggage storage, lockers, and coin laundry. The hostel organizes activities for guests, such as walking tours. The savvy staff can help you with your itinerary. Families and couples can reserve private rooms for themselves, but you have to do so *at least* a month in advance.

See map p. 102. 1009 11th St. NW (at K Street). ☎ 202-737-2333. Fax: 202-737-1508. hiwashingtondc.org. *Metro: Metro Center. From 11th Street exit, walk north on 11th Street 3 blocks. Parking: Use commercial garages in the area. Rack rates: $20–$29 per person. MC, V.*

Hotel Harrington
$ Downtown

When you think bargain and no frills, think Hotel Harrington. Family-owned since it opened in 1914, the Harrington caters to groups, families, and others looking for good value. It's an easy walk to the White House, the National Mall, and many other attractions, such as the FBI headquarters, Ford's Theatre, the National Theater, and MCI Center. In addition, the Metro Center Metrorail Station is 2 blocks away from access to anyplace else you'd like to go. If you're traveling with your kids, a family suite is a good idea. The suite includes two rooms (queen bed in one, two twin beds in the other), two bathrooms, compact refrigerator, and coffee/tea maker. Some extra-large rooms sleep up to eight. You can have a fridge put into many rooms. Toss in a load at the self-service laundry on the premises. The hotel has three on-site restaurants, all reasonably priced, and plenty of other nearby food options. Trivia note: In 1938, the Harrington became the first hotel in Washington to air-condition all of its rooms.

See map p. 102. 436 11th St. NW (at E Street). ☎ *800-424-8532 or 202-628-8140. Fax: 202-347-3924.* www.hotel-harrington.com. *Metro: Metro Center. From 11th Street exit, walk 2 blocks south to E. Parking, 4 blocks away: $10. Rack rates: $95 double, $105–$125 to sleep up to five, $149 suite, $155 extra-large. AE, DC, DISC, MC, V.*

Hotel Lombardy
$$ Foggy Bottom/West End

The Lombardy was built as an apartment building in 1929, and it keeps that old-fashioned elegant and homey feel today with the panel of brass mailboxes off the lobby, the elevator with white-gloved operator, and the touches of a comfortable past in the guest rooms. The rooms are large and furnished with antiques, wrought-iron beds, and brocade fabrics. Most have kitchenettes with dining areas, as well as bathrooms with the origi-nal tile and period pedestal sinks. In a nod to the modern, the innkeepers also provide two-line phones with data ports and voice mail, coffee makers, and terry robes. The multilingual staff is friendly. If you're looking to unwind after a tough day of touring or business, slip into a plush seat in the on-site Venetian Room, order a drink, and nibble *spuntino* (Italian and Italian-influenced snacks) from 5:30 to 9:30 p.m.

See map p. 102. 2019 Pennsylvania Ave. NW (actually on I Street. between 20th and 21st). ☎ *800-424-5486 or 202-828-2600. Fax: 202-872-0503.* hotellombardy.com. *Metro: Farragut West. From 18th Street exit, walk 2½ blocks west on I Street. Parking: $25. Rack rate: $199 double. Children stay free with parents in some rooms. AE, DC, DISC, MC, V.*

Hotel Madera
$$$ Dupont Circle

The Madera is one of several boutique hotels that have brought creative, avant-garde, sometimes way-over-the-top style to this traditionally but-toned-up city. The Madera is a strikingly attractive place with fairly large rooms, a complimentary evening "wine hour," and personalized service that focuses right down to the amenities you might find in your room. "Cardio rooms" have exercise equipment; "flash rooms" a computer with unlimited Internet access; "screening rooms" DVDs to go with the DVD player and extra TV; and "nosh rooms" a kitchenette, condiments, and grocery-shopping service. Some rooms have balconies. Others, on the upper floors, offer nice views.

See map p. 102. 1310 New Hampshire Ave. NW (north of N and west of 20th streets). ☎ *800-368-5691 or 202-296-7600. Fax: 202-293-2476.* hotelmadera.com. *Metro: Dupont Circle. From the Dupont Circle exit, walk south on 19th Street briefly, then right on Sunderland Place and across 20th to New Hampshire, and then turn left. Parking; $24. Rack rate: $259 double. Children stay free in parents' room. AE, DC, DISC, MC, V.*

Hotel Monaco
$$$$ Downtown

You get history with your sleep at the Monaco, a luxury hotel that resulted from a three-year rehabilitation of a 19th-century government palace that was designed by two noted architects and served first as Washington's general post office and then as the Tariff Commission headquarters. Robert Mills, architect of the Washington Monument, modeled his post office design on the Temple of Jupiter in Rome; it opened in 1842. Thomas Walter, an architect of the Capitol, designed the 1869 addition. As a guest, you get marble columns outside and a mixture of the 19th and 21st centuries inside. The spacious guest rooms have plush furnishings, workspaces, cordless phones, complimentary high-speed Internet access, and a bust of Thomas Jefferson. The hotel even pampers your pet or lend you a goldfish if you long for company during your stay. The Monaco also is well located in D.C.'s new and growing arts and entertainment district.

See map p. 102. 700 F St. NW (at 7th Street). ☎ *877-202-5411 or 202-628-7177. Fax: 202-628-7277.* www.monaco-dc.com. *Metro: Gallery Place-Chinatown. From the 7th and F streets exit, look for the gigantic building with marble columns diagonally across the intersection. Valet parking: $16. Rack rate: $309 double. Children stay free in parents' room. AE, DC, DISC, MC, V.*

Hotel Washington
$$$ Downtown

Overlooking the White House and an easy stroll from the National Mall, the Hotel Washington boasts convenience and one of the city's best views. (I find myself saying that about a lot of D.C. hotels!) From the Sky Terrace open-air restaurant on the hotel's top floor (open May to October), you can look down on the president's mansion while eating a light meal or relaxing with a drink. The adjacent, indoors, Sky Room is open year-round. Many guest rooms also feature views of the White House and/or the Washington Monument. (Ask about availability and price.) Once every four years, the inaugural parade marches by, as the president makes the quad-rennial pilgrimage from the Capitol to 1600 Pennsylvania Ave. Antique reproductions throughout the hotel help to create an atmosphere of historical charm.

See map p. 102. 515 15th St. NW at Pennsylvania Avenue. ☎ *800-424-9540 or 202-638-5900. Fax: 202-638-1594.* www.hotelwashington.com. *Metro: Metro Center. From the 12th and F streets exit, walk 3 blocks west on F to 15th. Parking: $25. Rack rates: $205–$265 double. Children younger than 12 stay free with parents in some rooms. AE, DC, MC, V.*

The Jefferson
$$$$ Downtown

The Jefferson was my wife's favorite Washington hotel when we lived in Ohio, and she made occasional business trips to D.C. (on a corporate credit card). More than two decades later, it's still considered one of the city's very best hotels because of the same intimate atmosphere and personalized service. It's small, quiet, elegant, and expensive, with a top-notch staff that remembers return guests by name. Antiques, original art, and reproductions grace the 67 rooms and 33 suites, many with balconies, some with wood-burning fireplaces. Some rooms include canopied beds, and each room features two-line telephones, speaker-phone, voicemail, fax machine, and Internet access, along with video and CD player. Double-glazed windows mute the traffic noise from 16th and M streets. The hotel has 24-hour room service, 24-hour multilingual concierge service, business services, a good restaurant, a comfortable lounge, and a fitness room. You pay $20 a pop for access to the indoor pool, exercise machines, steam room, and Jacuzzi at the University Club across the street.

See map p. 102. 1200 16th St. NW (at M Street). ☎ *800-235-6397 or 202-347-2200. Fax: 202-331-7982.* www.loewshotels.com/hotels/washington_jefferson. *Metro: Farragut North. From L Street exit, walk 2 blocks east on L, turn left on 16th, and then walk 1 block to M. Parking: $28. Rack rate: $399 double. Children under 12 stay free in parents' room. AE, DC, DISC, MC, V.*

Jurys Normandy Inn
$$ Dupont Circle

This relatively small, homey hotel is a bit out of the way, but not too far for the accommodations when you can get a discount. It's about 5 blocks north of the Dupont Circle Metrorail Station, in the neighborhood known as Kalorama, and about the same distance from the heart of Adams-Morgan, which are two of D.C.'s most popular entertainment districts, with plenty of restaurants and nightspots. The hotel is located in a neighborhood of imposing residences and diplomatic facilities. (Check out the French ambassador's digs at 2221 Kalorama Rd., for a truly jaw-dropping example.) If you stay here, you can call this intriguing neighborhood your own for a brief spell. Jurys Normandy also truly is a bargain. For relatively little money (for Washington), you get a comfortable room with high-speed

Internet access, two-line phone with dataport, minifridge, coffee maker, and use of the exercise room and outdoor pool at the nearby Courtyard by Marriott. Tea and coffee are served for free in the lounge in the afternoons, and a complimentary wine-and-cheese reception occurs on Tuesday nights. Maybe you can strike up a conversation with a traveling diplomat. Specials drop as low as $79 during slow times.

See map p. 102. 2118 Wyoming Ave. NW (west of Connecticut Avenue). ☎ ***800-424-3729*** *or 202-483-1350. Fax: 202-387-8241.* www.jurys-washingtondc-hotels.com. *Metro: Dupont Circle. From the Q Street exit, walk north 5 blocks on Connecticut Avenue and then turn left on Wyoming. Parking: $15. Rack rates: $175–$185 double. Children under 12 stay free in parents' room. AE, DC, DISC, MC, V.*

Jurys Washington
$$$ Dupont Circle

Unlike its sibling, Jurys Normandy, this hotel is not out of the way at all. It's right on the northeastern edge of the Dupont Circle action. With its more convenient location, Jurys Washington naturally is pricier than the Normandy. But it still often offers really good deals. The Jurys hotels are run by an Irish organization, Jurys Doyle Hotels of Dublin, and that's reflected in the Washington's eatery and drinkery — Claddagh's Restaurant, which serves contemporary American cuisine with what the owners describe as "a distinctive Irish flair," and Biddy Mulligans Bar, styled as an Irish pub with the bar itself imported from the Old Country. The rooms at Jurys Washington are large, pretty, and comfortable. They come with the usual amenities, including high-speed Internet access and — this isn't common! — a trouser press. The hotel offers concierge service, 24-hour room service, a business center, and an exercise room. Discounted rates sometimes drop below $100.

See map p. 102. 1500 New Hampshire Ave. NW (on northeast edge of Dupont Circle). ☎ ***800-424-3729*** *or 202-483-6000. Fax: 202-328-3265.* www.jurys-washingtondc-hotels.com. *Metro: Dupont Circle. From the Dupont Circle exit, walk around the circle counter-clockwise to New Hampshire. Parking: $15. Rack rate: $275 double. Children younger than 18 stay free in parents' room. AE, DC, DISC, MC, V.*

Lincoln Suites
$$ Downtown

The "suites" in this hotel actually are large rooms with kitchen facilities. All have at least a microwave, refrigerator, coffee maker, and wet bar, as well as phones with voice mail and dataports. "Double suites" contain two double beds and an activity table with two chairs. "Executive studio suites" have a full kitchen (full-sized refrigerator, oven, stove, microwave, sink, dishes, pots, and pans) and either two queen-size beds or one king. In 2002, the hotel completed a gradual overhaul that began in 1997 with the upgrading of the rooms and was completed with the entrance, lobby, and front desk. As a result, Lincoln now markets itself as "cool, hip, edgy, gorgeous" — and more expensive. The service didn't need to be upgraded;

it's always been great. Despite the new self-proclaimed ediginess, Lincoln still offers free milk and cookies every evening. (Ask nicely.) On site is Mackey's Public House, which serves tasty fish and chips, other light fare, and your favorite brews. Special discounts can bring room rates below $125.

See map p. 102. 1823 L St. NW, between 18th and 19th streets. ☎ **800-424-2970** or *202-223-4320. Fax: 202-293-4977.* www.lincolnhotels.com. *Metro: Farragut North. From the L Street exit, walk 1 block west on L, crossing 18th. Parking: $20. Rack rate: $200 suite. Rate includes continental breakfast. AE, DC, DISC, MC, V.*

One Washington Circle
$$$$ **Foggy Bottom**

This recently renovated hotel offers a variety of floor plans suitable for business travelers and families. All but 10 of the 151 units have kitchens, and most have balconies. Among the deluxe touches: coffee beans and grinder to go along with the coffee maker. All the units also have free high-speed Internet connection, two-line cordless telephones, a stereo with CD player, and a video-game console. The most luxurious units — the "grande staterooms" — feature a separate bedroom with king-size bed, a dining area with table and six chairs, living area with sofa bed, and a bath and a half. Even the simples "guest quarters" feel spacious, with sleeping and sitting areas in one large room that includes a double bed and fold-out sofa or two double beds. The strikingly modern decor is warmed with dark wood and fabrics in beige, gold, and blue. You can take advantage of an on-site fitness center, outdoor pool, concierge services, and a new, good restaurant, the **Circle Bistro.** Georgetown is an easy stroll away, and the Foggy Bottom-George Washington University Metrorail Station is just around the circle. Deep discounts below $100 per suite are sometimes available.

See map p. 102. 1 Washington Circle NW (Pennsylvania Avenue at New Hampshire Avenue). ☎ **800-424-9671** or *202-872-1680. Fax: 202-887-4989.* www.thecircle hotel.com. *Metro: Foggy Bottom-George Washington University. Walk north on 23rd Street 1 block to Washington Circle and then counterclockwise around the circle to New Hampshire Avenue at the northeast edge of the circle. Valet parking: $21.50. Rack rates: $345–$385 double. Children younger than 13 stay free in parents' room. AE, DC, DISC, MC, V.*

Red Roof Inn
$ **Downtown**

This hotel is not like the Red Roof Inns you breeze by on the Interstate. Hardly. Close to the Convention Center, MCI Center (sports and big-name entertainers), galleries, theaters, restaurants, nightspots, and Chinatown, this inn contains 197 rooms on 10 floors. It's a value find for business travelers and families. A king room includes a large desk in work area with dataport and speaker phone. Families can get rooms with two double beds. All rooms feature coffee makers and large bathrooms. The kids can work off excess energy using the in-room Nintendo (hourly charge). The hotel also has an exercise room and an on-site restaurant. Local phone calls are free. Rates below $100 are often available.

See map p. 102. 500 H St. NW (at 5th Street). ☎ **800-733-7663** *or 202-289-5959. Fax: 202-289-0754. www.redroof.com. Metro: Gallery Place-Chinatown. From 7th and H streets exit, walk 2 blocks east to 5th. Parking: $15. Rack rates: $110–$130 double. Children 16 and younger stay free in parents' room. AE, DC, DISC, MC, V.*

Renaissance Mayflower
$$$$ Downtown

I'll always have affection for the Mayflower because of some things that happened there long ago. Shortly after I graduated from college, a friend and I came here for a conference and were placed in a suite at no extra cost because of a room shortage. We were so worried about what we might have to pay that we triple-checked before unpacking our bags. The Mayflower also is where I covered my first inaugural ball: It's where Ohio Democrats celebrated Jimmy Carter's move into the White House in 1977. This hotel has been hosting those events since it opened in 1925 and Cal Coolidge's inauguration was celebrated here. The Mayflower is big, luxurious, and the setting for many meetings, conventions, and other public events. You can bump into any big shot here. The guest rooms, as well as the public areas, feature marble and mahogany. They also have your basic modern traveler's necessities — two-line phones, speaker phones, voice mail, and dataports. Parents can obtain cribs and child care. The hotel has a restaurant, coffee shop, lounge, 24-hour room service, concierge services, and exercise room. The location is ideal — midway between Dupont Circle and the White House, on top of the Farragut North Metrorail Station.

See map p. 102. 1127 Connecticut Ave. NW (between L and M streets). ☎ **888-236-2427** *or 202-347-3000. Fax: 202-776-9182. www.renaissancehotels.com. Metro: Farragut North. From the L Street exit, look for the hotel. Valet parking: $28. Rack rates: $299–$349 double. AE, DC, DISC, MC, V.*

Ritz-Carlton Washington
$$$$$ Foggy Bottom/West End

This hotel may be Washington's most luxurious — in terms of both facilities and services. You can choose, for example, a 2,250-square-foot suite: living room with fireplace, bedroom, dining room with seating for ten, Jacuzzi, and private terrace. Or you can stay on the private Club Level, where the lounge offers food and beverage service all day and a concierge is at your beck and call. If you like package deals, the Ritz offered a special for the 2005 presidential inauguration that included private jet transportation, a personal butler, inaugural ball tickets — and other stuff — for $150,000. The standard rooms feature marble in the bathrooms, goose down or nonallergenic pillows to suit your need, dataports, portable phones, and high-speed Internet access. And then you have the "fitness center," the adjacent Sports Club/LA — 100,000 square feet of just about any exercise and sports facility you can dream of for $10 a day. But it's the service that really marks the Ritz. Beyond daily attentiveness, managers here think creatively about what additional services you might want. For example, noting increased air-travel hassles, the hotel introduced "luggage-less" travel for frequent guests. Leave your clothes in your room, and the hotel will launder, dry clean, press, store them, and then place them in your room when you return. And, on your way out of D.C., grab some of the hotel's "flight bites" to eat on the airplane.

See map p. 102. 1150 22nd St. NW, at M Street. ☎ 800-241-3333 or 202-835-0500. Fax 202-835-1588. www.ritzcarlton.com/hotels/washington_dc. Metro: Foggy Bottom-George Washington University. Walk 1 block east on I Street, turn left on 22nd, and then walk 4 blocks to M. Self parking: $15. Valet parking: $30. Rack rate: $500 double. No charge for extra person in room. AE, DC, DISC, MC, V.

The River Inn
$$$$ **Foggy Bottom**

The facilities and services at this all-suites hotel focus on the needs of business travelers. But the kitchens in all units and separate bedrooms in some — coupled with discounts that can drop below $100 — make the River Inn a good option for families as well. Business travelers especially appreciate the large desk and good lighting, the lack of which drive me crazy in many hotels. Every unit also contains two-line phones, free high-speed Internet access, sofa bed, dressing alcove with vanity, and grinder with beans to go along with the coffee maker. The studios feel spacious. The one-bedroom suites are truly large, with two or three couches and king-size beds. The hotel also has an exercise facility.

See map p. 102. 924 25th St. NW (between I and K streets). ☎ 800-424-2741 or 202-337-7600. Fax: 202-337-6520. www.theriverinn.com. Metro: Foggy Bottom/ George Washington University. Walk 2 blocks west on I and then turn right on 25th. Parking: $20. Rack rates: $330–$360 suite. AE, DC, MC, V.

Sofitel Lafayette Square
$$$$ **Downtown**

The French-owned Sofitel promises "art de vivre" — "the art of French living" — and delivers with the excellent Cafe 15 French restaurant, a bar called Le Bar, Le Petit Bijou gift shop featuring French products, plus interior decor and staff uniforms created by French designers. Rooms in this 1928 office building — renovated in 2002 — are bright, airy, and cheerful. Velvet curtains, thick carpeting, rich-colored upholstery, and black lacquered desks with chrome legs provide the feel of luxury. The overall effect is a melding of early 20th-century Art Deco with 21st-century style and amenities. The bathrooms have separate tub and shower. Each room has three two-line telephones with a direct phone number and voice mail, data line, high-speed Internet access, television, radio, CD player, and WebTV. You can order room service around the clock and work out in the on-site fitness center.

See map p. 102. 806 15th St. NW (at H Streets). ☎ *800-763-4835* or 202-730-8800. Fax: 202-730-8500. www.sofitel.com. Metro: McPherson Square. From Vermont Avenue/White House exit, walk 1 block east on I Street and then turn right on 15th. Valet parking: $26. Rack rates: $340–$450 double. One child younger than 12 can stay free in parent's room. AE, MC, V.

State Plaza
$$ Foggy Bottom

The spacious accommodations at the all-suites State Plaza provide a home away from home for diplomats, business travelers, performing artists, and educators headed to the nearby World Bank, State Department, Kennedy Center, and George Washington University. The State Plaza is a find for families, too. Kids younger than 16 stay free in their parents' room, and you can save money by cooking meals in the suites' kitchens. On a quiet Foggy Bottom block, the State Plaza feels like a private residence in a condo or apartment building. Spacious is the operative word. The largest suites (the Grand Plaza) have a master bedroom, living room with queen sofa bed and easy chair, a stylish and well-equipped kitchen, and a separate dining area. Room service is available. The hotel also has an on-site fitness center, rooftop sundeck, and the **Garden Café,** which serves breakfast, lunch, and dinner, with outdoor dining in season. Discounts as low as $75 are sometimes available.

See map p. 102. 2117 E St. NW (between 21st and 22nd streets). ☎ *800-424-2859* or 202-861-8200. Fax: 202-659-8601. www.stateplaza.com. Metro: Foggy Bottom/George Washington University. Walk 2 blocks east on I Street, turn right on 21st Street, walk 4 blocks south, and then turn right on E Street. Parking: $18. Rack rates: $185–$245 double. AE, DC, DISC, MC, V.

Tabard Inn
$$ Dupont Circle

The Tabard is an eclectic and eccentric — and, yes, charming — place. If you've traveled in Europe under Frommer's tutelage, the Tabard will remind you of all those inexpensive but marvelous hostelries that have been cobbled together from adjacent buildings that measure their age in centuries. The Tabard isn't that old, but it was created from three adjacent town houses on a tree-lined street in the Dupont Circle neighborhood. Each of the 40 rooms is different, and they're furnished with a combination of antiques and — uh, well — pre-owned items. They're priced according to their size, view, location within the hotel, and whether they have private baths (five don't). All rooms come with free continental breakfast and free admission to the Tabard's fabulously equipped health club — the Capital YMCA around the corner. The Tabard's restaurant is wonderful, both for the setting and the New American cuisine. You can dine in the garden in warm weather or sip a drink beside a fireplace when it's cold. The lounge is the proverbial comfortable old shoe, a well-worn place for luxuriating by the fire, not for luxury. Be warned that the Tabard has no elevator.

See map p. 102. 1739 N St. NW (between 17th and 18th streets). ☎ *202-785-1277.* Fax: 202-785-6173. www.tabardinn.com. Metro: Dupont Circle. From the Dupont Circle exit, walk south on Connecticut Avenue 1 block, and then turn left on N and cross 18th. Valet parking: $22 when available. Also parking in nearby public garages: about $20. Rack rates: $101–$210. Additional person: $15. AE, DC, DISC, MC, V.

Willard Inter-Continental
$$$$$ **Downtown**

The Willard is another Washington hotel steeped in history. A stone's throw from the White House and the D.C. government's headquarters, it's been a prime spot for the powerful and the power-seekers to hang their hats since even before Henry Willard bought the old hotel that occupied the site in 1850. George Washington didn't sleep here, but Abraham Lincoln stayed for a while in Henry's hostelry. And Calvin Coolidge lived in the current building until Mrs. Harding vacated the White House following her husband's death in 1923. Heads of foreign states stay here now. The current Willard — built in 1901, closed in 1968, opened after thorough restoration in 1986, and given a major face-lift in 2000 — is a large, ornate, and luxurious domicile. Take a walk through Peacock Alley, the first-floor hallway, even if you don't stay here, and take a peek into the opulent **Willard Room** restaurant. If you do stay here, you'll have a room furnished in antique reproductions and equipped with the latest electronics. The Jenny Lind Romance Suite has a canopy bed and a Jacuzzi that sits beneath a large, circular window that centers on the Washington Monument. The 2,800-square-foot Presidential Suite will set you back just $3,800 or so, unless you opt for the two- or three-bedroom configuration, which costs a few hundred more. Deep discounts — sometimes below $200 — appear on weekends and off season.

See map p. 102. 1401 Pennsylvania Ave. NW (at 14th Street). ☎ *888-303-1758* or 202-628-9100. Fax: 202-637-7326. www.washington.interconti.com. Metro: Metro Center. From the F Street exit, walk 2 blocks west on F to the hotel's rear entrance between 14th and 15th streets. Parking: $25. Rack rates: $480–$620 double. Children under 18 stay free in parents' room. AE, DC, DISC, MC, V.

Washington's Runner-Up Hotels

Space limitations prevent me from publishing an encyclopedia of Washington's hotels. If you're stuck and can't find a room, check the Quick Concierge at the back of this book for hotel chains' toll-free reservation numbers or contact the following hotels, all tried and true (until readers of this book tell me otherwise). All offer lower weekend and off-peak rates. How low? Sometimes you can find a room for less than $100 a night, depending on availability.

Georgetown Inn

$$$$ **Georgetown** This well-soundproofed hotel in the heart of Georgetown offers one-bedroom suites and adjoining rooms that can be converted
to suites. *See map p. 102. 1310 Wisconsin Ave. NW (between N and O streets).*
☎ *800-424-2979 or 202-333-8900. Fax: 202-333-8308. www.georgetowninn.com.*

Hotel George

$$$$ **Capitol Hill** Modernistic posters of the first president adorn
the hotel, which attracts lobbyists, celebrities, and others who dig hip
surroundings and proximity to power. *See map p. 102. 15 E St. NW (at North
Capitol Street).* ☎ **800-576-8331** *or 202-347-4200. Fax: 202-347-4213.* www.hotel
george.com.

Hotel Rouge

$$$ **Downtown** This super-hip boutique hotel decorates in — take a
wild guess — red, serves free Bloody Marys on weekend mornings, and
offers a special Red Eye package with 6 a.m. check-in. *See map p. 102. 1315
16th St. NW (north of N Street).* ☎ **800-738-1202** *or 202-232-8000. Fax: 202-667-9827.*
www.rougehotel.com.

J.W. Marriott

$$$$ **Downtown** This convention hotel is huge, which means many
rooms are available and good deals abound when conventions aren't in
session. *See map p. 102. 1331 Pennsylvania Ave. NW (at 14th and E streets).* ☎ **800-
228-9290** *or 202-393-2000. Fax: 202-626-6991.* www.marriott.com.

Latham Hotel

$$$ **Georgetown** Between M Street and the C&O Canal, the Latham
offers a variety of units, including two-story carriage suites. *See map p. 102.
3000 M St. NW (at 30th Street)* ☎ **800-368-5922** *or 202-726-5000. Fax: 202-337-4250.*
www.thelatham.com.

Morrison-Clark Historic Inn and Restaurant

$$$ **Downtown** The rooms are individually decorated, some with
period antiques, in these two 1864 Victorian mansions that are listed in
the National Register of Historic Places. *See map p. 102. 1015 L St. NW (between
10th and 11th streets).* ☎ **800-332-7898** *or 202-898-1200. Fax: 202-289-8576.* www.
morrisonclark.com.

Omni Shoreham

$$$ **Upper Northwest** Another enormous — and opulent and historic —
hotel that hosts conventions and large meetings and therefore has com-
prehensive services and facilities and offers deals when the conventioneers
and meeters aren't around. *See map p. 102. 2500 Calvert St. NW (west of
Connecticut Avenue).* ☎ **800-843-6664** *or 202-234-0700. Fax: 202-265-7972.* www.omni
hotels.com.

Washington Plaza

$$$ Downtown   This 1960s hotel boasts recently redecorated and refurnished rooms, plus a large outdoor pool. *See map p. 102. 10 Thomas Circle NW (at M and 14th streets).* ☎ *800-424-1140 or 202-842-1300. Fax: 202/371-9602.* www.washingtonplazahotel.com.

Washington Suites Georgetown

$$$ Foggy Bottom/West End   This all-suites hotel offers bargains to families when special discounts bring rates as low as $120 a night. *See map p. 102. 2500 Pennsylvania Ave. NW (at 25th Street).* ☎ *877-736-2500 or 202-296-7600. Fax: 202-338-3818.* www.washingtonsuitesgeorgetown.com.

Washington Terrace

$$$ Downtown   Benefitting from a recent $12-million facelift, the Washington Terrace offers comfortable rooms and a superb restaurant named 15 ria in honor of the address and in celebration of lowercase letters. *See map p. 102. 1515 Rhode Island Ave. NW (west of 15th Street).* ☎ *866-984-6835 or 202-232-7000. Fax: 202/332-8436.* www.washingtonterracehotel.com.

Index of Accommodations by Price

$ (less than $125)
Hostelling International (Downtown)
Hotel Harrington (Downtown)
Red Roof Inn (Downtown)

$$ ($125–$200)
Georgetown Suites (Georgetown)
Hotel Lombardy (Foggy Bottom/West End)
Jurys Normandy Inn (Dupont Circle)
Lincoln Suites (Downtown)
State Plaza (Foggy Bottom)
Tabard Inn (Dupont Circle)

$$$ ($201–299)
Capitol Hill Suites (Capitol Hill)
D.C. Guest House (Downtown)
Four Points by Sheraton (Downtown)
Henley Park Hotel (Downtown)
Holiday Inn on the Hill (Capitol Hill)
Hotel Madera (Dupont Circle)
Hotel Rouge (Downtown)
Hotel Washington (Downtown)

Jurys Washington (Dupont Circle)
Latham Hotel (Georgetown)
Morrison-Clark Historic Inn and Restaurant (Downtown)
Omni Shoreham (Upper Northwest)
Washington Plaza (Downtown)
Washington Suites Georgetown (Foggy Bottom/West End)
Washington Terrace (Downtown)

$$$$ ($301–$400)
Georgetown Inn (Georgetown)
George Washington University Inn (Foggy Bottom)
Hotel George (Capitol Hill)
Hotel Monaco (Downtown)
The Jefferson (Downtown)
J.W. Marriott (Downtown)
One Washington Circle (Foggy Bottom)
Renaissance Mayflower (Downtown)
River Inn (Foggy Bottom)
Sofitel Lafayette Square (Downtown)

$$$$$ *(More than $400)* | Ritz-Carlton Washington (Foggy Bottom/West End)
Four Seasons (Georgetown) | Willard Inter-Continental (Downtown)
Hay-Adams (Downtown)

Index of Accommodations by Location

Capitol Hill
Capitol Hill Suites ($$$)
Holiday Inn on the Hill ($$$)
Hotel George ($$$$)

Downtown
D.C. Guest House ($$$)
Four Points by Sheraton ($$$)
Hay-Adams ($$$$$)
Henley Park Hotel ($$$)
Hostelling International ($)
Hotel Harrington ($)
Hotel Monaco ($$$$)
Hotel Rouge ($$$)
Hotel Washington ($$$)
The Jefferson ($$$$)
J.W. Marriott ($$$$)
Lincoln Suites ($$)
Morrison-Clark Historic Inn and Restaurant ($$$)
Red Roof Inn ($)
Renaissance Mayflower ($$$$)
Sofitel Lafayette Square ($$$$)
Washington Plaza ($$$)
Washington Terrace ($$$)
Willard Inter-Continental ($$$$$)

Dupont Circle
Hotel Madera ($$$)
Jurys Normandy Inn ($$)
Jurys Washington ($$$)
Tabard Inn ($$)

Foggy Bottom/West End
George Washington University Inn ($$$$)
Hotel Lombardy ($$)
One Washington Circle ($$$$)
Ritz-Carlton Washington ($$$$$)
River Inn ($$$$)
State Plaza ($$)
Washington Suites Georgetown ($$$)

Georgetown
Four Seasons ($$$$$)
Georgetown Inn ($$$$)
Georgetown Suites ($$)Latham Hotel ($$$)

Upper Northwest
Omni Shoreham ($$$)

Chapter 10

Dining and Snacking in Washington, D.C.

• •

In This Chapter

▶ Understanding Washington's eating habits

▶ Reviewing the best restaurants in all price ranges

▶ Finding snacks and meals to go

• •

*T*here's a joke around Washington that you can identify the world's trouble spots by checking out the new restaurants in town. People flee trouble overseas, whether it's famine, war, or oppression. Washington — the capital of the free world — is a beacon. Many refugees have started on the road to the American Dream by opening a restaurant (see Chapter 2). As a result, Vietnamese, Ethiopian, Afghan, and other exotic cuisines took root in the nation's capital when times were particularly bad in the lands that spawned them. Washington's international influences and community provide a hungry and knowledgeable audience for the Chinese, French, German, Indian, Italian, Japanese, Spanish, Thai, Latin American, and Middle Eastern restaurants you can find here. And, with Congress representing every corner of America, a variety of regional cuisines from throughout the United States are represented as well.

Getting the Dish on the Local Scene

This section brings you up to speed on a few trends and technicalities before you get down to the business of eating. You can find more news about D.C. dining in *The Washington Post* (www.washingtonpost.com), and *Washingtonian* magazine (www.washingtonian.com), under the Visitors Guide sections.

The current trends

A key sign that Washington's dining scene really is on a long-term up-tick is the creativity and diversity of its food and chefs.

- ✔ The biggest things in Washington dining right now are **little things.** We've discovered the pleasure of strolling into a good restaurant with a group of friends, ordering nice wine, and spending several hours sharing nibbles of small dishes. Mediterranean *meze* is on the menu at **Zaytinya,** a strikingly stylish new restaurant in the up-and-coming Penn Quarter arts-theater-entertainment district downtown. **Jaleo,** in the same downtown neighborhood and in two suburbs, offers an enormous choice of Spanish *tapas.* At **Minibar,** a special section within **Cafe Atlantico** (also in the neighborhood), chef Jose Andres whips up tiny creations that spring from his mind rather than one particular cuisine — potato mouse with caviar and vanilla oil, for example, or foie gras surrounded by cotton candy! Mexican *antojitos* ("little whims") and *apertivos* ("appetizers") are the rage at **Andale** in (yes!) Penn Quarter. Head up to Dupont Circle and dip little pieces of meats, fruits, vegetables, and breads into hot pots of cheeses, broths, and melted chocolate at the **Melting Pot,** a fondue emporium. The downtown (but *not* Penn Quarter) **Venetian Room** serves *spuntino* (Italian and Italian-influenced snacks) from 5:30 to 9:30 p.m. The **2Amys,** in Upper Northwest, offers Italian tidbits along with its superb Neapolitan pizzas.

- ✔ The trend among chefs is power to the **women.** In a profession traditionally dominated by men, women now run some of D.C.'s very best kitchens. **Ris** (short for Doris) **Lacoste** builds delicious tasting-menus around fresh foods at **1789 Restaurant** in Georgetown. At **Andale, Alison Swope** stirs New American with Mexican cooking to create what she calls "Contemporary Mexican" cuisine. Ann Cashion's take on American cuisine, at **Cashion's Eat Place** in Adams-Morgan, is informed both by her Mississippi roots and her cooking experience in Italy, France, and California.

- ✔ The other great new trend is the proliferation of not-your-father's **hotel restaurants.** A growing number of Washington hostelries are turning their dining space over to really good chefs. The **Venetian Room** and **15 ria** are in the **Hotel Lombardy** and **Washington Terrace Hotel** respectively. Other hotel restaurants include **Poste** in the **Hotel Monaco, Circle Bistro** in **One Washington Circle Hotel, Coeur de Lion** in the **Henley Park Hotel, Firefly** in the **Hotel Madera, Michel Richard's Citronelle** in the **Lathan Hotel, Bistro Bis** in the **Hotel George, Cafe 15** in the **Sofitel Lafayette Square, Dish** in the **River Inn, Nectar** in the **George Washington University Inn,** and the **Tabard Inn** in the **Tabard Inn.**

Dining in Washington, D.C.

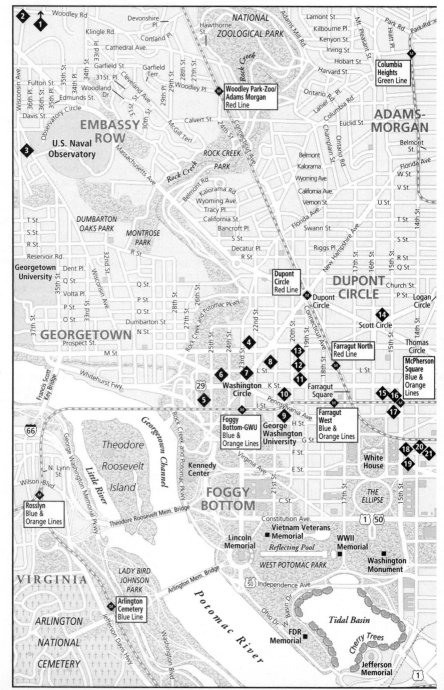

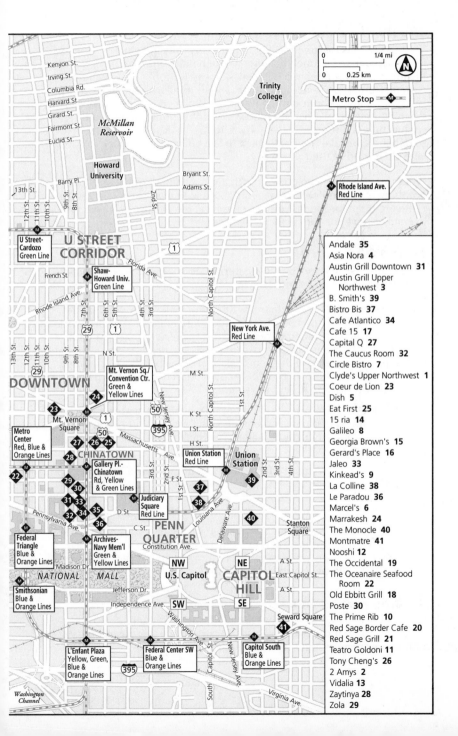

Andale **35**
Asia Nora **4**
Austin Grill Downtown **31**
Austin Grill Upper Northwest **3**
B. Smith's **39**
Bistro Bis **37**
Cafe Atlantico **34**
Cafe 15 **17**
Capital Q **27**
The Caucus Room **32**
Circle Bistro **7**
Clyde's Upper Northwest **1**
Coeur de Lion **23**
Dish **5**
Eat First **25**
15 ria **14**
Galileo **8**
Georgia Brown's **15**
Gerard's Place **16**
Jaleo **33**
Kinkead's **9**
La Colline **38**
Le Paradou **36**
Marcel's **6**
Marrakesh **24**
The Monocle **40**
Montmatre **41**
Nooshi **12**
The Occidental **19**
The Oceanaire Seafood Room **22**
Old Ebbitt Grill **18**
Poste **30**
The Prime Rib **10**
Red Sage Border Cafe **20**
Red Sage Grill **21**
Teatro Goldoni **11**
Tony Cheng's **26**
2 Amys **2**
Vidalia **13**
Zaytinya **28**
Zola **29**

The lunch scene

Washingtonians do lunch in just about every way imaginable. The infamous three-martini lunch has pretty much faded into the past. But business lunches remain a big deal — a way for lobbyists, lawmakers, administrators, political operatives, and journalists to share info in a relaxed setting without cutting into their crowded business days. Most Washingtonians on most days, however, gobble quick soups and sandwiches in lunch rooms, grab sandwiches and soft drinks and head for a park bench, or take their eats back to the office and get back to work with their food at their elbows.

What this routine means to you is that you can find lots of spots for grabbing decent quick lunches. And, because many of the top restaurants are open for lunch, you can sample some of the city's best dining in smaller portions for smaller prices at midday.

Eating like a local

Both high-class and inexpensive eateries are scattered throughout the city. Here's what makes some neighborhoods a bit distinctive, food-wise.

- ✔ **Capitol Hill:** Despite their low standing with the general public, members of Congress and their aides are in general a hard-working bunch, so you can find lots of spots for quick lunches on Capitol Hill. Restaurants, cafeterias, and carryouts are scattered throughout the Capitol and the congressional office buildings. The food court on the bottom floor of Union Station is one of the largest and most diverse you'll find anywhere.

- ✔ **Downtown:** This area is Washington's business center, so you can find many fine-dining establishments, plus delis and sandwich shops, on most corners. Buy a sandwich, chips, and soft drink and find a nearby park for people-watching.

- ✔ **Georgetown, Dupont Circle, and Adams-Morgan:** These areas are D.C.'s party spots, so lots of vibrant restaurants and saloons line the streets. You can eat, drink, dance, and check out the street scenes.

- ✔ **The National Mall:** The Mall is lined with museums and galleries, and the bigger ones will feed your stomach as well as your eyes. You can also find a lot of street vendors nearby, hawking hotdogs, sausages, chips, candy, and soft drinks.

Making reservations

While you can find lots of spots for lunch without much of a fuss or wait, accomplishing this feat is a bit trickier later in the day. Regarding restaurant dinner reservations: If you can make them, do!

Dining in Adams-Morgan and Dupont Circle

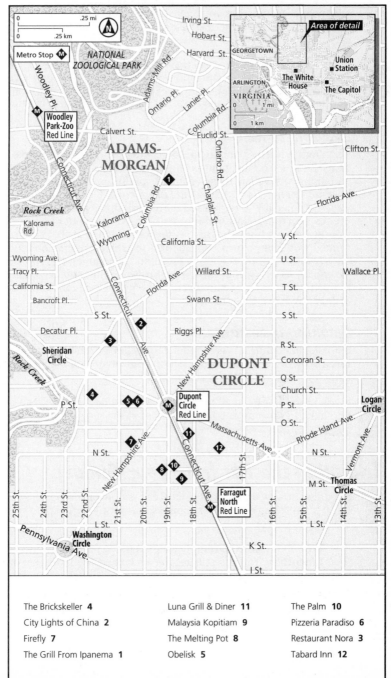

The Brickskeller **4**	Luna Grill & Diner **11**	The Palm **10**
City Lights of China **2**	Malaysia Kopitiam **9**	Pizzeria Paradiso **6**
Firefly **7**	The Melting Pot **8**	Restaurant Nora **3**
The Grill From Ipanema **1**	Obelisk **5**	Tabard Inn **12**

If you know your plans, make your reservations several days in advance — even before you leave home. Reserve for lunch, too, if you can. Otherwise, you can decrease the size of the lines you wait in by arriving before 11:45 a.m. or after 1:30 p.m.

If you're a Web head, you can make reservations at many D.C. restaurants by surfing over to OpenTable at www.opentable.com. OpenTable also provides descriptions of the restaurants, reviews, maps, and links to the restaurants' Web sites.

Dressing to dine

Washington is a working town, so it's filled with suits, wingtips, and "sensible" pumps. You'll encounter them in restaurants at breakfast, lunch, and dinner, as well as in government, media, and business offices. But Washington has a pretty forgiving dress code. Few restaurants block your entrance if you're dressed more casually. (I note those that do in the reviews that follow.) I doubt you'll get thrown out of many places for wearing jeans, although you may feel out of place at the nicer restaurants. If you love to dress up, go for it. Washingtonians don't look down on you for that, either. Though I wouldn't recommend it, you can wear a tux most places without raising eyebrows. Enough black-tie affairs occur in this town that people are used to seeing the penguin look on Metrorail or hustling down the street.

Smoking in restaurants

Smoking in restaurants isn't regulated by law in Washington. Most restaurants do provide nonsmoking sections, however, and many choose to ban smoking even without a legal mandate

If you prefer not to smell burning tobacco while you dine, you can find a list of nonsmoking restaurants at www.smokefreedc.org/restaurants.htm.

Trimming the Fat from Your Budget

Spending oodles on noodles (and steak and swordfish) is easy in D.C., but it's not required. Here are some suggestions for keeping your food bill under control:

- ✔ **When you want to sample an expensive restaurant, do so at lunchtime.** You can still get the acclaimed food, but you don't pay so much.

- ✔ **Buy carryout and picnic on a park bench or on the National Mall.** You can find many lovely, shaded spots among the memorials.

Dining in Georgetown

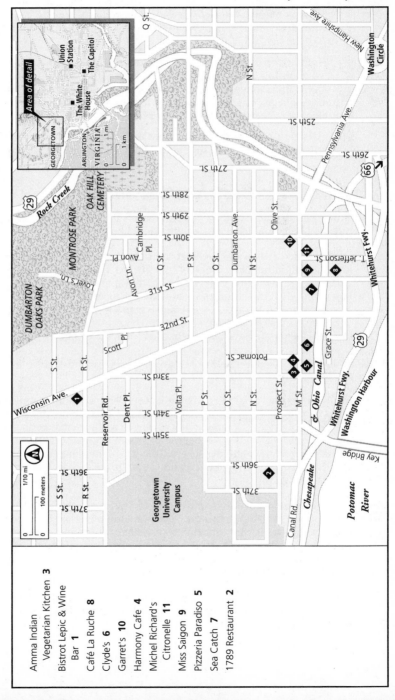

Amma Indian
Vegetarian Kitchen **3**
Bistrot Lepic & Wine
Bar **1**
Café La Ruche **8**
Clyde's **6**
Garret's **10**
Harmony Cafe **4**
Michel Richard's
Citronelle **11**
Miss Saigon **9**
Pizzeria Paradiso **5**
Sea Catch **7**
1789 Restaurant **2**

✔ **Take advantage of fixed-price, early bird, pretheater, and post-theater menus.** Check your watch as well as the hours restaurants offer specials. If you arrive five minutes late, you'll pay full price. You snooze, you lose.

✔ **Split appetizers and desserts — and even main courses — with your dining companions.** Many restaurants serve sinfully large portions. If you have access to a refrigerator and microwave, ask for doggy bags. You can heat up the leftovers for an in-room meal — like room service without the service (or the service fee).

✔ **Ask the prices of the dishes that are described by the waiter rather than listed on the menu.** They can shock you.

Washington's Best Restaurants

Now it's finally time to feed your faces, folks! While you loosen your belt buckle, I help you figure out where you'd like to eat.

I've compiled reviews of the best the best restaurants in all price ranges, arranged alphabetically for easy reference. The price range, location, and the type of cuisine follow each restaurant's name. After the reviews, you can find all the restaurants indexed by **location** so that you can find a place near the attractions you visit, by **price** so that you can budget accordingly, and by **cuisine** so that you can satisfy your individual tastes. The restaurants also are marked on handy maps.

Restaurants designated as kid-friendly in this chapter have a kids' menu and/or cuisine that appeals to a younger palate.

Each review contains two price indicators. There's a dollar symbol, for a quick look at the average price of a dinner without beverages. I also list the range of prices for main courses on the restaurant's menu. I added up the costs of the least expensive and most expensive appetizer or salad, main course, and dessert at dinner, not including taxes and tips, and then averaged the highest- and lowest-priced meals to come up with the dollar sign ranking.

Prices change over time, and the cost of your meal obviously depends on what you order. One reason I don't include beverage costs in my price categories is that ordering top-shelf cocktails and expensive wines can produce a $$$$$ bill at a $$$ restaurant. Sticking to a lower-priced entree and drinking coffee (or water) can squeeze a $$$$ restaurant into a $$$ bill (not that I recommend water over wine at gourmet restaurants).

Here's what you can expect meals to cost. Prices in Table 10-1 are per person, not including drinks.

Table 10-1	Key to Restaurant Dollar Signs
Dollar Sign(s)	*Price Range*
$	Less than $15
$$	$15–$25
$$$	$26–$40
$$$$	$41–$50
$$$$$	More than $50

Amma *Indian Vegetarian Kitchen*
$ Georgetown   INDIAN/VEGETARIAN

Amma is a wonderful example of the amusing diversity of Georgetown. This quiet, unassuming restaurant — with quiet, unassuming staff — sits right next to the Jinx Proof Tattoos & Piercing Parlor on bustling M Street. Amma offers you numerous ways to sample Indian vegetarian cooking at bargain prices. The Amma Special comes with rice, salad, bread, pickle, and two vegetables. The Kerala Thali House Special features three south Indian curries with mixed vegetables, spicy soup, rice, yogurt, pickle, grilled or deep-fried bread, and dessert. The Punjabi Thali House Special is built around three north Indian curries. Or you can mix and match à la carte.

See map p. 133. 3291 M St. NW (near 33rd Street). ☎ *202-625-6652. Reservations accepted. Take Georgetown Connection shuttle bus Route 2 from Dupont Circle or Rosslyn Metrorail Station. Full meals for $11 or less. AE, MC, V. Open: Mon–Thu 11:30 a.m.–2:30 p.m., 5:30–10 p.m.; Fri 11:30 a.m.–2:30 p.m., 5:30 p.m.–10:30 p.m.; Sat 11:30 a.m.–10:30 p.m.; and Sun 11:30 a.m.–4 p.m.*

Andale
$$$ Downtown   CONTEMPORARY MEXICAN

Chef/co-owner Alison Swope does everything right at this festive restaurant with lots of windows looking out on Seventh and D streets in the lively Penn Quarter neighborhood. The room is cheerful, brightened by sunny yellow walls hung with colorful prints. You can pick from 15 wines by the glass, a half dozen Margaritas, a half dozen bottled Mexican beers, and nearly a page of tequilas — or you can order Dos Equis on tap. The helpful menu describes the dishes and the drinks, and the staff is attentive and knowledgeable. Swope calls the cuisine here "Contemporary Mexican." She applies her knowledge of New American cooking to traditional Mexican recipes in order to create something new. You can make a meal by ordering several items from the lists of *antojitos* (little whims) and *apertivos* (appetizers). Susan and I particularly like the *totopos con mariscos* (tortillas with crab, shrimp, cheese, and avocado salsa). The jicama salad is a refreshing follow-up to spicy appetizers. For a main course, I highly recommend the smokey-tasting grilled pork chop in mole sauce with mashed sweet potatoes. For dessert, the warm pineapple upside-down cake with coconut ice cream and caramel sauce is wonderful.

See map p. 128. 401 7th St. NW (at D Street). ☎ *202-783-3133.* www.andaledc.com. *Reservations recommended. Metro: Archives/Navy Memorial. Walk north on 7th a half block to D. Main courses: $12–$27. AE, DC, DISC, MC, V. Open: Mon 11:30 a.m.– 9 p.m., Tues–Thurs 11:30a.m.–10 p.m., Fri–Sat 11:30 a.m.–11 p.m.*

Asia Nora
$$$$ Foggy Bottom/West End   ASIAN/ORGANIC

Like its older sister Nora (see upcoming review), Asia Nora cooks with organic ingredients. It's a gorgeous restaurant, decorated and furnished in warm tones, Asian artifacts, and soft chairs. The food, rather than pure Asian, is modern American with Asian touches. Thus, you may find the menu includes seared lemongrass beef with roasted butternut-scallion gnocchi, shiitake mushrooms, seared spinach, and Thai pesto, or roasted salmon with stir-fried rice noodles, assorted vegetables, coriander, and roasted peanuts. Top it off with a fruit tart and honey-lavender ice cream. I'm drooling as I write!

See map p. 128. 2213 M St. NW (at 22nd Street). ☎ *202-797-4860.* www.noras.com. *Reservations recommended. Metro: Foggy Bottom-George Washington University. Walk north on 23rd Street to M and then right. Main courses: $22–$28. AE, MC, V. Open: Mon–Thurs 5:30 p.m.–10 p.m., Fri–Sat 5:30 p.m.–10:30 p.m. Closed two weeks at end of Aug/early Sept.*

Austin Grill
$$ Downtown and Upper Northwest   SOUTHWESTERN

Our family hits the Austin Grill often. You get good Tex-Mex food in a festive atmosphere served by friendly staff. The grill gives you lots of choices. My wife tends to make a meal from several appetizers. My vegetarian daugher likes the portabella mushroom and spinach quesadilla, although I think it would benefit from some extra spices. My suggestion may be explained by the fact that what really turns me on here is the really hot stuff, such as the Roadhouse Burrito — spicy ground sirloin and red beans, topped with a cheese and jalapeño sauce. It's billed as a "heart attack on a platter." Also especially good is the Austin Special — one chicken and one cheese enchilada covered with three sauces. The kids' menu has Tex-Mex dishes, along with burgers, chicken sandwiches, and free ice cream for dessert. The original, which is a bit funky, is on Wisconsin Avenue above Georgetown. Tourists are more likely to encounter the new and spacious downtown grill in the up-and-coming arts-and-entertainment area near MCI Center.

See map p. 128. 750 E St. NW (between 7th and 8th streets). ☎ *202-393-3776. www.austingrill.com. Reservations not accepted. Metro: Gallery Place. From 7th and F Streets exit, walk 1 block south on 7th and then turn right on E. Main courses: $8–$18. AE, DC, DISC, MC, V. Open: Sun 11 a.m.– 9:30 p.m., Mon–Thurs 11 a.m.–10 p.m., and Fri–Sat 11 a.m.–11 p.m.*

See map p. 128. 2404 Wisconsin Ave. NW (near 37th and Calvert streets). ☎ *202-337-8080. On the 30-series Metrobus lines. Sun 11 a.m.–10:30 p.m., Mon 11:30 a.m.–10:30 p.m., Tues–Thurs 11:30 a.m.–11 p.m., Fri 11:30 a.m.–midnight, and Sat 11 a.m.–midnight.*

B. Smith's
$$$ Capitol Hill   SOUTHERN

Under the ornate, soaring Beaux Arts ceiling of what once was the President's Room in Union Station, Washingtonians now dine on innovative versions of Southern, Cajun, and Creole cooking. Share the red beans and rice appetizer before diving into your main courses. B. Smith's house special is called Swamp Thing, and it's mixed seafood over greens in a mustard-based seafood sauce. Other specialties include grilled lamb chops, fried green tomatoes, and spicy Cajun jambalaya. Executive chef Rahman Harper also has come up with a dish he calls Southern Surf & Surf. (Read it carefully; it's not a typo.) That would be Cajun crabcake, blackened shrimp, sautéed spinach, rice, and tomato. Traditional jazz groups entertain on Friday and Saturday nights and at Sunday brunch. Because of the 30-foot ceilings and hard surfaces, this place can get noisy.

See map p. 128. 50 Massachusetts Ave. NE (in Union Station). ☎ *202-289-6188. www.bsmith.com. Reservations recommended. Metro: Union Station. Main courses: $14–$30. AE, DISC, DC, MC, V. Open: Mon–Thu 11:30 a.m.–3 p.m. and 5 p.m.– 9 p.m., Fri–Sat 11:30 a.m.–3 p.m. and 5 p.m.– 10 p.m., Sun 11:30 a.m.–8 p.m.*

Bistro Bis
$$$$ Capitol Hill   FRENCH

The food at Bistro Bis is an excellent modern American interpretation of classic French bistro and brasserie cooking. The setting represents a modern American nod toward classic bistro style. From the zinc bar to the spacious leather booths, Bis is both eye-catching and comfortable. The menu changes frequently, but look for seared sea scallops with garlic, tomato, olives, parsley, and eggplant. The simplest dishes — grilled tuna, seared salmon, or braised short ribs, for example — often are the best.

See map p. 128. 15 E St. NW (west of North Capitol Street). ☎ *202-661-2700. www. bistrobis.com/bistro. Reservations recommended. Metro: Union Station. From Union Station Shops/Massachusetts Avenue exit, turn right on Massachusetts, then left on North Capitol, and then right on E. Main courses: $19.75–$29.75 AE, DC, DISC, MC, V. Open: Daily 7–10 a.m., 11:30 a.m.–2:30 p.m., and 5:30–10:30 p.m.*

Bistrot Lepic & Wine Bar
$$$ Georgetown   FRENCH

This neighborhood hangout is in upper Georgetown and is filled with diplomats, world travelers, and others who revel in real French food. Chef Bruno Fortin began to learn the art of French cooking in his parents' restaurant in Brittany and then hopped around Europe and North America before settling into Washington and opening Lepic (named for a street he lived on in Paris) in 1995. Like other good French chefs in America, Fortin offers traditional French dishes and his own improvisations on them. Start with the mussel soup with leeks and potatoes, and/or the lemon-lime risotto with shrimp. Then try the grilled trout with carrot sauce, potato-crusted salmon, or sautéed sea scallops with ginger broccoli mousse. The dining room is small, bustling, and pleasant, with sunny yellow walls. The new second-floor wine bar created added space for drinking and nibbling appetizers. It's also a place smokers can order from the full menu, but they must call ahead for reservations.

See map p. 133. 1736 Wisconsin Ave. NW (between R and S streets). ☎ 202-333-0111. www.bistrotlepic.com. Reservations recommended. Take Georgetown Connection Route 1 shuttle bus from Foggy Bottom/George Washington University Metrorail station or take a 30-series Metrobus. Main courses $16–$22. AE, DC, DISC, MC, V. Open: Tues–Thurs 11:30 a.m.–2:30 p.m. and 5:30–10 p.m., Fri–Sat 11:30 a.m.–2:30 p.m. and 5:30–10:30 p.m., Sun 11:30 a.m.–2:30 p.m. and 5:30–9:30 p.m. Wine bar open Tues–Sun 5:30 p.m.–midnight.

The Brickskeller
$$ Dupont Circle   AMERICAN

If you've left your college days long behind you, visiting the Brickskeller may make you think you've gone back. Your college town has to have a (smaller) hangout like this one. It's got red brick walls. It's got red-and-white checkered tablecloths. It's got beer cans and bottles as a primary decorating motif. It's got Janice Joplin on the jukebox. It's got surprisingly good food. And, my, does it have beer — more than 1,000 brands are advertised. The fish and chips here are really good. So is the *brotziet* — bratwurst simmered in beer with green pepper and onion, served on a toasted roll and with a side of German potato salad. You may find it's easier to eat with a fork. The juicy burgers, Buffalo wings, and French fries also are good choices. You get an enormous pile of fried onion rings for $3.25. If you crave alternatives to standard pub fare, you can order salmon, beef steaks, and several renditions of buffalo (not the kind with wings). One warning: If secondhand smoke bothers you, ask to be seated as far from the bar as possible.

See map p. 131. 1523 22nd St. NW (between P and Q streets). ☎ 202-293-1885. www.thebrickskeller.com. Reservations accepted for six or more people. Metro: Dupont Circle. From Q Street exit, walk west on Q to 22nd and then turn left. Main courses: $4.50 (plain burger)–16.95 (buffalo steak). AE, CB, DC, DISC, MC, V.

Open: Mon–Thurs 11:30 a.m.–2 a.m., Fri 11:30 a.m.–3 a.m., Sat 6 p.m.–3 a.m., Sun 6 p.m.–2 a.m.

Cafe Atlantico
$$$ Downtown   LATIN AMERICAN

Brightly decorated and filled with greenery and tables scattered over three open floors, Cafe Atlantico is a lively spot within an easy walk of many tourist attractions and cultural and entertainment venues. The Nuevo Latino cooking draws on the cuisines of South America, Central America, Mexico, and the Caribbean. The food is tasty and can be as rainbow-bright as the interior decorations. The cafe is noted for its exotic mixed drinks and extensive Latin American wine list. Come Saturday or Sunday from 11:30 a.m. to 2:30 p.m. for "Latino din-sum," culinary director Jose Andres and chef Katsuya Fukushima's innovative take on *tapas,* small dishes of Spain. At six-seat Mini Bar, on the second floor, Andres spins out small servings of whatever his imagination can conjure up in its wildest moments (foie gras in cotton candy, for example). The $65 tasting menu is offered Tuesday through Saturday with seatings at 6 and 8:30 p.m. A $45 tasting menu is in the main dining area, and a $22 pretheater menu runs from 5 to 6:30 p.m. weekdays.

See map p. 128. 405 8th St. NW (between D and E streets). ☎ ***202-393-0812.*** www. cafeatlanticodc.com. *Reservations recommended. Metro: Gallery Place-Chinatown. From F and 7th Streets exit, walk east on F to 8th and then turn left. Main courses: $18–$24. AE, DC, DISC, MC, V. Open: Sun–Thurs 11:30 a.m.–2:30 p.m. and 5–10 p.m. Fri–Sat 11:30 a.m.–2:30 p.m. and 5–11 p.m.*

Cafe 15
$$$$$ Downtown   FRENCH

Washington's only three-star Michelin chef is not a full-time fixture at Cafe 15, but Antoine Westermann's role as consulting chef here has brought lots of attention to this excellent French restaurant. Westermann earned the highest possible Michelin rating — possibly the most desired honor in the world of dining — for his Le Buerehiesel restaurant in Strasbourg, the German-influenced French town near the two countries' border. At Cafe 15, in the French-owned Sofitel Lafayette Square hotel, he designs the menu, trains the staff, and pops in from time to time to check how his instructions are being carried out. Cafe 15's full-time executive chef, Philippe Piel, worked for Westermann at Le Buerehiesel. Westermann describes his approach to cooking as "we create a new dish of tomorrow by basing it on the classics of yesterday." His variations on classical French cooking include a few dishes based on his grandmother's recipes. I particular enjoy Cafe 15's appetizer of sautéed frog legs accompanied by ravioli filled with a sweet onion compote, a Westermann signature dish; a main course of seared sea scallops with warm asparagus salad and mushrooms; and an unusual dessert of beer brioche with a caramelized pear and beer ice cream — a nod to that German influence, perhaps.

See map p. 128. 806 15th St. NW (at H Street). ☎ *202-730-8700. Reservations recommended. Metro: McPherson Square. From Franklin Square/14th Street exit, walk west on H to 15th. Main courses: $24–$34. AE, DC, DISC, MC, V. Open: Daily 6:30 a.m.–10:30 p.m.*

Cafe La Ruche
$$ Georgetown   FRENCH

My wife and daughter like to eat in this little restaurant off Georgetown's beaten path because it reminds them of France. From the outside, you can imagine it as a house in the French countryside (if you ignore the surrounding buildings). Inside, it's like a well-worn neighborhood hangout in Paris (though the TV at one end of the dining room intrudes upon the fantasy). Unfortunately, at times, indifferent service can remind you of Paris as well. To start, try the traditional French onion soup. You can make a meal of the salade Niçoise. The quiches are good. And the desserts are wonderful. (Get the fruit tart, and you can pretend it's health food. I do.) Weekend brunch, from 10 a.m. to 3 p.m., is a treat. When the weather's nice, you can eat outside.

See map p. 133. 1039 31st St. NW (between M and K streets). ☎ *202-965-2684.* www.cafelaruche.com. *Reservations accepted.. Take Georgetown Connection shuttle bus Route 2 from Foggy Bottom/GWU or Rosslyn Metrorail station to 31st and M and then walk south on 31st. Or take a 30-series Metrobus. Main courses: $6–$10. AE, DC, DISC, MC, V. Open: Mon–Fri 11:30 a.m.–11:30 p.m., Sat–Sun 10 a.m.–midnight.*

Capital Q
$ Chinatown   TEXAS BARBECUE

How's this for incongruity? In Washington's tiny Chinatown stands a tiny restaurant with autographed pictures of U.S. politicians on the walls and Texas barbecue on the menu. Most of the politicians are Texans, which is appropriate because this restaurant is run by transplanted Texan Nick Fontana. Capital Q is good enough and authentic enough to attract Texas expatriate diners and was picked to cater the party that House Majority Leader Dick Armey (of Texas) threw for 4,000 of his closest friends at the 2000 Republican National Convention in Philadelphia. Order the beef brisket or pulled pork from the sandwich menu. Or try the beef brisket plate, which comes with two side dishes. The "Chinese Cowboy Platter" gives you your choice of barbecued meat over rice. Service is cafeteria style. Wanna see what's going on here right now? Capital Q has a live cam on its Web site.

See map p. 128. 707 H. St. NW (between 7th and 8 streets). ☎ *202-347-8396.* www.capitalqbbq.com. *Reservations not accepted. Metro: Gallery Place-Chinatown. From 7th and 8th Streets exit, cross 7th on H and look for the restaurant. Sandwiches: $4.50–$5.95. Plates: $5.25–$24.95 (for an enormous serving of ribs). No credit cards. Open: Mon–Thurs 11 a.m.–7 p.m., Fri–Sat 11 a.m.–8 p.m.*

The Caucus Room

$$$$ Downtown STEAKHOUSE

This restaurant was created in that grand Washington tradition of Republican and Democratic lawmakers ripping each other's hearts out during the day and then visiting each other's hideaway offices to sip bourbon and swap stories at night. That doesn't happen so much in these highly partisan times, but Democratic lobbyist Tommy Boggs and former Republican National Committee Chairman Haley Barbour (who's now governor of Mississippi) joined the ownership group to make it happen at the Caucus Room, just off Pennsylvania Avenue, midway between the Capitol and the White House. The result is a near-caricature of what you'd expect from high-priced lobbyists. Cherry wood, marble, brass, and thick carpet define the decor. On the menu, you find Caesar salad and lots of steak. The food is good, the room is comfortable, and you just may spy some political VIPs moseying about.

See map p. 128. 401 9th St. NW (at D Street). ☎ *202-393-0777.* www.thecaucus room.com. *Reservations recommended. Metro: Archives-Navy Memorial. Walk west on Pennsylvania Avenue and then right 1 block on 9th to D. Main courses: $24–$36. AE, DISC, MC, V. Open: Mon–Fri11:30 a.m.–2:30 p.m. and 5:30 p.m.–10:30 p.m., Sat 5:30 p.m.–10:30 p.m.*

Circle Bistro

$$$ Foggy Bottom/West End AMERICAN/MEDITERRANEAN

The food at this young restaurant off Pennsylvania Avenue is excellent, and you can order it in an extraordinary number of different ways. The most obvious way is from the regular dinner menu in the comfortable dining room, which is sleek and modern but warmed by earth-toned decor and windows that look into greenery planted outside. But there's also a bar menu of small plates, salads, and sandwiches; a 5 to 7 p.m. happy hour when sophisticated snacks are served at a dollar a pop; an 11:30 a.m. to 2:30 p.m. Sunday brunch featuring fondues and small tortillas filled with scrambled eggs, shrimp, bacon, and other unexpected ingredients; barbecue by the pool from 4 to 10 p.m. weekends in the summer; a $28-dollar pretheater dinner from 5 to 7 p.m. daily; live jazz in the lounge from 8 p.m. to midnight Saturdays; and breakfast daily. Swiss-born executive chef George Vetsch says his cooking is influenced by the Mediterranean. Dinner starts with complementary fried chicken, calimari, and potatoes with four sauces, which sort of makes ordering an appetizer seem like overkill. Among the main courses, Susan and I especially like the grouper served on top of sliced zucchini and beneath a relish of mango, zucchini and red bell pepper. For dessert, you must taste the apple beignet, served with sugar, cinnamon, vanilla sauce, and cinnamon ice cream.

See map p. 128. 1 Washington Circle NW (at 23rd Street and New Hampshire Avenue). ☎ *202-293-5390.* www.circlebistro.com. *Reservations recommended. Metro: Foggy Bottom/George Washington University. Walk 1block north on 23rd and then go counterclockwise around Washington Circle to New Hampshire and 23rd. Main* *courses: $17–$23. AE, DC, DISC, MC, V. Open: Sun 8–10:30a.m., 11:30 a.m.–2:30 p.m., and 5–10 p.m,; Mon–Thurs 7–10 a.m., 11:30 a.m.–2:30 p.m., and 5–10 p.m., Fri 7–10 a.m., 11:30 a.m.–2:30 p.m., and 5–11 p.m., Sat 8–10:30 a.m., 11:30 a.m.–2:30 p.m., and 5–11 p.m. Bar open daily 10 a.m.–closing.*

City Lights of China
$$ Dupont Circle   CHINESE

Good food served by a friendly staff in pleasant surroundings — what more do you want in a Chinese restaurant? City Lights has a large and varied menu, and the owners invite you to ask the chef to accommodate your personal tastes. My family has become especially fond of the hot and sour soup, spring rolls, and Seafood Delight (shrimp, scallops, crab, and vegetables stir-fried in a light sauce). The restaurant also is noted for its Peking duck, crisp-fried Cornish hen, eggplant with garlic, and tangy Szechwan lamb. Many vegetable dishes are on the menu. In addition to serving you inside, City Lights has a substantial takeout menu and delivers to nearby hotels. Keep that thought in mind if you want to picnic on a park bench or collapse in your room after a particularly grueling day of seeing the sights.

See map p. 131. 1731 Connecticut Ave. NW (between R and S streets). ☎ *202-265-6688.* www.citylightsofchina.com. *Reservations recommended. Metro: Dupont Circle. From the Q Street exit, walk north on Connecticut Avenue past R Street. Main courses: $9–$22. AE, MC, V. Open: Mon–Fri11:30 a.m.–10:30 p.m., Sat noon–11 p.m., and Sun noon–10:30 p.m.*

Clyde's
$$$ Georgetown and Upper Northwest   AMERICAN

Like its sibling Old Ebbitt Grill, Clyde's of Georgetown was one of my favorite places to eat when I managed to find an excuse to visit Washington long before we moved here. Then, it was a comfortable old saloon with some unusually good food, especially (to my taste) the omelets. A 1996 renovation modernized the place, while aiming to maintain a saloonlike atmosphere — oak bar, plank flooring, checkered tablecloths. But the Garden Room now looks like all those other family-friendly pubs that hang artifacts all over the place. In this case, models of antique airplanes dangle below the skylight. Clyde's is still a place for hamburgers and other bar fare, but the ever-changing menu is quite ambitious, with special attention to incorporating fresh produce from mid-Atlantic farms. Always order the light and fluffy omelet if it's offered. We've also recently had good luck ordering pear salad with blue cheese and walnuts, linguini with mussels, rockfish, and crab cakes. Clyde's is a local chain now, and the Clyde's of Chevy Chase, just across the border in Maryland, is in the midst of the Friendship Heights upscale shopping area. It was forced to close during a construction project and was scheduled to reopen in mid-2005.

See map p. 133. 3236 M St. NW between Wisconsin Avenue and Potomac Street. ☎ *202-333-9180.* www.clydes.com. *Reservations recommended. Take the*

Georgetown Connection Route 2 shuttle bus from the Dupont Circle or Rosslyn Metrorail station to M and Potomac or 33rd street. Or hop a 30-series Metrobus to M and Wisconsin. Also in Chevy Chase, MD (see map p. 128): 70 Wisconsin Circle (northeast of the intersection of Wisconsin and Western avenues). ☎ *301-951-9600. Metro: Friendship Heights. From Western Avenue and Military Road exit, walk north on Wisconsin, cross Wisconsin Circle, and then turn right into the Chevy Chase shopping center parking lot. Reopening in mid-2005. Main courses: $8.50–$23. AE, DC, DISC, MC, V. Open: Mon–Thurs 11:30 a.m.–midnight, Fri 11:30 a.m.–1 a.m., Sat 10 a.m.–1 a.m., Sun 9 a.m.–midnight.*

Coeur de Lion
$$$$ Downtown   MODERN AMERICAN

This is one of Washington's more romantic dining venues, for young and old alike. The light is soft, the decor warm, the furnishings plush, the tables well spaced and lighted by candles, and the room touched by quiet jazz from the adjacent Blue Bar Thursday, Friday, and Saturday nights. Some older regulars seem to keep coming back because they like to be fussed over by maitre d' Ralph Fredericks and his hyper-attentive staff. Ralph definitely is a big part of the draw here. In fact, the owners lured him back in 2003 after he deserted Washington for two years to work in New Orleans and Beverly Hills. Some first-timers find Ralph a bit over the top, but it's smart to let him guide you through the menu. And don't hesitate to ask him for modifications to suit your taste. The rich, creamy crab cakes make a wonderful main course, for example, even if they appear only on the appetizer menu. The simplest dishes often are the best here.

See map p. 128. 926 Massachusetts Ave. NW (west of 9th Street, in the Henley Park Hotel). ☎ *202-638-5200.* www.henleypark.com. *Reservations recommended. Metro: Mt. Vernon Square. Walk 2 blocks south on 7th Street, go right across the top of Mt. Vernon Square to 9th, and then bear right on Massachusetts. Main courses: $17–$32. AE, DC, DISC, MC, V. Open: Mon–Sat 7–10:30 a.m., 11 a.m.–2:30 p.m., and 6–10 p.m., Sun 7–10:30 a.m., 11:30 a.m.–2:30 p.m., and 6–10 p.m.*

Dish
$$$ Foggy Bottom   AMERICAN

Executive chef Ron Reda starts with traditional American cooking and then recasts it with his own flare — sometimes a great deal, sometimes very little, sometimes not at all. He says the meatloaf is "Mom's recipe." The rest of the menu changes, so I can't recommend specific items unless those I liked come back when you're here. If you see them on the appetizer menu (called "First Dish"), grab the crispy blue point oysters or the fried shrimp. Among the main courses, the tasty fried chicken is moist and juicy and served with roasted tomato and a salad made with baby mizuna, a delicate Japanese green. The equally tasty blackened pork chop is salty and served with delicious saffron-vanilla poached pears. The best thing I've tasted for dessert here is called "Peachy Keen" — a fresh peach with brioche pudding, vanilla ice cream, and white chocolate sauce. Susan said it took a great deal of will power to prevent her from licking the plate.

See map p. 128. 924 25th St. NW (between I and K streets, in the River Inn). ☎ *202-338-8707.* www.dishdc.com. *Reservations recommended. Metro: Foggy Bottom/ George Washington University. Walk 2 blocks west on I Street and then go right on 25th. Main courses: $18–$25. AE, DC, MC, V. Open: Mon–Fri 7–10 a.m., 11 a.m.– 2:30 p.m., and 5–10:30 p.m., Sat–Sun 8–10 a.m. and 5–10:30 p.m.*

Eat First
$$ Chinatown   CHINESE

The name and the exterior appearance of Eat First don't scream "gourmet cooking," but the restaurant serves good food popular with the locals. You need to peruse the various sections of the lengthy menu to locate the best dishes. Try the steamed shrimp from among the house specialties, General Tso's chicken in the poultry section, sliced chicken with ginger and scallion from the clay pot preparations, and the barbecued pork and roasted duck entrees from the barbecue and soy sauce dishes. If you know your Chinese cooking, the chefs are happy to prepare items not on the menu. In an early-to-bed town, this place is one where you can satisfy late-late-late hunger.

See map p. 128. 609 H St. NW (between 6th and 7th streets). ☎ *202-289-1703. Reservations accepted. Metro: Gallery Place-Chinatown. From 6th and H Streets exit, walk less than 1 block east on H. Main courses: $6–$17. AE, MC, V. Open: Sun–Thurs 10 a.m.–2 a.m. and Fri–Sat 10 a.m.–3 a.m.*

15 ria
$$$ Downtown   AMERICAN/SOUTHERN

Let me say right up front that the food at 15 ria (the name is sort of an uncapitalized acronym for the address) is terrific. I need to do this lest you think all the whimsical creativity here is a substitute for good cooking. The dining room is relaxing, with warm earthy colors and comfortable upholstered chairs. The cuisine is Southern influenced, and some diners are tempted to give it the now-cliched description of "comfort food." 15 ria aspires to be a neighborhood restaurant and gathering place for those who work in the area, as well as an easy place for guests at the Washington Terrace Hotel to grab breakfast, lunch, or dinner. As such, it's continually tossing out gimmicks to attract folks to the establishment — a special Tuesday night bar menu for those watching the hit "Queer Eye for the Straight Guy" on the bar's TVs, for example, or free pastry baskets for Sunday brunch diners who can show a program from a religious service they attended that weekend. The restaurant offers a large selection of bourbons and single-malt scotches. The wine list sorts the offerings by taste ("crisp and refreshing," "spicy and aromatic"). The restaurant searches out fresh products from the mid-Atlantic region's farmers and fishermen, so the menu changes frequently. I can enthusiastically recommend, if you see them, the crab toast appetizer, the main course of braised short ribs, and a scrumptious crème brûlée bread pudding for dessert. *Note:* As we go to press, chef Jamie Leeds has left the restaurant. Time will tell how this change will affect the menu.

See map p. 128. 1515 Rhode Island Ave. (west of 15th Street, in the Washington Terrace Hotel). ☎ *202-742-0015. Reservations recommended. Metro: Farragut North. From the L Street exit, walk 1 block east on L, then left on 17th Street 2 blocks to Rhode Island, then right 2 blocks on Rhode Island, keeping north of Scott Circle, to 15th. Main courses: $13–$28. AE, DC, DISC MC, V. Open: Mon–Fri 6:30–11 a.m., 11:30 a.m.–2:30 p.m., and 6–10:30 p.m., Sat 7 a.m.–noon, 11:30 a.m.–5:30 p.m., and 6–11:30 p.m., Sun 7 a.m.–noon, 11:30 a.m.–4 p.m., and 6–10:30 p.m.*

Firefly
$$$ Dupont Circle   MODERN AMERICAN

I'm tempted to say the show is everything at Firefly, but that would be unfair to the good food served here. Firefly's promotional theme is "memories of summer nights spent lazing in the backyard" and, presumably, gazing upon fireflies flitting about over the lawn. When you walk in, you'll quickly note the "firefly tree," a floor-to-ceiling birch trunk with branches sporting candles in little copper lanterns. One wall in the main dining room is lined with birch logs, stood vertically to suggest a forest. More logs and stone dominate other sections of the small restaurant, which can be noisy when crowded. This restaurant is another of those young (opened in 2002) D.C. eateries that feature traditional American fare spiffed up for the 21st-century. The roast chicken comes with yellow tomato-onion compote; the grilled mackerel with stir-fried rapini (a leafy green with broccolilike buds), pickled jicama and chive oil; and a lamb minute steak with macaroni-and-cheese and chard. As I write this book, my favorite dishes from earlier meals here have unfortunately, vanished from the seasonally changing menu, with the exception of tasty spinach enlivened by slivers of garlic. Maybe you'll get lucky and the braised short ribs will return, or the dessert menu will offer the interesting apple tart and ice cream with salted pecans. Executive Chef John Wabeck recently initiated a 4:30 p.m. to 7 p.m. weekday happy hour, which features a different selection of small-batch wines each evening and four snacks from the restaurant, which starts serving dinners at 5:30.

See map p. 131. 1310 New Hampshire Ave. NW (north of N Street in the Hotel Madera). ☎ *202-861-1310.* www.firefly-dc.com. *Reservations recommended. Metro: Dupont Circle. From the Dupont Circle exit, walk south on 19th Street briefly, go right on Sunderland Place and across 20th to New Hampshire, and then turn left. Main courses: $16–$26.50. AE, DC, DISC MC, V. Open: Mon–Thurs 7–10 a.m., 11:30 a.m.–2:30 p.m., 5:30–10 p.m., Fri 7 a.m.–10 a.m., 11:30 a.m.–2:30 p.m., 5:30 p.m.– 10:30 p.m., Sat 7–10 a.m., 11 a.m.–2:30 p.m., 5:30 p.m.–10:30 p.m., Sun 7–10 a.m., 11 a.m.–2:30 p.m., 5:30–10 p.m.*

Galileo
$$–$$$$$ Downtown   NORTHERN ITALIAN

Talk about multipurposing! Galileo long has set the bar by which other D.C. Italian restaurants are measured — and charged for the quality. For several years, award-winning chef Roberto Donna also has been offering an even more expensive opportunity to taste additional outstanding dishes in *Laboratorio*, a private dining room where a 10- to 12-course tasting menu is served 5 nights a week for $110 on weekdays and $125 on weekends, with an additional $70 option for matched wines. Now he's gone the opposite direction and added bargain-priced meals at lunch and dinner in the bar area and outdoors in nice weather. Epicures are advised to reserve well ahead for one of the 30 coveted seats in *Laboratorio*, but you can't make reservations for the bar-area meals at lunch and dinner.

See map p. 128. 1110 21st St. NW (between L and M streets). ☎ *202-293-7191. Laboratorio* ☎ *202-331-0880.* www.robertodonna.com. *Reservations recommended for Galileo, required for Laboratorio, not accepted for bar area meals. Metro: Farragut North. Walk west on L Street 4 blocks and then right on 21st. Main courses $25–$35 at Galileo, $8–10 at the bar. AE, DC, DISC, MC, V. Open: Mon–Thurs 11:30 a.m.–2:15 p.m., 5:30–10 p.m, Fri 11:30 a.m.–2:15 p.m., 5:30–10:30 p.m., Sat 5:30–10:30 p.m.; Sun 5–10 p.m. Bar area bargains not available weekends at lunch or Sun and Mond at dinner.*

Garrett's
$$ Georgetown   AMERICAN

Garrett's is an old-fashioned saloon hangout with a surprisingly pretty little bright and airy dining room, with large windows and a glass roof tucked into a corner of the second floor. Take the stairs just east of the first-floor bar, and you may find the friendly, accommodating staff singing to a child celebrating a birthday. Garrett's menu features soups, salads, pastas, burgers, sandwiches, appetizers, finger food, and a few main courses that resemble Mom's home cooking. I like the chicken pot pie. It's tasty, with a flaky crust and so much gravy that it's served with a spoon. Also good is the "Huntington Hash" — pulled chicken and roasted potatoes topped with gravy and served with fresh fruit and cole slaw. The wine list is small, but the wines are good and priced from $4.50 to $7. You also have some interesting beer selections.

See map p. 133. 3003 M St. NW (west of 30th Street). ☎ *202-333-8282.* www. garrettsdc.com. *Reservations accepted. Take Georgetown Connection shuttle bus from Dupont Circle or Rosslyn Metrorail station to M and 30th or Thomas Jefferson street. Or ride 30-series Metrobus. Main courses: $8–$24. Sandwiches: $5.75–$8.25. AE, DC, DISC, MC, V. Open: Daily 11:30am–10 p.m.*

Georgia Brown's
$$$ Downtown   SOUTHERN

Ready for "nouveau soul food?" That's how the cuisine is described at Georgia Brown's, a Southern restaurant that bases its cooking on the traditions of South Carolina's Coastal Low Country — with a twist. And just what does that produce? How about fried green tomatoes stuffed with herbed cream cheese, served on green tomato relish with lemon-cayenne mayonnaise and watercress? It's a superb, rich dish that four can share. Or a salad of baby greens, apples, blue cheese, and toasted walnuts in apple

---

Dining with Dubya: Politico hangouts

So you wonder where the president likes to grab a bite outside the White House? Or where members of Congress and lobbyists feed their faces and bend their elbows between roll calls?

Well, President George W. Bush isn't known to frequent D.C. eateries, and when he does he seems to choose modest digs. Like his father, he's shown up at the **Peking Gourmet Inn** in suburban Falls Church, Virginia (6029 Leesburg Pike; ☎ 703-671-8088). My daughter ran into him one night at the **Cactus Cantina** (3300 Wisconsin Ave. NW, 1 block north of the National Cathedral; ☎ 202-686-7222), a good Tex-Mex spot near the National Cathedral. (Ironically, she had stopped there before going off to see a play that was highly critical of an execution Bush approved when he was Texas governor.) Nevertheless, one of her bolder classmates approached him and asked whether he would pose for a picture with the group, and he graciously agreed. Then, every kid with a cell phone — whether red state or blue state in their political leanings — immediately telephoned relatives and friends to tell who was eating at the next table.

You'll find senators, lobbyists, and Supreme Court justices at **The Monocle**. Senators, lobbyists and senate staffers at **La Colline** and **the Dubliner,** Senate staffers and lobbyists at **Bistro Bis**. House staffers and the occasional representative frequent **Bullfeathers**. White House folks hit the nearby **Occidental** and **Old Ebbitt Grill**.

The number-one see-and-be-seen place in town is **The Palm**. Actually, you might bump into lobbyists at any of the preceding restaurants because their jobs revolve around government folks, and they have the expense accounts to afford it.

---

vinaigrette dressing? Or a vegetarian croquette? You can find plenty of traditional home cooking, too, like fried chicken, pork chops, catfish, gumbo, shrimp, and grits. This New South is vegetarian-friendly, with several veggie selections on the menu, including a sampler that my vegetarian daughter rates highly. Portions are large. The dining room is warm and comfy. A popular jazz brunch occurs from 10 a.m. to 2:30 p.m. Sunday. The place is a hangout for local movers and shakers, and it's one of the most integrated dining rooms in town.

See map p. 128. 950 15th St. NW (between I and K streets). ☎ *202-393-4499.* www. gbrowns.com. *Reservations recommended. Metro: McPherson Square. From the Vermont Ave./White House exit, walk north on Vermont to I and then bear left on 15th. Main courses: $13–$24.50. AE, DC, DISC, MC, V. Open: Sun 10 a.m.–2:30 p.m., 5:30–9 p.m., Mon–Thurs 11:30 a.m.–10:30 p.m., Fri 11:30 a.m.–11:30 p.m., Sat 5:30–11:30 p.m.*

Gerard's Place
$$$$$ Downtown FRENCH

This intimate French restaurant serves top-notch food by Gerard Pangaud, one of the best French chefs in America, at top-notch prices. Pangaud changes the menu every other week, so you can't be sure what you'll find on any given day. If you have the chance, order Pangaud's signature poached lobster in a ginger, lime, and sauterne sauce, with red pepper, avocado, and mango. This delicious and unusual blending of flavors is typical of the twist he puts on traditional French cooking. One salad offering, for example, combines braised brisket of beef with a half-dozen vegetables and a pickled relish of gherkin cucumbers, capers, and shallots. Finish your taste adventure by marveling at a sweet souffle with a medley of fruits. If you're denied access to the lobster, look for Pangaud's take on roasted chicken or duck, or his fricassee of monkfish in red wine sauce. Gerard's proves the value of eating at lunch and ordering fixed-price meals. You can get a three-course, fixed-price lunch for $29.50. A tasting menu at dinner sets you back $85 or, if you order vegetarian, $62. (All prices are before wine.)

See map p. 128. 915 15th St. NW (between I and K streets). ☎ 202-737-4445. Reservations recommended. Metro: McPherson Square. From the Vermont Ave./ White House exit, walk north on Vermont to I and then east on 15th. Main courses: $25–$49.50. AE, MC, V. Open: Mon–Thurs 11:30 a.m.–2 p.m., 5:30–9 p.m., Friday 11:30 a.m.–2 p.m., 5:30 p.m.–9:30 p.m., Sat 5:30 p.m.–9:30 p.m.

The Grill From Ipanema
$$$ Adams-Morgan   BRAZILIAN

If you've never enjoyed the complex flavors of Brazilian cuisine, don't miss this favorite, known for its good food and lively neighborhood bar scene. Beneath the palm trees and tropical colors, get into a Latin American mood with Brazil's national dish, *feijoada* — a rich black bean stew with sausages, smoked meats, dried beef, and pork spooned over rice. Wash it down with Brazil's national cocktail, a *caipirinha,* made with lime, sugar, and sugarcane brandy. Other menu standouts include a variety of seafood stews called *moqueca.* If you want to avoid noise drifting in from the bar, ask for an outdoor table whenever the weather is nice.

See map p. 131. 1858 Columbia Rd. NW (at Mintwood Place). ☎ 202-986-0757. www.thegrillfromipanema.com. Reservations accepted except after 7:30 p.m. Fri–Sat. Metro: Woodley Park Zoo-Adams Morgan. From the Metrorail station, catch the No. 98 Metrobus to Calvert Street and Columbia Road and then walk south on Columbia 2 blocks. Bus runs 6 p.m.–3:15 a.m. weeknights from 9:50 a.m.–3:15 a.m. Sat, and 6 p.m.–midnight Sun. Or take a taxi. Main courses: $13–$25. AE, MC, V, DC, DISC. Open: Mon–Thurs 5–10:30 p.m., Fri 5–11:30 p.m., Sat noon–11:30 p.m., Sun noon–10 p.m.

Harmony Cafe
$ Georgetown   ASIAN

Tucked in the basement of an unassuming Georgetown storefront, the Harmony Cafe's attractive dining room can please vegetarians and omnivores alike. Most of the Asian dishes, from kung pao chicken to pork in garlic sauce, come in vegetarian versions, a testament to the ability of soy products to mimic other foods. The garden salad with a light Asian dressing is a refreshing accompaniment to the large list of entrees. For an appetizer, try the grilled shitake mushrooms. Don't see exactly what you want on the menu? Under the list of Chef's Specialties, one option is "Your Favorite Dish (ask for it)."

See map p. 133. 3287½ M St. NW (east of 33rd Street). ☎ *202-338-3881. Reservations accepted. Take Georgetown Connection shuttle bus Route 2 from Dupont Circle or Rosslyn Metrorail station to M and 33rd or Potomac street. Main courses: $5–$10. AE, V. Open: Mon–Sat 11:30 a.m.–11 p.m., Sun 5–11 p.m.*

Jaleo
$$ Downtown   SPANISH

Loosely translated, *jaleo* means revelry or racket. Neither is in short supply at this lively, colorful tapas bar and restaurant with walls of windows that look out onto bustling sidewalks. Enjoy flamenco music while perusing a menu of 50 tapas and main courses. Because sharing is an unspoken rule, Jaleo is fun with a group. The Sunday brunch (11:30 a.m.–3 p.m.) attracts locals en route to a nearby attraction or an afternoon siesta. You can graze here nightly for a week and not sample everything. Because I like so many things here, it's hard to focus on a few recommendations. Let me do my duty and steer you toward the spinach sauteed with pine nuts, apples, and raisons; chorizo sausage with garlic mashed potatoes; roasted eggplant with onions and tomatoes; fried calamari; grilled asparagus; and garlic shrimp. Don't eat too many of these choices, though, because you must sample dessert — and share it, too. The warm Basque cake with cream, cinnamon-vanilla sauce, and ice cream is wonderful, as is the flan and the chocolate-nut mousse with fresh strawberry. A world-traveler friend declared Jaleo's cafe con leche as "comparing favorably with what I've had in Mexico and Spain."

See map p. 128. 480 7th St. NW (at E Street). ☎ *202-628-7949.* www.jaleo.com. *Reservations accepted for lunch and between 5 and 6:30 p.m. Metro: Gallery Place/Chinatown. From 7th and F Streets exit, walk 1 block south on 7th to E. Main courses: $16–$18; tapas $3.25–$8. AE, DC, DISC, MC, V. Open: Sun–Mon 11:30 a.m.– 10 p.m., Tues–Thurs 11:30 a.m.–11:30 p.m., and Fri–Sat 11:30 a.m.–midnight.*

Kinkead's
$$$$ Foggy Bottom/West End   SEAFOOD

This restaurant is one of the very best in Washington. Everything is good, but chef-owner Bob Kinkead's signature dishes include pumpkin-seed-crusted salmon with crab, corn, and chilie ragout; as well as roasted cod accompanied by crab imperial, sweet potato puree, mustard cream sauce, and spoonbread (with ham, corn, and cheddar cheese). At the other extreme, Kinkead offers what he calls "simply prepared fish," such as grilled salmon or tuna with steamed fresh vegetables. You can choose from a variety of dining areas at Kinkead's. The main dining rooms upstairs are attractive and formal. An informal bar and cafe on the lower level plays live jazz from 6:30 to 10 p.m. Tuesday through Saturday. The "atrium" refers to a few tables outside the restaurant-proper in the adjacent indoor shopping mall. An added attraction at Kinkead's, unusual in today's restaurant world: sommelier Michael Flynn to advise you on selecting wine.

See map p. 128. 2000 Pennsylvania Ave. NW (actually on I Street between 20th and 21st streets). ☎ *202-296-7700.* www.kinkead.com. *Reservations recommended. Metro: Foggy Bottom. Walk 2½ blocks east on I. Restaurant entrance is on the right in the middle of the block. Main courses: $22–$29. AE, DC, DISC, MC, V. Open: Sun–Thurs 11:30 a.m.–10 p.m., Fri 11:30 a.m.–10:30 p.m., Sat 5:30–10:30 p.m.*

La Colline
$$$ Capitol Hill   FRENCH

Back in my newspaper days, La Colline (French for "The Hill") was my favorite place to take Capitol Hill sources for lunch — on the company's tab, of course. Beyond the fine food and the ideal location (the Capitol is practically outside the front door), La Colline has high-backed booths and well-spaced tables that offer some sense of privacy when you're engaged in confidential conversations. The restaurant is known for the classics, such as onion soup or lobster bisque to start a meal and crème brûlée for dessert. But, being a hangout for lawmakers and lobbyists, La Colline also fires up a grill for New York strip and other steaks.

See map p. 128. 400 N. Capitol St. NW (north of D Street). ☎ *202-737-0400.* www.restaurant.com/lacolline. *Reservations recommended. Metro: Union Station. From Union Station Shops/Massachusetts Avenue exit, walk right on Massachusetts and then left on North Capitol for 2 blocks. Main courses: $12.25–$23.75. AE, DC, DISC, MC, V. Open: Mon–Fri 7 a.m.–10 p.m., Sat 6–10 p.m.*

Le Paradou
$$$$$ Downtown   FRENCH

If you've got 135 bucks to spend on a *nine-course* tasting menu, Le Paradou is the place for you. Superstar chef Yannick Cam and business partner Michael Klein have spared no effort or expense in offering the finest dining experience at this contemporary French restaurant, which opened in mid-2004. And they've done it in a way that makes even a newcomer to this scene feel comfortable. The earth-toned decor with commissioned contemporary art is elegant but comfortable. The dark-suited waiters provide sophisticated but friendly service. From the pre-appetizer amuse of paper-thin smoked salmon with crème fraîche to the dessert of thin crispy pastry, caramel ice cream, nuts, and warm cherries and quince, Susan and I found the food to be exquisite. Ask the waiter's advice when ordering à la carte. If you spring for a fixed-price meal and something doesn't strike your fancy (put off by foie gras?), ask the waiter to suggest a substitute. Be real nice, and maybe he'll bring you the post-dessert dessert, a plate of thumbnail-sized mini treats. You can't eat cheap here, but you can taste Chef Cam's cooking for a lot less in the attractive bar and lounge, at the sidewalk tables in nice weather, or at lunch. Men are expected to wear jackets in the main dining room.

Where the chefs are

Washington can claim an expanding galaxy of star chefs. Antoine Westermann is the most acclaimed. But he's only here part time, as consulting chef at **Cafe 15**. Most of the year, you'll find him at his Le Buerehiesel restaurant in Strasbourg, France, where he earned his three Michelin stars (highest possible rating). For year-round quality, you can dine at **Gerard's Place**, run by Gerard Pangaud. Also serving up superb French food is Yannick Cam, who opened the exquisite **Le Paradou** in mid-2004. Cam became a D.C. superstar chef at Le Pavillon, which closed in 1990. His return downtown, after nearly a decade and a half in other ventures, was big D.C. dining news.

While these celebrity French chefs charge top dollar for their top-notch French cuisine, you can go down- or upscale to sample the work of Roberto Donna, D.C.'s preeminent Italian chef. Donna's **Galileo** has long been considered Washington's number-one Italian restaurant, with prices to match the reputation. The chef's private dining room, **Laboratorio,** costs even more, but Donna offers bargains at Galileo's bar.

See map p. 128. 678 Indiana Ave. NW (between 6th and 7th streets). ☎ *202-347-6780.* www.leparadou.net. *Reservations recommended. Metro: Archive/Navy Memorial. Walk east across square to Indiana. Restaurant is ahead on right. Main courses: $34–$38. Tasting menus: Two-course $58, three-course $75, six-course $100, nine-courses $135. AE, DC, DISC, MC, V. Open: Mon–Thurs noon–2:30 p.m., 6–10:30 p.m., Fri noon–2:30 p.m., 5:30–11 p.m., Sat 5:30–11 p.m.*

Luna Grill & Diner
$$ Dupont Circle   AMERICAN

At Luna, you can get bacon and eggs all day and much of the night. This diner offers you plenty of comfort food: meatloaf, mashed potatoes, grilled cheese, French fries, cheesesteak with fried onions and mushrooms . . . and burgers. You have alternatives to the traditional meat and potatoes, such as grilled vegetables and vegetarian pasta. Try the fried sweet potatoes or gravied mashed potatoes. Luna is a fun place, with whimsical murals on the walls and booths. The decor, the informality, and the home cooking make this restaurant a good place to take kids.

See map p. 131. 1301 Connecticut Ave. NW (at N Street). ☎ *202-835-2280.* www. lunagrillanddiner.com. *Reservations not accepted. Metro: Dupont Circle. From Dupont Circle exit, walk 1 block south on Connecticut. Main courses: $8–$16. AE, DISC, MC, V. Open: Mon–Thurs 8 a.m.–10:30 p.m., Fri 8 a.m.–midnight, Sat 10 a.m.–midnight, Sun 10 a.m.–10 p.m..*

Malaysia Kopitiam
$$ **Dupont Circle   MALAYSIAN**

There's a good chance you've never tasted Malaysian cooking. But, when you do, it'll remind you of other Asian cuisines, notably Chinese, Thai, and Indian. Washington is blessed with a good Malaysian eatery ready to help you understand the unfamiliar. First, the lengthy menu describes the dishes and contains photos to show you what they look like. Next, owner/host Leslie Phoon and his staff stand ready to answer questions and offer advice. (His wife, Penny, is the chef.) On your way in, check the chalkboard for specials. Try not to be distracted by the tiki bar decor. If you want suggestions from me, try the *wok wok* shrimp. It's served on a bed of lettuce with a sweetish cream sauce. A dining companion likened beef *hor fun* — stir-fried flat rice noodles with beef, bean sprouts, and Chinese spinach — to the ubiquitous Thai dish, *pad thai. Assam sambal* shrimp is stir-fried with red onions and red peppers in a spicy/sour sauce. *Nyonya* chicken is another spicy entree, this one with cucumbers. If you're not into hot stuff, don't worry: An entire menu section lists nonspicy entrees. Vegetarians will appreciate the section devoted to vegetable dishes.

See map p. 131. 1827 M St. NW (between 18th and 19th streets). ☎ *202-833-6232.* www.malaysiakopitiam.com. *Reservations accepted. Metro: Farragut North. From L Street exit, walk north on Connecticut Avenue and then left on M. Main courses: $7.50–$19, most under $10. AE, DISC, MC, V. Open: Mon–Thurs 11:30 a.m.– 10 p.m., Fri–Sat 11:30 a.m.–11 p.m., Sun noon–10 p.m.*

Marcel's
$$$$$ **Foggy Bottom/West End   FRENCH/FLEMISH**

The Restaurant Association of Metropolitan Washington named Marcel's the "Fine Dining Restaurant of the Year" in 2004. Chef/owner Robert Wiedmaier describes the fare here as "French cuisine with a Flemish flair." That combination produces such recommended dishes as rabbit with foie gras, mushrooms, and a grain mustard sauce; rockfish with potato crisp and ratatouille; and pan-seared New York strip with mushrooms, chive potato pureé, and cabernet sauce. Diners can hear live jazz drifting from the bar Monday through Saturday after 6:30 p.m. And Marcel's offers a unique pre/post-theater deal. For $48, you can eat the first two courses of a three-course dinner, take a complimentary limo to Kennedy Center, and then return in the limo for dessert after the performance. (In case you're curious, Wiedmaier named Marcel's for his son.)

See map p. 128. 2401 Pennsylvania Ave. NW (west of 24th Street). ☎ *202-296-1166.* www.marcelsdc.com. *Reservations recommended. Metro: Foggy Bottom-George Washington University. Walk west on I Street and then right on 24th 1½ blocks to Pennsylvania. Main courses: $29–$42. AE, MC, V. Open: Mon–Thurs 5:30 p.m.–10 p.m., Fri–Sat 5:30 p.m.–11 p.m., Sun 5 p.m.–9:30 p.m.*

Marrakesh
$$$ Downtown MOROCCAN

This Moroccan restaurant is just plain fun. Suspend your disbelief, and you can imagine you're out for a night with Humphrey Bogart and Sydney Greenstreet in old Casablanca. The adventure starts when you knock on the closed front door, it opens, and you're escorted through a curtain into an enormous dimly lighted dining room decorated from floor to ceiling in intricate colored patterns. After you settle into cushions around a low brass table, you wash your hands, which are your primary eating utensils for the evening. The seven-course meal is served family style, and you scoop up the food with bread or your fingers. Think eggplant, cucumber, phyllo pastry, almonds, cinnamon, olives, dates, raisins, honey, couscous, two meat courses (one perhaps a kebab), fruit, pastries, and mint tea. This restaurant is most fun with a group — I'd say about ten people — but the restaurant will serve any number. Oh, and there's a belly dancer.

See map p. 128. 617 New York Ave. NW (between 6th and 7th streets). ☎ *202-393-9393.* www.marrakeshwashington.com. *Reservations required. Metro: Mt. Vernon Square. Walk 2 blocks south on 7th and then go left on New York. Restaurant is on left, just before 6th. Fixed price meal: $26. No credit cards accepted. Open: Mon–Fri 6 p.m.–midnight, Sat 5:30 p.m.–midnight, Sun 5 p.m.–midnight.*

The Melting Pot
$$$ Dupont Circle FONDUE

As with Marrakesh, the Melting Pot is a great place to bring a group for a festive evening of drinking and dipping and dining (although you also have the choice of a "Lovers Lane" of dimly lighted booths for two). Here, however, you're not dipping your fingers into the pot in front of you. (It's not recommended with boiling oil!) Instead, you're strongly encouraged to use fondue forks. The ambience here is a melting pot of sophisticated and whimsical. The restaurant is modern and attractive. Lights come in the shapes of forks and pots and tiny spots suspended over the tables. Don't worry if steam from your fondue pot obscures your dining companions across the table. It's from the boiling water beneath the cooking chamber. (A member of my large party here once described the experience "like getting a facial.") The suggested way of proceeding here is to begin with melted cheese (my favorite is cheddar with beer, garlic, and other seasonings) into which you dip breads, vegetables, and apples. The main course (shrimp, steak, chicken, scallops, vegetables — even lobster) is dipped in a hot broth. The burgundy-based broth seems best for beef, but many like the simple oil because it doesn't import its own taste to the foods being cooked. You make dessert by dipping strawberries and other items — even marshmallows — into melted chocolate. The more dippers in your party, the more variety you can concoct with various ingredients to heat and to dip.

See map p. 131. 1220 19th St. NW (between M and N Streets). ☎ *202-857-0777.* www.meltingpot.com. *Reservations recommended. Metro: Dupont Circle. From the Dupont Circle exit, walk south on 19th about 1½ blocks. The restaurant is hiding* *underground on the right. Main courses: $18–25. AE, MC, V. Open: Sun 4–10 p.m., Mon–Thurs 5–10 p.m., Fri 5 p.m.–midnight, Sat 4 p.m.–midnight.*

Michel Richard's Citronelle
$$$$$ Georgetown   FRENCH/CALIFORNIA

Chef Michel Richard has earned a reputation as one of the best French chefs in America. His restaurant actually bills its offerings as "French/ California cuisine" — French recipes with American influences. Citronelle offers fixed-price dinners for $85 to $150 and a chef's table for $275 (all before beverages). The appetizers may include a lobster tart, foie gras, or white corn and crab soup. For the main course, how about squab a l'orange with apple risotto, or shallot-encrusted salmon with soybeans and mushrooms? For dessert, try an apple napoleon or petits fours. At these prices, gentlemen are expected to wear a jacket — and to be gentlemen! You can eat for less — but not for cheap — in the lounge or on the terrace. You also can test Citronelle's wares at breakfast.

See map p. 133. 3000 M St. NW (at 30th Street, in the Latham Hotel). ☎ *202-625-2150.* www.citronelledc.com. *Reservations required. Jacket required. Take Georgetown Connection shuttle bus from Dupont Circle or Rosslyn Metrorail station to M and 30th or Thomas Jefferson street. Or ride 30-series Metrobus. Fixed-price dinner: $85–275 without beverages. AE, DC, MC, V. Open: Sun–Thurs 6:30–10:30 a.m., 6:30–10 p.m., Fri 6:30–10:30 a.m., 6:30–10:30 p.m., Sat 6:30–10:30 a.m., 6–10 p.m. Closed Sun Aug 1 through Labor Day.*

Miss Saigon
$$$ Georgetown   VIETNAMESE

Decorated with potted palms and twinkling lights, Miss Saigon doesn't look like your typical Vietnamese restaurant. The food is definitely Vietnamese, however, and quite good. Eating in the comfortable dining room, you can choose from such house specialties as *bo luc lac,* which is cubed steak marinated in garlic, butter, and wine and then sautéed with onions; or *ca kho tieu,* which is salmon in a caramel sauce with cracked black pepper, served in a clay pot. For appetizers, try the shrimp-and-pork garden rolls. Finally, you can choose among some very un-Vietnamese desserts.

See map p. 133. 3057 M St. NW (between 30th and 31st streets). ☎ *202-333-5545. Reservations recommended. Take Georgetown Connection Route 2 shuttle bus from Foggy Bottom-GWU or Rosslyn Metrorail station to 30th or Thomas Jefferson streets. Or take a 30-series Metrobus. Main courses $9–$23. AE, DC, MC, V. Open: Mon–Fri 11:30 a.m.–10:30 p.m., Sat–Sun noon–11 p.m.*

The Monocle
$$$ Capitol Hill   AMERICAN

A stone's throw from the Senate office buildings, the Monocle is an old-style Washington institution. If you're a regular viewer of C-SPAN or CNN, you'll recognize some of the faces you see here (or at least the photos on the walls). John Kerry was a regular before he began his ultimately unsuccessful run in the 2004 presidential campaign and spent most of his life on the road. Presumably, you'll now have a good chance or running into him here again. The Monocle staff is solicitous. You can choose among several steaks, and a two-pound roasted lobster is on the menu. The pork rib chop with pommery mustard sauce is especially good. At lunch, go for the hamburger. Not surprisingly, the menu also has a good selection of martinis.

See map p. 128. 107 D St. NE (between 1st and 2nd streets). ☎ *202-546-4488.* www. themonocle.com. *Reservations recommended. Metro: Union Station. From Union Station Shops/Massachusetts Avenue exit, walk around the circle to 1st Street NE and then walk right 1 block to D and turn left. Main courses $14.50–$28.50. AE, DC, MC, V. Open: Mon–Fri 11:30 a.m.–midnight. Closed 2 weeks before Labor Day.*

Montmartre
$$$ Capitol Hill   FRENCH

Just a few blocks from the House office buildings and the U.S. Capitol itself — where France hasn't been such a popular place in recent years — this little restaurant reminds you of what you love about Paris. Appearances outside and in — including the sidewalk cafe — suggest a modest eatery on some French side street. The food tastes that way, too. The waitress doesn't speak clear English, but she does deliver a mean basket of crispy-crusted French bread. From then on, you have to choose, and I suggest a wonderful salad of endive, walnuts, and blue cheese to start. The sautéed cod with garlic mashed potatoes makes for a homey main course, and the roasted salmon with leeks and risotto tastes pretty darn good, too. For dessert, there's no contest. If it's offered, grab the berry tart.

See map p. 128. 327 7th St. SE (between Pennsylvania Avenue and C Street). ☎ *202-544-1244.* www.montmartre.us. *Reservations recommended. Metro: Eastern Market. Walk across Pennsylvania on 7th. Main courses: $16–$20. AE, DC, DISC, MC, V. Open: Tues–Thurs 11:30 a.m.–2:30 p.m., 5:30–10 p.m., Fri–Sat. 11:30 a.m.– 2:30 p.m., 5:30–10:30 p.m., Sun 11:30 a.m.–2:30 p.m., 5:30–9 p.m.*

Nooshi
$ Downtown   ASIAN

When the popular Oodles Noodles added sushi, it morphed into Nooshi. It still has an inventive array of Pan Asian noodle dishes such as *mee goreng* — a spicy marriage of Malaysian and Indian-style noodles with vegetables — as well as dishes sans noodles, such as chicken with basil, which you can have prepared mild or spicy. The sushi menu is large and reasonably priced. Other popular dishes include drunken noodles (with stir-fried minced chicken in basil, pepper, and onion sauce), spring rolls, and chicken *satay* (with slightly spicy peanut sauce). Of course, there's chicken noodle soup. The decor is sophisticated, and so is the presentation. Be sure to arrive early. At midday, office workers grab for all the tables.

See map p. 128. 1120 19th St. NW (between L and M streets). ☎ 202-293-3138. Reservations accepted for seven or more. Metro: Farragut North, exit west side From L Street, walk 2 blocks to 19th and turn right. Main courses $7–$12.50.AE, MC, V. Open: Mon–Thurs 11:30 a.m.–10 p.m., Fri–Sat 11:30 a.m.–10:30 p.m., Sun 5–10 p.m.

Obelisk
$$$$$ Dupont Circle   ITALIAN

Before Obelisk opened, you had to hop an Alitalia flight for food this authentic. Pure Italian cooking shines at this tiny Dupont Circle trattoria. The decor is simple, with a basket of fresh vegetables and crusty house-made bread forming the centerpiece. The fixed-price menu features several choices at each of the five courses. The pasta is handmade, the wines carefully selected, the ingredients fresh, and the staff knowledgeable and attentive.

See map p. 131. 2029 P St. NW (between 20th and 21st streets). ☎ 202-872-1180. Reservations recommended. Metro: Dupont Circle. From Q Street exit, walk south on 20th to P and turn right. Fixed-price dinner: $58. D, MC, V. Open: Tues–Sat 6 p.m.– 10 p.m.

The Occidental
$$$$ Downtown   AMERICAN

The Occidental Grill quite likely fits your image of a Washington power hangout. Two blocks from the White House, it projects an old-fashioned atmosphere with its dark wood paneling, classic bar, and spacious booths. The walls are covered with more than 2,000 autographed photos of Occidental diners, from Buffalo Bill Cody through Huey Long and various Kennedys up to Oprah Winfrey and contemporary politicians. The dining rooms (above the grill is a more formal room with the same menu) were opened in 1986, but the restaurant traces its roots on essentially the same site to 1906. The filet mignon is recommended at dinner, with one of the lobster appetizers. You can spend a lot less for a hamburger or other sandwich at lunch and still soak up the atmosphere..

See map p. 128. 1475 Pennsylvania Ave. NW (in the Willard Hotel complex between 14th and 15th streets). ☎ 202-783-1475. www.occidentaldc.com. Reservations recommended. Metro: Metro Center. From F & 12th Streets exit, walk 2 blocks east on F to 14th, then turn left 1 block to Pennsylvania, and then turn right. Main courses: $22–$39. AE, DC, MC, V. Open: Mon–Thurs 11:30 a.m.–3 p.m., 4:30–10 p.m., Fri–Sat 11:30 a.m.–3 p.m., 4:30–10 p.m., Sun 11:30 a.m.–3 p.m., 4:30–9:30 p.m.

The Oceanaire Seafood Room
$$$$ Downtown   SEAFOOD

My daughter and 11 of her friends had their high school preprom dinner at Oceanaire one year, because it's a festive place that's an especially good restaurant for larger parties. It also just happens to serve good seafood.

Many people walk into Oceanaire and feel as if they've stepped onto the set of a 1930s movie. The menu evokes that earlier age, and the restaurant was designed to suggest a 1930s ocean liner. The teens, however, debated whether they were supposed to be inside a ship — or under water, because of the fish mounted on the walls and the blue cast to the lighting. However you interpret the decor, oyster lovers can choose among a dozen varieties. The crab cakes are nearly all meat. The fried foods are tops. It's hard to go wrong ordering the fresh fish broiled. Portions are large — for sharing or taking home for another meal.

See map p. 128. 1201 F St. NW (west of 12th Street). ☎ *202-347-2277.* www.the oceanaire.com. *Reservations recommended. Metro: Metro Center. From the F and 12th Streets exit, look across the street. Main courses: $18–$40. AE, DISC, MC, V. Hours: Mon–Thurs 11:30 a.m.–10 p.m., Fri 11:30 a.m.–11 p.m., Sat 5–11 p.m., and Sun 5–9 p.m.*

Old Ebbitt Grill
$$$ **Downtown AMERICAN**

Before we moved to Washington, one of my favorite places to visit was the Old Ebbitt Grill, ensconced in a narrow, 19th-century building that made you feel that Teddy Roosevelt might walk through the door. That building was demolished in 1983, and the restaurant moved into new digs just around the corner from the White House. The new Old Ebbitt is a large, handsome establishment that evokes older times with mahogany, velvet, marble, and brass, as well as collections of antique steins, hunting trophies, and decoys. This place is a lunchtime and afterwork hangout for folks employed in the area — including White House staffers — so many customers order burgers and other bar fare. But the diverse menu changes daily, featuring what's fresh. For me, the highlight of one visit — other than spotting Newt Gingrich with his most recent wife — was superb strawberry shortcake with whipped cream. The Virginia farm that produced the berries was credited on the menu. The staff tends to be friendly and nice to kids, and many kid-friendly items are on the menu — from the very good burgers to finger-food appetizers.

See map p. 128. 675 15th St. NW (between F and G streets). ☎ *202-347-4800.* www. ebbitt.com. *Reservations recommended. Metro: Metro Center. Take 13th Street exit. Walk 2 blocks west on G. and then turn left at 15th. Main courses: $8 (hamburger)–$21 (steak). AE, DC, DISC, MC, V. Open: Mon–Fri 7:30 a.m.–1 a.m., Sat–Sun 8:30 a.m.–1 a.m.*

The Palm
$$$$$ **Dupont Circle STEAKHOUSE**

This is the ultimate old-school Washington power place, even though it's part of a chain that originated in New York. The walls are covered with autographed caricatures of Palm patrons past and present, many of whom will be familiar to you. And you can spot regulars seated at their favorite tables as easily as you can find them painted upon the walls. (Think Larry King, James Carville, and George Bush the First.) The last time Susan was here with an out-of-town companion, she no sooner finished describing the place as a celebrity magnet when Carville walked in. She also noticed the wall contained a sketch of Grimm (the dog star of Mike Peters' popular comic strip "Mother Goose and Grimm") saying "Bone apetite." Mike's base is my old newspaper, the *Dayton Daily News,* and Grimmy hangs on our wall at home, too — saying "Grimmy loves Juilie!" (We, however, are not likely ever to show up on the walls at the Palm!) The Palm bills itself as "the place to see and be seen," and that certainly is true. It's also the place to eat large steaks (how about a 36-ounce New York strip for two?) and large lobsters (3 pounds or more). The strip steaks and lobsters are top-notch, by the way, and the fried onions and creamed spinach come highly recommended as well. It's hard to summarize the cost of eating here. You can get soup and pasta for $21.50, or you can spend $90 for a three-pound lobster Newburg with a crab cocktail appetizer.

See map p. 131. 1225 19th St. NW, between M and N streets. ☎ *202-293-9091.* www. thepalm.com. *Reservations recommended. Metro: Dupont Circle. From Dupont Circle exit, walk 1½ blocks south on 19th. Main courses: $16.50–$76. AE, DC, MC, V. Hours: Mon–Fri 11:45 a.m. –10:30 p.m., Sat 5:30–10:30 p.m., and Sun 5:30–9:30 p.m.*

Pizzeria Paradiso
$ **Dupont Circle/Georgetown**   PIZZA

So crowded at meal times you may not be able to squeeze through the door, the original Pizzeria Paradiso owes its popularity to excellent pizza prepared in the traditional Italian manner. The light, thin crust is baked in a wood-burning oven and topped with whatever you request. To taste real Neapolitan pizza, order the Margherita, which comes with tomato, basil, and mozzarella cheese. The Atomica is spicy, thanks to the hot pepper flakes combined with the tomato, salami, black olives, and mozzarella. Paradiso also serves sandwiches, salads, and desserts. But it's the pizza that sets it apart from Washington's other restaurants, with the exception of the similar 2Amys in Upper Northwest. It's bustling and it serves pizza, so it's obviously a good place to take kids. It's also a good spot when you're looking for takeout.

See map p. 131. Dupont Circle: 2029 P St. NW (between 20th and 21st streets). ☎ *202-223-1245. Reservations not accepted. Metro: Dupont Circle. From the Q Street exit, walk 2 blocks south on 20th and then right on P. Georgetown (see map p. 133): 3282 M St. NW (west of Potomac Street).* ☎ *202-337-1245. Take the Georgetown Connection Route 2 shuttle bus from the Dupont Circle or Rosslyn Metrorail station to M and Potomac or 33rd street. Or hop a 30-series Metrobus to M and Wisconsin. Pizzas: $8–$16, higher with added ingredients. DC, MC, V. Open: Mon–Thurs 11:30 a.m.–11pm, Fri–Sat 11:30 a.m.–midnight, and Sun noon–10 p.m.*

Poste
$$$$ **Downtown** **MODERN AMERICAN**

I'm happy to report that Poste has a chef (Robert Weland) who says he plans to stay around for a while. That's a big deal for this extremely good-looking restaurant that has seemed capable of enticing chefs into its kitchen but incapable of developing a long-term relationship. When Weland arrived here in May 2004 (from Guastavino's in New York), he became Poste's third chef since the restaurant's opening in July 2002. Poste occupies one of the most striking, and historical, spaces in the D.C. dining world — the mail-sorting room of the 1842 General Post Office that, after an 1859 expansion, housed the Tariff Commission. Sixteen feet above the floor is the original cast iron ceiling with skylights. Floor-to-ceiling cupboards, filled with cooking utensils, covers one wall. Another is hung with large mirrors. The plush booths provide comfortable seating, and you have the choice of outdoor seating in nice weather. The place can get noisy, and the trip to the bathroom becomes an adventure. You have to walk through the lobby of the adjacent Hotel Monaco and then climb the stairs or take the elevator to the second floor. As for the food, Weland prepares a seasonal menu, and he's so into fresh he's put a greenhouse on the terrace so that he can take herbs straight from the plant to the kitchen as he cooks. My first meal at Weland's Poste started with a rich, tasty appetizer of foie gras, dates, and truffles. The main course of salmon poached in olive oil released a complex meld of flavors from horseradish and chives. The key lime tart made for a tart, refreshing dessert. Susan, a crème brûlée aficionado, proclaimed Poste's version "fabulous."

See map p. 128. 555 8th Street NW (between E and F streets). ☎ *202-783-6060. www.postebrasserie.com. Reservations recommended. Metro: Gallery Place/ Chinatown. From 7th and F Streets exit, walk 1 block south on 7th, then 1 block right on E, and then turn right on 8th. Or take a shortcut through the hotel entrance at 700 F Street (between 7th and 8th). Main courses: $18–$30. AE, DC, DISC, MC, V. Open: Mon–Fri 7–10 a.m., 11:30 a.m.–2:30 p.m., 5:30–10 p.m., Sat–Sun 7–10 a.m., 5:30–10 p.m.*

The Prime Rib
$$$$ **Downtown** **STEAKHOUSE**

If you want to visit the first half of the last century during your D.C. vacation, eat at Oceanaire one night and Prime Rib the next. At Prime Rib, the 1940s atmosphere comes from subdued lighting, black lacquered walls, brass trim, leather chairs and booths, tuxedoed waiters, a piano and bass playing supper club music, and the requirement that gentlemen wear jacket and tie. The food is impeccable — prime beef, of course, but also a wide selection of seafood, plus a litte lamb, pork, veal, and chicken. This place is called the Prime Rib for a reason, so you ought to have a good reason for ordering something else. If you crave seafood, order the crab cake for your appetizer.

See map p. 128. 2020 K St. NW (between 20th and 21st streets). ☎ *202-466-8811.* www.theprimerib.com. *Reservations recommended. Metro: Farragut West. From K Street exit, walk 3½ blocks west on K. Main courses: $20–$35. AE, DC, MC, V. Open: Mon–Thurs 11:30 a.m.–3 p.m., 5–11 p.m., Fri 11:30 a.m.–3 p.m., 5–11:30 p.m., and Sat 5–11:30 p.m.*

Red Sage Border Cafe
$$ Downtown   SOUTHWESTERN

Unlike its sibling Red Sage Grill downstairs (see next listing), the Border Cafe has settled into its role as a Southwestern/Latin American spot. Some colleagues and I used to come here after evening meetings in the area for beer and appetizers — a great way to share snacks, chat, and sample cooking from an establishment that can be quite expensive at dinner downstairs. (The margaritas here get rave reviews, too.) For a real meal, you can select from quesadillas, salads, chilis, (including eight-vegetable chili), and various entrees. On your way out, take a peek into the strikingly decorated dining rooms of the more expensive Grill.

See map p. 128. 605 14th St. NW (at F Street). ☎ *202-638-4444.* www.redsage.com. *Reservations not accepted. Metro: Metro Center. From F and 14th Streets exit, walk 3 blocks west on F. Main courses: $6–$15. AE, DISC, MC, V. Open: Mon–Sat 11:30 a.m.–11:30 p.m., Sun 5–11:30 p.m.*

Red Sage Grill
$$$$ Downtown   AMERICAN

When Red Sage opened, it was *the* hot spot to dine. The fad has passed, and now it's simply considered a good — and quite interesting — place to eat. The decor remains striking — a sort of Southwestern fantasyland that the designers at Disney World might have dreamed up. The menu, to say the least, is diverse. Forced to classify this place, I call it American — because all nationalities can hop into the American cooking pot, right? On one night alone, the menu offered such dishes as Hudson Valley foie gras, tuna carpaccio, Maine mussels and roasted tomato soup, Caesar salad, Mediterranean paella, Casco Bay cod, Colorado lamb chops, and an Italian meringue dessert. If you want to taste what made Red Sage a fad — without emptying your wallet — eat at the Border Cafe upstairs and sneak a peek at the Grill's dining rooms.

See map p. 128. 605 14th St. NW (at F Street). ☎ *202-638-4444. Reservations recommended. Metro: Metro Center. From F and 14th Streets exit, walk 2 blocks west on F. Main courses: $25–$37. AE, DISC, MC, V. Open: Mon–Thurs 11:30 a.m.–2 p.m., 5–10 p.m., Fri 11:30 a.m.–2 p.m., 5:30–10:30 p.m., Sat 5:30–10:30 p.m., Sun 5:30–10 p.m.*

Restaurant Nora
$$$$ Dupont Circle   AMERICAN/ORGANIC

This is PC food for people with lots of organically grown greenbacks. Everything possible on Nora's menu is produced without chemicals, hormones, or other additives. Anything that's not certified organic is marked with an asterisk. Most likely, it's wild fish or foraged mushrooms, for which no certification exists. The water is triple-filtered to remove chlorine, bacteria, and metals. The coffee is purchased from small, farmer-owned cooperatives that grow their crops beneath the forest canopy to protect native trees and wildlife. Even the staff's shirts are made from organic yarn, and Nora strives to patronize winemakers who don't use chemicals in their vineyards. Oh, and did I say the food is sophisticated and delicious and that the dining room — decorated with antique quilts — is attractive and comfortable?

See map p. 131. 2132 Florida Ave. NW (north of R Street). ☎ *202-462-5143.* www. noras.com. *Reservations recommended. Metro: Dupont Circle. From Q Street exit, walk 1 block north on Connecticut Avenue, then go left on R for 2 blocks, and then turn right on Florida. Main courses $24–$30. AE, MC, V. Open: Mon–Thurs 5:30– 10 p.m., Fri–Sat 5:30–10:30 p.m. Closed two weeks late Aug/early Sept.*

Sea Catch
$$$ Georgetown   SEAFOOD

Hidden in the back end of a courtyard off 31st Street, between M Street and the C&O Canal, Sea Catch is a surprisingly large restaurant that offers an attractive place to eat good food year-round. In warm weather, tables on an outdoor terrace overlook the canal. When it's cold, you still can overlook the canal through floor-to-ceiling windows. Fireplaces in two of the dining rooms make this restaurant a pleasant and romantic place to dine when it's really cold. I especially like the front dining room, which has stone walls, windows on the canal, wood paneling, ceiling beams, and one of those fireplaces. To start your meal here, try the rich, spicy, and delicious tomato-crab soup, or the mixed green salad topped with grapefruit, avocado, and crushed hazelnuts. You can't beat the crab cakes for your main course, although the lobster is quite good, too. If you like your tuna rare, Sea Catch holds that out as a signature dish. The signature dessert — key lime tart surrounded by sliced strawberries, blackberries, and kiwi — is a tart, refreshing way to end a meal. Susan's word for the crème brûlée here is "wonderful."

See map p. 133. 1054 31st St. NW (south of M Street at the C&O Canal). ☎ *202-337- 8855.* www.seacatchrestaurant.com. *Reservations recommended. Take Georgetown Connection Route 2 shuttle bus from Dupont Circle or Rosslyn Metrorail station to M and 31st or Thomas Jefferson street and then walk south on 31st and look for the courtyard on the right. Or take a 30-series Metrobus. Main courses: $15–$32. AE, DC, DISC, MC, V. Open: Lunch: Mon–Sat noon–3 p.m., 5:30–10 p.m.*

1789 Restaurant
$$$$ Georgetown   AMERICAN

The year 1789 marked the birth of the Unites States government and of Georgetown University, so it's an appropriate name for this comfortable restaurant, which sits in the nation's capital at the edge of the university's campus. It's an especially attractive place to dine in winter if you can land a table by the fireplace. The restaurant is in a federal-style house built in the mid-1800s and is decorated with antiques and historical prints. Ris (short for Doris) Lacoste has been chef here since 1995. For more than a decade before, she worked at several restaurants with Bob Kinkead, one of Washington's very best chefs. Lacoste always offers a tasting menu, based on what she can get that's fresh. In the summer, she calls it the "farmer's market menu," because she regularly shops local markets to find her ingredients. Over the years, she's developed especially close working relationships with a half-dozen area farmers. Throughout 2004, she did cooking demonstrations at local markets to show what could be done with locally grown foods. Because her emphasis is on fresh, Locoste's menu is always changing. You're well advised to sample what she suggests. Her tried-and-true specialties that regulars come back to ask for, however, include rack of lamb with creamy feta potatoes, garlic spinach, and rosemary-Shiraz sauce, pine-nut-crusted chicken with portobello mushrooms, roasted peppers, garlic, rapini, prosciutto, goat cheese, and lemon balsamic sauce, and simple grilled lobster. Men must wear jackets.

See map p. 133. 1226 36th St. NW (north of Prospect Street). ☎ *202-965-1789.* www. 1789restaurant.com. *Reservations recommended. From the Dupont Circle or Rosslyn Metrorail station, take the Georgetown Connection Route 2 shuttle bus to M and 33rd or 34th streets, walk up the hill 1 block on 33rd or 34th, then walk left on Prospect, and then turn right on 36th. Or take a taxi. Main courses: $18–$38. AE, DC, DISC, MC, V. Open: Mon–Thurs 6–10 p.m., Fri 6–11 p.m., Sat 5:30–11 p.m., Sun 5:30–10 p.m.*

Tabard Inn
$$$ Dupont Circle AMERICAN

This is one of my wife's favorite Washington restaurants — for the setting as much as for the food. It truly is an inn, with sleeping, eating, and drinking facilities scattered among three adjoining townhouses near Dupont Circle. The dining rooms are comfortable and lively at meal times. You can have a drink by the fireplace in the winter and dine in the garden when it's warm. Chef Pedro Matamoros worked at the Tabard under two previous, well-regarded, chefs — David Craig and Andrew Saba. Though Matamoros is a native of Nicaragua with a special interest in French and Italian cuisine, he is keeping alive the Tabard's tradition of New American cooking, with changing seasonal menus and an emphasis on fresh local ingredients. The seafood dishes always have tended to be the best here. Try fried oysters or crab-and-corn soup for an appetizer and roasted salmon or seared scallops for the main course.

See map p. 131. 1739 N St. NW (between 17th and 18th streets). ☎ *202-833-2668. Reservations recommended. Metro: Dupont Circle. From the Dupont Circle exit, walk south on Connecticut Avenue 1 block and then turn left on N and cross 18th. Main* *courses: $19–$26. AE, DC, MC, V. Hours: Mon–Thurs 7 p.m.–9:30 a.m., 11:30 a.m.–2:30 p.m., 6 p.m.–10 p.m., Fri 7–9:30 a.m., 11:30 a.m.–2:30 p.m., 6 p.m.–10:30 p.m., Sat 7 a.m.–9:30 a.m., 11 a.m.–2:30 p.m., 6 p.m.–10:30 p.m., Sun 7–9:30 a.m., 10:30 a.m.–2:30 p.m., 6 p.m.–9 p.m.*

Teatro Goldoni
$$$$ Downtown   ITALIAN/VENETIAN

The decor can distract your attention from the usually good food in this theatrically themed Venetian Italian restaurant. "Teatro Goldoni" means "Goldoni Theater," Goldoni was an 18th-century Venetian playwright and gastronome. The restaurant has a wall of Venetian masks, Harlequin-style panels of colored glass, pillars striped like barber poles, and a glass-enclosed kitchen raised up as if a stage. The table setting is part of the show, too, with bowls so large you'll wonder if they're meant for soup or for bathing. Chef/owner Fabrizio Aielli calls his food "Venetian world cuisine," which combines traditional Venetian cooking with modern twists and touches of cuisines from other parts of the world. The menu changes daily, but you may encounter these especially good dishes: endive salad with green apples, chives, gorgonzola cheese, and orange vinaigrette; Caesar salad with shaved parmesan cheese; and risotto with lobster, roasted tomatoes, truffle oil, and sweet basil.

See map p. 128. 1909 K St. NW (between 19th and 20th streets). ☎ *202955-9494.* www.teatrogoldoni.com. *Reservations recommended. Metro: Farragut West. From 18th Street exit, walk west on I Street, turn right on 19th, and then turn left on K. Main courses: $20.50–$35.50. AE, DC, DISC, MC, V. Open: Mon–Thurs 11:30 a.m.–2 p.m., 5:30–10 p.m., Fri 11:30 a.m.–2 p.m., 5–11 p.m., Sat 5–11 p.m.*

Tony Cheng's
$$$ Chinatown   CHINESE/SEAFOOD

Tony Cheng couldn't decide between fish and meat, so he put Tony Cheng's Seafood Restaurant on the second floor of this Chinatown building and Tony Cheng's Mongolian Restaurant on the first. The Seafood Restaurant is a bit of a misnomer, because you can order poultry, beef, pork, and vegetarian dishes there as well. But the seafood is the specialty, and it always pays to check what's fresh, including what's swimming in the tank. Downstairs, you pick your own ingredients for two different methods of cooking. Choose meats and vegetables for the chefs to sear quickly on the grill. Or pick vegetables, meats, and seafood that you cook yourself in a pot of boiling stock at your table. You finish the meal by eating the flavorful stock.

See map p. 128. 619 H St. NW (between 6th and 7th streets). ☎ *202-371-8669. Reservations accepted. Metro: Gallery Place-Chinatown. Take 7th & H Streets exit. Walk a half block east on H. Main courses: $10–$32. AE, MC, V. Open: Sun–Thurs 11 a.m.–11:30 p.m., Fri–Sat 11 a.m.–midnight.*

2 Amys
$$ Upper Northwest ITALIAN/PIZZA

This is real Neapolitan pizza, particularly the "pizze d.o.c." offerings, which follow the recipes of the Italian government's "denominazione di origine controllata" regulations. The pizzas here have thin, chewy crust. I like the d.o.c. Margherita, named after Italy's first queen and topped with tomato sauce, cheese, and basil. A Margherita "extra" enhances the flavor with whole, sweet, fresh cherry tomatoes. The d.o.c. versions are meatless, with fewer toppings than many Americans like. You can design your own pie from a list of two dozen toppings if you prefer. Be sure to sample the side dishes, such as the *polpettini al forno* (meatballs), *suppli a telefono* (breaded rice balls stuffed with cheese and fried), and deviled eggs with pesto sauce. The pizzas aren't big enough to make a shared meal, the way you're used to doing in a typical American pizzeria. But two can share a pizza when you add a couple of the sides or a salad. The restaurant is cheery, with shiny black-and-white tile and sunny paint on the walls. The decor makes for noise, which is one reason it's kid-friendly. Others are the food, the highchairs, and the cheerful staff. For big folk, there's a wine bar in one corner.

See map p. 128. 3715 Macomb St. NW (just west of Wisconsin Avenue near Washington National Cathedral). ☎ *202-885-5700.* www.marketing-specialists.com/2Amysindex.htm. *Reservations not accepted. Metro: Tenleytown. Then take a 30-series Metrobus south on Wisconsin. Or take a 30-series bus from anywhere on its route. Or catch a cab. Pizzas from $8–$13, or more if you add lots of ingredients. Sides and salads from $4–$6.75. MC, V. Open: Tues–Sat 11 a.m.–11 p.m., Sun 11 a.m.–10 p.m.*

Vidalia
$$$$ Downtown AMERICAN/SOUTHERN

Maybe it's because I like jazz clubs, but it never bothered me that Vidalia is located below street level. Others, however, seem to hesitate at the top of the stairs. So let me reassure you that at the bottom you find a cheerful restaurant with good food. Vidalia brought modern Southern cooking to Washington as Arkansan Bill Clinton was moving into the White House. Proprietor/chef Jeffrey Buben calls Vidalia's cooking "American cuisine with a Southern accent." That means five-onion soup for an appetizer, shrimp and grits for the main course, and Georgia pecan pie with praline ice cream for dessert, for example. When Buben puts more emphasis on the modern, he comes up with dishes like mustard-seed-crusted tuna with portobello mushrooms, fennel, mustard greens, creamy cornpone, and mustard-tarragon sauce.

See map p. 128. 1990 M St. NW (between 19th and 20th streets). ☎ *202-659-1990.* www.vidaliadc.com. *Reservations recommended. Metro: Dupont Circle. From Dupont Circle exit, walk 2 blocks south on 19th and then turn right on M. Main courses: $23–$29.50. AE, DC, DISC, MC, V. Open: Mon–Thurs 11:30 a.m.–2:30 p.m., 5:30–10 p.m., Fri 11:30 a.m.–2:30 p.m., 5:30 –10:30 p.m., Sat 5:30 p.m.–10:30 p.m., Sun 5:30–10 p.m.*

Zaytinya
$$ Downtown MEDITERRANEAN

The worst thing about Zaytinya is that you can make reservations only for lunch and from 5 to 6:30 p.m. when patrons can be assured of a table before they head off to a nearby theater. This popular spot fills up rapidly after that. So the best solution may be to arrive here around 6:30 and then linger over several rounds of Mediterranean *mezes* (small plates) while enjoying the view of the bustling street scene outside the floor-to-ceiling windows. This strategy is especially good in spring or autumn, when you can watch night fall outside and the dining room become warmed by soft lighting inside. This stunningly attractive, modern restaurant is two stories high in the main dining room, with dark wood tables and chairs, white walls, and tiers of candles that cast soft light from the wall opposite the windows. While entrees are on the menu, let your waiter help you select mezes to share. If you're a vegetarian, you'll be pleased to note that 70 percent of these dishes were made for you. The *kolokithokeftedes* (zucchini-cheese patties) are light and tasty, fried crisp on the outside but creamy within. Susan usually doesn't think much of lamb, but she loved Zaytinya's ground lamb with eggplant puree *(kasarli ali zazik kebabi)*. Chef Jose Andres is especially proud of the *manty nejla,* little pastas stuffed with beef in a yogurt sauce. The preparation is so labor-intensive that it can't turn a profit, he said, but it belongs on the menu as a statement of the restaurant's intentions.

See map p. 128. 701 9th St. NW (north of G Street). ☎ *202-638-0800.* www. zaytinya.com. *Reservations accepted only for lunch and 5–6:30 p.m. Metro: Gallery Place/Chinatown. From the 9th and G Streets exit, look for the building with two stories of floor-to-ceiling windows and the big sign over the door that says "Zaytinya." Mezes: $3.50–$9. AE, DC, DISC, MC, V. Open: Sun–Mon 11:30 a.m.–10 p.m., Tues–Thurs 11:30 a.m.–11:30 p.m., Fri–Sat 11:30 a.m.–midnight.*

Zola
$$$ Downtown MODERN AMERICAN

This spy-themed restaurant next to the International Spy Museum has garnered mixed reviews within our family and from our friends. Certainly, it's a clever, fun place to dine. The staff dresses in black. Decorations include declassified intelligence documents and film noir stills. Peep holes in the frosted glass beside the booths let you spy on the kitchen or folks on the other side of the wall, depending on where you're sitting. The booths are big and comfortable — perhaps too big for people of smaller stature, who may prefer to sit at a table. As befitting a spot for spies, the service here is attentive yet discrete. An example: The waiter replaced my white napkin with a black one so that lint wouldn't mar my charcoal slacks. The quality of the food brings out the disagreements. Susan really liked it, for example, while I found it uneven. We can agree on recommending some dishes, however. The corn and mussel chowder with bacon is a good starter, and the broiled jumbo prawns make for a good main course. The crispy french fries may be the best thing on the menu. If it's offered, order the pineapple upside-down cake with Tahitian vanilla ice cream for dessert. From 5 to 7 p.m., Zola serves a $28, three-course "pre-event menu." (You might be going to the theater or to a basketball game — or to a tractor-pull for that matter.)

See map p. 128. 800 F St. NW (west of 8th St). ☎ 202-654-0999. www.zoladc.com. *Reservations recommended. Metro: Gallery Place/Chinatown. From the 7th and F streets exit, walk 1 block west on F. Main courses: $16–$24. AE, DC, DISC, MC, V. Open: Mon–Fri 11:30 a.m.–midnight, Sat 5 p.m.–midnight, Sun 5–10 p.m.*

Dining and Snacking on the Go

Washington is full of workaholics who eat at their desks and tourists who eat on the run, so the city is full of places where you can grab snacks and light meals. Because Washington has so many parks — from huge expanses like the National Mall to small green areas suitable for al fresco dining scattered all around town — getting picnic food to go is a great idea.

Quick and cheap

Because of office workers downtown, you'll find an inexpensive lunch spot on nearly ever corner and at many points midblock. Elsewhere, they're not as common. But you'll be hard-pressed to find a neighborhood that doesn't have a few modest eateries that are quick and cheap.

One of my favorites goes by the nonsense name **Booeymonger** (3265 Prospect St. NW at Potomac Street in Georgetown, ☎ 202-333-4810; and 5252 Wisconsin Ave. NW at Jenifer Street near the D.C.-Maryland border in Upper Northwest, ☎ 202-686-5805). The Wisconsin Avenue deli is a Price family hangout, because it's just a few blocks from home, the eat-in and takeout service is fast, and the food is good. (We've got Booeymonger frequent-eater cards!) My wife has a thing for the Manhattan — roast beef, spinach, bacon, cheddar cheese, and dressing on a baguette — and the carrot cake. In delis, I tend to go for hot pastrami on rye with mustard. When in a healthy mood, however, I order Booey's Pita Pan, a veggie and cheese sandwich. The menu has lots of sandwiches, salads, and sides to choose from (some with silly names), and you can get a full breakfast in the morning. The Georgetown Booey opens at 7:30 a.m. Monday through Friday and 8 a.m. weekends, and closes at midnight. The Wisconsin Booey opens at 7:30 a.m. every day and closes at 1 a.m. Sunday through Thursday, 2 a.m. Friday and Saturday.

Another place I like a lot is **Chipotle** (1837 M St. NW, ☎ 202-466-4104; 1629 Connecticut Ave. NW, ☎ 202-387-8261; 2600 Connecticut Ave. NW, ☎ 202-299-9111; 4301 Wisconsin Ave. NW, ☎ 202-237-0602; 601 F St. NW, ☎ 202-347-4701; 3255 M St. NW, ☎ 202-333-8377). I know it's a chain, but it's much more attractive — and the food is much better — than the typical fast-food joint. Burritos and tacos are made fresh as you order them in the cafeteria line and instruct the cooks on which ingredients you want. And you can grab a beer or margarita to quench your thirst.

Coffee shops

Besides a zillion branches of a certain West Coast coffee empire, Washingtonians have many sources for their caffeine fixes.

One of the most interesting is **Kramerbooks & Afterwords Cafe** (1517 Connecticut Ave. NW, just above Dupont Circle; ☎ **202-387-1400**). Bookish coffee swillers have been gathering at the cafe inside this bookstore since long before the national chains discovered how to sell food and drink with reading materials. You can get a caffeine or lit fix here just about any time you need one, because this place is open Monday through Thursday from 7:30 a.m. to 1 a.m., and 'round the clock from 7:30 a.m. Friday to 1 a.m. Monday.

The local chain of **Firehook Bakeries** (1909 Q St. NW at Connecticut Ave., ☎ **202-588-9296**; 912 17th St. NW between I and K streets, ☎ **202-429-2253**; 441 4th St. NW between D and E streets, ☎ **202-347-1760**; 3411 Connecticut Ave. NW between Newark and Ordway streets, ☎ **202-362-2253**; 215 Pennsylvania Ave. SE between 2nd and 3rd streets, ☎ **202-544-7003**; 555 13th St. NW between E and F streets, ☎ **202-393-0952**) provides a great fix of fresh-made pastries and locally roasted coffee. My daughter and her friends liked to hang out at the one near her school. Firehook makes the pastries and sells Quartermaine's coffee, which is roasted nearby in suburban Maryland. Hours vary, but all the stores tend to open at 7 a.m. weekdays and 8 a.m. weekends and stay open until at least 7 p.m. Call the location you're interested in for specifics.

Breakfast spots

To check out the power breakfast scene, head for a hotel dining room near the White House or Capitol. The **Lafayette Room** at the Hay-Adams (One Lafayette Square at 16th and H streets NW; ☎ **202-638-6600**) and the **Willard Room** at the Willard Inter-Continental (1401 Pennsylvania Ave. NW between 14th and 15th streets; ☎ **202-628-9100**) are good places to start. So is the **Old Ebbitt Grill** (675 15th St. NW between F and G streets; ☎ **202-347-4800**).

At **La Colline** (400 N. Capitol St. NW at D Street; ☎ **202-737-0400**), just down the street from the Capitol, lobbyists meet lawmakers over glasses of OJ. At **Kramerbooks & Afterwords Cafe** (1517 Connecticut Ave. NW, just north of Dupont Circle; ☎ **202-387-1400**; www.kramers.com), you can crack a book with your soft-boiled egg.

If you want to jump-start *your* engine, not the economy's, try the **Luna Grill and Diner** (1301 Connecticut Ave. NW at N Street; ☎ **202-835-2280**). Another place for a fast, cheap — and good — breakfast is a

Dining and Snacking on the Go

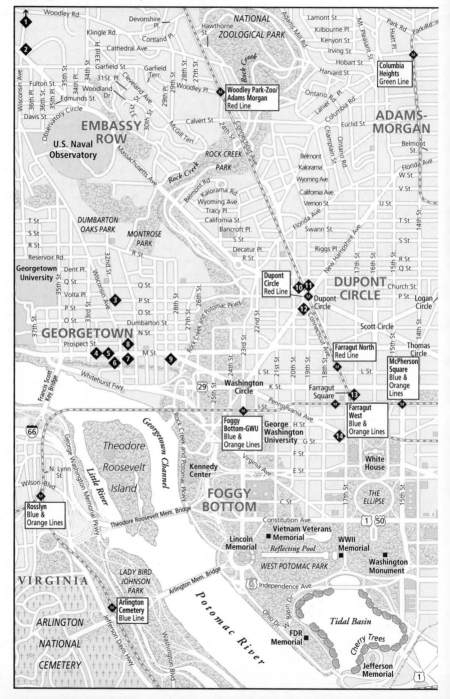

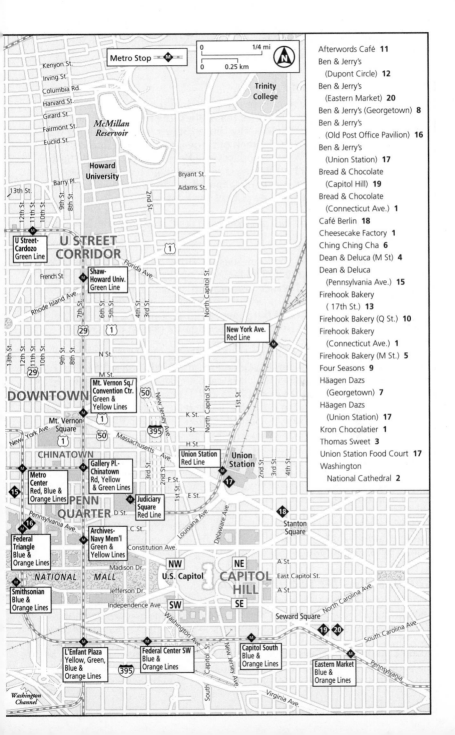

Afterwords Café **11**
Ben & Jerry's
 (Dupont Circle) **12**
Ben & Jerry's
 (Eastern Market) **20**
Ben & Jerry's (Georgetown) **8**
Ben & Jerry's
 (Old Post Office Pavilion) **16**
Ben & Jerry's
 (Union Station) **17**
Bread & Chocolate
 (Capitol Hill) **19**
Bread & Chocolate
 (Connecticut Ave.) **1**
Café Berlin **18**
Cheesecake Factory **1**
Ching Ching Cha **6**
Dean & Deluca (M St) **4**
Dean & Deluca
 (Pennsylvania Ave.) **15**
Firehook Bakery
 (17th St.) **13**
Firehook Bakery (Q St.) **10**
Firehook Bakery
 (Connecticut Ave.) **1**
Firehook Bakery (M St.) **5**
Four Seasons **9**
Häagen Dazs
 (Georgetown) **7**
Häagen Dazs
 (Union Station) **17**
Kron Chocolatier **1**
Thomas Sweet **3**
Union Station Food Court **17**
Washington
 National Cathedral **2**

Booeymonger (3265 Prospect St. NW at Potomac Street in Georgetown, ☎ 202-333-4810; and 5252 Wisconsin Ave. NW at Jennifer Street in Upper Northwest, ☎ 202-686-5805).

Tea for two (or one)

The Americans may have beaten the English in the American Revolution, but if the war had been a battle of tea parties, the Brits would have massacred the Yanks. Nevertheless, the United States has come a long way since the Boston Tea Party. Instead of throwing it into the harbor, Americans drink it. In Washington, several hotels are doing their part to perpetuate the upper-crust British tradition of high tea. In this context, *high tea* is a light meal with small, trimmed sandwiches (no crusts!), little cakes, and — of course — pots of fresh-brewed tea.

If you take high tea, you can pass on a big meal at dinnertime and opt for a snack later in the evening.

Get fancy and refined at the Four Seasons Hotel (2800 Pennsylvania Ave. NW at 28th Street; ☎ 202-342-0444). Soak up the view of Rock Creek Park from the **Garden Terrace Lounge** and nibble on finger sandwiches, breads, tartlets, scones with Devonshire cream, fresh-brewed tea, and a nip of sherry (for medicinal purposes only). Teatime is 2 to 5 p.m. daily. (Beginning at 3 p.m. Tuesday through Sunday, a pianist performs.)

You can learn Chinese tea ritual at **Ching Ching Cha** (1063 Wisconsin Ave. NW near the C&O Canal in Georgetown; ☎ 202-333-8288). The setting is serene and enhanced by classical Chinese music. The parlor lists more than two dozen teas from China and Taiwan, plus meals, snacks, and desserts. You also can purchase loose tea to take home. The restaurant is open Tuesday through Saturday from 11:30 a.m. to 9 p.m. and Sunday from 11:30 a.m. to 7 p.m.

You can tour and take tea at the **Washington National Cathedral** (Massachusetts and Wisconsin avenues NW; ☎ 202-537-8993), on Tuesdays and Wednesdays, except for some holidays. The tour starts at 1:30 p.m. inside the West Entrance on Wisconsin and finishes high up in the Pilgrim Observation Gallery, where you can gaze through arched windows at the city and beyond. Cost is $22 per person. Reservations are required — often far in advance — and are accepted up to six months ahead of time.

Food stores for picnic supplies

Visitors intent on cramming in a lot of sights often prefer quick bites to spending an hour or two in a restaurant. Most delis and coffee shops — as well as many full-service restaurants — gladly pack your order to go.

Don't think of this to-go service as just fast food, however. Think of it as a picnic. You can find park benches all over the place, as well as many small park areas. I particularly like Lafayette Square, across Pennsylvania

Avenue from the White House, and you can find lots of room on the Mall and around the Tidal Basin. (I'll pray for the pigeons and squirrels to leave you alone. You can do your part by not feeding them.)

Dean & Deluca is a great place to put together a picnic. There's a downtown cafe (1299 Pennsylvania Ave. NW, just east of 13th Street; ☎ 202-628-8155), open Monday through Friday from 7:30 a.m. to 4:30 p.m. Take your food to Lafayette Square or to Pershing Park (Pennsylvania Avenue and 15th Street) or hike on to the Mall. The Georgetown shop (3276 M St. NW, east of 33rd Street; ☎ 202-342-2500) is much larger and has a wide selection of sandwiches, salads, and desserts, as well as gourmet groceries. It's open daily from 10 a.m. to 8 p.m. You can picnic in Dean & Deluca's outdoor cafe, take your food south of M to the C&O Canal National Park, or go further south to the Georgetown waterfront.

You can find good, basic sandwich shops throughout the city — several per block in many places. Among those that I can vouch for, should you pass them in your wanderings, are **Au Bon Pain, Booeymonger, Bread & Chocolate, Chipotle, Corner Bakery, Firehook Bakery, La Madeleine, Vie de France,** and the **Wall Street Deli** — all with multiple locations.

Chocolates and sweets

Sweet tooth crave a fix? Head for **Bread & Chocolate** (666 Pennsylvania Ave. SE, between 6th and 7th streets, on Capitol Hill, ☎ 202-547-2875; 2301 M St. NW, in the West End, ☎ 202-833-8360; or 5542 Connecticut Ave. NW, at Morrison Street, in Upper Northwest, ☎ 202-966-7413). This bakery/restaurant bakes marvelous pastries. Sample the strudels, tortes, and pies at **Cafe Berlin** (322 Massachusetts Ave. NE east of 3rd Street; ☎ 202-543-7656), also located on the Hill.

Back in Upper Northwest, buy a Cheesecake at the **Cheesecake Factory** (5345 Wisconsin Ave. NW between Jenifer Street and Western Avenue; ☎ 202-364-0500). Choose among 35 varieties of calorie-laden, artery-clogging cheesecakes — or a bunch of other sweets. (You may find a slice too rich to consume in one sitting and want to share with your companions. I can't imagine why.) **Kron Chocolatier** (5300 Wisconsin Ave. NW; ☎ 202-966-4946) is across the street in the Mazza Gallerie. This shop sells all manner of world-class chocolate. Try the chocolate-dipped strawberries.

We all scream for ice cream

Washington's gone kind of ice-cream-crazy, with lots of shops, many of them local, some of them unusual.

At the **Cold Stone Creamery** (3508 Connecticut Ave. NW, north of Ordway Street in Upper Northwest; ☎ 202-237-2605), you pick your ice cream flavor and goodies to mix into it — candy bar chunks, for example, or hot fudge sauce. The clerk scoops the ice cream onto a cold stone (natch) and then mashes your additives into it.

For another unique treat, check out **Isee Icy** (1560 Wisconsin Ave. NW at Q Street in Georgetown; ☎ 202–333-4646). Here you get Argentinean ice cream — extra creamy and rich.

For locally made traditional U.S. ice cream in Georgetown, head for **Thomas Sweet** (3214 P St. NW, east of Wisconsin Avenue; ☎ 202-337-0616). If the ice cream craving strikes you at Dupont Circle, walk on up to **Larry's** (1633 Connecticut Ave. NW between Q and R streets; ☎ 202-234-2690). Nearby competition comes from **Sweet Licks** (1704 R St. NW, west of 17th Street; ☎ 202-797-2736).

On Capitol Hill, **Ben & Jerry** (☎ 202-842-2887) and **Häagen Dazs** (☎ 202-789-0953) both dish up their rich and creative flavors in Union Station. You'll also run into **Ben & Jerry's** at the Hill's Eastern Market (327 7th St. SE, between Pennsylvania Avenue and C Street; ☎ 202-546-2253) and Downtown in the Old Post Office Pavilion (1100 Pennsylvania Ave. NW at 11th Street; ☎ 202-842-5882). Ben, Jerry, Häagen, and Dazs pop up in several other spots around town, as well.

Food court extraordinaire

The lower level of Union Station houses the largest and most diverse **food court** I've ever seen. Sure, you can buy hamburgers and pizzas, and if that's what the kids desire, that's fine. Those with more cosmopolitan tastes will want to take a stroll around the entire court before making their selections.

You can find the usual national chains, but also branches of local restaurants and a wide range of cuisines — French, Indian, Greek, Cajun, barbecue, seafood, pasta, sushi, deli items, baked goods, and gourmet coffee among the vast selection of edibles. If that doesn't satisfy you, you can take the escalator up to the next level, where other food establishments — from fast-food stands to full-serve restaurants — are scattered among the train gates and boutiques.

Meals on the Mall

You'll be spending lots of time in the museums along the National Mall — and trudging from one to the other. You can ease your hunger and quench your thirst in many of them. Some 3 million people eat in the Smithsonian Institution's cafeterias and restaurants each year. The food spots tend to be open when the museums are. All are happy to add to your AE, DISC, MC, or V bills.

Here are your options:

✔ **National Museum of American History:** The Main Street Café offers pizza, hamburgers, sandwiches, salads, soups, and pastries. The Palm Court Coffee Bar serves sandwiches, salads, coffee, espresso, cappuccino, cookies, and pastries.

- ✔ **National Museum of Natural History:** At the Fossil Cafe, you can eat sandwiches, salads, and desserts at tables that themselves are natural history exhibits. The self-service Atrium Café offers continental breakfast, burgers, pizza, pasta, rotisserie chicken, soups, salads, and sandwiches. From 5:30 to 10 p.m. Fridays, you can eat, drink, and listen to live music at the Smithsonian Jazz Café for a $5 cover charge.

- ✔ **National Air and Space Museum:** The Wright Place, renovated in 2001 and 2002, sells Donato's pizza, Boston Market's rotisserie chicken, and the usual McDonald's fare. The Mezza Café serves pastries, salads, and sandwiches. Spring through early fall, food carts on the terrace sell ice cream, soda, and hot dogs. An outdoor cafe serves panini, pastries, sandwiches, and salads,

- ✔ **The Castle:** Seattle's Best Coffee operates a kiosk here. In addition to caffeine, you can pick up breakfast items, sandwiches, pastries, fruit, and juice.

- ✔ **Hirshhorn Museum:** There's an outdoor cafe here from late spring through summer.

- ✔ **National Museum of the American Indian:** Not surprisingly, the Mitsitam Café here serves Native-American inspired food, including sandwiches, entrees, soups, and desserts.

- ✔ **National Gallery of Art:** In addition to fine art, the National Gallery offers the best dining options on the Mall. The Cascade Café, in the concourse between the East and West buildings, with a view of the cascade waterfall, is a large cafeteria with a wide choice of food. The dining area is bright and airy, the walls hung with prints from the gallery's collection. For $6.50, you can get one of the best dining deals in Washington here — soup and half a big sandwich. The wild mushroom soup is spicy and rich. When I'm at the nearby D.C. courts building on jury duty — which, in Washington, comes every two years like clockwork — I often wander down here during lunch break. It's open 10 a.m. to 3 p.m. Monday through Saturday, and 11 a.m. to 4 p.m. Sunday.

Another good spot at the gallery is the Pavilion cafe, a glass-enclosed shelter in the Sculpture Garden. We stopped in one noon after a seven-inch snowfall, warmed ourselves with chili and tomato-herb bread, and gazed at the serene winter view outside. They hand out enormous salads here, and sandwiches so stuffed that a dining companion complained of the tuna salad sandwich: "There's too much tuna." Healthful side dishes include roasted vegetables and pasta. In winter, you can sit inside and watch the ice skaters outside. In warm weather, you can eat at outdoor tables. The cafe is open 10 a.m. to 4 p.m. Monday through Saturday, and 11 a.m. to 5 p.m. Sunday.

Brunch, accompanied by live jazz, is offered from 11 a.m. to 3 p.m. Sundays on the terrace level of the East Building. The East Building has an espresso bar on the concourse level where you can get gelato, panini, and sweets from 10 a.m. to 4:30 p.m. Monday through Saturday and 11 a.m. to 5:30 p.m. Sunday. The Garden Café is open in the West Building from 11:30 a.m. to 3 p.m. Monday through Saturday and noon to 6 p.m. Sunday. My wife likes the setting, but I find the selection too small and the prices to large.

Drinks, with a view

Enjoy a cocktail while drinking in a primo view at the **Sky Terrace** of the Hotel Washington (515 15th St. NW at Pennsylvania Avenue; ☎ **202-638-5900**). Between May and October, this spot is a favorite for catching a sundowner. Keep it simple and stick to a cheese platter or a sandwich if you eat here. While you ogle the landscape, see how many buildings you can identify. You can almost peer into the East Wing of the White House.

For a view of the Potomac River — and of younger Washingtonians hustling for companionship of the opposite sex — mosey on down to Georgetown's **Washington Harbour** complex (3000 K St. at Thomas Jefferson Street) on a warm evening. Grab a table at one of the outdoor watering holes, sip a drink, nibble on some appetizers, and watch the people strolling along the riverwalk, the boats sailing on the river, and the planes flying into and out of National Airport.

Index of Restaurants by Neighborhood

Adams-Morgan

The Grill from Ipanema (Brazilian, $$$)

Capitol Hill

Ben & Jerry's (Ice Cream)
Bistro Bis (French, $$$$)
Bread & Chocolate (American, $$)
B. Smith's (Southern, $$$)
Cafe Berlin (German, $$)
Firehook Bakery (American, $)
Häagen Dazs (Ice Cream)
La Colline (French, $$$)
The Monocle (American, $$$)
Montmartre (French, $$$)
Union Station Food Court (Various Cuisines, $)

Chinatown

Capital Q (Barbecue, $)
Eat First (Chinese, $$)
Tony Cheng's (Chinese $$$)

Downtown

Andale (Mexican, $$$)
Austin Grill (Southwestern, $$)
Ben & Jerry's (Ice Cream)
Bread and Chocolate (American, $$)
Cafe Atlantico (Latin American, $$$)
Cafe 15 (French, $$$$$)
The Caucus Room (Steakhouse, $$$$)
Chipotle (Mexican, $)
Coeur de Lion (Modern American, $$$$)
Dean & Deluca (American, $$)
15 ria (American/Southern, $$$)

Firehook Bakery (American, $)
Galileo (Italian, $$–$$$$$)
Georgia Brown's (Southern, $$$)
Gerard's Place (French, $$$$$)
Jaleo (Spanish, $$)
Lafayette Room (Modern American, $$$$$)
Le Paradou (French, $$$$$)
Marrakesh (Moroccan, $$$)
Nooshi (Asian, $)
The Occidental (American, $$$$)
The Oceanaire Seafood Room, (Seafood, $$$$)
Old Ebbitt Grill (American, $$$)
Poste (Modern American, $$$$)
The Prime Rib (Steakhouse, $$$$)
Red Sage Border Cafe (Southwestern, $$)
Red Sage Grill (American, $$$$)
Sky Terrace (American, $$$)
Teatro Goldoni (Italian/Venetian, $$$$)
Vidalia (American/Southern, $$$$)
Willard Room (Modern American, $$$$$)
Zaytinya (Mediterranean, $$)
Zola (Modern American, $$$)

Dupont Circle

The Brickskeller (American, $$)
Chipotle (Mexican, $)
City Lights of China (Chinese, $$)
Firefly (Modern American, $$$)
Firehook Bakery (American, $)
Kramerbooks & Afterwords (American, $$)
Larry's (Ice Cream)
Luna Grill & Diner (American, $$)
Malaysia Kopitiam (Malaysian, $$)
The Melting Pot (Fondue, $$$)
Obelisk (Italian, $$$$$)
The Palm (Steakhouse, $$$$$)
Pizzeria Paradiso (Pizza, $)
Restaurant Nora (American/Organic, $$$$)
Sweet Licks (Ice Cream)
Tabard Inn (American, $$$)

Foggy Bottom/West End

Asia Nora (Asian/Organic, $$$$)
Bread and Chocolate (American, $$)
Circle Bistro (American/Mediterranean, $$$)
Dish (American, $$$)
Kinkead's (Seafood, $$$$)
Marcel's (French/Flemish, $$$$$)

Georgetown

Amma Indian Vegetarian Kitchen (Indian/Vegetarian, $)
Bistrot Lepic (French, $$$)
Booeymonger (American, $)
Café La Ruche (French, $$)
Ching Ching Cha (Chinese, $$)
Chipotle (Mexican, $)
Clyde's (American, $$$)
Dean & Deluca (American, $$)
Garden Terrace Lounge (American, $$$)
Garrett's (American, $$)
Harmony Cafe (Asian, $)
Isee Icy (Ice Cream)
Michel Richard's Citronelle (French/California, $$$$$)
Miss Saigon (Vietnamese, $$$)
Pizzeria Paradiso (Pizza, $)
Sea Catch (Seafood, $$$)
1789 Restaurant (American, $$$$)
Sweet Licks (Ice Cream)
Thomas Sweet (Ice Cream)

Upper Northwest

Austin Grill (Southwestern, $$)
Booeymonger (American, $)
Bread and Chocolate (American, $$)
Cheesecake Factory (American, $$)
Chipotle (Mexican, $)
Clyde's (American, $$$)
Cold Stone Creamery (Ice Cream)
Firehook Bakery (American, $)
Kron Chocolatier (Candy)
2 Amys (Italian/Pizza, $$)

Index of Restaurants by Cuisine

American

Booeymonger (Georgetown/Upper Northwest, $)
Bread and Chocolate (Capitol Hill, Downtown, West End & Upper Northwest, $$)
The Brickskeller (Dupont Circle, $$)
Cheesecake Factory (Upper Northwest, $$)
Circle Bistro (Foggy Bottom/West End, $$$)
Clyde's (Georgetown & Upper Northwest, $$$)
Coeur de Lion (Downtown, $$$$)
Dean & Deluca (Downtown & Georgetown, $$)
Dish (Foggy Bottom, $$$)
15 ria (Downtown, $$$)
Firefly (Dupont Circle, $$$)
Firehook Bakery (Capitol Hill, Downtown, Dupont Circle & Upper Northwest, $)
Garden Terrace Lounge (Georgetown, $$$)
Garrett's (Georgetown, $$)
Kramerbooks & Afterwords (Dupont Circle, $$)
Lafayette Room (Downtown, $$$$$)
Luna Grill & Diner (Dupont Circle, $$)
The Monocle (Capitol Hill, $$$)
The Occidental (Downtown, $$$$)
Old Ebbitt Grill, (Downtown, $$$)
Poste (Downtown, $$$$)
Red Sage Grill (Downtown, $$$$)
Restaurant Nora (Dupont Circle, $$$$)
1789 Restaurant (Georgetown, $$$$)
Sky Terrace (Downtown, $$$)
Tabard Inn (Dupont Circle, $$$)
Vidalia (Downtown, $$$$)
Willard room (Downtown, $$$$$)
Zola (Downtown, $$$)

Asian

Asia Nora (Foggy Bottom/West End, $$$$)
Harmony Cafe (Georgetown, $)
Nooshi (Downtown, $)

Barbecue

Capital Q (Chinatown, $)

Brazilian

The Grill From Ipanema (Adams-Morgan, $$$)

Candy

Kron Chocolatier (Upper Northwest)

Chinese

Ching Ching Cha (Georgetown, $$)
City Lights of China (Dupont Circle, $$)
Eat First (Chinatown, $$)
Tony Cheng's (Chinatown, $$$)

Fondue

The Melting Pot (Dupont Circle, $$$)

French

Bistro Bis (Capitol Hill, $$$$)
Bistrot Lepic & Wine Bar (Georgetown, $$$)
Cafe 15 (Downtown, $$$$$)
Café La Ruche (Georgetown, $$)
Gerard's Place (Downtown, $$$$$)
La Colline (Capitol Hill, $$$)
Le Paradou (Downtown, $$$$$)
Marcel's (Foggy Bottom/West End, $$$$$)
Michel Richard's Citronelle (Georgetown, $$$$$)
Montmartre (Capitol Hill, $$$)

German

Cafe Berlin (Capitol Hill, $$)

Hamburgers

The Brickskeller (Dupont Circle, $)
Clyde's (Georgetown & Upper Northwest, $$$)
Old Ebbitt Grill (Downtown, $$$)

Ice Cream
Ben & Jerry's (Capitol Hill & Downtown)
Cold Stone Creamery (Upper Northwest)
Häagen Dazs (Capitol Hill)
Isee Icy (Georgetown)
Larry's (Dupont Circle)
Sweet Licks (Dupont Circle)
Thomas Sweet (Georgetown)

Indian
Amma Indian Vegetarian Kitchen, (Georgetown, $)

Italian
Galileo (Downtown, $$–$$$$$)
Obelisk (Dupont Circle, $$$$$)
Teatro Goldoni (Downtown, $$$$)
2 Amys (Upper Northwest, $$)

Latin American
Café Atlantico (Downtown, $$$)

Malayasian
Malaysia Kopitiam (Dupont Circle, $$)

Mexican
Andale (Downtown, $$$)
Chipotle (Downtown, Dupont Circle, Georgetown & Upper Northwest, $)

Mediterranean
Circle Bistro (Foggy Bottom/West End, $$$)
Zaytinya (Downtown, $$)

Moroccan
Marrakesh (Downtown, $$$)

Organic
Asia Nora (Foggy Bottom/West End, $$$$)

Restaurant Nora (Dupont Circle, $$$$)

Pizza
Pizzeria Paradiso (Dupont Circle & Georgetown, $)
2 Amys (Upper Northwest, $$)

Seafood
Kinkead's (Foggy Bottom/West End, $$$$)
The Oceanaire Seafood Room (Downtown, $$$$)
Sea Catch (Georgetown, $$$)
Tony Cheng's (Chinatown, $$$)

Southern
B. Smith's (Capitol Hill, $$$)
15 ria (Downtown, $$$)
Georgia Brown's (Downtown, $$$)
Vidalia (Downtown, $$$$)

Southwestern
Austin Grill (Downtown & Upper Northwest, $$)
Red Sage Border Cafe (Downtown, $$)

Spanish
Jaleo (Downtown, $$)

Steakhouse
The Caucus Room (Downtown, $$$$)
The Palm (Dupont Circle, $$$$$)
The Prime Rib (Downtown, $$$$)

Vegetarian
Amma Indian Vegetarian Kitchen (Georgetown, $)

Vietnamese
Miss Saigon (Georgetown, $$$)

Index of Restaurants by Price

$

Amma Indian Vegetarian Kitchen (Georgetown, Indian/Vegetarian)
Booeymonger (Georgetown/Upper Northwest, American)
Capital Q (Chinatown, Barbecue)
Chipotle (Downtown, Dupont Circle, Georgetown & Upper Northwest, Mexican)
Firehook Bakery (Capitol Hill, Downtown, Dupont Circle & Upper Northwest, American)
Harmony Cafe (Georgetown, Asian)
Nooshi (Asian, Downtown)
Pizzeria Paradiso (Dupont Circle & Georgetown, Pizza)
Union Station Food Court (Various Cuisines, $)

$$

Austin Grill (Downtown & Upper Northwest, Southwestern)
Bread and Chocolate (Capitol Hill, Downtown, West End & Upper Northwest, American)
The Brickskeller (Dupont Circle, American)
Cafe Berlin (Capitol Hill, German)
Cafe La Ruche (Georgetown, French)
Capitol City Brewing Company (Capitol Hill/Downtown, American)
Cheesecake Factory (Upper Northwest, American)
Ching Ching Cha (Georgetown, Chinese)
City Lights of China (Dupont Circle, Chinese)
Dean & Deluca (Downtown & Georgetown, American)
Eat First (Chinatown, Chinese)
Galileo (Downtown, Italian)
Garrett's (Georgetown, American)
Jaleo (Downtown, Spanish)
Kramerbooks & Afterwords (Dupont Circle, American)
Luna Grill & Diner (Dupont Circle, American)

Malaysia Kopitiam (Dupont Circle, Malaysian)
Red Sage Border Cafe (Downtown, Southwestern)
2 Amys (Upper Northwest, Italian/Pizza)
Zaytinya (Downtown, Mediterranean)

$$$

Andale (Downtown, Mexican)
B. Smith's (Capitol Hill, Southern)
Bistrot Lepic & Wine Bar (Georgetown, French)
Cafe Atlantico (Downtown, Latin American)
Circle Bistro (Foggy Bottom/West End, American/Mediterranean)
Clyde's (Georgetown & Upper Northwest, American)
Dish (Foggy Bottom, American)
15 ria (Downtown, American/Southern)
Firefly (Dupont Circle, Modern American)
Garden Terrace Lounge (Georgetown, American)
Georgia Brown's (Downtown, Southern)
The Grill From Ipanema, (Adams-Morgan, Brazilian)
La Colline (Capitol Hill, French)
Marrakesh (Downtown, Moroccan)
The Melting Pot (Dupont Circle, Fondue)
Miss Saigon (Georgetown, Vietnamese)
The Monocle (Capitol Hill, American)
Montmartre (Capitol Hill, French)
Old Ebbitt Grill (Downtown, American)
Sea Catch (Georgetown, Seafood)
Sky Terrace (Downtown, American)
Tabard Inn (Dupont Circle, American)
Tony Cheng's (Chinatown, Chinese)
Zola (Downtown, Modern American)

$$$$

Asia Nora (Foggy Bottom/West End, Asian/Organic)
Bistro Bis (Capitol Hill, French)
The Caucus Room (Downtown, Steakhouse)
Coeur de Lion (Downtown, Modern American)
Kinkead's (Foggy Bottom/West End, Seafood)
The Occidental (Downtown, American)
The Oceanaire Seafood Room (Downtown, Seafood)
Poste (Downtown, Modern American)
The Prime Rib (Downtown, Steakhouse)
Red Sage Grill (Downtown, American)
Restaurant Nora (Dupont Circle, American/Organic)
1789 Restaurant (Georgetown, American)

Teatro Goldoni (Downtown, Italian/Venetian)
Vidalia (Downtown, American/Southern)

$$$$$

Cafe 15 (Downtown, French)
Galileo (Dupont Circle, Italian)
Gerard's Place (Downtown, French)
Lafayette Room (Downtown, Modern American)
Le Paradou (Downtown, French)
Marcel's (Foggy Bottom/West End, French/Flemish)
Michel Richard's Citronelle (Georgetown, French/California)
Obelisk (Dupont Circle, Northern Italian)
The Palm (Dupont Circle, Steakhouse)
Willard Room (Downtown, Modern American)

Part IV
Exploring
Washington, D.C.

The 5th Wave   By Rich Tennant

"I want a lens that's heavy enough to counterbalance the weight on my back."

In this part . . .

You're here to see the sights, and this part points you to the best. I start with the biggies — the Capitol, the Washington Monument, and the like. I also cover places that may be less familiar to you, such as the Capital Children's Museum and Old Stone House. In case you're interested in buying as well as looking, I introduce you to the best of Washington's shopping scene. I also give tips on things to do outside of Washington, including some suggested itineraries — for the government groupie, for example, or the family with kids. If you don't want to take responsibility for your entire D.C. visit, I point you to some guided tours.

Chapter 11

Discovering Washington, D.C.'s Best Attractions

*Y*ou came to Washington to see the sights, and this chapter gives you the scoop on Washington's premier attractions (memorials, galleries, topless bars — just wanted to see if you were paying attention — and so on).

The following reviews give you the lowdown on what you find at each place, as well as the specifics on hours, admission fees (if any), and any specific tips or heads-up you need for an attraction.

One of the most pleasant things I reveal is that, in the capital of the land of the free, most of the attractions are free.

The Top Attractions from A to Z

For more information on the architecture and historical background of some of D.C.'s attractions, see Chapter 2.

Arlington National Cemetery
Virginia

There's something overwhelming about the tens of thousands of simple grave markers that march in perfect formation across Arlington's hills and valleys. In their presence, it's impossible not to be moved by the enormity of the sacrifice of the military men and women who fought to preserve

The Top Attractions in Washington, D.C.

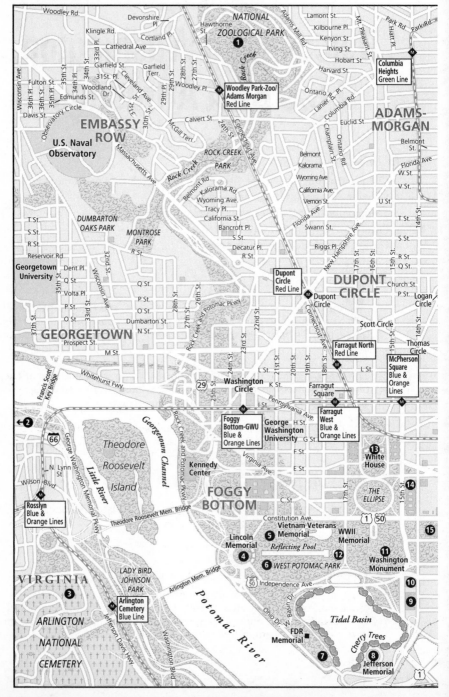

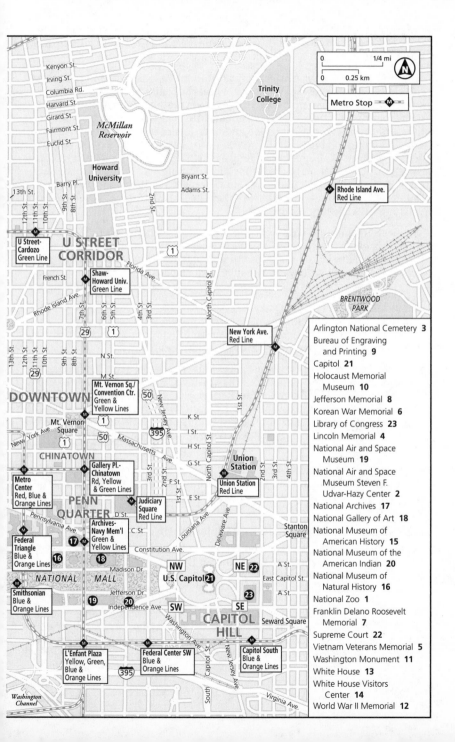

Trinity College

Metro Stop Ⓜ

McMillan Reservoir

Howard University

Kenyon St.
Irving St.
Columbia Rd.
Harvard St.
Girard St.
Fairmont St.
Euclid St.

Bryant St.
Adams St.

Rhode Island Ave.
Red Line

13th St.

Barry Pl.

U Street-Cardozo
Green Line

U STREET CORRIDOR

French St.

Shaw-Howard Univ.
Green Line

Florida Ave.

BRENTWOOD PARK

DOWNTOWN

New York Ave.
Red Line

Mt. Vernon Sq./Convention Ctr.
Green & Yellow Lines

Mt. Vernon Square

CHINATOWN

Gallery Pl.-Chinatown
Rd, Yellow & Green Lines

Union Station

Union Station
Red Line

Metro Center
Red, Blue & Orange Lines

PENN QUARTER

Judiciary Square
Red Line

Archives-Navy Mem'l
Green & Yellow Lines

Federal Triangle
Blue & Orange Lines

Stanton Square

NATIONAL MALL

Smithsonian
Blue & Orange Lines

NW
U.S. Capitol Ⓜ 21

NE 22

SW

SE 23

CAPITOL HILL

Seward Square

L'Enfant Plaza
Yellow, Green, Blue & Orange Lines

Federal Center SW
Blue & Orange Lines

Capitol South
Blue & Orange Lines

Washington Channel

Arlington National Cemetery **3**
Bureau of Engraving
  and Printing **9**
Capitol **21**
Holocaust Memorial
  Museum **10**
Jefferson Memorial **8**
Korean War Memorial **6**
Library of Congress **23**
Lincoln Memorial **4**
National Air and Space
  Museum **19**
National Air and Space
  Museum Steven F.
  Udvar-Hazy Center **2**
National Archives **17**
National Gallery of Art **18**
National Museum of
  American History **15**
National Museum of the
  American Indian **20**
National Museum of
  Natural History **16**
National Zoo **1**
Franklin Delano Roosevelt
  Memorial **7**
Supreme Court **22**
Vietnam Veterans Memorial **5**
Washington Monument **11**
White House **13**
White House Visitors
  Center **14**
World War II Memorial **12**

America's freedom and to enforce its sometimes-controversial foreign policies. More than 260,000 war dead and veterans (and their dependents) are buried here.

Stop first at the **visitor center,** look around, pick up a map, and then take the short walk to the memorial to the nearly 2 million women who have served in the military since the American Revolution. Return to the visitor center and buy a ticket for the **Tourmobile.** The sprawling cemetery is hilly. Unless you're in great shape and have lots of time, I don't advise covering it entirely on foot. The Tourmobile stops at the major sights. You can get off, explore the cemetery as long as you like, and then reboard to continue your tour. Before boarding for the first time, use the visitor center's restrooms — you won't find more until you get to **Arlington House,** where Robert E. Lee once lived with his wife, Mary Custis Lee, Martha Washington's great-granddaughter.

The first Tourmobile stop is at the grave of President John F. Kennedy, where his widow, Jacqueline Kennedy Onassis, also is buried, along with their two infants who died before the president. The president's brother, Robert F. Kennedy, who was assassinated during his own presidential campaign in 1968, is buried nearby. These gravesites have commanding views of the capital city.

The next Tourmobile stop is at the Tomb of the Unknowns, where the guard is changed every hour on the hour from October to March and every half-hour April to September. It's a somber ceremony.

When you get to Arlington House, also known as the Custis-Lee Mansion, you can take a free self-guided tour between 9:30 a.m. and 4:30 p.m., except December 25 and January 1. The Robert E. Lee Museum at the house opens at 8 a.m. The grave of Pierre L'Enfant, who drew up the plans for the capital at George Washington's request, is nearby. He was moved here from a pauper's grave and now enjoys a breathtaking panorama of his masterwork.

After you return to the visitor center, you can take a ten-minute walk to the Marine Corps Memorial, yet another moving scene that portrays the immortal photograph of Marines raising the U.S. flag on Iwo Jima during World War II.

Expect to spend two to three hours at these sights.

Remember that Arlington is a cemetery, so please conduct yourself — and make sure that your children conduct themselves — accordingly. Burials quite likely will be taking place while you visit. An average of 15 burials occur each day.

See map p. 184. In Arlington, Virginia, across the Arlington Memorial Bridge from the Lincoln Memorial. ☎ 703-607-8000. www.arlingtoncemetery.org. *Metro: Arlington National Cemetery. Tourmobile stops here. Admission: Free. Tourmobile tour: Adults $6, children 3–11 $3. Open: Daily Apr–Sept 8 a.m.–7 p.m., Oct–Mar 8 a.m.– 5 p.m. Tourmobile leaves visitor center Apr–Aug 8:30 a.m.–6:30 p.m., Sept–March 9:30 a.m.–4:30 p.m.*

The Mall

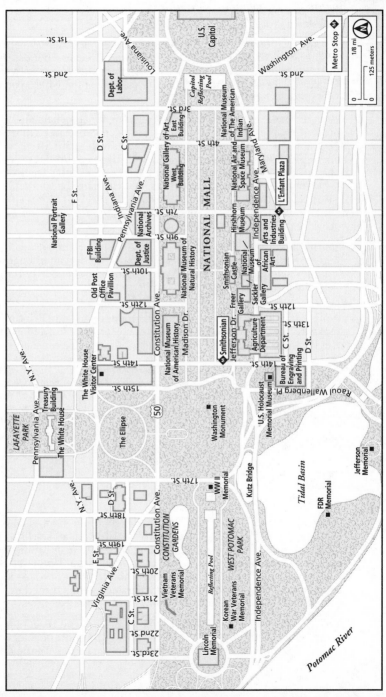

Bureau of Engraving and Printing
Tidal Basin

The buck may stop in the White House, but it starts here, where printers and engravers make money, postage stamps, Treasury bonds, and White House invitations. No free samples! But you can purchase a souvenir (such as uncut or shredded currency) in the visitor center, where you can play with interactive displays.

March through September, you must get free, timed tickets on the day you tour, and people line up early. One person can get up to eight tickets. The ticket kiosk is on Raoul Wallenberg Place on the 15th Street side of the building. The kiosk opens at 8 a.m. Monday through Friday, except federal holidays, and tickets usually are gone by 9 a.m. Evening tours are offered May through August. Without tickets, you can skip the tour and enter the visitor center through the tour entrance on the 14th Street side. Tickets aren't required for tours October through February. *Figure on spending an hour here (not including the wait to get in).*

Security has been tightened substantially at government facilities since the terrorist attacks of September 11, 2001. The Bureau of Engraving and Printing closes to the public when the Homeland Security Department raises the terrorist threat level to code orange.

Your U.S. representative and senators can help you with tickets to government buildings, such as the Bureau of Engraving and Printing. Phone them way ahead of time, tell them what you want to do, and ask them what they can do for you.

See map p. 184. 14th and C streets SW. ☎ *866-874-2330 (toll-free) or 202-874-2330.* www.moneyfactory.gov. *Metro: Smithsonian. From the Independence Avenue exit, walk west on Independence 1 long block and then left on 14th (to the tour entrance) or 2 blocks and then left on Raoul Wallenberg Place (for the ticket kiosk). Admission: Free. Tours: May–Aug Mon–Fri 10 a.m.–2 p.m. and 5–7 p.m., Sept–April Mon–Fri10 a.m.–2 p.m. Visitor center open: May–Aug 8:30 a.m.–7:30 p.m., Sept–April 8:30 a.m.–3:30 p.m. Closed: Federal holidays and Dec 25 through Jan 1.*

Capitol
Capitol Hill

As the home to Congress and the most common symbol of American democracy, the Capitol belongs on every visitor's must-see list. The familiar architecture, the historic art inside, and the ornate decoration are other aspects that make the Capitol an interesting stop. Unfortunately, construction of a visitor center under the Capitol's East Lawn — along with various makeshift, post-9/11 security barriers — has turned much of the area around the Capitol into an eyesore and obstacle course.

The Capitol dominates the Washington landscape. The 180-foot-high dome is topped by a statue titled *Freedom.* Inside, the Rotunda serves as the heart of the Capitol. Above the Rotunda, in the canopy of the dome, you

Monuments & Memorials

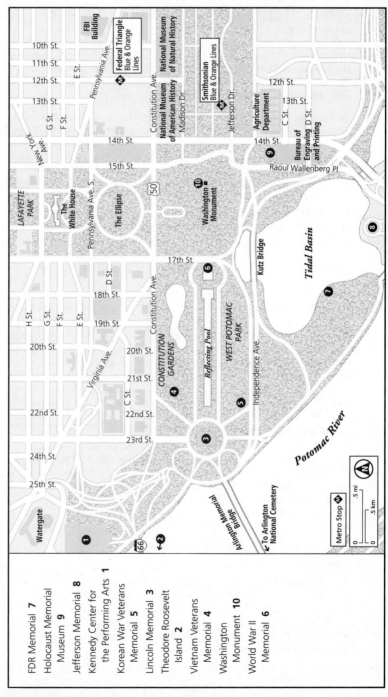

10th St.
11th St.
12th St.
13th St.
E St.
FBI Building
Pennsylvania Ave.
Federal Triangle
Blue & Orange Lines
Constitution Ave.
National Museum of Natural History
National Museum of American History
Madison Dr.
Smithsonian
Blue & Orange Lines
Jefferson Dr.
12th St.
13th St.
C St.
Agriculture Department
Bureau of Engraving and Printing
D St.
G St.
F St.
New York Ave.
14th St.
14th St.
9
Raoul Wallenberg Pl.
15th St.
LAFAYETTE PARK
The White House
Pennsylvania Ave. S.
The Ellipse
50
10
Washington Monument
Tidal Basin
8
Kutz Bridge
17th St.
6
D St.
18th St.
H St.
G St.
F St.
E St.
19th St.
Constitution Ave.
CONSTITUTION GARDENS
Reflecting Pool
WEST POTOMAC PARK
7
20th St.
20th St.
Virginia Ave.
C St.
21st St.
4
Independence Ave.
22nd St.
22nd St.
5
23rd St.
3
Potomac River
24th St.
25th St.
Watergate
1
2
66
To Arlington National Cemetery
Arlington Memorial Bridge
Metro Stop
.5 mi
.5 km
0
0

FDR Memorial **7**
Holocaust Memorial Museum **9**
Jefferson Memorial **8**
Kennedy Center for the Performing Arts **1**
Korean War Veterans Memorial **5**
Lincoln Memorial **3**
Theodore Roosevelt Island **2**
Vietnam Veterans Memorial **4**
Washington Monument **10**
World War II Memorial **6**

see Constantino Brumidi's fresco, *The Apotheosis of Washington,* which portrays the first president as a godlike character flanked by such allegorical figures as Liberty, War, Victory, and Fame. Statues of prominent Americans — and some not so prominent — fill Statuary Hall and stand throughout the building. Most important, of course, the building contains the House and Senate chambers — which you see on C-SPAN's coverage of congressional floor debates — and the offices of top congressional leaders and some of the most powerful committees.

You can obtain free tickets for guided tours from a member of Congress or first-come, first-served at the Capitol Guide Service Kiosk along the curving sidewalk near First Street SW and Independence Avenue beginning at 9 a.m. Monday through Saturday. Lines can get quite long in spring and summer, which is why contacting your representative or senators ahead of time is a good idea. Expect to spend one to two hours here, not counting the time you wait to get in.

Your U.S. representative and senators can arrange for you to join a special Capitol Guide Service tour that's conducted before the public tours. Some members of Congress — and their aides — are happy to lead constituents on tours themselves. Call your state's representative or senators far ahead of your visit and ask what they might do for you.

If the House or Senate is in session, you can watch the proceedings from a visitor's gallery. Call your representative or a senator for tickets.

If you do take a seat in a visitors gallery, don't be surprised if nothing exciting is going on. While the chambers fill for roll-call votes and during extremely important debates, usually only a handful of members is on the floor. You can witness the surreal scene of a grandiloquent senator propounding profoundly on the greatest issues of the day, with only one or two other members, one or two reporters, a few congressional staffers — and the C-SPAN cameras — looking on.

See map p. 184. Capitol Guide Service Kiosk, near 1st Street SW and Independence Avenue. ☎ *202-225-6827. (Call senators at* ☎ *202-224-3121, representatives at* ☎ *202-225-3121.)* www.aoc.gov. *Metro: Capitol South. Walk north 1 block on 1st Street SE, turn left on Independence Avenue for 3 blocks, and then go right on 1st Street SW for 1 block. Admission: Free. Tours: 9 a.m.–4:30 p.m. Mon–Sat except Thanksgiving and Dec. 25. First-come, first-served tour tickets distributed at kiosk beginning at 9 a.m.*

Franklin Delano Roosevelt Memorial
Tidal Basin

This monument to a U.S. president illustrates the latest trend in monument architecture. It is, shall I say, monumental in size — telling the 32nd president's biography as well as honoring him on a 7½-acre site. Walking through four open-air "rooms," one for each of Roosevelt's terms, you revisit the Great Depression, World War II, and other notable aspects of his 12-year presidency, the longest ever. The memorial features statues of

National Zoological Park

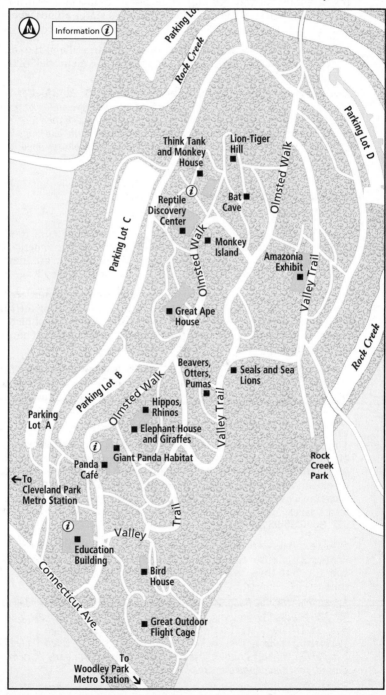

his first lady, Eleanor, an important public figure in her own right, and Roosevelt's beloved dog Fala. Note how Fala's statue shines where visitors pet it.

You can see FDR's wheelchair and other memorabilia in the information center. Restrooms are located at each end of the memorial. Allow 30 minutes to an hour to visit.

See map p. 189. West Basin Drive SW at Ohio Drive. ☎ *202-426-6841.* www.nps. gov/fdrm. *Metro: Smithsonian. From the Independence Avenue exit, walk west on Independence until you're sure that you've gone too far and then turn left on West Basin Drive; total walking time about 30 minutes. The Tourmobile stops here, or you can take a taxi. Admission: Free. Open: Outdoor memorial always open; staffed daily 8 a.m.–11:45 p.m. except Dec 25.*

Holocaust Memorial Museum
Tidal Basin

I have yet to meet a soul unmoved by a visit to this museum. Prepare to be emotionally drained when you leave. The museum recommends that children younger than 11 not visit the permanent collection, but they can view other exhibits. Prepare your older children for what they'll see and hear.

The museum remembers the 6 million Jews who were murdered and the millions of others who were murdered or oppressed during the Holocaust. Multimedia exhibitions document this obscene chapter of history. Upon entering, each visitor picks up an identity card of a Holocaust victim, which personalizes the museum experience.

The self-guided tour begins with the rise of Nazism. Then, the Nazis' "Final Solution" is depicted. Aboard a freight car that was used to transport Jews to Treblinka, visitors listen to recordings of survivors. Another section is dedicated to the liberation of the concentration camps and to the non-Jews who, at great risk, hid Jews.

Time-specific tickets are required to view the permanent exhibits, which occupy the bulk of most visitors' time at the museum. They're free at the museum for same-day visits, but usually are depleted quickly. People line up as early as 8 a.m., though distribution doesn't begin until 10 a.m. at the museum's pass desk by the 14th Street entrance. One person can pick up four passes. You can get tickets ahead of time for $1.75 from Tickets.com (☎ **800-400-9373;** www.tickets.com).

Other exhibits don't require tickets. Among them is "Daniel's Story," which is appropriate for elementary and middle-school children. Most people spend two to three hours in the museum; many visitors spend a lot more time.

See map p. 184. 100 Raoul Wallenberg Place SW (south of Independence Avenue). ☎ *202-488-0400.* www.ushmm.org. *Metro: Smithsonian. From the Independence Avenue exit, walk west on Independence 2 blocks and then go left on Raoul Wallenberg Place. Admission: Free. Advance tickets: $1.75. Open: Daily 10 a.m.–5:20 p.m., extended hours until 7:50 p.m. Tues and Thurs from early April to mid-June. Closed: Yom Kippur and Christmas.*

The White House Area

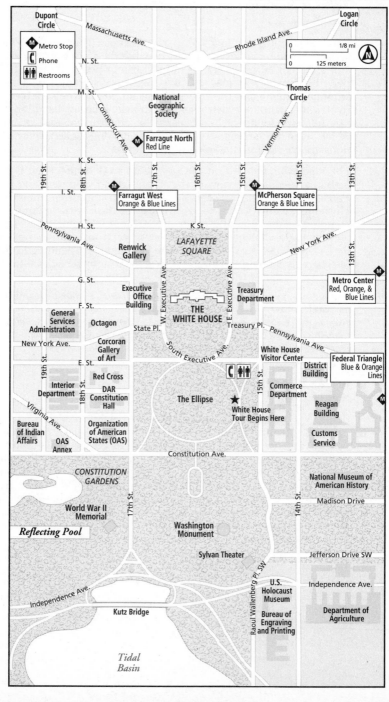

Legend:
- Ⓜ Metro Stop
- 🅲 Phone
- 🚻 Restrooms

Scale: 0 — 1/8 mi / 0 — 125 meters

Dupont Circle
Logan Circle
Massachusetts Ave.
Rhode Island Ave.
N. St.
Thomas Circle
M. St.
National Geographic Society
Vermont Ave.
L. St.
Connecticut Ave.
Farragut North
Red Line
K. St.
19th St.
18th St.
17th St.
16th St.
15th St.
14th St.
13th St.
I. St.
Farragut West
Orange & Blue Lines
McPherson Square
Orange & Blue Lines
H. St.
Pennsylvania Ave.
K St.
New York Ave.
13th St.
Renwick Gallery
LAFAYETTE SQUARE
G. St.
Metro Center
Red, Orange, & Blue Lines
Executive Office Building
W. Executive Ave.
E. Executive Ave.
THE WHITE HOUSE
Treasury Department
F. St.
General Services Administration
Octagon
State Pl.
Treasury Pl.
Pennsylvania Ave.
New York Ave.
Corcoran Gallery of Art
South Executive Ave.
White House Visitor Center
District Building
Federal Triangle
Blue & Orange Lines
19th St.
E. St.
Red Cross
18th St.
Interior Department
DAR Constitution Hall
The Ellipse
White House Tour Begins Here ★
15th St.
Commerce Department
Reagan Building
Virginia Ave.
Bureau of Indian Affairs
OAS Annex
Organization of American States (OAS)
Customs Service
Constitution Ave.
CONSTITUTION GARDENS
National Museum of American History
17th St.
14th St.
Madison Drive
World War II Memorial
Washington Monument
Reflecting Pool
Sylvan Theater
Jefferson Drive SW
Raoul Wallenberg Pl. SW
U.S. Holocaust Museum
Independence Ave.
Independence Ave.
Department of Agriculture
Kutz Bridge
Bureau of Engraving and Printing
Tidal Basin

Jefferson Memorial
Tidal Basin

This memorial is my favorite, partly because Thomas Jefferson is my favorite founding father and partly because the setting is marvelous. A 19-foot statue of Jefferson stands atop a six-foot pedestal inside the memorial's columned rotunda, which is akin to Jefferson's designs for his Monticello home and the University of Virginia. (When we toured U.Va.-rival William and Mary with my then-college-hunting daughter, the guide said Jefferson founded U.Va. because his children couldn't get into W&M, which Jefferson himself attended — as now does Julie!) Jefferson quotations are carved into the memorial's interior.

The memorial, located on the southeast bank of the Tidal Basin, commands a spectacular view of the Washington Monument and the White House to the north. The scene is gorgeous in the spring when the cherry blossoms bloom, and awe-inspiring after dark with Jefferson's statue standing behind you and other of Washington's illuminated landmarks glowing in the distance. A bookstore and restrooms are in the basement. Park rangers deliver talks upon request. Count on spending 15 to 45 minutes here depending on whether you listen to a ranger's talk — more if you get mesmerized by the view.

See map p. 184. East Basin Drive SW on southeast side of Tidal Basin. ☎ *202-426-6841.* www.nps.gov/thje. *Metro: Smithsonian. From the Independence Avenue exit, walk 2 blocks west on Independence and then left on Raoul Wallenberg Place to the Tidal Basin path. It's a 15- to 25-minute walk. A Tourmobile stop is at the memorial, or you can take a taxi. Admission: Free. Open: Always.*

Korean War Veterans Memorial
National Mall

Before Vietnam, another undeclared war helped to drive a once-popular president (Truman) from office, cost more than 50,000 American lives, and left the nation in a mood more inclined to forget a conflict than to memorialize it. Finally, on the 42nd anniversary of the armistice that ended the fighting — but which has not yet officially sealed the peace — the Korean War Veterans Memorial was dedicated on July 27, 1995, by the presidents of the United States and South Korea, Bill Clinton and Kim Young Sam. The focal point of the memorial is statues that depict an infantry unit on patrol. Park rangers give talks upon request. A bookstore, restrooms, and concessions are at the site. Allocate at least 15 minutes to tour this memorial.

See map p. 184. French Drive SW and Independence Avenue, southeast of the Lincoln Memorial. ☎ *202-426-6841.* www.nps.gov/kowa. *Metro: Foggy Bottom-George Washington University. Walk south 8 blocks on 23rd Street to the Lincoln Memorial and then left on French Drive. Or walk from the Tourmobile's Lincoln Memorial stop. Or take a taxi. Admission: Free. Open: Always.*

Library of Congress
Capitol Hill

The general public can't borrow books at this library, the world's largest, but you can do research here (and I have). The collection — 120 million items on 530 miles of bookshelves — is built upon Thomas Jefferson's personal library of 6,487 volumes.

The main building, named for Jefferson, is an ornate Italian Renaissance structure that you can tour. If you saw the movie *All the President's Men,* you'll remember a mind-boggling overhead shot of Woodward and Bernstein doing research in the Main Reading Room, which you can view. Another highlight, the Great Hall, soars 75 feet from marble floor to stained glass ceiling. The *Gutenberg Bible* and the *Giant Bible of Mainz* are among artifacts on permanent display. The building also houses changing exhibits, as well as film showings and concerts.

Stop first at the Jefferson Building's visitor center, inside the ground level First Street SE entrance. Get tour tickets and ask what's going on, not only in the Jefferson Building, but in the library's nearby Madison and Adams buildings as well. Figure on spending one to two hours here if you take the tour. Naturally, at Congress' library, a representative or senator can get you into a special tour.

See map p. 184. 1st Street SE (between East Capital Street and Independence Avenue). ☎ *202-707-8000.* www.loc.gov. *Metro: Capitol South. Walk north on 1st Street 1½ blocks to Jefferson Building. Admission: Free. Open: Jefferson Mon–Sat 10 a.m.–5:30 p.m., Madison: Mon–Fri 8:30 a.m.–9:30 p.m., Sat 8:30 a.m.–6:30 p.m., Adams Mon, Wed, Thurs 8:30 a.m.–9:30 p.m., Tues, Fri, Sat 8:30 a.m.–5:30 p.m. Tours: Mon–Fri 10:30 and 11:30 a.m., 1:30 p.m., 2:30 p.m., and 3:30 p.m., Sat 10:30 and 11:30 a.m., 1:30 and 2:30 p.m. Congressional tours: Mon–Fri 8:30 a.m. and 2 p.m.*

Lincoln Memorial
National Mall

Okay, I confess: The Lincoln Memorial is up there with the Jefferson. If you were forced to pick the greatest president, Lincoln would be in the Final Four. And, like Jefferson's, Lincoln's memorial is an awe-inspiring place. Once again, you have an oversized sculpture of the president inside a structure that, in this case, has become as familiar as the Capitol and the White House. (It's on the back of the penny!) The Gettysburg Address and Lincoln's second inaugural address are inscribed on the walls. And the vista is spectacular, looking the length of the Mall, past the World War II Memorial and the Washington Monument to the Capitol.

The Lincoln Memorial has been the sight of some of America's most important political demonstrations, from Marian Anderson singing here in 1939, to Martin Luther King's "I Have a Dream" speech in 1963, to the Vietnam War protests. The Memorial has a visitor center and restrooms, and rangers give talks on request. You can spend 15 to 45 minutes — or more — here, depending on your interest, and it's awe-inspiring at night. From the back, you look into Arlington National Cemetery and see the perpetual flame on Kennedy's grave.

See map p. 189. West end of the Mall at 23rd Street between Constitution and Independence avenues. ☎ 202-426-6841. www.nps.gov/linc. *Metro: Foggy Bottom. Walk south 8 blocks on 23rd Street. Tourmobile stops here, or you can take a taxi. Admission: Free. Open: Always.*

National Air & Space Museum
National Mall

This museum is crammed with significant artifacts of flight and exhibits that teach the history and science of flight. You can stand beside John Glenn's *Friendship 7* capsule, in which he became the first American to orbit Earth, while gazing upon Neil Armstrong's *Columbia* command module, which first carried men to the moon. You can see Charles Lindbergh's ocean-crossing *Spirit of St. Louis,* Chuck *(The Right Stuff)* Yeager's sound-barrier-breaking *X-1,* a space station, a space rock . . . I have no room to do the collection justice.

Orville and Wilbur Wright's *Flyer* used to hang from the ceiling in the **Milestones of Flight Gallery,** near Glenn's and Armstrong's capsules. There, in a few feet of museum space, the 20th century progressed from "man cannot fly" to "man can walk on the moon" — in just 65 years! To mark the centennial of the Wrights' first flight — December 17, 1903 — the museum moved the Flyer to a special exhibit about "The Wright Brothers & the Invention of the Aerial Age." That exhibit is scheduled to run at least into late 2005.

Because the Air and Space Museum is on every visitor's agenda, arriving when the doors open or late in the day is wise. Get a map at the information desk and decide whether you want to take a free guided tour, rent an audio tape tour, or fend for yourself. Next, purchase tickets for one of the movies on the multistory IMAX screen and consider buying tickets for the Albert Einstein Planetarium's tour of the universe.

An hour can slip by in what seems like seconds in this enormous, exhibit-packed place. Kids love it here. Allow *at least* two to three hours. If you're with me or my pilot-in-training nephew Jason, you'll be here all day!

See map p. 184. Between Independence Avenue SW, Jefferson Drive and 4th and 7th streets. ☎ 202-357-2700; tours & reservations 202-633-2563; IMAX Theater & planetarium 877-932-4629 (202-633-4629); lectures & programs 202-633-2398. www.nasm.si.edu. *Metro: L'Enfant Plaza. From Smithsonian Museums exit, walk north 1 block on 7th Street SW, across Independence, and then turn right. Admission: Free. Fees for Imax Theater, Einstein Planetarium. Open: Daily 10 a.m.–5:30 p.m. Closed: Dec 25.*

National Air & Space Museum Steven F. Udvar-Hazy Center
Washington Dulles International Airport, Virginia

You can fit just so many flying machines into a building in the middle of Washington, so the Air and Space Museum decided to expand out into the countryside — in a corner of Washington Dulles International Airport, about 25 miles away, to be exact. The product of this expansion is the Steven F. Udvar-Hazy Center, an enormous structure that opened in late 2003 and nearly quintupled the museum's display space.

There's now plenty of room for such large artifacts as the Enola Gay, the B-29 Superfortress that dropped the first atomic bomb; the Space Shuttle Enterprise, the first shuttle, which was used in tests; and the SR-71 Blackbird reconnaissance plane, the fastest and highest-flying jet aircraft ever built with a top speed over 2,200 mph at altitudes exceeding 85,000 feet. More than 200 aircraft and 135 spacecraft now call Udvar-Hazy home. It also has an aircraft control tower and a giant-screen IMAX Theater.

Knowledgeable docents enrich the visitor's experience by explaining displays and answering questions. The overall organization of the exhibits — especially the signage, or lack thereof — needed improving during my last visit.

A shuttle bus carries visitors between the two facilities. If you plan to use it, buy your tickets as soon as you enter the first museum you visit to guard against sellouts.

You'll spend one to two hours here — more if you really study the exhibits.

See map p. 184. 14390 Air and Space Museum Parkway, Chantilly, VA (off U.S. 28, south of Washington Dulles International Airport main entrance). ☎ *202-357-2700; IMAX Theater 202-275-2371; shuttle bus tickets 202-633-4629.* www.nasm.si.edu/ museum/udvarhazy. *Parking on site. Shuttle bus runs between the two Air and Space Museum facilities, leaving each place at 9 and 10:30 a.m., noon, 1:30, 3, and 5 p.m. Admission: Free. Parking: $12. Shuttle bus round trip: $7, discounts for groups of four or more. Open: Daily 10 a.m.–5:30 p.m. Closed Dec 25.*

National Archives
Downtown

The Declaration of Independence, the Constitution of the United States, the Bill of Rights, a 1297 version of the Magna Carta, and numerous other historical documents reside in the Archives, which recently underwent an extensive renovation and continues to make its display spaces more viewer-friendly. Those familiar with the old Archives, where you squinted to see documentary treasures behind thick glass, will be especially pleased with the new Archives, where history is explained with multimedia presentations, interactive exhibits, and other state-of-the-art technologies. While tourists are most interested in the famous documents, the National Archives and Records Administration preserves *billions* of federal records. As at the Library of Congress, members of the public can conduct research here. Figure on spending at least a half hour viewing the main exhibits.

See map p. 184. 700 Pennsylvania Ave. NW (between 9th and 7th streets). ☎ *202-501-5000.* www.archives.gov. *Metro: Archives-Navy Memorial. Walk across Pennsylvania Avenue. Admission: Free. Open: Daily 10 a.m.–9 p.m. Memorial Day weekend through Labor Day, to 5:30 p.m. daily after Labor Day through March, to 7 p.m. April to Memorial Day weekend. Closed Dec 25.*

National Gallery of Art
National Mall

The National Gallery is two buildings — East and West — connected by an underground walkway. The Gallery owns more than 100,000 works from the Middle Ages to the present. Important works are on exhibit throughout both buildings, and the gallery always is mounting special exhibitions, some of international importance.

The West Building is a treasure chest of European art from the 13th into the early 20th centuries and American art from the 18th to the early 20th. Notable is the only painting by Leonardo da Vinci in the Western Hemisphere.

I.M. Pei designed the starkly modern East Building, which, appropriately, houses the gallery's 20th-century and contemporary art. An immense Calder mobile dominates the soaring central court. You also see works by Henri Matisse, Joan Miró, Pablo Picasso, and Jackson Pollock here.

In the Micro Gallery, near the Mall entrance to the West Building, you can use a computer terminal to identify the works you want to see and then print a map that shows you where they're located. In addition to the exhibits, the Gallery presents daily tours of the collection, a concert series, lectures, and films. The shops sell some of Washington's best souvenirs — reproductions of the gallery's masterworks in many forms. The Gallery even has a children's shop. You need at least two hours for a cursory taste of the National Gallery's treasures.

Families take note: Kids — as well as adults — enjoy the outdoor Sculpture Garden, across 7th Street from the West Building. It even has an ice-skating rink in the winter.

In addition to housing sculpture, the garden hosts live jazz performances 5 to 8 p.m. on Fridays from Memorial Day through Labor Day.

See map p. 184. Constitution Avenue NW between 3rd and 7th streets. ☎ *202-737-4215.* www.nga.gov. *Metro: Archives-Navy Memorial. Walk 1½ blocks east on Pennsylvania Avenue and then right on 6th Street. Admission: Free. Open: Mon–Sat 10 a.m.–5 p.m., Sun 11 a.m.–6 p.m. Memorial Day–Labor Day. Closed: Dec 25, Jan 1.*

National Museum of American History
National Mall

If the Smithsonian is the nation's attic — as it's often called — then this museum is the corner where the heirlooms are kept: three million pieces of vintage Americana.

A highlight here always has been the original Star-Spangled Banner, the giant flag that inspired the National Anthem during the battle for Fort McHenry in Baltimore in 1814. Since late 1998, the flag has been undergoing an extensive cleaning and preservation project, most of which has occurred in a museum laboratory where visitors can witness the work. The museum plans to put the flag back on display on Flag Day, June 14, 2006.

You also can take a look at first ladies' gowns, a Samuel Morse telegraph, an Alexander Graham Bell telephone, George Washington's military uniform, Abraham Lincoln's top hat, Muhammad Ali's boxing gloves, Duke Ellington's sheet music, Julia Child's kitchen . . . even Howdy Doody. And that's not even scratching the surface.

Exhibition halls let you concentrate on things (agriculture equipment, power machinery, musical instruments), while others explore social phenomena (First Ladies' roles in politics, American at war, sports in American life).

The hands-on history and science rooms are designed for youngsters (or oldsters) 5 and older. Kids conduct experiments in the science room. In the history room, they can climb on a high-wheel bicycle or transmit a telegram. When the rooms are busy, you're given timed tickets that let you in later in the day.

You need at least two hours here, and this museum is another one in which you could spend an entire day and then come back for more.

See map p. 184. Between Constitution Avenue NW, Madison Drive, and 12th and 14th streets. ☎ *202-633-1000.* http://americanhistory.si.edu. *Metro: Smithsonian. From the Mall exit, walk north across the Mall to the museum on your left. Admission: Free. Open: Daily Memorial Day weekend through Labor Day weekend 10 a.m.–6:30 p.m., till 5:30 p.m. rest of year. Closed Dec 25.*

National Museum of the American Indian
National Mall

The Smithsonian's newest museum has caused quite a stir. Not only has it proved to be enormously popular (even after getting your timed tickets, you'll battle big crowds), it's also been quite controversial. Leaders of Indian organizations were intimately involved in the planning of the museum, and critics complain that it's too heavy on Native American myths and too light on hard science.

You can decide for yourself by perusing the contents of the 250,000-square-foot facility which opened in fall 2004. The museum has acquired 10,000 years worth of artifacts from all the Americas — far more than can be displayed at one time. You also can shop at two museum stores and eat in the Mitsitam Café. ("Mitsitam" means "let's eat!" in the Delaware and Piscataway Indian language.) The cafe serves native foods from throughout the Western Hemisphere.

The museum's exterior architecture is designed to evoke a stone mass carved over time by wind and water.

Tickets are distributed free at the museum until the day's quota is filled. To assure entry, you can buy tickets in advance for $1.75 through the museum's Web site, at www.tickets.com, or by calling ☎ 866-400-6624.

See map p. 184. Independence Ave. SW at 4th St. ☎ 202-633-1000. www.nmai.si.edu. *Advance tickets: ☎ 866-400-6624;* www.tickets.com. *Metro: L'Enfant Plaza. From 7th Street/Maryland Avenue/Smithsonian Museums exit, walk 2 blocks northeast on Maryland, then right on Independence and left on 4th. Admission: Free. Advance tickets: $1.75. Open: Daily 10am–5:30pm. Closed Dec 25.*

National Museum of Natural History
National Mall

Kids dig dinosaurs, right? And bugs. And giant 3-D movies. So they gotta love this place! From the moment you walk in and encounter the huge African elephant in the Rotunda, your children will be squealing with delight. And the museum has plenty to interest the bigger folks, too. While the National Gallery may boast that it has artworks stretching back 800 years, artifacts at the Natural History Museum measure their years in *billions.*

When you're done ogling the elephant, pick up a museum map at the nearby information desk. Then consider buying tickets for the 90-foot-high IMAX theater. If you'd like to join a tour, they leave from the Rotunda, September through June, Monday through Friday at 10:30 a.m. and 1:30 p.m. No tours are scheduled in July or August.

Children go gaga at the insect zoo, where they can touch creepy crawly critters and slither through a model of a termite mound, and they love to explore Dinosaur Hall. Other highlights, for visitors of all ages, include the Hall of Geology, Gems, and Minerals — where you find a moon rock, the 45.5 carat Hope Diamond, and many other baubles — and the exhibit on Ice Age mammals, which includes a giant ground sloth, a saber-toothed cat, and an American mastodon.

Humans are part of natural history, too, so the museum contains exhibits about evolution and various human cultures. One may argue that a high mark in human evolution was the development of jazz, and the Natural History Museum displays that art from 6 to 10 p.m. every Friday when it presents live music, food, drinks, and IMAX films for a $10 cover.

Plan on spending two to four hours here (not counting jazz night).

See map p. 184. Between Constitution Avenue NW, Madison Drive, and 9th and 12th streets. ☎ 202-633-1000. www.mnh.si.edu. *Metro: Smithsonian. From the Mall exit, walk north across the Mall to the museum on your right. Admission: Free. Jazz night: $10 cover. IMAX Theater: $8 adult, $6.50 children 2–12 and seniors 55 and older. Open: Daily 10 a.m.–5:30 p.m., till 7:30 p.m. Memorial Day weekend through Labor Day weekend. Closed Dec 25.*

National Zoo
Upper Northwest

Hands-down *the* most kid-friendly place in town, the National Zoological Park (that's "zoo" to you) shows off more than 5,800 critters big and small around 163 acres of hills and valleys, with most of the animals in compounds designed to resemble their natural habitat. Be sure to wear your walking shoes and comfortable clothing, 'cause you'll be doing lots of hiking here.

Grab a map and schedule of events at the Education Building near the Connecticut Avenue entrance. Zookeepers conduct demonstrations and give talks throughout the park. It's always fun to be around at feeding time. And the elephants and the seals put on performances.

The zoo obtained a new pair of giant pandas from China in 2000, thus assuring that pandas will remain the park's most popular inhabitants. Come meet Mei Xiang and Tian Tian.

Here are other highlights.

Think Tank: Look in as scientists study animal thinking, including inquiring into orangutans' language. Researchers test apes' ability to use and understand word symbols.

The **Orangutan Transportation System:** The apes use an outdoor overhead cable to commute between buildings.

Amazonia: The Amazon River Basin's tropical habitat is recreated to accommodate macaws, sloths, monkeys, avocadoes, cocoa trees, piranhas, poison frogs, and others. It's a great place to warm up in the winter.

The **Reptile Discovery Center:** Lizards and turtles and snakes, oh my. Yucky for grownups, groovy for kids.

The **Pollinarium:** Hummingbirds and butterflies flit about, pollinating plants.

You can spend two to five hours at the zoo. Take it easy. Flop for a while under a tree. Bring some food or grab lunch or a snack at one of the — let's call them "adequate" — refreshment stands.

Despite its name, Woodley Park-Zoo is not the best Metrorail station to use on the way to the zoo. Here's what the locals do: On the way *to* the zoo, use the Cleveland Park station and then walk south on Connecticut Avenue from the East Side exit. When *leaving* the zoo, walk south on Connecticut to the Woodley Park-Zoo station. You walk a tad further, but more downhill and less uphill. The L1, 2, and 4 Metrobuses run from Dupont Circle all the way up Connecticut Avenue to Maryland, stopping at the zoo.

See map p. 191. 3001 Connecticut Ave. NW (north of Cathedral Avenue). ☎ *202-673-4821.* www.natzoo.si.edu. *Metro: Cleveland Park and Woodley Park-Zoo. Going to Zoo, walk down Connecticut from Cleveland Park. Leaving, walk down Connecticut to Woodley Park-Zoo. Admission: Free. Grounds open daily 6 a.m.–8 p.m. April–Oct, till 6 p.m. Nov–March. Buildings open daily 10 a.m.–6 p.m. April–Oct, till 4:30 p.m. Nov–March. Closed Dec 25.*

Supreme Court
Capitol Hill

The majestic Supreme Court building looks as if it has been standing since the birth of the republic — the Roman Republic, that is. In fact, the court was the last of the three government branches to get its own digs. The nine justices didn't move into this classic temple until 1935. Previously, they occupied a nook in the Capitol. This place is another one where a member of Congress — with lots of notice — can get you into a guided tour. Otherwise, you can wander around yourself, check out the exhibits on the ground floor, and attend a lecture in the courtroom.

By far, the best thing to do here is attend a one-hour argument. The topic can be front-page news around the world — defining freedom of speech, setting limits on the death penalty — or it can pick at arcane details of a commercial contract. No matter, it can be grand entertainment — with justices interrupting the lawyers, casting wry asides, or convulsing the courtroom in laughter with an on-the-money wisecrack. The court's right wing is most notable in the comment department. Antonin Scalia is the most humorous — or scathing, depending on the moment — justice. Clarence Thomas almost never opens his mouth.

The court hears arguments between 10 a.m. and 3 p.m. (sometimes only in the morning) on many Mondays, Tuesdays, and Wednesdays from October into late spring. Lines form on the plaza when arguments are being heard — one for listening to an entire argument, the other for taking a three-minute peek. Come early if the argument is big news. You can spend an hour here, more if you attend an argument or take a tour.

See map p. 184. 1 1st St. NE (at Maryland Avenue). ☎ *202-479-3030.* www.supreme courtus.gov. *Metro: Capitol South. Walk north 2½ blocks on 1st Street. Admission: Free. Open: Mon–Fri 9 a.m.–4:30 p.m. Closed federal holidays.*

Vietnam Veterans Memorial
National Mall

Depending on your age and your circumstances, this memorial can be the most emotional spot in Washington. The war divided the country, and the surviving soldiers came home feeling unappreciated. The private Vietnam Veterans Memorial Fund lobbied for a memorial on the Mall and raised money to build it. The organizers wanted to honor the soldiers and steer clear of the war's politics. Maya Lin — a Chinese-American Yale University student who grew up in Ohio — created the winning design.

Like the war, the simple memorial — a black granite V carved into the ground — was controversial. To appease those who wanted a more traditional, patriotic monument, a flagpole and a statute of three soldiers was placed near the wall. Later a statue of three female military nurses, tending to a wounded soldier, was added.

Nevertheless, it's the Wall — with its 58,245 names of the dead and missing — that commands the attention of visitors and eloquently commemorates the soldiers' sacrifice. Park rangers are available to discuss the memorial and help if you're looking for individual names. So, usually, are Vietnam-era vets. You can find a bookstore, restrooms, and concessions in the area. You can spend as little as 15 minutes here, more as you're moved.

See map p. 184. Bacon Drive at Constitution Avenue NW, just northeast of the Lincoln Memorial. ☎ *202-426-6841.* www.nps.gov/vive. *Metro: Foggy Bottom. Walk south 7 blocks on 23rd Street, then left 1@bf1/2 blocks on Constitution, and then right on Bacon. The Tourmobile stops at the nearby Lincoln Memorial, or you can take a taxi. Admission: Free. Open: Always.*

Washington Monument
National Mall

This towering marble obelisk is one of the most recognizable sights in America. The view from the top is the most spectacular in Washington. You can get free time-specific tickets for riding the elevator to the top on the day of your visit at the monument's ticket kiosk near 15th Street and Madison Drive. They're usually gone before noon, so arrive early. You can buy tickets in advance by calling ☎ **800-967-2283** or on the Internet at www.reservations.nps.gov. The charge is $1.50 per ticket, plus 50 cents per order.

The ride to the top takes just 70 seconds. You can stare out the windows as long as you like. You descend at a slower speed so that you can view the monument's interior. The grounds contain exhibits, a bookstore, restrooms, and concessions. On summer evenings, military bands perform here, and the monument provides a gleaming exclamation point for the 4th of July fireworks.

You pass through security screening to enter the monument. Food, drinks, and large bags are prohibited. If you wear a pacemaker or other medical device that a magnetometer may affect, tell a ranger so that you can go through alternative screening. Figure on a 30-minute visit, not counting time in line.

 The Washington Monument has undergone a great deal of security enhancement, some of which turned this once-pristine lawn into a concrete-barrier farm. The work got so intense in the fall of 2004 that the monument was closed, with reopening scheduled for spring 2005.

See map p. 184. Between Constitution Avenue NW, Independence Avenue SW, and 15th and 17th streets. ☎ *202-426-6841; advance tickets 800-967-2283.* www.nps.gov/wash; *advance tickets* www.reservations.nps.gov. *Metro: Smithsonian.*

From the Mall exit, walk west on Jefferson Drive 2 long blocks. Admission: Free. Fee for advance tickets: $1.50 per ticket, plus 50 cents per order. Open: Daily 9 a.m.–4:45 p.m.; ticket kiosk 8 a.m.–4:30 p.m. or when tickets run out. Closed Dec 25.

White House
Downtown

Is it just me, or does everybody wonder why, if security can screen passengers to get on airplanes, they can't screen visitors for White House tours? As I write this book, things are looser than during the first couple years after 9/11. But you still can't just walk up to the White House gate and get into a tour line. You must form a group of at least ten people and make a reservation — up to six months ahead — through a senator or representative. Check by Internet or phone to see whether things improve for your visit.

If you do get in, you'll see just a fraction of the president's mansion, which is not only the president's home and office but also work space for the highest ranking presidential aides and the White House press corps. The best time to visit is when the place is decorated wonderfully for Christmas.

If you can't get in, you'll have to content yourself with strolling around the grounds, gazing through the fence, and marveling at the bizarre architecture of the Old Executive Office Building next door. You also can visit the **White House Visitor Center,** which, strangely enough, is located in the Great Hall of the Commerce Department building, on Pennsylvania Avenue between 14th and 15th streets. There, you find ranger talks, exhibits, a gift shop, and restrooms.

See map p. 184. 1600 Pennsylvania Ave. NW (between 15th and 17th streets). ☎ 202-456-7041. www.whitehouse.gov/history/tours. Metro: McPherson Square. From the Vermont Avenue-White House exit, walk 1 block south on Vermont and then across Lafayette Square. It's that big white house in front of you. Admission: Free for groups of at least ten who obtain tickets from a member of Congress. Tours: Tues–Sat 7:30 a.m.–12:30 p.m. Closed federal holidays.

See map p. 184. Visitor Center: 1450 Pennsylvania Ave. NW (between 14th and 15th streets). ☎ 202-208-1631. www.nps.gov/whho. Metro: Federal Triangle. Walk half block north on 12th Street and then go left on Pennsylvania 2½ blocks. Keep the parks on your right, and the visitor center will show up on your left. Admission: Free. Open: Daily 7:30 a.m.–4 p.m. Closed Thanksgiving, Dec 25, Jan. 1.

World War II Memorial
National Mall

Like the Mall's newest museum (the National Museum of the American Indian), the newest memorial arrived awash in controversy. First was the controversy over why it took so long to erect this memorial to the troops who fought America's biggest war — even after memorials to the later Korean and Vietnam conflicts were dedicated. It was opened finally on April 29, 2004, and was dedicated on Memorial Day weekend May 29.

Second was the controversy over the location, smack dab in the middle of the Mall between the long-standing **Lincoln Memorial** and the **Washington Monument.** Critics objected that it would disrupt the hallowed view from Lincoln's seat to the **Capitol** dome, which had been interrupted only by Washington's thin obelisk. Finally was the controversy over the design. After Maya Lin's spare plan for the **Vietnam Veterans Memorial** had been emulated in later memorials all around the country, the World War II Memorial came in big and bulky and ornate. There's a tall pillar with a wreath for each state and territory that fought in the war, a free-standing arch for each of the major theaters of the war, fountains, and a reflecting pool. A field of 4,000 gold stars represents the more than 400,000 U.S. lives lost in the conflict.

The beauty of America, of course, is that each visitor can decide for himself. You can check the view from the Lincoln Monument's steps. You can trek from Lincoln to Washington, pausing first to study the new memorial up close. As with the Vietnam memorial, the time you choose to spend here depends to a great extent on your personal relationship with this war. Plan on at least 15 to 30 minutes.

See map p. 184. 17th Street, between Constitution and Independence Avenues. ☎ *202-426-6841.* www.nps.gov/nwwm. *Metro: Smithsonian. From the Independence Avenue exit, walk west to 17th, then turn right. Admission: Free. Open: Always.*

Finding More Cool Things to See and Do

As a world capital — arguably *the world's capital* — Washington really does have something to interest everyone, or at least *nearly* everyone. In this section, I identify places of particular appeal to kids, historians, art aficionados, gardeners, and architecture buffs.

Especially for kids

If you have children with you, you should make a point to check out the following sights, perfectly suited for young visitors. Washington is both a fun and important destination for the younger members of the family, with most of the national monuments and museums having a child-focused aspect. Children love several of Washington's top sights. In the preceding section, be sure to check out the **Bureau of Engraving and Printing,** the **National Air and Space Museum,** the **National Museum of American History,** the **National Museum of Natural History,** and, of course, the **National Zoo.** Here are some more spots that are particularly attractive to kids — and, luckily, to their parents as well.

FBI
Downtown

The one-hour FBI tour is one of the most popular in Washington among children — especially little boys who like things that go BANG. The tour covers such topics as the Ten Most Wanted list, famous FBI cases, and how the FBI operates. Participants walk through a crime laboratory; don't be surprised to see technicians analyzing hair, fibers, and blood for clues. Usually the tour has a bang-up finish with a demonstration at the firing range, which can be scary for some of the youngest children.

The best way to get into this tour is to ask your representative or senator to make a reservation for you at least three months before your visit. Reservations aren't required, but waits can reach two hours, and high demand can cause the later tours to fill up early.

If you have a reservation, plan on arriving at least 15 minutes early. Be prepared to pass through a security check.

The tour was suspended for building renovations in 2004 and scheduled to resume during 2005. To check whether you can tour, visit the FBI Web site (www.fbi.gov/aboutus/tour/tour.htm) or phone ☎ **202-324-3447.**

See map p. 208. 935 Pennsylvania Ave. NW. Tour entrance on E Street at 9th Street. ☎ *202-324-3447.* www.fbi.gov/aboutus/tour/tour.htm. *Metro: Archives-Navy Memorial. Walk west on Pennsylvania and then right on 9th 1 block to E. Admission: Free. Previously, tours were offered Mon–Fri 8:45 a.m.–4:15 p.m. Closed federal holidays.*

National Aquarium
Downtown

Locals bring their tadpoles here long before they're ready for the heavy-duty museums. At the National Aquarium, hidden in the Commerce Department building, youngsters can watch sharks, eels, and koi (Japanese carp) get along swimmingly. (It's lucky for the rest of the fish that a separate tank holds the piranhas.) Although this aquarium doesn't boast the latest in technological advances, you can find more than 200 species of aquatic life here, including alligators. Kids can dip their hands into the touch tank and pet a horseshoe crab. Feeding time is 2 p.m. Monday through Saturday. A visit here sets you back a half-hour or more.

See map p. 208. 14th Street NW between Constitution and Pennsylvania avenues, lower level of Commerce Department building. ☎ *202-482-2825.* national aquarium.com. *Metro: Federal Triangle. Walk half block north on 12th Street, left on Pennsylvania 2 blocks, and then left on 14th. Admission: $5, seniors and military personnel $4, children 2–10 $2, younger than 2 free. Open: Daily 9 a.m.–5 p.m.; last admission 4:30 p.m. Closed Thanksgiving, Dec 25.*

National Geographic Society's Explorers Hall
Downtown

The National Geographic Society explores the universe, so you can encounter exhibits on just about anything in Explorers Hall. Kids can be enthralled by some of the changing topics. As I'm writing this book, for example, visitors can see a display of photographs, videos, and artifacts from Africa and play with interactive exhibits about making maps. Call or check the Web site to find out what's going on before you decide to attend.

While you're here, you also can check out the National Geographic Store's stock of nature books, photography, globes, maps, and back issues of the magazine. Plan on spending at least an hour.

See map p. 208. 17th and M streets NW. ☎ **202-857-7588.** www.national geographic.com/explorer. *Metro: Farragut North. From L Street exit, walk east on L 1 block and then go left at 17th. Admission: Free. Open: Mon–Sat 9 a.m.–5 p.m., Sun 10 a.m.–5 p.m. Closed Dec 25. Open Mon–Sat and holidays 9 a.m.–5 p.m., Sun 10 a.m.–5 p.m. Closed Dec 25.*

National Postal Museum
Capitol Hill

This museum, dedicated to the history of stamps and the postal service, delivers, by extension, a large slice of American history. Interactive exhibits make it a hit with children. Tour a Southern Railway mail car, look up at mail planes, and discover the real story of the Pony Express. The museum is located in the old City Post Office Building, which operated from 1914 through 1986. Plan on spending an hour or more.

See map p. 208. 2 Massachusetts Ave. NE, west of Union Station. ☎ **202-633-5555.** www.postalmuseum.si.edu. *Metro: Union Station. From Union Station Shops/Massachusetts Avenue exit, walk across 1st Street NE. Admission: Free. Open: Daily 10 a.m.–5:30 p.m. Closed Dec 25.*

Especially for teens

I have it on good authority, from teenagers who wish to remain anonymous, that the zoo is a cool place for teens to hang out. So is the Air and Space Museum (see "The Top Attractions from A to Z," at the beginning of this chapter, for both listings). And the FBI is a cool tour (see "Especially for kids"). Here are some other places where local teenagers like to go and that visiting teens likely would enjoy as well.

International Spy Museum
Downtown

The interactive exhibits and gee-whiz spyware and spylore grab young folks' attention and that of many older visitors as well. This museum has been very popular, so you're advised to purchase your time-specific tickets in advance. That's right, I said "purchase." This spot is a privately operated enterprise and one of the few museums in town where you have to pay to enter.

Because of the subject matter here — violence, deception, terrorism — the museum recommends that visitors be at least 12 years old, even though discounted tickets are available for children ages 3 to 11.

Once inside, you encounter the latest in interactive museum technology, along with old and new spy tools. You can see a Revolutionary War letter written by George Washington to authorize establishment of a spy network in New York in 1777. You can enter a mockup of an intelligence agency's

More Cool Things to See and Do

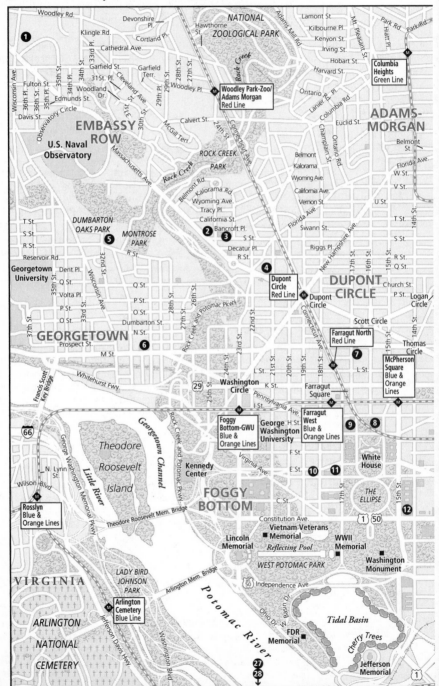

Woodley Rd.
Devonshire Pl.
Klingle Rd.
Cortland Pl.
Cathedral Ave.
NATIONAL
ZOOLOGICAL PARK
Hawthorne St.
Lamont St.
Kilbourne Pl.
Kenyon St.
Irving St.
Hobart St.
Harvard St.
Mt. Pleasant St.
Park Rd.
Hiatt Pl.
Park Rd.

Columbia
Heights
Green Line

Garfield St.
Garfield Terr.
31St. Pl.
Woodland Dr.
Cleveland Ave.
Woodley Pl.
Woodley Rd.
Calvert St.
McGill Terr.
Rock Creek

Woodley Park-Zoo/
Adams Morgan
Red Line

Ontario Rd. Pl.
Lanier Pl.
Columbia Rd.
Euclid St.

ADAMS-
MORGAN

Wisconsin Ave.
Fulton St.
Woodland
Edmunds St.
Davis St.
Observatory Circle

EMBASSY
ROW
U.S. Naval
Observatory
Massachusetts Ave.

ROCK CREEK
PARK

Belmont
Kalorama
Wyoming Ave.
California Ave.
Vernon St.
Belmont
Florida Ave.
W. St.
V St.

Rock Creek
Belmont Rd.
Kalorama Rd.
Wyoming Ave.
Tracy Pl.
California St.
Bancroft Pl.

Florida Ave.
Swann St.
U St.
T St.
S St.

DUMBARTON
OAKS PARK
MONTROSE
PARK
R St.

Decatur Pl.
R St.

Riggs Pl.
New Hampshire Ave.
Q St.
R St.
S St.

Georgetown
University
Dent Pl.
Q St.
Volta Pl.
P St.
O St.
Dumbarton St.
N St.

Dupont
Circle
Red Line
Dupont
Circle

DUPONT
CIRCLE
Church St.
P St.
Logan
Circle

GEORGETOWN
Prospect St.
M St.

Scott Circle
Thomas
Circle

Farragut North
Red Line

McPherson
Square
Blue &
Orange
Lines

Whitehurst Fwy.
Washington
Circle
Pennsylvania Ave.
Farragut
Square

Francis Scott
Key Bridge

Foggy
Bottom-GWU
Blue &
Orange
Lines
George
Washington
University

Farragut
West
Blue &
Orange Lines

White
House

Theodore
Roosevelt
Island

Kennedy
Center

FOGGY
BOTTOM

THE
ELLIPSE

Rosslyn
Blue &
Orange Lines

Constitution Ave.
Vietnam Veterans
Memorial
Reflecting Pool
Lincoln
Memorial
WWII
Memorial
Washington
Monument

LADY BIRD
JOHNSON
PARK

WEST POTOMAC PARK

VIRGINIA

Arlington
Cemetery
Blue Line

Independence Ave.

ARLINGTON
NATIONAL
CEMETERY

Potomac River
FDR
Memorial

Tidal Basin
Cherry Trees
Jefferson
Memorial

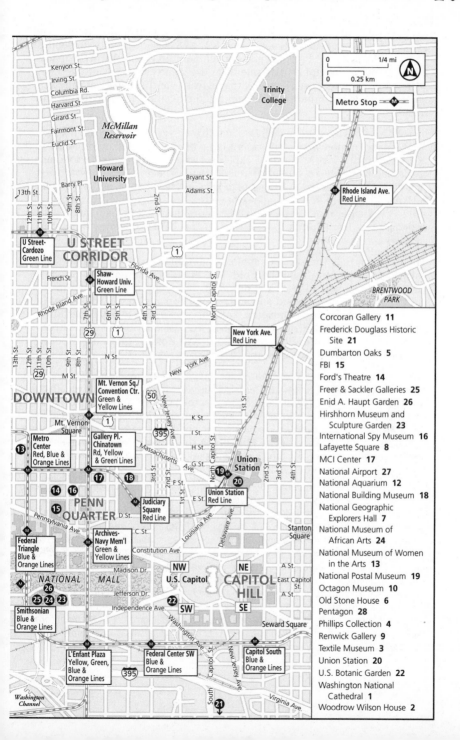

21st-century operations center, which displays information about the latest developments in espionage. Among the 68,000-square-foot museum's many artifacts are an Enigma cipher machine from World War II Germany, a U.S. Army M-209 cipher machine from the same era, a Soviet overcoat with a buttonhole camera, a CIA disguise kit, and (shades of Maxwell Smart!) a shoe with microphone and radio transmitter concealed in the heel.

Instruments of violence, as well as of intelligence-gathering, are on display. A U.S.-made bomb was disguised as a lump of coal to be planted in enemy coal bins during World War II; it exploded when shoveled into a locomotive's engine, a ship's boiler, or a factory's furnace. A double-barreled poison-gas gun enabled KGB agents to kill silently with a spray of cyanide. Another KGB weapon — a single-shot pistol — was disguised as a lipstick tube. On a lighter note, some exhibits explore the public's fascination with espionage — from Junior G-Man toys in the 1930s to James Bond and Austin Powers movies today.

The museum tells the story of spying from Biblical times to the present, with a heavy emphasis on the Cold War. Visitors are invited to adopt a secret identity and to try to maintain it under interrogation, to break codes, to identify disguised spies, to eavesdrop, and to be the target of eavesdroppers. There's a museum store, of course, and two eateries operated by the folks who run the popular Red Sage Grill and the Border Cafe — **Spy City Cafe,** for quick meals, and **Zola,** a full-scale Modern American restaurant. See Chapter 10 for listing information.

Peter Earnest (what a great name for a spy!), the museum's executive director, spent 36 years with the CIA. His advisory board includes two former CIA directors, two former CIA disguise chiefs, and a retired KGB general. The museum is located in five restored buildings, one of which once housed a Communist Party district headquarters. It's within easy eavesdropping distance of the FBI across the intersection. The average visitor spends two hours with the permanent exhibits, an hour and a quarter in the special exhibits.

See map p. 208. 800 F Street NW (between 8th and 9th streets). ☎ ***866-779-6873*** *or 202-393-7798.* www.spymuseum.org. *Metro: Gallery Place-Chinatown. From 9th and G Streets exit, walk 1 block south on 9th, cross F, and then turn left on F. Admission to permanent exhibits: $13, children 5–11 $10, under 4 free, seniors 65 and older, active duty military personnel, intelligence workers, and college students $12. Admission to special exhibits: $5, children 5–11 $3, under 4 free, seniors 65 and older, active duty military personnel, intelligence workers, and college students $4. Combined admisison: $17 children 5–11 $12, under 4 free, seniors 65 and older, active duty military personnel, intelligence workers, and college students $16. Open: Daily 10 a.m.–8 p.m. April–Oct, 10 a.m.–5 p.m. Nov–March. Last admission to permanent exhibits 2 hours before closing. Last admission to special exhibits 1¼ hours before closing. Last admission on combination tickets to all exhibits 3¾ hours before closing. Closed Thanksgiving, Dec 25, Jan1.*

Georgetown

Teens have been making Georgetown their own since the days of pegged pants and poodle skirts. Shops, restaurants, and the overall scene entertain teenagers in this historic neighborhood, which is centered on the intersection of Wisconsin Avenue and M Street NW. You can eye a wide variety of people for people-watching. And — teens can be cruel — some youngsters get great joy from observing the frustration of drivers inching along in Georgetown's always-gummed-up traffic.

Commander Salamander (1420 Wisconsin Ave.), **Urban Outfitters** (3111 M St.), and **Up Against the Wall** (3219 M St.) are among the shops that cater to younger shoppers. The Commander ("Nobody calls it the Commander!" my teenager daughter admonishes me) offers punk-style clothing, colored wigs, and off-the-wall gifts — think "devil ducks," red rubber duckies with devil's horns. The Outfitters stock slightly offbeat clothing and accoutrements in a wide price range — fuzzy lamps (why not?) for decorating a teen's bedroom and lots of CD accessories. The Wall folks may be distinguished primarily by what's free — lots of loud music. Check out **Deja Blue** (3005 M St.) for used blue jeans and **Beyond Comics** (1419 Wisconsin Ave.) for comic books and related toys, dolls, T-shirts, and other such stuff. If your kids are suffering shopping-mall withdrawal, they can find scores of chain stores in **Georgetown Park** (3222 M St.). I won't tell them about **Jinx Proof Tattoos and Piercing Parlor** (3281 M St.) or **Mrs. Natalie** the palm reader (1500 Wisconsin Ave.).

A kajillion restaurants are in Georgetown, give or take a few bazillion, many of them inexpensive and many ideal for carryout food. Before they actually entered college, Julie and her chums liked to sample college life by getting sandwiches at **Wisemiller's Grocery & Deli** (1236½ 36th St.), near the Georgetown University campus and then finding a seat on a convenient wall or set of steps or heading to the little park south of M near 34th. **Dean & Deluca** (3276 M St.) is a great place for gourmet carryout, and it has outdoor tables.

Georgetown is especially well-stocked with ice cream parlors. **Isee Icy** (1560 Wisconsin Ave. at Q Street) scoops Argentinean ice cream. **Thomas Sweet** (3214 P St. east of Wisconsin) is locally grown. If your kids are into national brands, Georgetown invites them to **Ben & Jerry's** (3135 M St.) or **Häagen-Dazs** (3120 M St.).

The 30-series **Metrobuses** run along Pennsylvania Avenue, M Street, and Wisconsin Avenue. **Georgetown Connection** shuttle buses connect with the Dupont Circle, Foggy Bottom-George Washington University, and Rosslyn Metrorail stations. Energetic teens have no trouble walking from the Foggy Bottom station, north on 23rd Street to Washington Circle, left around circle to Pennsylvania Avenue, and then left on Pennsylvania to M.

Dupont Circle

Like Georgetown, Dupont Circle has all the necessities for people-watching, eating, and shopping. The park in the circle is a haven for chess players, recuperating bicycle messengers, and assorted other characters.

Beadazzled (1507 Connecticut Ave.) sells beads (you couldn't guess?) from $1 to $100 a piece, plus already-made jewelry and crafts. **Kramerbooks & Afterwords** (1517 Connecticut Ave.) is a bookstore where you can eat, drink, listen to music, and . . . well . . . browse for books. **Pizzeria Paradiso** (2029 P St.) is one of the two best pizza parlors in the city and also makes sandwiches to go. Look at three doorways, and one probably leads into a place to eat. Dupont Circle has its own Metrorail Station, so it's really easy to get to.

Union Station

Young people are drawn to Union Station like iron filings to a magnet. Come here any afternoon or weekend if you don't believe me. Who'd have thought that a train station would morph into an upscale mall and entertainment center? Union Station has all the right stuff that young people crave: a nine-screen movie theater complex, more than 50 retailers, and a lower-level food court with dozens of vendors. You can eat in a restaurant or in the brightly decorated food court. Or you can carry your food outside to the fountain. A Metro stop is right in the basement.

Sports

If your teens are sports buffs, they'll find Washington to be one of the best professional sports towns in the country. We've got the NFL **Redskins,** the NBA **Wizards,** the NHL **Capitals,** the WNBA **Mystics,** and the Major League Soccer **D.C. United. Georgetown University** plays big-time college basketball. **The University of Maryland,** in suburban College Park, has been fielding nationally ranked basketball and football teams recently. And, as I write this book, it looks like **Major League Baseball** is going to send the city a team (the hapless Montreal Expos, to be named something like the Senators, the Nationals, or maybe the Grays) after a three-decade absence. Negotiations over the size of D.C.'s bribe — say, a publicly built ballpark — were in progress.

MCI Center (601 F St. NW) is a superb arena and home to the Wizards, Mystics, Capitals (when the NHL is actually playing hockey), and some Georgetown games.

RFK Stadium (2400 East Capitol St.) is a beautiful setting for soccer and baseball. A new soccer stadium is supposed to be built along with the new baseball field. A Metrorail station is practically in MCI Center's basement, and RFK has a station, too. The Redskins' **FedEx Field** (1600 FedEx Way, Landover, MD) is not easily accessible, but 'Skins tickets are nearly impossible to get anyway.

Music

MCI Center and RFK Stadium also are venues for big-time pop-music concerts, as are other stages around town. To keep up with who's performing, check the ads and listings in *The Washington Post* — particularly the Friday "Weekend" section — as well as *The Post*'s online entertainment guide (http://eg.washingtonpost.com).

Especially for history buffs

Deciding which attractions fall into this category is a tough call, because history infuses everything here. When you're done with the monuments, memorials, and federal buildings I cite earlier in this chapter, take a look at these attractions:

Ford's Theatre & Peterson House
Downtown

Closed for more than a century after President Lincoln was assassinated here on April 14, 1865, Ford's Theatre became a showcase for plays and concerts again in 1968. You can attend a performance here. And you can tour the scene, viewing the presidential box as it looked the night John Wilkes Booth shot the president during a performance of *Our American Cousin.*

In the basement, the **Lincoln Museum** displays the clothing Lincoln was wearing that night, the .44 caliber Derringer that Booth used, and other memorabilia associated with Lincoln and the assassination. Across the street, you can visit the place where Lincoln died, the Petersen House, 516 10th St. NW. You can spend about an hour touring the two locations.

See map p. 208. 511 10th St. NW (between E and F streets). ☎ *202-426-6924.* www.nps.gov/foth. *Performance information: 202-347-4833;* www.fords theatre.org. *Metro: Metro Center. From 11th Street exit, walk 1 block south on 11th, go left on F, and then right on 10th. Admission: Free. Fee for performances. Open: Daily 9 a.m.–5 p.m., except Dec 25. Theater closed during performances, rehearsals, and work on set.*

Frederick Douglass National Historic Site
Anacostia

This 21-room house was home to Frederick Douglass, the 19th-century abolitionist and civil rights leader, who was born a slave and eventually served as a District of Columbia Council member, D.C.'s U.S. marshal, and U.S. minister to Haiti. The home and visitor center feature original furnishings and tell the story of Douglass' remarkable life. Be sure to see the short film for an overview of his life. A bookstore and restrooms are on site. Space is limited, so call ahead to find the best time to visit and to make a reservation. Plan to spend an hour here.

See map p. 208. 1411 W St. SE at 14th Street. ☎ *800-426-5961.* www.nps.gov/frdo. *Take a taxi. Or take Tourmobile's Frederick Douglass tour (*☎ *202-554-5100;* www.tourmobile.com.*) Admission: $2. Open: April 15–Oct 15 9 a.m.–5 p.m., Oct. 16–April 14 9 a.m.–4 p.m. Closed Jan 1, Thanksgiving, Dec 25.*

Old Stone House
Georgetown

In the heart of Georgetown — and easy to pass given its diminutive size — is Washington's oldest house. Built in 1765, it predates the United States and the District of Columbia. It's furnished as it was when Georgetown was a thriving tobacco port. Ask the ranger to tell you about the place. Most visitors are struck by the interior space, or lack thereof. Be sure to look out back at the lovely garden, abloom from April to November. You're invited to bring lunch and join picnickers who brown-bag it on the lawn. Plan to spend 15 minutes here, more if you do lunch.

See map p. 208. 3051 M St. NW (between 30th and 31st streets). ☎ *202-426-6851.* www.nps.gov/olst. *Take Georgetown Connection shuttle bus from Dupont Circle or Rosslyn Metrorail station to M and 30th or Thomas Jefferson Street or ride 30-series Metrobus. Admission: Free. Open: Daily 9 a.m.–5 p.m., except Dec 25.*

The Pentagon
Virginia

Shortly after the terrorist attacks of Sept. 11, 2001, on weekends, when most of the building's 23,000 employees stay home, members of the public were allowed to drive into a section of the Pentagon parking lots and walk to a grassy rise that overlooks the side of the building that was struck by American Airlines Flight 77. The area became a spontaneous memorial, built by visitors leaving flowers, flags, notes, and other items of tribute. My family went several times and found it quite moving.

Built during the early years of World War II to be U.S. military headquarters, this five-sided building usually is described in terms of its enormous size: 3.7 million square feet of floor space, 100,000 miles of telephone cable, and the like. Unfortunately, the once-popular Pentagon tour was a casualty of the 9/11 attacks. As I write this book, tours are available to some groups, but not to individuals. When you visit Washington, you can call to find out whether tours for the general public have resumed or if you happen to be in a group that qualifies.

See map p. 208. Arlington, Virginia. ☎ *703-697-1776.* dod.mil/pubs/pentagon. *Metro: Pentagon. From the Pentagon exit, take the escalator up. Admission: Free. At press time, closed to the general public.*

Woodrow Wilson House
North of Dupont Circle

After his term ended in 1921, Woodrow Wilson, America's 28th president, lived the last three years of his life in this Georgian Revival home, which was built in 1915. Many of the gifts Wilson received from world leaders — as well as his inaugural Bible, specs, and a shell casing from World War I — are among the artifacts displayed in the house. According to the docents, the residence/museum looks very much as it did when Wilson lived in it. Touring the place properly takes about an hour.

See map p. 208. 2340 S St. NW. (between 23rd and 24th streets). ☎ *202-387-4062. www.woodrowwilsonhouse.org. Metro: Dupont Circle. From the Q Street exit, walk 2 blocks west on Q, right on Massachusetts Avenue 4 blocks, right on 24th St. 1 block, and then right on S. (Note: It's uphill.) Or take an N-series Metrobus up Massachusetts. Or take a taxi. Admission $5, seniors $4, students $2.50 students, children under 7 free. Open Tues–Sun 10 a.m.–4 p.m. Closed major holidays.*

Especially for art lovers

Art galleries paint many D.C. neighborhoods, but the biggest concentration is in **Georgetown,** around 7th Street NW in the **Penn Quarter** neighborhood, **Downtown,** and on the **National Mall.** For the Georgetown galleries, take the Metro to Foggy Bottom, walk north to Pennsylvania Avenue, and then walk to where Pennsylvania ends at M Street. You also can take the Georgetown Connection shuttle bus from the Foggy Bottom, Dupont Circle, or Rosslyn Metrorail station. Many galleries are on M and along Wisconsin Avenue between M and R streets. To reach the 7th Street galleries, between D and G streets, take the Metro to the Archives-Navy Memorial station and walk north on 7th.

The top gallery in town, of course, is the National Gallery, which I tell you about in the first section of this chapter. Here are the other main galleries and museums:

Corcoran Gallery
Downtown

You can find Washington's first art museum — and D.C.'s largest private art museum — just a block from the White House. The Corcoran was founded in 1869 "for the purpose of encouraging the American genius." Its collection traces America's artistic development from colonial times to the present. It also contains a significant number of European works. My teenage daughter likes to come here to see the works of students in the Corcoran College of Art and Design. The Corcoran has a cafe, a noteworthy museum shop, and an auditorium, which hosts concerts, films, and other activities. Tours of the collection leave from the information desk daily at noon except Tuesday, plus 7:30 p.m. Thursday, and 2:30 p.m. Saturday and Sunday. Figure on spending about an hour here.

See map p. 208. 500 17th St. NW (between New York Avenue and E Street). ☎ *202-639-1700. www.corcoran.org. Metro: Farragut West. From the 17th Street exit, walk 5 blocks south on 17th. Admission: $6.75, seniors $4.75, students 12–18 $3, under 12 free, families with children under 18 $12, free for everyone Mon (donations accepted). Open: Wed–Mon 10 a.m.–5 p.m., Thurs until 9 p.m. Closed Thanksgiving, Dec 25, and Jan 1.*

Freer and Sackler Galleries of Art
National Mall

Although these neighboring galleries store and display their collections in separate buildings, they're connected by underground exhibition space and together comprise the Smithsonian's museum of Asian art. The Freer also contains the world's finest collection of Whistlers (James McNeill Whistler, that is). If you've never seen the Peacock Room, that alone is reason to visit the Freer. Take the guided tour (daily 11:30 a.m. except Wednesday and July 4) to discover the fascinating history behind Whistler's stunning dining room, created for a London town house and moved to the Mall after the owner's death.

The Freer houses a world-renowned collection of art from Asia and the Near East. Highlights include Chinese paintings, Japanese folding screens, Korean ceramics, Buddhist sculpture, and Indian and Persian manuscripts. The Sackler's highlights include early Chinese bronzes and jades, Chinese paintings and lacquerware, ancient Near Eastern ceramics and metalware, South and Southeast Asian sculpture, and Islamic arts. Budget at least a half-hour for each museum.

The Freer's auditorium hosts music, dance, film, lectures, and dramatic presentation relating to the collections.

See map p. 208. Between the Smithsonian Castle, Independence Avenue and 12th Street. ☎ *202-357-4880.* www.asia.si.edu. *Metro: Smithsonian. From The Mall exit, walk southeast across Jefferson Drive. Admission: Free. Open: Daily 10 a.m.–5:30 p.m., Thurs till 8 p.m. in summer. Closed Dec 25.*

Hirshhorn Museum and Sculpture Garden
National Mall

I get a charge out of standing directly beneath Kenneth Snelson's 60-foot-high "Needle Tower," just outside the Hirshhorn, and looking straight up. I must admit that much abstract and contemporary art is not to my taste. But some of it turns me on, and this aluminum-and-steel, TV-tower-like structure is one example.

If modern and contemporary art is *your* thing, then the Hirshhorn is your museum. All the top guns are here: Benton, Christo, Close, Gorky, Miró, O'Keeffe, Warhol, Bacon, de Kooning, Matisse . . . you get the — uh — picture. And, of course, the museum has many special exhibits. Across Jefferson Drive is the sunken Sculpture Garden, with more than 60 works by Rodin, Moore, Calder, and others (a particularly neat place in winter when the statues are draped in snow).

You can catch a museum tour daily at noon, plus 2 p.m. weekends. September through May there also are tours at 10:30 a.m. weekdays. Sculpture Garden tours are offered (weather permitting) Monday through Saturday in summer at 10:30 a.m., and in May, September, and October Monday through Saturday at 12:15 p.m. Inquire at the information desk about tours of special exhibitions. No tours are given on holidays

See map p. 208. Independence Avenue at 7th Street SW. ☎ *202-633-4674.* hirshhorn.si.edu. *Metro: L'Enfant Plaza. From Smithsonian Museums exit, walk north 1 block on 7th and cross Independence. Admission: Free. Open: Daily 10 a.m.–5:30 p.m. Plaza: 7:30 a.m.–5:30 p.m.; Sculpture Garden 7:30 a.m.–dusk. Closed Dec 25.*

National Museum of African Art
National Mall

Art from throughout Africa — traditional and contemporary — is the focus of this Smithsonian museum. In addition to mounting exhibits, the museum serves as a research and reference facility, with photo archives and a library. Its permanent exhibits include "The Art of the Personal Object," which explores the artistic content of everyday things, and "Ceramics," which shows traditional and modern works.

See map p. 208. 950 Independence Ave. SW (midway between 7th and 12th streets) ☎ *202-357-4600.* www.nmafa.si.edu. *Metro: Smithsonian. From Independence Avenue exit, cross Independence and walk to the right. Admission: Free. Open: Daily 10 a.m.–5:30 p.m., except Dec 25.*

National Museum of Women in the Arts
Downtown

Housed in a landmark Downtown building that once served as a Masonic Temple, the privately managed National Museum of Women in the Arts has compiled a collection of 2,700 works by more than 800 artists since Wilhelmina Cole Holladay and Wallace F. Holladay began compiling their personal collection in the 1960s. That collection comprised the core of the museum when it was incorporated in 1981 and moved into its current quarters in 1987. The museum seeks to acquire the works of women artists of all periods and all nationalities.

See map p. 208. 1250 New York Avenue NW (at 13th Street). ☎ *800-222-7270, 202-783-5000.* www.nmwa.org. *Metro: Metro Center. From 13th Street exit, walk 2 blocks north on 13th. Admission: $5, seniors 60 and older and students with ID $3, children 18 and younger free. Free for everyone first Sun and Wed of every month. Open: Mon–Sat 10 a.m.–5 p.m., Sun noon–5 p.m. Closed Thanksgiving, Dec 25, Jan 1.*

Phillips Collection
Dupont Circle

In the former home of collector and benefactor Duncan Phillips, you find the works of modern artists and of the earlier artists who influenced them. The Phillips bills itself as America's first museum of modern art, but it also believes in showing "the continuum of art and artists influencing their successors through the centuries." Duncan Phillips collected El Greco, for example, because he was the "first impassioned expressionist."

The Phillips is noted for impressionist and post-impressionist paintings. You find Renoir's *Luncheon of the Boating Party* here, as well as works by such other notable artists as van Gogh, Monet, Degas, Gauguin, Cézanne, Rothko, Matisse, de Kooning, Hopper, and O'Keeffe. The museum has a shop, cafe, and Sunday concerts at 5 p.m. September through May.

The Phillips sent approximately 50 of its European masterpieces on tour during a remodeling project. The works — including the *Boating Party* — were scheduled to return home in summer 2005.

See map p. 208. 1600 21st St. NW (at Q Street). ☎ *202-387-2151.* www.phillips collection.org. *Metro: Dupont Circle. From Q Street exit, walk 1 block west on Q. Admission charged on weekends and for special exhibitions: $13, seniors over 65 and students $11, children 18 and younger free. Donations accepted. Open: Sun noon–7 p.m., Tues–Sat 10 a.m.–5 p.m., until 8:30 p.m. Thurs. Closed federal holidays.*

Renwick Gallery
Downtown

Across from the White House, this striking Second Empire building shows off American crafts from the 19th century to the present. Rotating exhibits from the gallery's permanent collection are displayed in the second floor galleries.

Among the more notable are Larry Fuente's *Game Fish,* with its glittering scales of game pieces, buttons, and beads, and Albert Paley's *Portal Gates,* made from forged steel, brass, copper, and bronze. Temporary exhibits of American crafts and decorative arts are shown on the first floor. Wood turning, leaded glasswork, and quilts are just a few of the crafts to be featured. Tours start in the lobby Monday through Friday at noon, May through August, except Memorial Day and July 4.

See map p. 208. 1661 Pennsylvania Ave. NW (east of 17th Street). ☎ *202-633-2850.* americanart.si.edu/renwick. *Metro: Farragut West. From 17th Street exit, walk 2 blocks south on 17th and then left on Pennsylvania. Admission: Free. Open: Daily 10 a.m.–5:30 p.m., except Dec 25.*

Textile Museum
North of Dupont Circle

More than 17,000 objects, dating from 3,000 B.C. to the present, are held in the Textile Museum's collection. It all started with George Hewitt Myers's Chinese silks, tapestries, and hand-woven Oriental rugs. The gift shop is noteworthy, too, featuring silk scarves and ties, Tibetan rug squares, and other interesting items.

See map p. 208. 2320 S St. NW (between 23rd and 24th streets). ☎ *202-667-0441.* www.textilemuseum.org. *Metro: Dupont Circle. From Q Street exit, walk 2 blocks west on Q, right on Massachusetts Avenue 4 blocks, right on 24th Street 1 block, and then right on S. (**Note:** It's uphill.) Or take an N-series Metrobus up Massachusetts. Or take a taxi. Admission: Suggested donation $5. Open: Mon–Sat 10 a.m.–5 p.m., Sun 1–5 p.m. Closed federal holidays, Dec 24.*

Stopping to smell the roses: Gardens and peaceful spots

You can find a lot of green spaces in and around Washington, many dating back to the founding of the city, and some even before that time. The temperate climate (well, in the spring and fall, anyway) means that the gardens are blooming pretty much throughout the year.

Dumbarton Oaks
Georgetown

Usually, this is a spot for indoor and outdoor activities. Unfortunately, the indoor displays of Byzantine and pre-Columbian art are closed because of an extensive renovation project. They're scheduled to reopen in 2007. That leaves only the gardens to explore now, but the gardens are great. They, in fact, are what prompted my wife to visit Dumbarton Oaks in the first place, when we brought our then-little daughter here. It's a great place for little kids to run around and let off steam.

Robert and Mildred Bliss — wealthy collectors of Byzantine and pre-Columbian art and of books on gardens — purchased this 19th-century mansion in 1920 and then restored and expanded it over the years. In 1940, they donated the building, some of the grounds, their collections, and an endowment to Harvard University, which uses the property as a study center and museum.

The mansion hosted the Dumbarton Oaks Conversations — international discussions that laid the foundations for the United Nations — in 1944. The art from the Byzantine Empire is considered by many the most important Byzantine collection in America. Mildred Bliss employed noted landscape gardener Beatrix Farrand to design the gardens, which were envisioned as a unique American incorporation of elements from traditional French, English, and Italian gardens. They're in bloom from early spring through fall. Blooming starts in mid-March and April with cherry trees, forsythia, wisteria, azaleas, dogwood, lilacs, and magnolias and ends in October with chrysanthemums.

See map p. 208. 1703 32nd St. NW (between R and S streets). Garden entrance at R and 31st. ☎ **202-339-6401.** www.doaks.org. *Take Georgetown Connection Route 1 shuttle bus from Foggy Bottom-George Washington University Metrorail station to Wisconsin and R streets and then walk 1 block east on R. Or take a 30-series Metrobus to Wisconsin and R. Admission: $6, children and seniors $4. Open: Daily March 15–Oct 2–6 p.m., Nov–March 14 2–5 p.m. Closed in inclement weather, federal holidays, Dec 24.*

Enid A. Haupt Garden
The Mall

This 4.2-acre park, located between the Smithsonian Castle and Independence Avenue, is a pleasant place to rest when you're touring the

National Mall. It's named for the woman who endowed it, an heir to the Annenburg publishing fortune and a one-time editor and publisher of *Seventeen* magazine who loved gardens and could afford to finance them.

The Haupt Garden actually is a collection of gardens that grow above the underground sections of the Arthur M. Sackler Gallery of Asian Art, the National Museum of African Art, and the S. Dillon Ripley Center's International Gallery. The Parterre is a large flower bed, lined with benches, in which designs are formed with the dirt, grass, shrubs, and flowers. The Moongate Garden was inspired by the Temple of Heaven in Beijing; it features a circular granite "island" and granite walkways that bridge the water. Catch your breath, rest your feet, and reflect before moving on to the next museum.

See map p. 208. Independence Avenue SW at 10th Street ☎ *202-663-1000. www.gardens.si.edu/horticulture/gardens/Haupt/hpt_home.htm. Metro: Smithsonian. From the Independence Avenue exit, cross Independence and walk to the right. Admission: Free. Open: Memorial Day–Labor Day from 7 a.m.–9:15 p.m., rest of the year until 5:45 p.m., except Dec 25. Tours: May through fall Wed 1 p.m. from the south patio of the Castle.*

Lafayette Square
Downtown

Once part of the White House North Lawn and now separated from the lawn by Pennsylvania Avenue and the White House fence, Lafayette Square is a marvelous place for sitting, snacking, or even stretching out on the grass. Gazing to the south, you see the White House with the Washington Monument peeking over the roof in the near distance. To the west are historic houses that lead you to feel you're visiting a 19th-century town square. You can check out an ethnically diverse collection of statues — Marquis de Lafayette, for whom the square is named, the Comte Jean de Rochambeau, Thaddeus Kosciusko, Baron Frederick von Steuben, and Andrew Jackson on horseback.

The park attracts lunching workers from nearby office buildings, resting tourists, and a diverse collection of demonstrators who like to display their signs at the president's door. Over the centuries, the land has accommodated a farmhouse, an apple orchard, a cemetery, and a racetrack. According to the National Park Service, it's also home to "the highest density of squirrels per square acre ever recorded."

See map p. 208. Bordered by Pennsylvania Avenue NW and 15th, 17th, and H streets. Metro: McPherson Square. From the Vermont Avenue-White House exit, walk south 1 block on Vermont Avenue, cross H Street, and enter the park. Admission: Free. Open: 24 hours.

United States Botanic Garden
Capitol Hill

The nation's greenhouse sits in a sort of no-man's land just west of Capitol Hill, but not really on the National Mall. Because it's run by Congress, I call it a Capitol Hill attraction. And attractive it is, having just been through a major-major-major renovation.

About 4,000 plants are on display inside the Conservatory. More are in the gardens just outside the Conservatory and across Independence Avenue in Bartholdi Park. The park also contains the Bartholdi Fountain, created for the 1876 International Centennial Exhibition in Philadelphia by Frederic Auguste Bartholdi, the French designer of the Statue of Liberty.

Ask at the information desk about free 45-minute tours of the Conservatory that are conducted from time to time. Or you can just wander about on your own. The conservatory is particularly appealing in winter, when it serves as a tropical respite from the cold. It's a great place to visit in the Christmas season, when poinsettias brighten holiday spirits.

See map p. 208. 100 Maryland Avenue SW (at 1st Street). ☎ *202-225-8333.* www.usbg.gov. *Metro: Federal Center Southwest. Walk 3 blocks north on 3rd Street and then turn right on Maryland. Admission: Free. Open: Daily 10 a.m.–5 p.m.*

Especially for architecture buffs

Just about every building on the D.C. tourist itinerary has something to offer architecture enthusiasts. You can spend hours — days — studying the details of the great government buildings, such as the Capitol, the White House, the Supreme Court, and the Library of Congress. Many of the monuments are architectural triumphs, like the Jefferson Memorial, the Lincoln Memorial, the Vietnam Veterans Memorial, and the Washington Monument, to name a few. If you take the train to Beaux Arts Union Station or fly into National Airport, you're instantly exposed to fascinating architecture.

National Airport
Virginia

Because travelers often heed advice to get to the airport early, they find themselves with lots of time on their hands. If you find yourself in those shoes, you may want to tour National Airport on your way out of town. Here's how much of an attraction this place is: Just before the new terminal opened in 1997, thousands of Washingtonians (including my family) showed up for an open house.

What you find here is the historically interesting old Terminal A and the modern new terminal. Because of heightened security, only ticketed passengers are allowed access to the gate concourses. But you can see much of the interesting stuff from outside those security checkpoints.

State-of-the-art when it opened in 1941, Terminal A was designed to be both "modern" and reflective of the area's Colonial and Neoclassical architecture. It was built on curve and features a multilevel waiting room with picture windows that look over the runways to the Washington skyline across the Potomac River. It will be restored to its 1941 condition and continue to house gates, ticket counters, and concessions.

The new terminal also offers picture-window views of Washington land-marks. The first things you notice, of course, are the glass and metal in the walls, ceilings, and roof, with 54 domes designed to suggest Thomas Jefferson's contributions to architecture. Works by 30 artists are incorporated into the floors, walls, windows, and other elements of the terminal in various materials, including stained glass, marble, terrazzo, cast bronze, hammered aluminum and copper, painted steel, porcelain, enamel, paint on board, and paint on canvas. As a practical, functioning airport, it's easy to navigate and has an unusually good collection of eating and shopping spots.

See map p. 208. Off George Washington Memorial Parkway in Arlington, Va. ☎ *703-417-8000.* www.metwashairports.com/national. *Admission: Free. Metro: National Airport. Open: 24 hours.*

National Building Museum
Downtown

The best place to begin an architecture tour of Washington is the National Building Museum, dedicated to architecture, design, engineering, construction, and urban planning. The museum itself occupies a fascinating building. Designed in 1881 and opened in 1887, it was constructed to house the Pension Bureau, a predecessor of today's Department of Veterans Affairs.

Among the building's most striking features is a three-foot-high terra-cotta frieze that wraps for 1,200 feet around the entire exterior. Designed by Caspar Buberl, the frieze depicts a parade of Civil War soldiers. Working before the advent of modern air-conditioning and efficient electric lighting, architect Montgomery C. Meigs employed a system of windows, vents, and open archways to bathe the Great Hall in light and air. The Great Hall has a central fountain and eight 75-foot-tall Corinthian columns that are among the tallest interior columns in the world. Its monumental dimensions and spectacular appearance make the Great Hall a popular site for major events, including presidential inaugural balls. (If you'd like to host a party here, rental fees start at $11,000.)

The focus of the museum is on the building process, architectural styles, and construction techniques. The collection contains 40,000 photographs, 68,000 prints and drawings, 100 linear feet of documents, and 2,100 objects such as construction materials and architectural fragments. Exhibits planned for 2005 included "New Designs for Public Space," a post-9/11 look at how Americans design public places that are both open and secure, and "Tools of the Imagination," about the tools architects have used over the last 250 years, from pencils to the latest computer software. A long-term exhibit is "Washington: Symbol and City," which tells the story of how the nation's capital grew to its current form.

At the information desk, you can get free activity booklets for children ages 6 to 13. Family-oriented programs are scheduled throughout the year; call or check the museum's Web site for details. Exhibits sometimes contain interactive elements aimed at youngsters. Brief hands-on programs are conducted from 2:30 to 3 p.m. each Saturday and Sunday.

See map p. 208. 401 F Street NW between (4th and 5th streets). ☎ *202-272-2448.* www.nbm.org. *Metro: Judiciary Square. From the F Street exit escalator, look in front of your nose. Admission: Free, but a $5 donation is requested. Open: Mon–Sat 10 a.m.–5 p.m. and Sun 11 a.m.–5 p.m. Guided tours Mon–Wed 12:30 p.m., Thurs–Sat 11:30 a.m., 12:30, 1:30 p.m., Sun 12:30, 1:30 pm. Call or check Web site for tours of current exhibitions. Closed Jan 1, Thanksgiving, Dec 25, and during special events.*

The Octagon Museum
Downtown

The Octagon is a museum of architecture and an architecturally interesting building. It's also a place where international history was made. The Treaty of Ghent, which ended the War of 1812, was signed here. During that war, President and Mrs. Madison fled here after the British set fire to the White House. The OSS, predecessor to the CIA, set up shop in the Octagon during World War II, and the National Trust for Historic Preservation was headquartered here immediately afterward.

Built between 1799 and 1801, the Octagon is one of the oldest structures in the Capital and one of the best examples of Federal architecture in the country. The Octagon was designed by William Thornton, the first architect of the U.S. Capitol. Strangely, it doesn't have eight sides. While it's not known how the Octagon acquired its name, it may have come from the round entrance hall. According to the American Architectural Foundation, round rooms in the 18th century often were formed from eight angled walls that were plastered smooth in a circle and were referred to as "octagon salons." The house was built for John and Ann Ogle Tayloe, who raised 15 children in the Octagon and continued to live here until their deaths — John's in 1828, Ann's in 1855.

Visitors can tour the house and explore exhibits. If you tour the building, you see the Octagon as it looked during the last 11 years of John Tayloe's life. The museum collection includes more than 100,000 architectural drawings, 30,000 historic photographs, 760 pieces of decorative arts, and nearly 14,000 archeological artifacts and architectural fragments from the building and its grounds, as well as scrapbooks, sketchbooks, manuscripts, and models.

See map p. 208. 1799 New York Ave. NW (at 18th Street). ☎ *202-638-3221.* www.arch foundation.org/octagon. *Metro: Farragut West. From the 18th Street exit, walk 5 blocks south on 18th. Admission: $5, children and seniors $3. Open: Tues–Sun from 10 a.m.–4 p.m. Closed Thanksgiving, Dec 25, and Jan 1.*

Union Station
Capitol Hill

This is Washington's back-to-the-future headquarters. After years of blight, Union Station has become the most bustling hub in town. The train is the very best way to travel in the Washington-New York corridor today. Hordes of subway travelers use the Metrorail station here daily. Maryland and Virginia commuter trains converge here. Cabs line up for business. Tour buses come and go. And — as I detail in Chapter 12 and elsewhere in the book — Union Station is a great place for shopping, eating, movie-going, and teens hanging out. More than 25 million people pass through this place every year.

The building is, indeed, a railroad palace. It was designed in grand Beaux-Arts style by Daniel Burnham, who gathered inspiration from the Diocletian Baths and the Arch of Constantine in Rome. When construction was completed in 1908, Union Station occupied more land area than any other U.S. building and there was no bigger train station in the world. Presidents really used the President's Room (now home to B. Smith's Restaurant), and kings, queens, and other world leaders passed through with regularity.

Airplanes and interstate highways drove the station into a long decline. But a monumental renovation campaign led to a spectacular reopening in 1988, and now you can gaze upon the grandeur that welcomed travelers nearly a century ago — with a lot of new amenities.

A fountain and statue of Columbus stand outside the building, along with a replica of the Liberty Bell. The facade is festooned with eagles. Inside, sculptures of Roman soldiers by Augustus Sant-Gaudens stand guard over the Main Hall, which features a 96-foot high barrel-vaulted ceiling. The East Hall boasts stenciled skylights. At the east end of the East Hall, be sure to peek into B. Smith's to see the soaring ceilings and ornate architecture of the President's Room.

See map p. 208. 50 Massachusetts Ave. NE (at 1st Street). ☎ *202-289-1908.* www.unionstationdc.com. *Metro: Union Station. Admission: Free. Open: All the time.*

Washington National Cathedral
Upper Northwest

The cathedral, founded to serve all faiths (though it's affiliated with the Episcopal denomination), raises its towers higher than anything else in Washington and can be seen throughout D.C. and into the Virginia suburbs. President Theodore Roosevelt and the bishop of London participated in the laying of the foundation stone, which came from a field near Bethlehem, in 1907. Like its European predecessors, this cathedral — officially named the Cathedral Church of Saint Peter and Saint Paul — wasn't built in a day. Constructed in the traditional "stone-on-stone" method (no structural steel), the building was completed in 1990.

You can find much to see and do here, outside as well as inside. You can catch a 30- to 45-minute guided tour at the Cathedral's west end Monday through Saturday from 10 to 11:30 a.m.; Tuesday, Thursday, Friday, and Saturday from 12:15 to 3:15 p.m.; Monday and Wednesday from 1:15 to

3:15 p.m.; and Sunday from 12:45 to 2:30 p.m. A donation of $3 is requested for adults, $2 for seniors, and $1 for children. Several other specialized tours also are offered; phone or check the Cathedral's Web site for details. You can rent an audio tour or wander about on your own. Whatever you do, be sure to check out the gardens as well as the interior.

The real business of the church — weddings, funerals, worship services, and the like — supercedes touring. Some programs are offered on irregular schedules, so calling before you visit is wise.

 Kids 5 and older enjoy the medieval crafts workshop, held in the Crypt Saturday from 10 a.m. to 2 p.m. For $7, they can work on an anvil, carve limestone, create a clay gargoyle, illuminate a manuscript, make a brass rubbing, and build a stone arch. Tours for youngsters to explore the cathedrals gargoyles and grotesques (including Darth Vader!) run from April through Halloween (boo!); bring binoculars. You can find out about other special youth and family tours by calling ☎ **202-537-2934.**

 The cathedral is a bit off the standard tourist path, but you can grab a good lunch or dinner at several neighborhood restaurants:

- ✔ **2 Amys** (see review in Chapter 10). This place offers real Neapolitan pizza, with thin, chewy crust. It's a great spot for kids.

- ✔ **Cactus Cantina** (3300 Wisconsin Ave. NW, north of Macomb Street; ☎ **202-686-7222**), a large, boisterous Tex-Mex spot with an outdoor dining area and where my daughter once encountered President Bush II and his entourage.

- ✔ **Cafe Deluxe** (3228 Wisconsin Ave., south of Macomb; ☎ **202-686-2233**), a stylish bistro with indoor and outdoor tables and an eclectic menu of New American and traditional comfort foods with a twist: burgers, pasta, chicken pot pie, grilled meatloaf with Creole sauce, lemon pepper-crusted sea bass, and penne pasta with chicken and asparagus).

You can take tea after a tour of the Cathedral itself on Tuesdays and Wednesdays, except for some holidays, beginning at 1:30 p.m. inside the West Entrance. Tea is served at tour's end in the Pilgrim Observation Gallery, where you can gaze through arched windows at the city and beyond. It costs $22 per person, and you need to make reservations as much as six months ahead of time by calling ☎ **202-537-8993.**

See map p. 208. Massachusetts and Wisconsin avenues NW. (You can't miss it!) General info ☎ 202-537-6200; recorded info 202-364-6616; tour info 202-537-5596. www.cathedral.org/cathedral. *Take an N-series Metrobus up Massachusetts Avenue from Dupont Circle. Or catch a 30-series bus, which runs along Pennsylvania Avenue, M Street, and Wisconsin Avenue. Or take a taxi. Admission: Free, offerings accepted. Fees vary for tours, programs. Open: Mon–Fri 10 a.m.–5 p.m. (late May to early Sept until 8 p.m.), Sat 10 a.m.–4:30 p.m., and Sun 8 a.m.–6:30 p.m. Gardens open until dusk.*

Seeing Washington by Guided Tour

Travelers with limited time and/or limited mobility can benefit from
taking a general orientation tour. So can visitors who like to check out
the forest before inspecting the trees. Guided tours also make sense for
those with kids in tow, seniors, and travelers with special interests. In
Washington, you can tour historic, cultural, and even scandal-ridden
sites. And you can do it by bus, bike, boat, motorized scooter, and
foot — for an hour or for a day or more.

General orientation tours

Tourmobile (☎ 888-868-7707 or 202-554-5100; www.tourmobile.com)
takes the prize as the best general tour operator in the city. The area's
largest sightseeing organization is licensed by the National Park Service
and operates its trams year-round.

The company's **American Heritage Tour** makes about two dozen tram
stops on or near the Mall and Pennsylvania Avenue and then heads off
to Arlington Cemetery for another four stops. You can get off and on the
trams as often as you like during the day. Some visitors remain on board
for an entire loop, listening as the Tourmobile guide points out places of
interest and discusses their history, and then take a second go-round,
getting off at spots that interest them.

Using Tourmobile is an excellent way to familiarize yourself with the
major tourist areas. One-day tickets cost $20 for adults, $10 for kids 3 to
11, and free for younger tots. You can purchase tickets from the driver
or at ticket booths at select boarding points along the tram route.
Tourmobile runs from 9:30 a.m. to 4:30 p.m. daily except December 25
and January 1. Final reboarding is 3:30 p.m.

If you find the prospect of tackling both D.C. and Arlington in one day
too taxing, Tourmobile offers a separate Arlington Cemetery Tour. The
cost is $6 for adults, $3 children 3 to 11, and free for those younger. You
can purchase tickets at the Arlington Cemetery Visitors Center. This tour
departs the visitor center daily except December 25 from 8:30 a.m. to
6:30 p.m. from April through August and 9:30 a.m. to 4:30 a.m. the rest of
the year.

You also can take the Tourmobile to the Frederick Douglass National
Historic Site, which is off the beaten tourist path. (See "Especially
for history buffs" section, earlier in this chapter.) This tour operates
from mid-June through Labor Day and costs $7 for adults, $3.50 for
children 3 to 11, and is free for those younger. The tour departs from the
Washington Monument and Arlington Cemetery Visitors Center. Call
Tourmobile for tour times.

Old Town Trolley (☎ 202-832-9800; www.historictours.com/
washington) operates much like Tourmobile, except you ride in a bus
outfitted to look like an old-time trolley car. You can get on and off the

Tourmobile Route

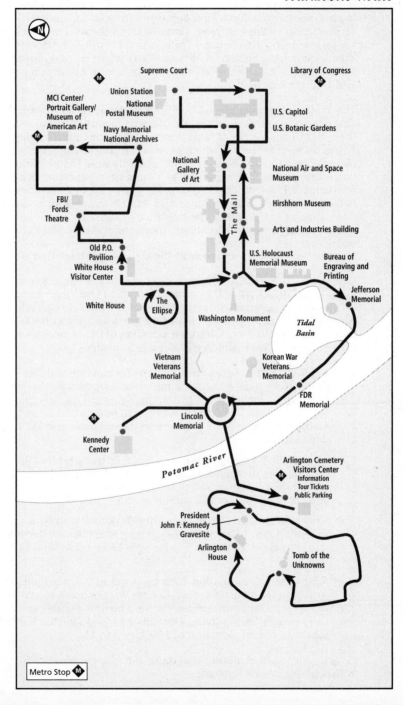

N

Supreme Court

Library of Congress

MCI Center/
Portrait Gallery/
Museum of
American Art

Union Station

National
Postal Museum

U.S. Capitol

U.S. Botanic Gardens

Navy Memorial
National Archives

National
Gallery
of Art

National Air and Space
Museum

FBI/
Fords
Theatre

The Mall

Hirshhorn Museum

Arts and Industries Building

Old P.O.
Pavilion
White House
Visitor Center

U.S. Holocaust
Memorial Museum

Bureau of
Engraving and
Printing

Jefferson
Memorial

White House

The
Ellipse

Washington Monument

*Tidal
Basin*

Vietnam
Veterans
Memorial

Korean War
Veterans
Memorial

FDR
Memorial

Kennedy
Center

Lincoln
Memorial

Potomac River

Arlington Cemetery
Visitors Center
Information
Tour Tickets
Public Parking

President
John F. Kennedy
Gravesite

Arlington
House

Tomb of the
Unknowns

Metro Stop

trolley whenever the spirit moves you. It takes about 2¼ hours for a trolley to complete one loop. First departure from Union Station is 9 a.m. Trolleys stop running at 5 p.m. (Inquire about the final departure from the last stop you plan to use.) Trolleys don't run July 4, December 25, Thanksgiving, the Sunday of Memorial Day weekend, and during the Marine Corps Marathon. Prices are $28 for adults, $14 children 4 to 12, and younger kids free.

The Trolley also takes you on a 2½-hour **Monuments by Moonlight** tour that lets you see D.C.'s memorials and monuments illuminated in all their nighttime glory — at least during part of the tour. The guides let you in on such secrets as which president's ghost haunts Congress. (Which ones don't?) The tour departs nightly from Union Station at 6:30 p.m. during fall and winter and 7:30 p.m. in spring and summer. It doesn't run January 1, July 4, Thanksgiving, December 25, or December 31. Cost is $30 for adults; $15 for children ages 4 to 12; and free for younger kids. Reservations are required. The best time to take this tour is late fall and winter, when you entire Moonlight Tour actually takes place after dark.

You can buy discounted tickets at the Old Town Trolley Web site.

Gray Line (☎ 800-862-1400; www.grayline.com) offers an extensive array of D.C. tours, as well as trips to Maryland and Virginia attractions by motor coach, usually from the Gray Line terminal in Union Station. Always call ahead to confirm departure times and points because they're subject to change. Here's a sampling of the company's touring options. For all tours, children under age 3 ride free.

- ✔ **L'il Red Trolley Tours** are similar to Tourmobile and Old Town Trolley and make a 2¼-hour continuous loop around Washington. Some stops include the Capitol, the National Zoo, Arlington Cemetery, and Georgetown. Riders can hop on and off as they choose. The tour costs $28 for ages 12 and older and $12 for kids ages 3 to 11.

- ✔ The **Public Buildings Tour** is a nine-hour trek past and through monuments, museums, memorials, government buildings, and historical sites. The tour starts at 8:30 a.m. Monday through Saturday and costs $45 for ages 12 and older and $22 for kids 3 to 11.

- ✔ Gray Line starts its three-hour **after-dark tour** nightly at 7:45 p.m. except on Jan. 1, July 4, Thanksgiving, December 24, December 25, and December 31. Cost is $35 for ages 12 and older and $17 for ages 3 to 11.

- ✔ A nine-hour **Combination Tour** takes in top D.C. sites plus visits to Arlington National Cemetery, George Washington's Mount Vernon home, and Old Town Alexandria, Va. The tour departs at 8:30 a.m. daily except Thanksgiving, December 25, and January 1. It costs $50 for those 12 and older and $27 for kids 3 to 11.

Gray Line also offers multilingual tours and tours to Monticello, Colonial Williamsburg, and Gettysburg.

DC Ducks (☎ 202-966-3825; www.historictours.com/washington) supplies an entertaining combination of history and silliness, utilizing amphibious vehicles that transported troops and supplies during World War II. Each Duck ferries up to 28 visitors to several major D.C. sights before plunging into the Potomac for a half-hour swim. The 90-minute keels-on-wheels tours depart daily on the hour from Union Station 10 a.m. to 4 p.m. in spring and summer. Tours may be cancelled in bad weather, so it pays to phone ahead. Tickets cost $28 for ages 13 and up, $14 for children 4 to 12. Younger kids ride free and discounts are available at the Web site. The drivers will be wise-quacking, and eventually so will you.

DC Ducks seating is first-come, first-seated, so show up early or you may have to wait another hour for your ride.

Walking tours

If your feet aren't too tired, consider a walking tour to discover historic sights and architectural gems up close. **Anthony S. Pitch** — author, historian, journalist, and charming guide with encyclopedic memory — doles out an impressive amount of historical and architectural information during the various tours he leads around town. C-SPAN filmed one of his treks. His various walking tours include Lincoln's assassination, Georgetown homes of the famous and infamous, Adams-Morgan, the Lafayette Square/White House area, and the British burning of the Capitol and the White House. Pitch leads public tours, which you can join for $15, as well as tours for groups for $300. Get details at www.dcsightseeing.com or ☎ 301-294-9514.

River tours

Hit the deck and see the capital city's pretty face from the Potomac. For a 45-minute narrated float, take one of the Capitol River Cruises' boats from Georgetown's Washington Harbour dock (bottom of 31st Street). The cruise runs hourly noon to 8 p.m. every day April through October, and till 9 p.m. Memorial Day through Labor Day . The cost is $10 for adults and $5 for kids 3 to 12. Call ☎ 800-405-5511 or 301-460-7447 or visit its Web site at www.capitolrivercruises.com.

Canal rides

Board a mule-drawn canal boat for a trip along the historic C&O Canal. *The Georgetown* is berthed in (where else?) Georgetown, near the Chesapeake and Ohio Canal National Historical Park visitor center, 1057 Thomas Jefferson St. NW, just south of M Street. From spring into early fall, the boat plies the canal for delightful 70-minute rides, manned (and womaned) by volunteers in period clothing, while National Park Service rangers narrate. Schedules vary, so call ☎ 202-653-5190 or check the Web at www.nps.gov/choh for details. Tickets are $8, seniors 62 and older $6, kids 4 to 14 $5, and under 4 free.

Bike tours

Several guided bicycle tours are available through **Bike the Sites**
(☎ **202-842-2453;** www.bikethesites.com). The Capital Sites Package
is two tours that you can take back-to-back or at any time within a week.
One focuses on museums, the other on monuments. Each tour involves
5 miles of easy pedaling on flat land. The museums tour lasts two hours,
the monuments tour two and a half hours. The guide stops frequently so
that bikers can consume some history and humor with their granola
bars. The package costs $55 ($45 for children 12 and younger) and
includes bike, helmet, and water bottle. Tours leave from a purple and
yellow kiosk on 12th Street NW between Pennsylvania and Constitution
avenues, across 12th from the Federal Triangle Metrorail Station. Call for
times and to make reservations.

Bike the Sites, in conjunction with **City Scooter Tours** (☎ **888-441-7575;**
www.cityscootertours.com) also offers three-hour guided tours of the
Mall and Tidal Basin areas on sit-upon powered "mobility scooters."
Tours leave from the Bike the Sites pavilion year-round at 10 a.m.
Sundays and Wednesdays (except Wednesdays in November) and 7 p.m.
Fridays. Cost is $75. Call for reservations.

Chapter 12

Shopping the Local Stores

. . . .

In This Chapter

▶ Visiting the big brands indoors and markets outdoors

▶ Exploring great shopping neighborhoods

▶ Shopping for specific needs

▶ Finding the right shop

. . . .

I know that shopping isn't your top reason for coming to Washington. And I know that, to the extent you'd like to taste some of the shopping Washington has to offer; you don't want to visit the same national chains that you can find back home. So, as I consider the shopping that you may want — or need — to do here, I clue you in to the local shops, as well as the familiar names.

Surveying the Shopping Scene

You won't find much clothing, furniture, or fashion made in D.C. Washington focuses more on making laws, rules, regulations, and headlines. But the Washington area does have artists and craftspeople whose work is displayed in D.C. galleries. Certain shops seek out interesting products that aren't found in run-of-the-mill retail establishments.

You find the best buys here at the museum and gallery shops, because they make an effort to sell things related to their collections that you can't locate in your average suburban shopping mall.

It's impossible to talk about the best times to find sales or general shopping hours anymore. Shoppers demand sales, so the typical retailer puts on some kind of sale most of the time. Retailers also set their shopping hours according to their perceptions of their customers' work schedules and shopping habits and as part of special promotions.

Call ahead if you want to know a certain store's hours. Otherwise, you can be fairly confident that most D.C. stores will be open at least from late morning to early evening. You're more likely to find late-night shops in late-night entertainment areas.

Shopping in Washington, D.C.

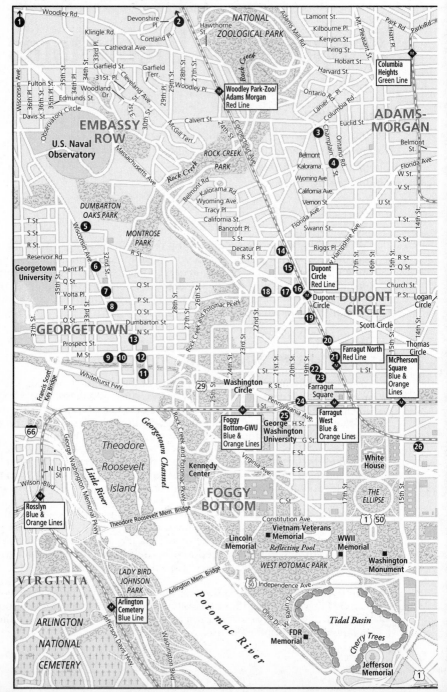

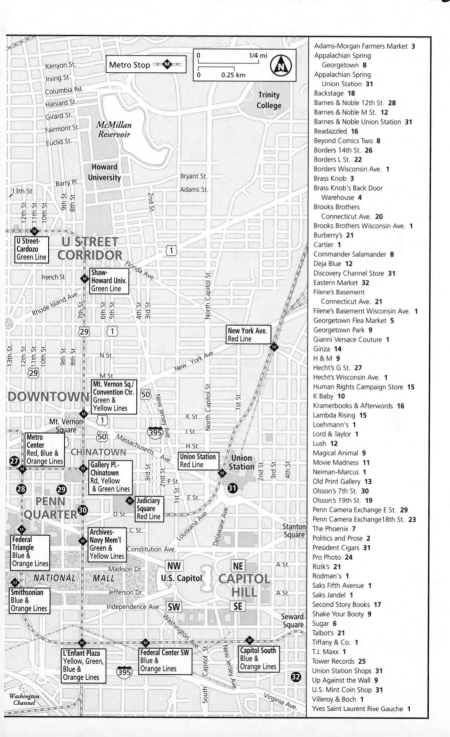

Adams-Morgan Farmers Market **3**
Appalachian Spring
   Georgetown **8**
Appalachian Spring
   Union Station **31**
Backstage **18**
Barnes & Noble 12th St. **28**
Barnes & Noble M St. **12**
Barnes & Noble Union Station **31**
Beadazzled **16**
Beyond Comics Two **8**
Borders 14th St. **26**
Borders L St. **22**
Borders Wisconsin Ave. **1**
Brass Knob **3**
Brass Knob's Back Door
   Warehouse **4**
Brooks Brothers
   Connecticut Ave. **20**
Brooks Brothers Wisconsin Ave. **1**
Burberry's **21**
Cartier **1**
Commander Salamander **8**
Deja Blue **12**
Discovery Channel Store **31**
Eastern Market **32**
Filene's Basement
   Connecticut Ave. **21**
Filene's Basement Wisconsin Ave. **1**
Georgetown Flea Market **5**
Georgetown Park **9**
Gianni Versace Couture **1**
Ginza **14**
H & M **9**
Hecht's G St. **27**
Hecht's Wisconsin Ave. **1**
Human Rights Campaign Store **15**
K Baby **10**
Kramerbooks & Afterwords **16**
Lambda Rising **15**
Loehmann's **1**
Lord & Taylor **1**
Lush **12**
Magical Animal **9**
Movie Madness **11**
Neiman-Marcus **1**
Old Print Gallery **13**
Olsson's 7th St. **30**
Olsson's 19th St. **19**
Penn Camera Exchange E St. **29**
Penn Camera Exchange18th St. **23**
The Phoenix **9**
Politics and Prose **2**
President Cigars **31**
Pro Photo **24**
Rizik's **21**
Rodman's **1**
Saks Fifth Avenue **1**
Saks Jandel **1**
Second Story Books **17**
Shake Your Booty **9**
Sugar **6**
Talbot's **21**
Tiffany & Co. **1**
T.J. Maxx **1**
Tower Records **25**
Union Station Shops **31**
Up Against the Wall **9**
U.S. Mint Coin Shop **31**
Villeroy & Boch **1**
Yves Saint Laurent Rive Gauche **1**

Don't forget to factor in your contribution to the local government's coffers when you consider the price of an item. The sales tax is 5.75 percent in Washington, 5 percent in Maryland, and 4.5 percent in Virginia.

Checking Out the Big Names

Hecht's (www.hechts.com) is the only local name left in the Washington department store scene, and it's part of the May Co. chain. The other department stores within the city are Lord & Taylor and Neiman Marcus, in the Upper Northwest/Maryland neighborhood that I describe later in this chapter as Washington's Rodeo Drive. Saks Fifth Avenue has a men's store on Wisconsin Avenue just south of the Washington-Maryland border and a women's and children's store just north.

Hecht's flagship store is at 1201 G St. NW, at the Metro Center Metrorail Station (☎ 202-628-6661). Another store is located just north of the Washington-Maryland line at 5400 Wisconsin Ave. NW, at the Friendship Heights Metrorail Station (☎ 301-654-7600). Hecht's is Washington's most comprehensive department store and also the most moderately priced, so my family shops here fairly often.

Neiman-Marcus — the Texas-based emporium that sells six-figure Christmas gifts and is picketed regularly by antifur activists — anchors one side of the Mazza Gallerie, an urban shopping mall at 5300 Wisconsin Ave. (☎ 202-966-9700; www.neimanmarcus.com). It's across Western Avenue from Hecht's and right at the Friendship Heights Metrorail Station.

Lord & Taylor, best known for women's clothing, is at 5255 Western Ave. NW, also near the Friendship Heights Metrorail Station (☎ 202-362-9600; www.lordandtaylor.com).

Saks Fifth Avenue's Maryland store is a rather regal structure that stands oddly alone in the midst of its own large parking lot at 5555 Wisconsin Ave. (☎ 301-657-9000; www.saksfifthavenue.com). The Saks Fifth Avenue **Men's Store** sits across Mazza Gallerie's main lobby from Neiman-Marcus, at 5300 Wisconsin NW (☎ 202-363-2059).

Taking It to the Street

Old-fashioned markets of various kinds are still alive and kicking in Washington. The early dog gets the flea — or something like that — when shoppers battle for bargains at flea markets. And don't be afraid to bargain for your bargain. A lot of folks think that's the main reason to frequent flea markets. Here are a couple of interesting spots:

✔ Capitol Hill's **Eastern Market** (7th Street SE, between C Street and North Carolina Avenue; ☎ **202-544-0083;** Metro: Eastern Market) is a riot of activity on weekends. Scores upon scores of farmers, grocers, artists, craftsmen, and vendors peddle their wares inside the historic market building and in the open spaces and storefronts that surround it. Chefs join the locals and party-givers who shop here on Saturday, when the produce and flowers are especially plentiful. Activity occurs all week long inside the Victorian-era building, where various butchers, bakers, fishmongers, and grocers have their permanent stands in the South Hall. The North Hall has been turned into an arts-and-crafts center, open Saturday from 10 a.m. to 5 p.m. The indoor market is open Tuesday through Friday from 10 a.m. to 6 p.m., Saturday from 8 a.m. to 6 p.m., and Sunday from 8 a.m. to 4 p.m. The flea market is open Sunday from 10 a.m. to 5 p.m. Both are closed Mondays.

✔ The **Georgetown Flea Market** (☎ **202-775-3532**) is flooded every Sunday with frenzied shoppers hoping for that once-in-a-lifetime bargain. Nearly 100 vendors sell antiques, furniture, clothing, and the odd knickknack. Former Secretary of State Madeleine Albright and Supreme Court Justice Stephen Breyer are among the bargain-hunting and antique-questing Washingtonians who have been spotted here. The flea market takes place in a parking lot at S Street NW, west of Wisconsin Avenue on Georgetown's north end. Take the Georgetown Connection Route 1 shuttle bus from the Foggy Bottom/George Washington University Metrorail station or take a 30-series Metrobus. The market is open from 8 a.m. to 4 p.m. Sundays year-round.

Hunting Down Best Buys in D.C.'s Prime Shopping Zones

During your time in D.C., perhaps as a break from all that sightseeing, you may want to check out the following shopping areas. Each neighborhood has its own unique characteristics.

Adams-Morgan

Adams-Morgan is jammed with restaurants, clubs, and interesting shops — and with people trying to get into them. The heart of this ethnically diverse neighborhood beats at 18th Street NW and Columbia Road. Take Metrorail to the Woodley Park-Zoo-Adams-Morgan Station, walk south 1 long block on Connecticut Avenue, left 5 long blocks on Calvert Street, and then bear right a half block to 18th and Columbia. In evenings and on weekends, you can take the No. 98 Metrobus from the station to Calvert and Columbia. The bus runs weeknights from 6 p.m. to 2 a.m., Saturdays from 10 a.m. to 2 a.m., and Sundays from 6 p.m. to midnight. After dark, many people prefer to take the bus or a taxi.

You can enjoy a number of secondhand and one-of-a-kind stores here selling clothing, antiques, foodstuffs, and other items. On Saturday, you can find a **farmers' market** at 18th Street and Columbia. Check out a haunt of decorators and do-it-yourselfers at **The Brass Knob** (2311 18th St. NW; ☎ **202-332-3370**), and The Brass Knob's **Back Door Warehouse** (2329 Champlain St. NW; ☎ **202-265-0587**), for architectural acquisitions recovered from demolished houses and office buildings.

When you enter a Metrorail station to begin your trip, get a transfer ticket from the machine on the mezzanine level. Hand the bus driver the transfer and 25 cents.

Carry exact fare; the drivers don't make change. You don't get a discount when you transfer from bus to train.

Connecticut Avenue/Dupont Circle

The shopping on Connecticut Avenue changes flavor as you walk north from the Farragut North Metrorail Station at K Street to Dupont Circle and beyond. Between K and M streets, where many lawyers and lobbyists ply their not-unrelated trades, you can browse such traditional clothiers as **Brooks Brothers** (1201 Connecticut Ave.; ☎ **202-659-4650**); **Talbot's** (1122 Connecticut Ave.; ☎ **202-887-6973**); and **Burberry's** (1155 Connecticut Ave.; ☎ **202-463-3000**); Clothing bargain hunters will like Filene's Basement (1133 Connecticut Ave.; ☎ **202-872-8430**). Women who need a little something to wear to a black-tie affair at the White House shop at **Rizik's** (1100 Connecticut Ave.; ☎ **202-223-4050**), which has been offering designer garments and excellent service for nearly a century.

As you get closer to Dupont Circle, shoppers and shopkeepers are less likely to be wearing suits and carrying briefcases and more likely to be outfitted in jeans and unnatural hair colors. Check out the galleries, booksellers, secondhand stores, and specialty boutiques in this lively neighborhood, which is one of Washington's major entertainment centers, home to many nonprofit organizations, and the heart of D.C.'s gay community. Try **Kramerbooks & Afterwords** for books, drink, and food into the wee hours (1517 Connecticut Ave.; ☎ **202-387-1400**) or **Backstage** (2101 P St.; ☎ **202-775-1558**) for scripts, sheet music, and theatrical makeup. The staff at **Beadazzled** (1507 Connecticut Ave.; ☎ **202-265-2323**) can help you make a necklace from a large selection of beads. In search of a kimono and fan? Look no further than **Ginza** (1721 Connecticut Ave.; ☎ **202-331-7991**). **Lambda Rising** (1625 Connecticut Ave.; **202-462-6969**) is D.C.'s leading gay/lesbian-oriented bookstore. The **Human Rights Campaign,** America's largest gay rights political action organization, runs a store at 1629 Connecticut (☎ **202-232-8621**).

Georgetown

Many art galleries, antique stores, and specialty shops help make Georgetown one of Washington's liveliest neighborhoods from morning until after midnight. This community is truly diverse, sporting some of the city's most expensive residences, Georgetown University and its student rooming houses, and folks from all walks of life strolling the commercial blocks defined by M Street NW, Wisconsin Avenue, and nearby side streets. You see old women with blue hair and young women with blue hair — just different tints.

You'll recognize the major national chain stores when you walk past them, so let me concentrate on some others — local, or at least unusual.

- **Movie Madness** (1083 Thomas Jefferson St.; ☎ **202-337-7064**) sells movie posters.

- **Commander Salamander** (1420 Wisconsin Ave.; ☎ **202-337-2265**) sells punkish clothing, colored wigs, and off-the-wall gifts. This store is popular with teens.

- **The Phoenix** (1514 Wisconsin Ave.; ☎ **202-338-4404**) has been selling Mexican folk art and bric-a-bracs, handcrafted silver jewelry, and those peasant blouses once favored by Joan Baez since 1955.

- At **Deja Blue** (3005 M St.; ☎ **202-337-7100**), you can buy used blue jeans and other clothing.

- For some comic relief, — and more — check out **Beyond Comics 2** (1419 Wisconsin Ave.; ☎ **202-333-8650**) for comic books and the toys, dolls, T-shirts, and other paraphernalia that the comic characters spawn.

- **Up Against the Wall** (3219 M St.; ☎ **202-337-9316**) sells trendy clothes for teens and young adults.

- **Shake Your Booty** (3225 M St.; ☎ **202-333-6524**) supplies boots — and shoes — to folks inclined to shake their thing.

- **Lush** (3036 M St. NW; ☎ **202-333-6950**), popular in Great Britain, opened one of its first U.S. stores here to sell fresh-made bath bombs, soaps, and other natural beauty products.

- **H & M** (3222 M St. NW; ☎ **202-298-6792**), from Sweden, a hip international chain store, offers trendy, inexpensive clothing for the whole family.

- **Old Print Gallery** (1220 31st St. NW; ☎ **202-965-1818**) offers the area's largest selection of antique prints and maps.

- **K Baby** (3112 M St., NW; ☎ **202-333-3939**) targets babies — and their mommies who crave high-end clothing and nursery accessories.

✔ **Sugar** (1633 Wisconsin Ave. NW; **202-333-5331**) boutique attracts celebrities in search of hot designers' clothes plus jewelry made by local designers.

✔ **Appalachian Spring** (1415 Wisconsin Ave. NW; **202-337-5780**) carries a wide selection of American crafts made of wood, glass, and fiber. If you suffer mall withdrawal, you can find a slew of upscale national chains at **Georgetown Park** (3222 M St.; ☎ **202-298-5577**). To explore something a bit different in the mall, check out the **Magical Animal** (☎ **202-337-4476**), which features contemporary American jewelry and crafts, many with an animal theme. Billing itself as "the gift shop for people who love animals," this establishment is quick to assure shoppers that its gifts are "not made from any animal-derived materials."

Union Station

A magnificent railway station, **Union Station** (50 Massachusetts Ave. NE; ☎ **202-289-1908;** www.unionstationdc.com.) serves Washington in multiple ways as it approaches its 100th birthday in 2007 — train station, Metrorail station, intercity bus depot, tour bus departure point, fast-food station, full-service restaurant station, and super shopping destination. National chains are well represented here. But you also encounter some unique shops as well.

The most interesting spot here is the **East Hall Gallery.** The gallery's central open area contains small stands that sell a variety of jewelry, arts, and crafts. Encircling the open area are stores, one of which, **Appalachian Spring** (☎ **202-682-0505**), is a favorite of my family. My daughter acquired a wonderful monkey puppet (whom she named "Fred") here when she was young. Each time we return, we check to assure ourselves that Fred's younger relatives do, indeed, still hang out here. (Fred still hangs out in Julie's bedroom, even though she now spends most of the year away at college.) The quilt on Susan and my bed comes from the Appalachian Spring Georgetown store, the first, which opened in 1964. Originally, Appalachian Spring dealt exclusively in arts and crafts from the Appalachian Mountains. Now it carries original works from throughout the United States.

Right outside the East Hall is a **coin shop** operated by the **U.S. Mint** (☎ **202-289-0609**). Elsewhere in the station are a cigar shop that goes by the moniker **President Cigars** (☎ **202-289-3778**) and a **Discovery Channel Store** (☎ **202-842-3700**), run by the TV/Internet empire that's headquartered in Washington's Maryland suburbs.

If you get hungry here, you'll have no trouble finding something to eat. Several full-service **restaurants** are scattered around the station. (See Chapter 10 for **B. Smith's.**) The lower-level **food court** is enormous and offers a wide variety of cuisines.

Upper Wisconsin Avenue

Just outside the Friendship Heights Metrorail Station is what I call **Washington's Rodeo Drive.** A few blocks of Wisconsin Avenue, on both sides of the Washington-Maryland border, provide retail space for some of the best-known names in up-up-up-scale shopping. (I happen to live near here, so I tell you about the downscale stores — where I shop — as well.)

If Tiffany and friends appeal to you, gather up your titanium credit cards and follow me to **Saks Fifth Avenue** (5555 Wisconsin Ave.; ☎ 301-657-9000); **Saks Jandel** (5510 Wisconsin Ave.; ☎ 301-652-2250); **Saks Fifth Avenue Men's Store** (5300 Wisconsin Ave.; ☎ 202-363-2059); **Tiffany & Co.** (5500 Wisconsin Ave.; ☎ 301-657-8777); **Gianni Versace Couture** (5454 Wisconsin Ave.; ☎ 301-907-9400); **Cartier** (5454 Wisconsin Ave.; ☎ 301-654-5858); **Neiman-Marcus** (5300 Wisconsin Ave.; ☎ 202-966-9700); **Brooks Brothers** (5504 Wisconsin Ave.; ☎ 301-654-8202); **Yves Saint Laurent Rive Gauche** (5510 Wisconsin Ave.; ☎ 301-652-2250); and **Villeroy & Boch** (5300 Wisconsin Ave.; ☎ 202-364-5180). **Lord & Taylor** (5255 Western Ave. NW; ☎ 202-362-9600) is just two blocks southwest of Wisconsin.

At this writing, a major construction project is underway on the east side of Wisconsin Avenue at Western, which will create even more stores. The modernized and expanded Chevy Chase Center is slated to partially open in the latter half of 2005. It isn't scheduled to be completed until at least some time in 2006.Now, just so you don't get the wrong idea about my neighborhood, let me tell you that you can have an eclectic shopping experience here if you want it. Neiman's and Saks' men's stores are major anchors of the **Mazza Gallerie** (5300 Wisconsin) shopping mall. So is discounter **Filene's Basement** (☎ 202-966-0208). Across Jenifer Street from Mazza and across 44th Street from Lord & Taylor sits another discounter, **T.J. Maxx** (☎ 202-237-7616). This area also contains Washington's major local department store, **Hecht's** (5400 Wisconsin Ave.; ☎ 301-654-7600). Across Wisconsin from Mazza is another indoor mall, **Chevy Chase Pavilion.** Next door is **Loehmann's** (5333 Wisconsin Ave. NW; ☎ 202-362-4733), an off-price mecca since the first store opened in Brooklyn in 1921. New merchandise, including a small amount for men, appears regularly, and women flock to the famous Back Room for their favorite designers' clothes at 30 to 65 percent off regular retail.

The easiest way to get to the area is to take Metrorail to the Friendship Heights Station and follow the signs to the Western Avenue exits. After you go through the Metro gate and up the escalator, you find yourself in a sort of rotunda, with four exits to choose from. The hard left takes you to the Western Avenue and 44th Street exit and Mazza Gallerie. The soft left takes you to the Wisconsin and Western avenues exit, where you can enter Hecht's or continue up to the sidewalk, turn left, and walk up Wisconsin toward the upscale stores in Maryland. Straight ahead is the

Western Avenue and Military Road exit, which takes you toward Clyde's restaurant, expected to reopen in 2005, and the rest of the Chevy Chase Center construction project. The doors to your right take you right into Chevy Chase Pavilion.

This neighborhood presents you with numerous dining options. See reviews of **Clyde's, Booeymonger,** and **Chipotle** in chapter 10. You can get good, *huge* meals at the **Cheesecake Factory** (5335 Wisconsin Ave.; ☎ 202-364-4623) in the Pavilion, but you may have to wait at meal times because they don't take reservations. At **Maggiano's Little Italy** (5333 Wisconsin Ave.; ☎ 202-966-5500), they take reservations but don't seem to know what they're for; you can make a reservation, show up on time, and still have to wait. In the front end of Maggiano's, the **Corner Bakery** (☎ 202-237-2200) serves sandwiches, salads, and pastas. **Chadwick's** (5247 Wisconsin, ☎ 202-362-8040) is a neighborhood hangout; I find the burgers, salads, and crab cakes to be best. **Bambule** (5225 Wisconsin Ave.; ☎ 202-966-0300) serves tapas and has comfortable lounge seating and outdoor dining in good weather. Fancier and more expensive is the French/Mediterranean restaurant Matisse (4934 Wisconsin Ave.; ☎ 202-244-5222). The Pavilion has a small food court.

For a look at a real Friendship Heights neighborhood institution, walk south on Wisconsin Avenue to Garrison Street and check out **Rodman's** (5100 Wisconsin Ave.; ☎ 202-363-3466). It's sort of a 21st-century general store. Someone from our house comes here nearly every day — to buy milk or bread or wine or toothpaste or bath beads or toilet paper or a kitchen gadget or a birthday card or to get a watch repaired or to pick up a prescription. This place is, after all, a pharmacy . . . and an international food emporium and an electronics shop. Okay, you get the picture. (And you can get film and developing services, including digital prints.) If you need something that fits on a shelf, you just may find it here. If you're here at the right time, you may catch Roy Rodman roaming the aisles, negotiating a deal with a wholesaler on his portable phone. I was here once, after a blizzard, when grocers around town were running out of basics, and I noticed with surprise that Rodman's had lots of milk. I commented on this irony to a clerk, who told me that a milk truck had broken down in front of the store the day before, and Mr. Rodman had negotiated to buy the whole load.

Shopping for Specialties in D.C.

Are you looking to buy a specific product rather than to browse a shopping area? Check this section to find what you're looking for.

Bookstores

Washington is a literary town, so you can buy books in lots of places. Here's a sampling.

✔ It's off the beaten tourist path, but **Politics and Prose** (5015 Connecticut Ave. NW; ☎ 202-364-1919) is a wonderful bookstore. It's a neighborhood institution in a neighborhood that happens to have lots of writers. So, beyond the books for sale, something is always going on here. C-SPAN is taping a writer who's reading from or talking about his book. An author is signing books or celebrating a new publication. (The coming-out party for the first book my wife and I wrote was here.) You may bump into George Will or Tim Russert while browsing in the current affairs section. A funky coffee house is in the lower level. Take an L-series Metrobus from Dupont Circle or catch a cab.

✔ Before it became a universal requirement that bookstores house cafes, **Kramerbooks & Afterwords** (1517 Connecticut Ave. NW; ☎ 202-387-1400) was serving up food, drink, and live music with its printed products. I'm talking full bar, breakfast, lunch, dinner, and late supper. This place is open from 7:30 a.m. to 1 a.m. daily, and around the clock from Friday morning until Sunday night. Brunch is served Saturday and Sunday, including all night. Did I mention that they sell books?

✔ **Olsson's Books & Records** is Washington's local bookstore chain, with two shops in the city and others in the suburbs, including one at Reagan National Airport (☎ 703-417-1087). The stores survive in an era dominated by national chains by focusing on their communities. Each store's manager stocks reading matter and music that he knows his clientele is most interested in. You can find more theater, film, and history — plus a cafe and high-speed Internet access — at the location that's next door to the Shakespeare Theater (418 7th St. NW; ☎ 202-638-7610 for books, 202-638-7613 for music), and more ecology and politics for the activists who work around Dupont Circle at that branch (1307 19th St. NW; ☎ 202-785-1133 for books, 202-785-2662 for music).

✔ Bargain hunters and collectors browse the shelves of **Second Story Books** by Dupont Circle (2000 P St. NW; ☎ 202-659-8884). It's Washington's premier used and rare books store and also has two locations in the suburbs. Proprietor Allan Stypeck is a host of "The Book Guys" radio show. Together, the three stores have more than a million books, manuscripts, maps, prints, paintings, and vintage posters.

✔ You can get your **Borders Books & Music** fix downtown at 600 14th St. NW (☎ 202-737-1385) and 1801 L St. NW (☎ 202-466-4999) and in Upper Northwest's Friendship Heights shopping district (5333 Wisconsin Ave. NW; ☎ 202-686-8270).

✔ **Barnes & Noble** stores are downtown (555 12th St NW; ☎ 202-347-0176), in Union Station (☎ 202-289-1724), and in Georgetown (3040 M Street NW; ☎ 202-965-9880).

Cameras

If you need to get a camera repaired, want to buy some photographic equipment, or need expert advice on the best film for what you plan to shoot, here are two reputable companies that buy, sell, and repair equipment and sell and process film.

- ✔ **Penn Camera Exchange** has two shops downtown: 840 E St. NW (☎ 202-347-5777) and 1015 18th St. NW (☎ 202-785-7366).

- ✔ I've bought a camera, other equipment, and film from **Pro Photo** (1902 I St. NW; ☎ 202-223-1292). I was referred there in the first place by a professional photographer.

Music

So, what you really want is music for your ears? Here are some places to find it.

- ✔ **Tower Records** has an enormous store inside 2000 Pennsylvania Ave. NW (☎ 202-331-2400). You can browse music in all its styles — and videos — over two floors.

- ✔ **Olsson's, Borders,** and **Barnes & Noble** sell music as well as books. See the previous section for details.

Bibliophiles, music lovers, and collectors shouldn't overlook the museum and gallery stores.

Index of Stores by Merchandise

Saks Fifth Avenue Men's Store (Upper Northwest)
Saks Jandel (Upper Northwest/Maryland)
Shake Your Booty (Georgetown)
Sugar (Georgetown)
Talbot's (Downtown and Upper Northwest)
Up Against the Wall (Georgetown)
Yves Saint Laurent Rive Gauche (Upper Northwest/Maryland)

Department Stores

Hecht's (Downtown and Upper Northwest/Maryland)
Lord & Taylor (Upper Northwest)
Neiman Marcus (Upper Northwest)
Saks Fifth Avenue (Upper Northwest/Maryland)

Discount Shopping

Filene's Basement(Downtown and Upper Northwest)
Loehmann's (Upper Northwest)
T.J. Maxx (Upper Northwest)

Gifts and Souvenirs

Appalachian Spring (Georgetown and Union Station)
Ginza(Dupont Circle)
Discovery Channel Store (Union Station)

Magical Animal (Georgetown)
The Phoenix (Georgetown)
U.S. Mint
Villeroy & Boch (Upper Northwest)

Jewelry

Beadazzled (Downtown)
Tiffany & Company (Upper Northwest/Maryland)

Malls

Chevy Chase Pavilion
Georgetown Park
Mazza Gallerie

Markets

Eastern Market (Capital Hill)
Georgetown Flea Market (Georgetown)

Miscellaneous

Backstage (Dupont Circle)
Beyond Comics 2 (Georgetown)
Human Rights Campaign (Dupont Circle)
Movie Madness (Georgetown)
Old Print Gallery (Georgetown)
President Cigars (Union Station)
Rodman's (Upper Northwest)
Tower Records (Downtown)

Chapter 13

Following an Itinerary: Three Great Options

So many sights, so little time! Is that your problem? Allow me to help with some suggested itineraries for seeing the top Washington sights in just three days, for seeing government in action, and for exploring D.C. with kids.

Refer to Chapter 10 for restaurant reviews and Chapter 11 for details about the top sites.

Exploring Washington in Three Days

Direct from the Rectangular Office (sorry, mine's not oval), here is a three-day agenda for visiting the cream of Washington's top sights and getting a taste of the city.

As of this writing, the **White House** is not open for tours by the general public. If it does reopen — or if you're in a group that qualifies for a tour — you'll want to put it on your itinerary, too. Call ☎ **202-456-7041** or check `www.whitehouse.gov/history/tours` for information and updates.

Save your Washington time for touring, not for standing in line, by buying advance tickets to the **Washington Monument** and the **Holocaust Museum.**

Day one

Start your Washington touring by getting an overview on the **Tourmobile.** Board at the stop closest to your hotel (drivers sell tickets) or at **Union**

Station. Ride the whole route, taking in the sights from the comfort of your seat. Then continue on the Tourmobile to the **Smithsonian Institution** museum on the **National Mall** that interests you most. (Depending on where you first boarded the Tourmobile, you may save time by getting off across the Mall from your museum destination rather than riding all the way to the museum's door.) Spend some time at that museum and have lunch there or at a nearby museum on the Mall.

In the afternoon, take the Tourmobile to **Arlington National Cemetery** and transfer to Tourmobile's Arlington tour. Get off at each of the stops to visit the **Kennedy gravesites,** witness the changing of the guard at the **Tomb of the Unknowns,** and explore **Arlington House.**

Have dinner in **Georgetown.** After dinner, stroll M Street and Wisconsin Avenue to absorb the Georgetown nightlife. Treat yourself to an ice cream cone at **Isee Icy** or **Thomas Sweet.**

Day two

If the **Supreme Court** is hearing arguments today, get in line on the court plaza before 10 a.m. and take a look. One line lets you take a quick peek; the other enables you to see the entire hour-long performance. Whether or not you take in an argument, plan on touring the Court, the **Capitol,** and the **Library of Congress.**

Before you leave home, contact your representative or a senator for tickets to the special congressional tours conducted in each of these buildings.

Act like an insider and grab lunch in a **congressional cafeteria.** Enter any House or Senate office building and ask a guard for directions.

When you're done on Capitol Hill, if you have time, visit another **museum on the Mall.** Then return to the Hill for a quick, inexpensive dinner in **Union Station's spacious lower-level food court** or at one of the informal restaurants that are scattered around the building. Afterward, take Gray Line's three-hour **Washington After Dark Tour,** which leaves from the bus line's terminal in the station.

Day three

Use your advance tickets for a morning visit to the **Holocaust Museum** and a late afternoon ride to the top of the **Washington Monument.** In between, try to squeeze in some time at the **National Gallery of Art,** where the **Cascade Cafe** inside or the **Pavilion Cafe** in the **Sculpture Garden** is a good place for lunch. After you leave the Washington Monument, stroll down the Mall to take in the **memorials** to those who fought in **World War II, Vietnam,** and **Korea,** as well as the **Lincoln Memorial.**

If fine dining interests you and you don't mind paying for it, eat at **Kinkead's,** one of Washington's very best restaurants and one of my favorites. Otherwise, check out the reviews for the $ and $$ restaurants in Chapter 10. In warm weather, cap off your D.C. visit by having a drink with a view on the **Sky Terrace** at the top of the Hotel Washington.

Washington for Government Groupies

Many put their faith in oysters and chocolate, but Henry Kissinger declared that — based on personal experience — power is the greatest aphrodisiac. Should you agree with Henry — the former secretary of state, national security adviser, and all-around powerful person — join the government groupie patrol at the following sights. (Even if you're not a government groupie or a political junkie, you may want to tag along just to see where all those tax dollars of yours go.)

Contact your U.S. representative or one of your senators far in advance of your visit to Washington. Ask him or her for **VIP touring tickets** and for a pass to the visitors galleries in the **House and/or Senate chambers**. Also ask about stopping by to see the office — or all three of them — while you're in town.

Government Groupie Morning is much like Day Two of the three-day tour. If the **Supreme Court** is hearing arguments today, get in line on the court plaza before 10 a.m. As a government groupie, you'll want to witness the entire hour-long event. When you're not in the courtroom, tour the Court, the **Capitol,** and the **Library of Congress.** If they're in session, stop by the chambers to watch Congress at work.

You'll definitely want to have **lunch in a government cafeteria.** Ask a guard in any House or Senate office building for directions. If you feel more judicial than legislative, eat in the Supreme Court cafeteria.

If you contact one of your members of Congress at least three months before your D.C. visit, you can secure a reservation for an afternoon tour of the **FBI;** arrive at least 15 minutes before your tour is to start. A reno-vation project closed the tour in 2004, but it was scheduled to resume during 2005. To find out whether the tour is back in business during your visit, check www.fbi.gov/aboutus/tour/tour.htm or phone ☎ 202-324-3447.

Post-9/11 security has wreaked havoc on Government Groupie Day by severely restricting tours of the **White House** and the **Pentagon.** To get into the White House as I write this book, you have to be in a group of at least ten people and make reservations through a member of Congress. The Pentagon also is restricted to certain groups. Check the White House status at ☎ **202-456-7041** or www.whitehouse.gov/history/tours or the Pentagon at ☎ **703-697-1776** or dod.mil/pubs/pentagon. If you can't get into the president's mansion, you can stop by the **White House Visitor Center** — which is at 1450 Pennsylvania Ave. NW — and then take a stroll over to 1600 Pennsylvania and gaze longingly through the fence.

Now, head back to the Hill and grab a drink at **Bullfeathers** (410 1st St. SE at D Street), a popular hangout for House staffers, or the **Dubliner** (520 North Capitol St. NW at F Street), which draws folks from the Senate side. For dinner, drop some bucks at one of these government groupie gathering places:

- ✔ **The Monocle,** a dining spot for senators, Senate staffers, the occasional Supreme Court justice, and others who have business on the Senate side of Capitol Hill

- ✔ **The Palm,** where you may run into Larry King or James Carville or at least see their caricatures on the wall

- ✔ **The Caucus Room,** a fairly new restaurant owned by Democratic and Republican lobbyists who are out to prove that Washington power-brokers still can eat and drink together in bipartisan conviviality

Touring Washington Family Style

Don't despair if the grandparents change their minds about staying with the children so that you can enjoy a nice, relaxing adult vacation. Bring the younger generation along! Washington is a very kid-friendly place. Just take lots of breaks and carry snacks.

With kids younger than 8

Go directly to the **National Zoo.** Do not pass go. Do not collect $200. Go to the zoo. Pick up a map and schedule of events at the Education Building near the Connecticut Avenue entrance when you arrive. Children particularly enjoy watching the **animals being fed** and the **training sessions.** The more active the animals, the more enthralled the kids will be. That makes the **seals** and the **monkeys** good bets. Check out the **Orangutan Transportation System,** to see whether any apes are using their high-strung cable to swing from building to building right over your head. Small kids sometimes find it easier to identify with the small animals in the **Small Mammal House.** Children like the lizards and snakes at the **Reptile Discovery Center** so much that I wonder if they also identify with slippery slime. Everyone, of course, loves the **pandas.**

If you don't spend the entire day at the zoo (It can happen!), head for the **National Mall** and the old-fashioned **carousel** in front of the Smithsonian's **Arts and Industries Building.** Other kid-friendly happenings on the Mall include

- ✔ The **Insect Zoo** and **Dinosaur Hall** in the **Museum of Natural History**

- ✔ The hands-on history and science rooms in the **American History Museum**

- ✔ Just about any of the airplanes and space vehicles in the **Air and Space Museum**

- ✔ The **sculpture gardens** outside the **National Gallery** and the **Hirshhorn Museum**

In addition, not far from the Mall is the **National Aquarium,** where children can pet a horseshoe crab in the touch tank.

With kids 8 and older

The **National Zoo** and the **Air and Space Museum** work for kids of all ages (including me!). So do the **IMAX Theater** presentations in Air and Space and the **Natural History** museums. Buy a **kite** in Air and Space and fly it on the Mall — a long-standing tradition. These older kids also like the **FBI** and **Bureau of Engraving and Printing** tours.

The beauty of Washington for families is that it's hard to have an interest that isn't represented in the city somewhere. Ask your youngsters what they're interested in, and you should be able to find a museum — or at least a museum section — that's dedicated to the subject. Washington also has **sports, music, movies,** and **pizza.**

With teens

Touring Washington with teens is easy (knock on wood). At the very least, they'll be interested in the places they've read about in their History classes.

To avoid feeling like you're dragging your teens around the city, ask them to thumb through this book, especially Chapter 11, and let them take the lead in planning some of your family's activities. See Chapter 11 for specific ideas.

Chapter 14

Going Beyond Washington, D.C.: Three Great Day Trips

● ●

In This Chapter

▶ Visiting Old Town in Alexandria, Virginia

▶ Touring Mt. Vernon

▶ Exploring Annapolis, Maryland

● ●

*I*f time permits, you may want to get out of Dodge for a day or longer. Excursion opportunities abound in the region. You can reach historic sites, shopping outlets, state parks, national parks, and theme parks faster than Congress can answer a roll call. This chapter describes three destinations within an hour or less of the White House (in case that's where you stay). Using your hotel as a base, you can spend a day at one of the following locations and still return in time for a nightcap and the news.

Day Trip #1: Discovering Old Town in Alexandria, Virginia

With its scenic riverfront setting, historic sites, and myriad dining and shopping choices, Alexandria's **Old Town** charms all who visit. George Washington was a teenage surveyor's assistant when Alexandria became a city in 1749. The once-thriving colonial port on the western shore of the Potomac River is about 8 miles south of D.C. Picturesque and steeped in history, Old Town boasts fine 18th- and 19th-century buildings, an active waterfront, a large artists cooperative, boutiques, and fine and casual dining. In February, locals and visitors unpack their powdered wigs for the giant Washington's Birthday Parade.

Getting to Old Town

If you drive to Old Town, go west on Independence Avenue. As you approach the Lincoln Memorial, watch closely for signs to Arlington Memorial Bridge. After you cross the bridge, turn right out of the traffic circle and then exit left, following the signs to National Airport.

Old Town Alexandria

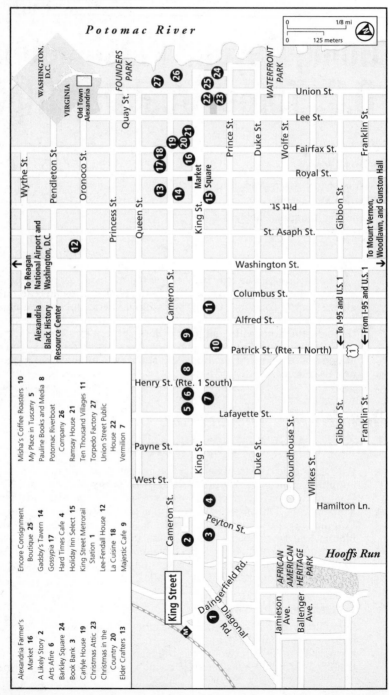

Potomac River

After you pass the airport, the parkway becomes Washington Street in Alexandria. The heart of Old Town is along **King Street,** both left and right of Washington Street.

Thumbs down on driving here in rush hour, when the 8 miles from D.C. may feel more like 80. And be prepared that traffic almost always creeps on Old Town's narrow streets, and finding parking is a hassle, especially on weekends.

Out-of-town visitors can get **free 24-hour parking** permits at the **Ramsay House Visitors Center** (221 King St., east of Fairfax Street; ☎ 703-838-4200; www.funside.com). Park your car at a two-hour meter and put in some change. At the visitor center, give your license number and show identification that proves you're from out of the area. Then put the pass in your car. You can renew it once. Old Town has 14 **parking lots and garages,** most of them on or near King Street on the river side of Washington Street.

Especially if you're coming for the day and aren't lugging luggage, **Metrorail** is a better transportation bet. Take the Yellow Line train toward Huntington or a Blue Line toward Franconia-Springfield. Get off at the **King Street Station.** You're now at the western edge of Old Town. You can start strolling east on King to explore everything Old Town has to offer. (The first couple blocks don't look like much, but you'll soon start using words like quaint and charming to describe what you're seeing.) Or you can catch a **DASH bus** (☎ 703-370-3274; www.dashbus.com) at the Metrorail Station. The 2, 5, and 7 buses travel from the station to near the eastern end of King Street. Fare's a buck — or a quarter with a Metrorail transfer. The Dash About shuttle takes passengers for free between the Metro station and the visitors center Friday night and all day Saturday and Sunday.

Taking a tour

Alexandria offers so many tours that they bump into each other as they move around town. The **Ghost and Graveyard Tour** seems to be the most popular, but I liked the **History Tour** and the **Horse Drawn Carriage Ride** better during a recent visit.

A guide wearing 18th-century clothes and carrying a lantern leads Alexandria Colonial Tours' **Ghost and Graveyard Tour** (☎ 703-519-1749; www.alexcolonialtours.com), which, of course, takes place at night. The guide leads his group through Old Town's old streets, his patter a mixture of real cultural history and stories about old-time Alexandria residents who supposedly died in some unfortunate way that caused them to return to haunt the living. The group is "abandoned" in a graveyard, but it's not too hard to find your way out. The one-hour tour starts from the Ramsay House Visitors Center, 221 King St. (east of Fairfax Street), at 7:30 and 9 p.m. Friday and Saturday, and 7:30 p.m. Sunday March through November, weather permitting. During June to November, tours also are scheduled on Wednesday and Thursday at 7:30 p.m. Tickets are $7 for tourists 13 and older, $5 for children ages 7 to 12, and free for those younger than 7.

Although you have to make an appointment for Alexandria Colonial Tours' 90-minute **History Tour** (☎ **703-519-1749;** www.alexcolonial tours.com), you may end up, as Susan and I did, with your own private guide.

Our guide was a retired university history professor who led us around Old Town, telling us the true history of a city that predates the United States and the national capital to the north. The price — $15 for adults, $10 for children 17 and younger — seemed, to us, quite the bargain.

Another fun way to see Old Town is in a horse-drawn carriage. Our driver/ guide was Ann Crump, an Alexandria native who runs **Olde Towne Horse and Carriage** (☎ **703-765-8976**). She and her little guard dog Hobo have been riding behind horse Penny for quite some time. As a native and longtime guide, Ann knows the town inside-out — and not just the usual historical record. As we clip-clopped slowly through the quieter back streets, Ann pointed out the house John Dean lived in during Watergate, the headquarters of one candidate in a particularly heated local political race, and a cat with a propensity to wander far from home. It proved to be a quiet, relaxing excursion on a lovely autumn afternoon. Ann asks that reservations be made at least 24 hours in advance.

As a river city, Alexandria also offers a number of **boat tours** from the marina at Cameron and Union streets.

With the **Potomac Riverboat Company** (☎ **877-511-2628,** 703-548-9000; www.potomacriverboatco.com), you can cruise to, tour, and return from George Washington's Mount Vernon home; see Washington's monuments from the water; or take a water taxi round-trip or one-way between Alexandria and 31st Street NW in Georgetown. Prices range from $8 to $27 for adults, $7 to $26 for seniors, and $5 to $15 for children ages 6 to 10 (children 1 to 5 are free). Boats run on varied schedules from April to mid-October.

Seeing the sights

Write, call, or stop at the **Ramsay House Visitors Center** (221 King St., east of Fairfax Street; ☎ **703-838-4200;** www.funside.com), a replica of the early 18th-century house built by William Ramsay, a Scottish merchant and a founder of Alexandria. The center provides brochures, maps, and a special events calendar. Pick up the free **Official Visitors Guide,** which contains, among other things, directions for an **Old Town walking tour**. You also can purchase admission tickets for many historic homes and sights. Ramsay House is open daily from 9 a.m. to 5 p.m.

If you plan to visit historic Gadsby's Tavern, Carlyle House, and Lee-Fendall House, you can save a bit by buying the Tricorn Ticket, which gets you into all three places for $9 for adults and $5 for children 11 to 17.

The two buildings that comprise **Gadsby's Tavern** (134 N. Royal St., south of Cameron Street; ☎ 703-838-4242; www.gadsbystavern.org) were constructed in 1785 and 1792 and were operated by John Gadsby from 1796 to 1808. Many Revolutionary leaders slept, ate, met and were entertained here — including George and Martha Washington, John Adams, Thomas Jefferson, James Monroe, and the Marquis de Lafayette. The buildings and furnishings have been restored to their 18th-century appearance. Guided tours are conducted a quarter before and past each hour: April through October Tuesday through Saturday from 10 a.m. to 5 p.m. and Sunday and Monday from 1 to 5 p.m.; November through March Wednesday through Saturday from 11 a.m. to 4 p.m. and Sunday 1 to 4 p.m.; and closed major holidays. Tours cost $4 for adults, $2 for children 11 to 17, free for younger children who are with a paying adult. The tavern is still functioning, so you can eat here daily from 11:30 a.m. to 3 p.m. and from 5:30 to 10 p.m. or take Sunday Brunch from 11 a.m. to 3 p.m. The ham and crab in puff pastry is pretty good.

We heard a fascinating and thorough recounting of the history and archi-tecture of the **Carlyle House** (121 N. Fairfax St., south of Cameron Street; ☎ 703-549-2997; www.carlylehouse.org) during a 45-minute tour of this impressive 18th-century mansion. It was built of stone in 1752 by John Carlyle, a Scottish merchant and another founder of the city. The home's Colonial Georgian architecture is said to be patterned on a Scottish country house. British Gen. Edward Braddock set up headquar-ters here for a while during the French and Indian War, and five colonial governors met here to plan the campaign against the French and Indians along the Ohio River. You can take a break from touring by relaxing in the gardens out back. Tours are conducted on the hour and half hour Tuesday through Saturday from 10 a.m. to 4 p.m. and until 4:30 p.m. April through October. Tickets cost $4 for adults, $2 for children ages11 to 17, and free for younger kids.

Historical figures from the 18th to the 20th centuries owned the prop-erty on which the **Lee-Fendall House** (614 Oronoco St., east of N. Washington Street; ☎ 703-548-1789; www.leefendallhouse.org) stands. Gen. "Light Horse Harry" Lee — a Revolutionary War leader and the father of Confederate Gen. Robert E. Lee — sold the lot for the house to his cousin Philip Richard Fendall in 1784. The last of the Lee family moved out in 1903. In 1937, the house became the property of United Mine Workers President John L Lewis, one of the most important labor leaders in U.S. history. Lewis lived here until his death in 1969. The house is restored to its Victorian appearance when Lee family members lived here during the 1850 to 1870 period. Guided tours begin on the hour Tuesday through Saturday from 10 a.m. to 3 p.m. and Sunday from 1 to 3 p.m. The house is open till 4. Admission is $4 for adults, $2 for students ages 11 to 17, and free for younger children.

Shopping in Old Town

Right after World War I and again during World War II, the **Torpedo Factory** (105 N. Union St. at Cameron Street; ☎ 703-838-4565; www.torpedofactory.org) did manufacture torpedoes. Now, it's an arts center, with 84 working studios, 6 galleries, and more than 160 painters, sculptors, weavers, and other artists who work in full view of the public. Visitors are invited inside the artists' studios to observe and make purchases. While you're here, take a look at the unearthed artifacts on display in the **Alexandria Archaeology Museum** (☎ 703-838-4399; oha.ci.alexandria.va.us/archaeology), which occupies space in the factory. The factory is open daily from 10 a.m. to 5 p.m., and admission is free. It's also free to visit the museum, which is open Tuesday through Friday from 10 a.m. to 3 p.m., Saturday from 10 a.m. to 5 p.m., and Sunday from 1 to 5 p.m. The museum is closed Jan. 1, Easter, July 4, Thanksgiving, and Dec. 25.

Farmers have been displaying their produce in Alexandria's Market Square since the city was born. Today, the **Farmer's Market** (301 King St., between Royal and Fairfax streets) occupies the square in front of City Hall from 5 to 10:30 a.m. every Saturday year-round. As befitting a market in a 21st-century tourist area, the market offers arts and crafts, as well as fruits, vegetables, and baked goods. It's a great place to nibble your breakfast while strolling around and looking at what's for sale. Get some coffee, some fresh-squeezed orange juice, and a couple of pastries. You can find a place to sit on a wall or some steps if you have trouble chewing and walking — and juggling several cups and bags — at the same time.

I can't begin to do justice to the multitude of shops that stretch from the river to the King Street Metrorail Station. So I just highlight a few of the most interesting ones.

Ten Thousand Villages (824 King St.; ☎ 703-684-1435; www.tenthousandvillages.com) is a very interesting shop that sells "fairly traded" crafts from around the world — mostly from poorer countries or neighborhoods. The shop is part of a global organization that pays the craftsmen or farmers (coffee is sold here) more than they usually earn. But the prices remain attractive. Also importing folk arts and crafts — most from Latin America — is **Gossypia** (325 Cameron St.; ☎ 703-836-6969; www.gossypia.com). Here you encounter decorative items, rugs, pillows — and bridal dresses. **Elder Crafters** (405 Cameron St.; ☎ 703-683-4338; www.eldercrafters.com) specializes in crafters older then 55. Some of you might think that's a bit early to be called "elder," but AARP is out recruiting 50-year-olds now, so there you go. You can find a wide range of products here, from the kind of simple crafts you run into at a church bazaar to gorgeous quilts with prices tags that flirt with $1,000. Much of the stuff here is kid-oriented — clothes, toys, and the like. **Arts Afire**

(1117 King St.; ☎ **703-548-1197;** www.artsafire.com) sells primarily —
but not exclusively — American-made arts and crafts. It probably won't
surprise you to learn that **My Place in Tuscany** (1127 King St.; ☎ **703-
683-8882;** www.myplaceintuscany.com) sells brightly colored handmade ceramics from Italy.

For upscale discount shopping (does that make sense?), visit **Encore
Consignment Boutique** (110 S. Union St.; ☎ 703-683-1756; pages.
areaguides.com/EncoreConsignmentBoutique), where used, expensive clothes and accessories are sold for less than you'd pay new. For
real decadence, leap over to **Barkley Square Gourmet Dog Bakery &
Boutique** (101 Whales Alley; ☎ **703-519-7566**), which proffers exactly
what its name implies. Get your dog some gourmet biscuits, or some
fancy toys, or some exclusive clothing.

If cooking's your thing, drop in on **La Cuisine** (323 Cameron St.; ☎ **703-
836-4435**). The foodies there sell cooking utensils, cookbooks, spices,
oils, and chef's clothing. **Misha's Coffee Roasters** (102 South Patrick St.;
☎ **703-548-4089**) roasts coffee (duh!) on the premises and sells brewed
coffee for consumption inside or on a bench on the sidewalk.

A Likely Story (1555 King St.; ☎ **703-836-2498;** www.alikelystory
books.com) is a children's bookstore, as well as a place to buy toys,
games, puzzles, stuffed animals, and other kid stuff . The nearby **Book
Bank** (1510 King St.) sells used books. A really big religious bookstore,
Pauline Books and Media, sits at 1025 King. St.

The Christmas Attic (125 S. Union St.; ☎ **703-548-2829;** christmas
attic.com) is an enormous Christmas store, open year-round, that
became so big and successful it opened a second shop (107 N. Fairfax St.;
☎ **703-548-4267**). The second shop is called **Christmas in the Country,**
but you can find some pretty uncountrified things here. "Christmas" is
defined broadly enough there to encompass other holidays, such as with
scary Halloween accoutrements.

Where to dine in Alexandria

The best meal I've had in Alexandria recently was at **Vermilion**
(1120 King St., west of Henry Street; ☎ **703-684-9669;** www.vermilion
restaurant.com), a warm and comfortable New American spot. Try to
get a table by a second floor window, where you can look down at the
activity along King Street while savoring the quiet, soft atmosphere
inside. In keeping with the name, most of the interior is done in shades
of red — a red brick wall, red fabric draped from the ceiling and along
another wall. The floor is a warm wood. Gas lights glow along the brick
wall. Candles burn on the tables. We started with superb French bread
and a generous serving of steamed mussels in a rich, salty, buttery sauce.
Also coming with a rich taste was a delicious salad of spinach, pecans,

apple, goat cheese, and a warm bacon dressing. The pan-seared halibut was cooked perfectly. The tender pork chop came in a tasty sweet and salty sauce, with garlic mashed potatoes. Lots of revelers crowd into the downstairs bar, which has its own menu, but it's a bit too smokey for my nostrils. Main courses run from $17 to $25. Vermilion is open daily from 11:30 a.m. to 3 p.m. Dinner is 5:30 to 10 p.m. Sunday through Thursday and until 11 p.m. Friday and Saturday. Reservations are recommended.

The hottest dining spot in town, as I write this book, is the **Majestic Cafe** (911 King St, between Patrick and Alfred streets; ☎ 703-837-9117; www. majesticcafe.com), a Modern American restaurant with strong Southern influences. This spot is historic — 20th-century historic, that is. As you approach the Majestic, the Art Deco facade and the movie-theater-like neon sign proclaim its movie-theater-like name. An earlier majestic cafe fed Alexandrians a couple blocks away in the '30s and '40s, and at this site from 1949 to 1978. This Majestic, opened in 2001, reclaims that heritage. The dining room is bright, bustling, noisy and filled at 6 p.m. on a Saturday night. Chef/owner Susan McCreight Lindeborg presides from the dining room side of her open kitchen, directing her staff, garnishing plates, serving some of the tables, and schmoozing with regulars. The complimentary hush puppies that open the meal are very good. The scalloped oysters appetizer with country ham and cracker crust is rich and delicious. The sautéed sea scallops seemed to be the best main course. The Majestic brags about its American Cake, chocolate with a mountain of very sweet white frosting, but I prefer the poached pear in flaky pastry with a vanilla cream filling. Nice touches here: Susan always offers a vegetarian main course, and she serves kids half portions (at half price) of whatever's on the menu. Main courses range from $17 to $22.50. Lunch is served 11:30 a.m. to 2:30 p.m. Tuesday through Saturday, with brunch from 11 a.m. to 2:30 p.m. Sunday. Dinner starts at 5:30 p.m. Tuesday through Sunday and ends at 10 p.m. Tuesday through Thursday and Sunday and at 11 p.m. Friday and Saturday. Reservations are required.

The **Hard Times Cafe** (1404 King St., at West Street; ☎ 703-837-0050; www.hardtimes.com) earns a spot in my family's heart because of the bizarre focus of its menu — Texas and Cincinnati chili. When we lived in Dayton, Cincinnati chili parlors were all around, and I developed a fondness for the spicy stuff. For the uninitiated, Texas chili is made with coarse-ground or chunked beef. Cincinnati chili, originally concocted by Greek immigrants, uses fine-ground beef in a tomato sauce with sweeter spices, including cinnamon. Adding to Cincinnati chili's uniqueness is the tradition of serving it with spaghetti, beans, onion, and cheese — or any combination thereof. Keeping up with the new times, the Hard Times folks now offers vegetarian chili. It's open daily from 11 a.m. to 11 p.m. No reservations are necessary. Hard Times opens at 11 a.m. daily and closes at midnight Sunday through Thursday and 1 a.m. Friday and Saturday. A bowl of chili costs $5 to $10, with chili dogs running about $8. No reservations are required.

The **Union Street Public House** (121 S. Union St., between King and Prince streets; ☎ 703-548-1785; www.usphalexandria.com) has long been a favorite for its casual, neighborhood saloon ambiance, bar food, and local beer. Old brickwork, gas lamps, and polished wood enhance the pubby-clubby atmosphere. Dinner entrees — crab cakes, fish and chips, lobster, ribs, and pasta — range from $10 to $25, with sandwiches from $7.50 to $15. A kids' menu is available. It's open Monday through Thursday from 11:30 a.m. to 10:30 p.m.; Friday and Saturday from 11:30 a.m. to 11:30 p.m.; and Sunday from 11 a.m. to 10:30 p.m., with Sunday brunch from 11 a.m. to 3 p.m. and lighter fare available until 1:15 a.m. Reservations are required for parties of eight or more.

Spending the night in Alexandria

The best-located hotel in Alexandria is a **Holiday Inn Select** (480 King St., east of Pitt Street; ☎ 800-465-4329, 703-549-6080). But it's not, as they say, your father's Holiday Inn. This six-story, red brick hotel stands a block from Market Square in the heart of Old Town. The decor — from the lobby to the rooms — is replica colonial, not Holiday Inn traditional. Rooms tend to be large. Some have balconies overlooking a courtyard. Complimentary coffee and pastries are set out in the lobby in the mornings, tea and cookies in late afternoon. The hotels offers a pool, exercise equipment, concierge, and the usual in-room amenities. On-site parking costs $10 a night. Rack rates run from $179 to $229 for a double, although discounts are often available.

Day Trip #2: Exploring Mount Vernon

Mount Vernon (☎ 703-780-2000; www.mountvernon.org) lies on the Potomac River, about 15 miles and more than 200 years away from modern-day D.C. A stop at George Washington's riverfront estate, meticulously restored down to the original paint colors on the walls, is the perfect complement to a visit in the federal district bearing his name. The land was granted to Washington's great-grandfather in 1674. G.W. lived here most of his life, with time out for being a soldier and a president. He died and was buried here in 1799. What a setting! He certainly had an eye for prime real estate. The house is restored to look as it did the last year that he lived here.

Getting to Mount Vernon

Getting there really can be half the fun when you take the 6½-hour **cruise** to and from Mount Vernon from Washington on the *Potomac Spirit* (Pier 4 at 6th and Water streets SW; ☎ 866-211-3811, 202-484-2320; www.cruisetomountvernon.com). The boat leaves Pier 4 at 8:30 a.m., arrives at Mount Vernon around 10 a.m., and sets your ashore to tour the mansion and grounds. At 1:30 p.m., the boat starts its return trip, arriving back in D.C. at 3 p.m. Cruises are offered Tuesday through Sunday from mid-March to early September and Friday through Sunday from early September to late October. Roundtrip fare, include Mount Vernon admission, is $32 for adults, $31 for senior, $22 for children 6 to 11, and free for younger kids.

If you plan to drive, follow the directions to Alexander in section "Day Trip #1: Discovering Old Town in Alexandria, Virginia" and keep going. The George Washington Memorial Parkway ends at Mount Vernon. It's that easy.

Gray Line (☎ **800-862-1400;** www.grayline.com) offers a four-hour excursion to Alexandria and Mount Vernon. The tour departs Union Station at 8:30 a.m. daily all year and also at 2 p.m. from late June to late October. Cost is $35 for adults and $17 for children ages 3 to 11. No tours are offered Thanksgiving, December 25, and January 1.

Seeing the sights

Mount Vernon is open daily April through August from 8 a.m. to 5 p.m.; March, September, and October from 9 a.m. to 5 p.m.; and November through February from 9 a.m. to 4 p.m.

Aside from the addition of air-conditioning in 1998, Mount Vernon is a typical 18th-century aristocratic estate. Explore the house and grounds on your own. Guides are stationed throughout the mansion to answer your questions. Take a minute, especially with youngsters, to inspect the family kitchen and outbuildings where baking, weaving, and washing took place. George and other family members are interred in a tomb a short walk from the mansion.

Mount Vernon commemorates the **Presidents' Day** holiday, the third Monday in February, by admitting visitors for free and hosting a wreath-laying at Washington's tomb, with music and military exercises by the U.S. Army Old Guard Fife and Drum Corps. On February 22, Washington's actual birthday, anyone who is named George or was born on that date gets free admission.

From late November to early December, candlelight tours of the mansion are conducted from 5 to 8 p.m. Friday through Sunday. Costumed characters, including Martha Washington, speak with the tourists. Outside are caroling, cookies, hot cider, and a campfire. Tickets — $15 for adults, $8 for children younger than 12 — go on sale at the beginning of November at Mount Vernon's main gate or through Ticketmaster (☎ **800-527-6384,** 703-573-7328; www.ticketmaster.com) for an additional fee.

Regular admission to the mansion is $11 for adults, $10.50 for seniors 62 and older, $5 for children 6 to 11, and free for children younger than 6 when accompanied by an adult. You can rent an audio tour recording for $4.

Mount Vernon hosts special events throughout the year, including hands-on activities especially for children. Call to find out what's going on during your visit. The grounds are a great place for youngsters to explore while their parents take turns touring the house.

Where to dine

Outside the main gate, a **food court** sells pizza, burgers, sandwiches, desserts, and beverages. Pizza and sandwiches go for $4 to $7. Also outside the gate, the **Mount Vernon Inn** (☎ **703-780-0011**) is a full-service restaurant in colonial style with costumed servers, candlelit dinners, and two fireplaces. Dinner main courses range from $13.50 to $25. Lunch entrees and sandwiches are $5.75 to $8. The inn is open daily except Dec. 25 from 11 a.m. to 3:30 p.m. and Monday through Saturday from 5 to 9 p.m. Reservations are suggested.

A picnic ground is located 1 mile north at Riverside Park and elsewhere along the parkway. Or stop on the way back to D.C. and dine in Old Town, Alexandria. (See the section "Day Trip #1: Discovering Old Town, Alexandria, Virginia," earlier in this chapter.)

Day Trip #3: Visiting Annapolis, Maryland

Cruise up to Annapolis, about 30 miles from Washington as the gull flies. (Bet your heart rate slows.) A port since the 18th century, Annapolis still supports hundreds of maritime-related businesses and is a magnet for boaters from all over the world. This home of the **U.S. Naval Academy,** Maryland's state capitol, St. John's College, and exemplary 18th- and 19th-century architecture has a small-town feel. With more than 30,000 registered pleasure craft, Annapolis stakes claim to the title "sailing capital of the United States."

A vocal and active preservation group oversees the historic district, some think with an iron fist. But the efforts have paid off handsomely: No high-rises, billboards, fast-food restaurants, or out-of-place modern buildings interfere with the architectural integrity of downtown.

Getting there

Traveling to Annapolis is one time during your Washington visit when a car comes in handy. The drive from downtown D.C. takes about an hour. Leave Washington to the east via New York Avenue, which is U.S. 50, and follow 50 all the way. As you approach Annapolis, take Exit 24, Rowe (rhymes with cow) Boulevard. Continue about 1 mile, hang a right at the governor's mansion (or you'll crash the iron fence), and go halfway around Church Circle. Take a right at the Maryland Inn (Duke of Gloucester Street) and follow signs to Main Street, City Dock, and the Historic District.

Annapolis

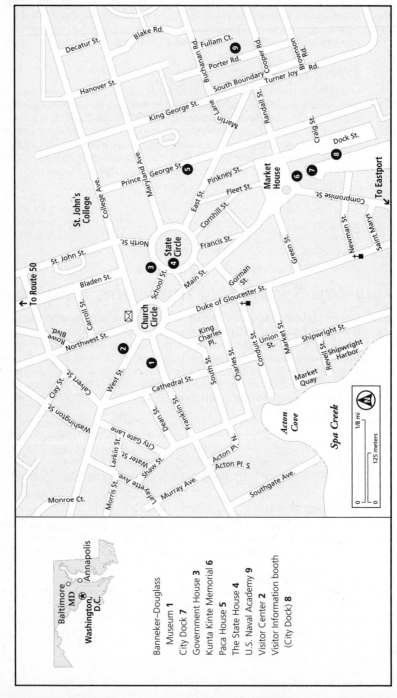

Banneker–Douglass
Museum 1
City Dock 7
Government House 3
Kunta Kinte Memorial 6
Paca House 5
The State House 4
U.S. Naval Academy 9
Visitor Center 2
Visitor Information booth
(City Dock) 8

Tune your radio to **1620 AM** as you approach the city for warnings about **parking** during special events.

On-street parking is 50 cents an hour from 10 a.m. to 7:30 p.m. daily. After two hours, you must move the car. You'll find it a lot easier to park in a garage or at the Navy-Marine Corps Stadium, which is off Rowe at Taylor Avenue.

Stadium parking is $4 all day, $5 during special events. Free **shuttles** (☎ 410-263-7964; www.annapolis.gov/government/depts/transport/parking.asp) run every 15 to 20 minutes to and from the Historic District weekdays from 6:30 a.m. to 7 p.m. year-round. From May to October, they also run weekends 10 a.m. to 6 p.m. The **Gotts Court Garage,** off Calvert or Northwest Street by the visitor center, is free for the first hour, but you pay $1 for each additional hour, with a maximum of $8 weekdays and $4 weekends. Off Main Street closer to the City Dock, the **Hillman Garage** charges $8 maximum every day and tends to fill earlier.

The local traffic agents are as vigilant as vultures awaiting fresh road kill. You really don't want to park in an illegal spot.

Dillon's Bus Service (☎ 800-827-3490, 410-647-2321; www.dillonbus.com) operates limited service between D.C. and Annapolis for $4.25 one way. **Greyhound's** (☎ 800-229-9424; greyhound.com) limited service is $16.75 one way, $32.50 round trip.

Seeing the sights

Annapolis is a working state capital whose history stretches back more than 300 years. More than 1,500 historic buildings are scattered among the narrow brick streets and alleys — more colonial buildings than in any other town in the country. The city is almost always crowded with people working, playing, sailing, eating, and studying.

To work out how you want to spend your time in Annapolis, write to the **Annapolis and Anne Arundel County Conference and Visitors Bureau,** 26 West St., Annapolis, MD 21401 (☎ 888-302-2852, 410-280-0445), open 9 a.m. to 5 p.m. daily except Thanksgiving and Dec. 25, or surf over to www.visit-annapolis.org. Once you arrive, you can get information from the bureau, which is just off Church Circle. You also can pick up maps and literature and ask questions at visitor information booth next to the public restrooms at the City Dock. It's open the same hours.

Three Centuries Tours (☎ 410-263-5401) leads two-hour walking tours of the historic district and the Naval Academy daily April through October. Reservations aren't available, so just show up at 10:30 a.m. at the visitor bureau, 26 West St., or at 1:30 p.m. at the City Dock information booth. Thursday through Saturday, a sunset tour departs the dock at 6:30 p.m. During November through March, the tours are offered only at 1:30 p.m. on Saturdays from the dock. Tickets are $11 for adults, $6 for children 17 and younger.

Discover Annapolis Tours (☎ 410-626-6000; www.discoverannapolis.com) shuttles visitors through 350 years of history and architecture aboard minibuses with big windows. The hour-long tours depart several times a day from the visitor bureau April through November and most weekends December through March. Call or check the Web site for departure times, which vary from week to week. Make reservations at the visitor bureau. The cost is $14 for adults, $7 for ages 11 to 15, $3 for kids 6 to 10, and free for kids under 6. This tour is good for persons with disabilities, those who can't walk long distances, and the terminally lazy. All others should get out there and walk!

For $5, you can rent an **Historic Annapolis audiocassette tour** narrated by Walter Cronkite or an **African-American Heritage audiocassette tour,** from the **Historic Annapolis Foundation Museum Store** (77 Main St.; ☎ 410-268-5576). The recordings are available Sunday through Thursday from 10 a.m. to 8 p.m. and Friday and Saturday until 10 p.m. Each tour takes most people about 90 minutes.

Watermark Cruises (☎ 410-268-7600; www.watermarkcruises.com) sails from the City Dock to view Annapolis Harbor, as well as the U.S. Naval Academy on the banks of the Severn River. Go with the flow. The 40-minute narrated tour leaves every hour on the hour from noon to 3 p.m. weekdays and 11 a.m. to 6 p.m. weekends late March to mid-May; from 11 a.m. to 4 p.m. weekdays and 11 a.m. to 7 p.m. weekends mid-May to early September; and from noon to 4 p.m. weekdays and 11 a.m. to 6 p.m. weekends from early September to early October. Some tours are offered on an irregular basis until late November. Cost is $8 for adults and $4 for ages 3 to 11. Kids younger than 3 cruise free.

Walk the length of City Dock to the water and enjoy the panorama from **Susan Campbell Memorial Park.** Get a double-scooper from **Storm Brothers Ice Cream Factory** (130 Dock St.; ☎ 410-263-3376) and drip across the street to the seawall along **Ego Alley,** appropriately named for the informal parade of boats and flesh that takes place on summer weekends. Where Ego Alley dead-ends, across from **Market House,** is a life-size bronze of *Roots* author **Alex Haley** reading to several children. The sculpture commemorates the landing of Haley's ancestor, Kunta Kinte, aboard the slave ship *Lord Ligonier* in 1767.

Check out the architecture as you ascend **Main Street** from City Dock to **Church Circle** and the harbor view from the **Maryland Inn** (58 State Circle; ☎ 410-263-2641). Independently owned businesses are **A.L. Goodies General Store** (112 Main St.; ☎ 410-269-0071) for souvenirs, T-shirts, and fudge; **Avoca Handweavers** (141 Main St.; ☎ 410-263-1485) for woolens and household accessories from the British Isles; **Snyder's Bootery** (170 Main St.; ☎ 410-263-4500) with a large selection of boat shoes; and **Chick and Ruth's Delly** (165 Main; ☎ 410-269-6737), an Annapolis institution since the 1960s. (See the next section, "Where to dine," for more information).

History buffs may want to detour to the **Banneker-Douglass Museum** (84 Franklin St.; ☎ 410-216-6180), dedicated to preserving Maryland's African-American heritage; it's named for Benjamin Banneker, who helped survey and lay out the District of Columbia, and Frederick Douglass, who escaped slavery to become a leader of the abolition movement. From the top of Main Street, go left at Church Circle and then left at Franklin. The museum is housed in the old **Mount Moriah A.M.E. Church.** The museum's exhibits change periodically. Call ahead to find out about current shows. It's open Tuesday through Friday from 10 a.m. to 3 p.m. and Saturday from noon to 4 p.m. Admission is free.

If you go right onto Church Circle from Main Street and right again at School Street to State Circle, you discover Annapolis as state capital. The **State House** (☎ 410-974-3400), the oldest state capitol building in continuous use, still watches over the town below. Construction began in 1772, and the original section was completed in 1779. It served as the U.S. Capitol from November 1783 to August 1784 when the Continental Congress met in the Old Senate Chamber. View the grounds and public areas on your own or take the free tour, daily at 11 a.m. and 3 p.m. When you exit the rear of the building, cross **Lawyers Mall,** with its statue of **Thurgood Marshall,** to **Government House,** the official residence of Maryland's governor. Because the governor lives here, you can't just walk in to tour.

On State Circle are some of the town's premier shops and galleries. **Annapolis Pottery** (No. 40; ☎ 410-268-6153; www.annapolispottery. com) is a workshop/gallery with a wide selection of attractive and functional pieces. The **Maryland Federation of Art Gallery** (No. 18; ☎ 410-268-4566; www.mdfedart.org), in a restored 1840 building with exposed brick and modern lighting, mounts solo and small group exhibits of multimedia works and three national shows per year.

From State Circle, turn down Maryland Avenue, with its many home design and antiques shops, boutiques, and galleries. Reminiscent of a gentler era and a lot less touristy than Main Street, Maryland Avenue merits exploration. Shops line the cobblestone street from State Circle to Prince George Street. Stop in the **Aurora Gallery** (No. 67; ☎ 410- 263-9150) a few doors from the State House, with its American-made crafts, pottery, jewelry, paintings, and sculpture (some created by the artist-owners). Across the street is the **Briarwood Book Shop** (No. 66; ☎ 410-268-1440) for used and out-of-print books. The **Dawson Gallery** (No. 44; ☎ 410-269-1299) sells 18th-, 19th-, and early 20th-century American and European paintings. Among the gallery's better-known customers is Harrison Ford, who purchased paintings here while filming *Patriot Games* in Annapolis.

Anyone who's been in Annapolis five minutes knows it's a sailing mecca. Many people come here from all over the country to learn to sail. If you're one of them, try the Annapolis Sailing School (601 6th St.; ☎ 800-638-9192, 410-267-7205; www.annapolissailing.com), where I'm told you can learn the basics in a weekend.

If you're not going to take the helm yourself, feel the wind on your face aboard the 74-foot schooner *Woodwind* (☎ 410-263-7837; www.schoonerWoodwind.com), which sails from behind the Marriott Hotel at 80 Compromise St. Several cruises run at varying times daily April through November. Call or check the Web site for details. The two-hour cruise costs $25 to 29 for adults, $23 to 27 for seniors, and $15 for kids younger than 12.

Annapolis lays claim to numerous fine examples of 18th- and 19th-century architecture. As you tour, notice the colored plaques on many buildings designating their historic status and the period in which they were built. (An explanation is provided in the *Annapolis Visitors Guide,* available at the visitor center) Check out the **William Paca House and Garden** (186 Prince George St.; ☎ 410-263-5553; www.annapolis.org). Paca (pronounced *Pay*-ca) was a wealthy planter who signed the Declaration of Independence. The Georgian mansion, built between 1763 and 1765, nearly succumbed to the wrecker's ball in 1965. The Historic Annapolis Foundation stepped in, restoring the house and gardens to their former grandeur. The mansion is open Monday through Saturday from 10 a.m. to 5 p.m. and Sunday from noon to 5 p.m. from late March through December and Saturday from 10 a.m. to 5 p.m. and Sunday noon to 5 p.m. from late January to late March. The building is closed most of January, as well as Thanksgiving Day, December 25, and December 30. Call or check the Web site for details. Admission to the house or gardens alone is $5 for adults, $4 for seniors, $3 for children 6 to 17, free for younger kids, and $15 for families. Touring both costs adults $8, seniors $7, and children 6 to 17 $5. Younger kids are still free and families are $15.

Many people use the words "Annapolis" and **"U.S. Naval Academy"** interchangeably. Whatever you call it, the academy is a must-see. If you park downtown, it's a five-minute walk from City Dock via Randall Street to King George Street and Gate 1, the visitors' entrance. Since September 11, 2001, tourists aren't permitted to drive onto the academy grounds (or "onboard," as the sailors say). The exception is a vehicle with a hand-icapped license plate or permit, which is allowed on campus through Gate 1 after an inspection. To get information before you arrive, call ☎ 410-263-6933 or visit the academy's Web site for tourists at www.navyonline.com.

Stop first at the **Armel-Leftwich Visitor Center,** just inside Gate 1 and next to the Field House, for a map and to see the short film *To Lead and to Serve.* Check out the interactive exhibits and the gift shop and stroll the waterfront promenade behind the building. You can view exhibits on life at the Naval Academy and see *Freedom 7,* the space capsule in which Navy Commander Alan Shepard became the first American to take a sub-orbital flight into space. The center is open daily from 9 a.m. to 5 p.m. March through December and from 9 a.m. to 4 p.m. in January and February. It's closed Thanksgiving, December 25, and January 1.

Then hop onto a guided tour, which is free for preschoolers and costs $5 for elementary and secondary students, $6 for seniors older than 62, and $7 everyone else. July through August, the tours run from 9:30 a.m. to 3 p.m. Monday through Saturday and 12:30 to 3 p.m. Sunday. From December through March, they run Monday through Saturday from 10 a.m. to 2:30 p.m. and Sunday from 12:30 to 2:30 p.m. April through June, the tours run Monday through Friday from 10 a.m. to 3 p.m., Saturday from 9:30 a.m. to 3 p.m., and Sunday from 12:30 to 3 p.m.

During the academic year (September through May), try to hook up with a morning tour that allows you to see noon meal formation in front of Bancroft Hall. Drills and music precede the procession into the 65,000-square-foot dining hall, which can accommodate all 4,000 midshipmen at one time.

Lejeune Hall, across from the visitor center, contains athletic trophies and photographs. You may also be able to catch swim practice in the Olympic-size pool. Close by is **Dahlgren Hall,** where a biplane "flies" from the ceiling, the Navy's ice hockey team plays, and the site of figure skating competitions and ice shows. Cross the yard to the awesome **Navy Chapel** and John Paul Jones's crypt. Nearby is the **Naval Academy Museum,** Preble Hall (☎ 410-293-2108), filled with 200 years of naval art and artifacts; see the ground floor Gallery of Ships, many of which are original builder's models. The **Robert Crown Center** is headquarters for the academy's sailing program. Bancroft Hall (known as "Mother B") is the dormitory for all the midshipmen. For information and tickets to athletic events, call the Naval Academy Athletic Association (☎ 800-874-6289).

Where to dine

Café Normandie (185 Main St.; ☎ 410-263-3382) is a cozy, plant-filled French bistro. Come for a hearty breakfast on weekends (eggs, omelets, and French toast). All week, it's is a good place for lunch (tomato-crab or onion soup, grilled chicken Caesar salad, or crêpes), or dinner (veal, shrimp, beef many ways, seafood-filled crêpes, or pasta). Except for the ice-cream or fruit-filled crêpes, the desserts are ho-hum. The restaurant is open Monday through Friday from 11 a.m. to 4 p.m. and 5 to 10:30 p.m., Saturday from 8 a.m. to 4 p.m. and 5 to 11 p.m., and Sunday from 8 a.m. to 4 p.m. and 5 to 10 p.m. Main courses run from $13 to $28. Reservations are recommended.

From May to October, visit **Cantler's Riverside Inn** on Mill Creek (458 Forest Beach Rd.; ☎ 410-757-1311; cantlers.com) and dig into a pile of steamed Maryland blue crabs. This place is packed in summer, especially on weekends (when the restaurant doesn't take a reservation). The best strategy is to arrive at off times. Have an early or late lunch or a *very* early dinner. Otherwise, you may find the crabs AWOL. Also try the steamed shrimp, crab-vegetable soup, soft-shell crab sandwich, and fried or broiled fish. The inn is about a 15-minute ride from City Dock. Cantler's opens daily at 11 a.m. and closes at midnight Friday and Saturday and 11 p.m. the rest of the week.

A bit of advice I picked up from an old crab picker: At Cantler's, order large or jumbo males *(jimmys)*. The mediums are too much work for too little meat. The roe in the female crabs *(sooks)* puts most people off.

With its long wooden bar, chatty bartender, high-decibel noise level, and garage-sale accessories, **Riordan's** (26 Market Space; ☎ 410-263-5449; www.riordans.com) is a quintessential neighborhood saloon. The servers are pleasant and efficient, the food is consistent and reasonably priced, and the beer is cold. Start with potato skins with the works or a seafood appetizer and then move on to a burger or roast beef sandwich. The soups are, um, super, especially the New England clam chowder and crab vegetable. The à la carte Sunday brunch (mimosa or glass of champagne included) is an Annapolis tradition and also a bargain, with entrees less than $10. At lunch and dinner, a kids' menu for the 10-and-under set lists burgers, chicken, and pasta. Hours are Monday through Saturday from 11 a.m. to 1:30 a.m. and Sunday 10 to 1:30 a.m. Main courses are $9 to $17.

Chick and Ruth's Delly (165 Main St.; ☎ 410-269-6737; www.chickand ruths.com) has anchored the corner of Main and Conduit streets since the '60s, before Annapolis became a yuppie outpost. Come for the breakfast platters (served all day), the tasty sandwiches (named for Maryland politicians and local characters), milkshakes, malts, or banana splits. Try the *delly fries* (home fries with plenty of pepper and onions). The kitschy decor — orange Formica countertops and bagel light-pulls are decor? — is pure 1950s. So are the cheeky waitresses and the prices. Except for the crabs, almost everything's under $10. It's open Monday and Tuesday from 6:30 a.m. to 4 p.m.; Wednesday, Thursday, and Sunday until 10 p.m., and Friday and Saturday until 11:30 p.m.

Part V
Living It Up After Dark: D.C. Nightlife

The 5th Wave   By Rich Tennant

"Yes, we are going to hear Pachelbel's
Canon next, but maybe I should explain..."

In this part . . .

Read my lips: D.C. ain't Vegas! For many, Washington is a place to work. Period. But that doesn't mean you can't enjoy your D.C. nights. This part gives you the lowdown on where to find the best movies, shows, concerts, neighborhood watering holes, music/dance clubs, and after-dark tours — plus I tell you about D.C.'s high culture (symphony, opera, and dance), which is top-notch and getting better.

Chapter 15

Applauding the Cultural Scene

● ●

In This Chapter

▶ Getting information and tickets

▶ Dining before the curtain goes up

▶ Knowing what's hot on the cultural scene

▶ Taking in a play, concert, or dance performance

● ●

*U*nlike the famous cherry trees, Washington's cultural scene knows no particular season and blooms year-round. Over the years, a dazzling array of theatrical venues has sprouted for residents and visitors alike.

Getting the Inside Scoop on the D.C. Arts Scene

You could spend your entire Washington visit in the **John F. Kennedy Center for the Performing Arts** (2700 F St. NW, between New Hampshire Avenue and Rock Creek Parkway; concerts ☎ **800-444-1324** or 202-467-4600, tours 202-416-8340; www.kennedy-center.org) and partake of just about every type of performance you enjoy.

The center, a living memorial to the martyred president, is both a performance venue and a tourist attraction in its own right. It also was a long time a-borning.

President Eisenhower signed legislation creating a "national cultural center" in 1958. Kennedy himself was an ardent fundraiser for the project. After Kennedy's assassination, Congress designated the center as his memorial. President Johnson broke ground in 1965. The center finally opened in 1971, during the Nixon presidency, with a performance of Leonard Bernstein's "Requiem" for Kennedy.

The Performing Arts Scene in Washington, D.C.

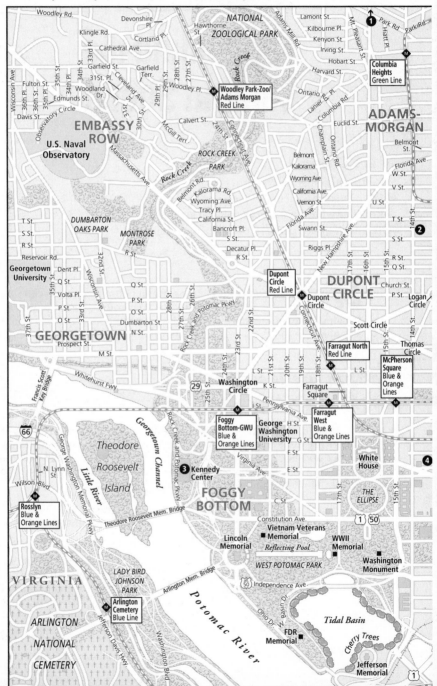

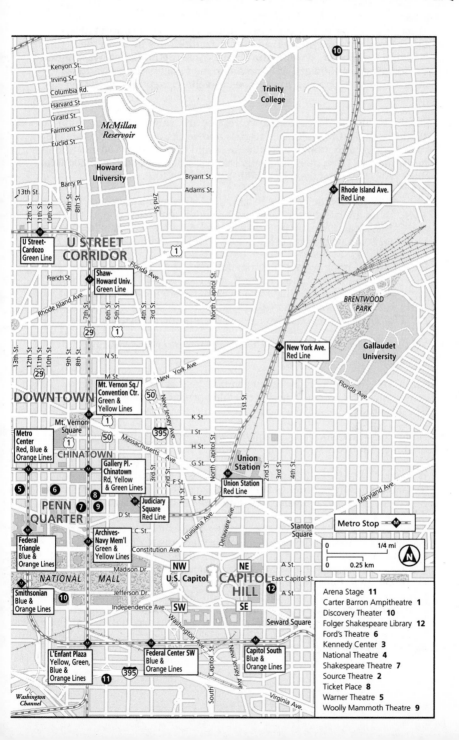

Kenyon St.
Irving St.
Columbia Rd.
Harvard St.
Girard St.
Fairmont St.
Euclid St.

McMillan Reservoir

Trinity College

Howard University

Bryant St.
Adams St.

Barry Pl.

13th St.
12th St.
11th St.
10th St.
9th St.
8th St.
2nd St.

U Street-Cardozo
Green Line

U STREET CORRIDOR

French St.

Shaw-Howard Univ.
Green Line

Florida Ave.

North Capitol St.

Rhode Island Ave

Rhode Island Ave.
Red Line

BRENTWOOD PARK

Gallaudet University

New York Ave.
Red Line

Florida Ave.

13th St.
12th St.
11th St.
10th St.
9th St.
8th St.
7th St.
6th St.
5th St.
4th St.
3rd St.

(29)
(1)

N St.

(29)

DOWNTOWN

M St.

New York Ave.

New Jersey Ave.

1st St.

Mt. Vernon Sq./Convention Ctr.
Green & Yellow Lines

Mt. Vernon Square

(1)
(50)

Metro Center
Red, Blue & Orange Lines

(1)
(50)

Massachusetts Ave.

K St.
I St.
H St.
G St.

North Capitol St.

CHINATOWN

Gallery Pl.-Chinatown
Rd, Yellow & Green Lines

3rd St.
2nd St.

Union Station

Union Station
Red Line

2nd St.
3rd St.
4th St.

Maryland Ave.

5   **6**

8

PENN QUARTER

7   **9**

F St.
E St.

Judiciary Square
Red Line

D St.

Louisiana Ave.

Delaware Ave.

Stanton Square

Metro Stop ═══ Ⓜ

Federal Triangle
Blue & Orange Lines

Archives-Navy Mem'l
Green & Yellow Lines

C St.

Constitution Ave.

0   1/4 mi
0   0.25 km

NATIONAL MALL

Madison Dr.

NW   **NE**

U.S. Capitol   **CAPITOL**   East Capitol St.

A St.

12

Smithsonian
Blue & Orange Lines

10

Jefferson Dr.

HILL

A St.

Independence Ave.

SW   **SE**

Seward Square

L'Enfant Plaza
Yellow, Green, Blue & Orange Lines

11

(395)

Federal Center SW
Blue & Orange Lines

Capitol St.

New Jersey Ave.

Capitol South
Blue & Orange Lines

South

Virginia Ave.

Washington Channel

Arena Stage **11**
Carter Barron Ampitheatre **1**
Discovery Theater **10**
Folger Shakespeare Library **12**
Ford's Theatre **6**
Kennedy Center **3**
National Theatre **4**
Shakespeare Theatre **7**
Source Theatre **2**
Ticket Place **8**
Warner Theatre **5**
Woolly Mammoth Theatre **9**

Today, the center is a world-class cultural venue, with **concert hall, opera house, movie theater,** and other facilities. It's home to the **National Symphony, Washington Opera, Washington Ballet, Washington Performing Arts Society,** and the American Film Institute's **National Film Theater.** It also hosts numerous traveling troupes in all the performing arts.

The halls outside the performance venues are truly grand. More than 40 nations donated building materials and works of art. Great views are to be had from the top-floor restaurants and promenade. You can attend performances here, including daily free performances on the Millennium Stage. And you can take a free, hour-long guided tour.

The center is open daily from 10 a.m. until 30 minutes after last performance. Tours are conducted Monday through Friday from 10 a.m. to 5 p.m. and Saturday and Sunday from 10 a.m. to 1 p.m. Admission is free to the building. You pay, of course, for tickets to most performances.

Free shuttle service is available from the Foggy Bottom-George Washington University Metrorail Station every 15 minutes from 9:45 a.m. until midnight Monday through Friday, 10 a.m. until midnight Saturdays, noon until midnight Sundays, and 4 p.m. until midnight on federal holidays. Look for signs to the left as you get off the station escalator.

 You can obtain tickets for "VIP" tours of the center from members of Congress.

All these events occurs at just one venue. Year-round, on any given day, you can count on finding performing artists on many stages in Washington.

 Half-price tickets for many Kennedy Center performances are available in limited numbers to full-time students through graduate school, seniors 65 and older, people with permanent disabilities, enlisted military personnel in grades E1-E4, and people on fixed low incomes. If you have a disability, you can order tickets by phone. Others must get them at the box office. Tickets are available in advance for opening nights and some other performances. The rest are sold on performance day beginning at noon for matinees and 6 p.m. for evening shows. Except for primary and secondary school students, you must produce proof of eligibility — student or military ID card, Medicare card, driver's license, or other government document indicating age or income. Those with disabilities can show an ID card obtained from Kennedy Center. The box office, in the Kennedy Center Hall of States, is open Monday through Saturday 10 a.m. to 9 p.m., and Sundays and holidays from noon to 9 p.m. For an extra charge, you can place a phone order from 10 a.m. until 6 p.m. daily by calling ☎ **202-416-8529** or 202-416-8528. For additional information, call ☎ **800-444-1324** or 202-467-4600.

Fabulous freebies

The best news for those traveling on a tight budget is that **free performances** are as much a part of Washington as spin doctors and negative campaign advertising.

The Kennedy Center offers free performances on the Millennium Stage in the Grand Foyer daily at 6 p.m. Audiences enjoy midsummer nights' freebies when the **Shakespeare Theatre** plays outdoors in Rock Creek Park's Carter Barron Amphitheatre, off 16th Street and Colorado Avenue NW. The **National Symphony** and military bands present free outdoor concerts at several sites from Memorial Day through Labor Day. The National Mall — most recently between 4th and 7th streets, has become an outdoor theater for screening classing movies in the summer. In 2004, the fare included *All the President's Men, Dr. Jekyll and Mr. Hyde, Whatever Happened to Baby Jane, The Thin Man,* and *Mr. Smith Goes to Washington.*

The play's the thing

In a city that generates more than its share of political theater, dramatic and musical theater also thrives. Broadway-bound shows and resurrected classics account for much theatrical activity at the **Kennedy Center** (2700 F St. NW, between New Hampshire Avenue and Rock Creek Parkway; ☎ **800-444-1324** or 202-467-4600; www.kennedy-center.org).

Arena Stage (1101 Sixth St. SW, at Maine Ave; ☎ **202-488-3300;** www.arenastage.org), on the other hand, presents new works, reinterprets older works, and practices diversity. Now more than 50 years old, Arena can brag about a distinguished life so far: It was the first not-for-profit theater in the United States, the first regional theater to transfer a production to Broadway, the first regional theater invited by the U.S. State Department to tour behind the Iron Curtain, and the first regional to win a Tony.

D.C.'s diminutive Theater District — I don't think I'll compare it to New York's — is downtown, east of the White House. The most active stages are

- ✔ **National Theatre** (1321 Pennsylvania Ave. NW, between 13th and 14th streets; ☎ 202-628-6161; www.nationaltheatre.org).

- ✔ **Warner Theatre** (13th Street NW, between E and F streets; ☎ 202-783-4000; www.warnertheatre.com).

- ✔ **Ford's Theatre** (511 10th St. NW, between E and F streets; ☎ 202-347-4833; www.fordstheatre.org).

- ✔ **Shakespeare Theatre** (450 7th St. NW, between D and E streets; ☎ 202-547-1122; www.shakespearetheatre.org).

Don't overlook the smaller, innovative **Source Theatre** (1835 14th St NW, between S and T streets; ☎ 202-462-1073; www.sourcetheatre.com) and the **Woolly Mammoth Theatre** (☎ 202-393-3939; www.woolly mammoth.net). As I write this book, Woolly Mammoth is performing in the Kennedy Center and other venues while a new Mammoth lair is scheduled to open at 7th and D streets NW in the spring of 2005.

The **Folger Shakespeare Library** (201 E. Capitol St. SE, at 2nd Street; ☎ 202-544-7077; www.folger.edu/public/theater/menu.asp) provides D.C.'s most interesting setting for theater-going. It's a replica of an Elizabethan theater. While Shakespeare's plays obviously provide the core of the Folger's offerings, works by other playwrights are performed as well, and the theater presents poetry readings and early-music concerts.

Hearing the sounds of music

The **National Symphony Orchestra,** one of the world's best, plays in the Kennedy Center Concert Hall (2700 F St. NW between New Hampshire Avenue and Rock Creek Parkway; ☎ 800-444-1324, 202-467-4600; www. kennedy-center.org/nso). Leonard Slatkin is the conductor, with other world-renowned conductors and musicians making guest appearances. The symphony's performances frequently sell out, so make your reservations early.

Hot time: Summer in the city

If you visit Washington in summer and enjoy classical music, check out the **National Symphony's free concerts** on the **West Lawn of the Capitol,** on the Sunday of the Memorial Day and Labor Day weekends, and on July 4. These events are some of the top perks of summer in this city. You also can catch a free concert by the **NSO** several times in summer at the **Carter Barron Amphitheatre** in Rock Creek Park (16th Street and Colorado Avenue NW; ☎ 202-426-0486; www.nps.gov/rocr/cbarron). The Capitol Lawn concerts are enormously popular, so you need to arrive early and be prepared to go through security screening.

The rousing **4th of July concert** on the **West Lawn of the Capitol** features the **National Symphony,** guest artists, celebrity hosts, and an enthusiastic audience. The evening ends with a bang when the 1812 Overture accompanies the **fireworks** display on the Mall (or vice versa, depending on your viewpoint). Arrive early, be braced for crowds, and bring something to sit on. You also can catch a live broadcast of the concert on public television.

A night at the opera

Snagging tickets for the **Washington National Opera** (2700 F St. NW, between New Hampshire Avenue and Rock Creek Parkway, in Kennedy Center; ☎ 800-876-7372, 202-295-2400; www.dc-opera.org) was hard enough *before* Placido Domingo became artistic director. After his arrival, getting opera tickets became tougher than getting elected. A move to other venues during renovation of the Kennedy Center Opera House discouraged some regulars, so seats became easier to come by. Patrons wondered what would happen after the opera's scheduled return to its regular KC digs in early 2005. To increase your chances of getting the seats you want, call the box office in August or as soon after that as you can. If tickets aren't available, you can get in the standing-room-only line at the Kennedy Center Box office before 10 a.m. on Saturdays during the season. SRO tickets for Saturday and the following week are sold then, one per customer.

Enjoying an evening of dance

The best in the dance world grace Washington's stages. Alvin Ailey, the American Ballet Theatre, the Bolshoi, Merce Cunningham, Paul Taylor, and many other stellar companies take their turns performing here. The city also is quite proud of its own **Washington Ballet** (☎ **202-362-3606;** www.washingtonballet.org). The Washington Ballet performs at Kennedy Center the Warner Theater.

Finding Out What's Playing and Getting Tickets

If you want to take in a play, concert, or dance performance during your D.C. visit, it pays to do a little homework before you arrive. Surf to the Washington, D.C., Convention and Tourism Corp. Web site (www.washington.org) and click Events in the upper-left corner of the page. Or call ☎ **202-789-7000.** You also can peruse *The Washington Post's* daily Style section, Sunday Arts section, and Friday *Weekend* magazine or visit *The Post's* online entertainment guide at http://eg.washingtonpost.com.

Tickets, please!

Competition for tickets to a popular performance can be keen. To get the best seats (or any seats!) for a hit show, you need to buy tickets as far in advance as possible.

If you order tickets over the phone, ask about the seat location; at the box office, ask to see a diagram of the theater.

To order tickets to most events, call **TicketMaster** (☎ **800-551-7328** or 202-432-7328) or visit TicketMaster's Web site, www.ticketmaster.com. Expect to pay an outlandish surcharge. **Tickets.com** (☎ **800-955-5566;** www.tickets.com) pretty much covers what TicketMaster doesn't. Like TicketMaster, expect to pay a high surcharge. If your hotel has a concierge, he or she should be able to get tickets to many events. You may have to pay a surcharge, and you should tip the concierge for the service.

For cut-rate tickets to same-day performances, go to Ticket Place, which moved in 2004 to a new location at 407 7th St. NW between D and E Sts., near the Gallery Place/Chinatown and Archives/Navy Memorial Metrorail stations. After adding on service charges, Ticket Place sells same-day tickets for 62 percent of face value if you go to the ticket booth Tuesday through Saturday from 11 a.m. to 6 p.m. Tickets are sold online at www. ticketplace.org for 67 percent of face value Tuesday through Friday from noon to 4 p.m. Ticket Place doesn't sell tickets by phone but does provide recorded information at ☎ 202-842-5387. Because Ticket Place is closed Sunday and Monday, you can sometimes purchase tickets for those days Saturday. Ticket Place also serves as a TicketMaster outlet.

The best pre-theater dining

If you're catching a theater performance, be seated for dinner no later than 6 p.m., as most curtains go up at 7:30 or 8 p.m. Choose someplace near the theater, in case the service is slow. (Wouldn't you rather sprint a couple of blocks than hail a cab and maybe miss Act I?) When you sit down, tell the host or waiter (or both) that you're going to an event and need to be out by a certain time. Order soon after you're seated and save the soufflé and other dishes requiring lots of preparation for a nontheater evening.

Many restaurants offer pre-theater, fixed-price menus. This dinner usually includes an appetizer or salad, entree, and dessert. Pre-theater specials usually are available from 4:30 or 5 p.m. to 6 or 6:30 p.m. You can spend considerably less than you would if you ordered à la carte.

If you have tickets for a show, consider the following pre-theater deals:

- ✔ **Marcel's** (2401 Pennsylvania Ave. NW, at 24th Street; ☎ 202-296-1166) has the coolest pre- (and post-) theater deal. This highly acclaimed restaurant serves you dinner between 5:30 and 7 p.m., sends you by limo to the Kennedy Center for your show, and then brings you back to the restaurant for dessert after the show, all for $48.

- ✔ The pre-theater dinner at **Circle Bistro** (1 Washington Circle NW, at 23rd Street and New Hampshire Avenue; ☎ 202-293-5390) is served from 5 to 7 p.m. and costs $28.

- ✔ **701**, near the Shakespeare and Ford's theaters (701 Pennsylvania Ave. NW; ☎ 202-393-0701), serves its pre-theater meal from 5:30 to 6:45 p.m.

- ✔ The restaurants in the **Kennedy Center** don't offer pretheater specials, but they certainly are handy places to eat before a show. Reservations are recommended at the full-service **Roof Terrace Restaurant** (2700 F St. NW; ☎ 202-416-8555). They're not accepted at the **KC Cafe**, which also is located on the roof terrace level.

See Chapter 10 for reviews of other restaurants. Ask restaurants near your theater whether they offer a pretheater special.

Some theaters set aside tickets for seniors and full-time students and sell them the day of the performance. If you don't ask, you don't get! Gamblers are advised to arrive at the box office a half-hour before curtain time; sometimes unclaimed reserved tickets are available. If you're determined to attend a performance that's sold out, ask about SRO (Standing Room Only) tickets. If someone leaves at intermission, you may get lucky and snag a seat.

Curtain calls

Some people blame it on the preponderance of bureaucrats in D.C. For whatever reason, Washingtonians are a punctual lot, so you can count on the curtain rising on time. A good general rule is to arrive at least 15 minutes early so that you can visit the restroom and buy your over-priced snack. (I've seen the line to the ladies room snake all the way to Kentucky five minutes before a performance.) Many venues will not seat latecomers until a break in the program occurs — which may mean intermission.

Dressing the part

A night at the theater no longer demands a suit and tie or dress and high heels. Most Washington theatergoers are a shade or two less formal and flamboyant. Knock yourself out and preen your feathers if that's your style, but the usher will show you to your seat no matter what your attire — well, within reason. When in doubt, follow your mother's advice and "wash behind your ears, comb your hair, and look presentable." Try slacks or a skirt, a shirt or blouse, a jacket or sweater, a tie if you want. Now, go make your entrance.

Finding Things for the Kids

Washington offers wonderful cultural opportunities for families, especially during the school year. Look to the following for entertaining productions that are geared to youngsters:

- ✔ The **Discovery Theater,** in the **Smithsonian's Arts and Industries Building** (900 Jefferson Dr. SW; ☎ 202-357-3030; discovery theater.si.edu). During renovation of the Arts and Industries Building, enter the theater through the garden on from the west side of the building.

- ✔ Youth and family programs at the **Kennedy Center** (2700 F St. NW, between New Hampshire Avenue and Rock Creek Parkway; ☎ 800-444-1324 or 202-467-4600; www.kennedy-center.org/programs/family).

- ✔ The free children's program, "Saturday Morning at the **National Theatre**" (1321 Pennsylvania Ave. NW, between 13th and 14th streets; ☎ 202-783-3372; www.nationaltheatre.org). Tickets are given away — first-come, first-served — a half hour before each of the 9:30 and 11 a.m. programs. Recent programs included Pinocchio; the Jungle Book; the Lion, the Witch and the Wardrobe; Snow White and the Seven Dwarfs; Jack And The Beanstalk; and the Blues Alley Youth (jazz) Orchestra.

✔ The **Washington Ballet's** *Nutcracker,* performed during the Christmas season at the Warner Theatre (13th Street NW, between E and F streets; ☎ **202-783-4000;** www.warnertheatre.com).

✔ The "petting zoo" before the **National Symphony's Family Concerts** (2700 F St. NW between New Hampshire Avenue and Rock Creek Parkway, in the Kennedy Center; ☎ **800-444-1324**, 202-467-4600; www.kennedy-center.org/nso) is a treat for budding young musicians and even those who don't know they're budding yet. The concerts are designed to appeal to anyone 7 or older. During the "petting zoo," one hour before each concert, kids can go up to the stage and handle instruments. After 3 p.m. concerts, performers stay to answer children's questions and to tell stories about what it's like to be a musician.

Chapter 16

Bars, Stars, and Gee-Tars: D.C. at Night

. . . .

In This Chapter

▶ Hunting for jazz in Georgetown
▶ Discovering dance clubs in Adams-Morgan
▶ Rocking downtown
▶ Cruising for comedy near the White House
▶ Getting out to gay bars in Dupont Circle

. . . .

*T*aking in Mozart at the Kennedy Center or *Hamlet* at the Shakespeare Theatre may quench your cultural appetite. But it also may leave you thirsty for a chilled cocktail and some hot jazz. When your high-culture sensibilities have been fed, but you feel the urge to get down or wet your whistle, you won't lack for a place to go in D.C. Rest assured, after the lights go off in the White House, you can take the party elsewhere, such as Adams-Morgan or Georgetown. Washington's large international population has spawned clubs, bars, and other nightspots that appeal to its multicultural citizenry.

Before you head off to strut your stuff, keep in mind that Washington, D.C. is not New York City. Washington's subway system doesn't run around the clock. But Metrorail does run later — and earlier — than it used to. The system opens at 5 a.m. weekdays and 7 a.m. weekends. It closes at midnight Sunday through Thursday and 3 a.m. Friday and Saturday. Check when the last train leaves from the station you plan to use at the end of your night of revelry. Leave yourself plenty of time to get to the station, or you may find yourself having to hail a cab. Be aware: D.C. cabs, plentiful as grains of sand during business hours, make like Cinderella's coach at night.

For a comprehensive listing of the entertainment happenings, see the "Weekend" section of the Friday *The Washington Post.* The free *City Paper* — available in bookstores, restaurants, bars, and cafes all around town — is another good source for information on what's going on.

Washington, D.C. Clubs and Bars

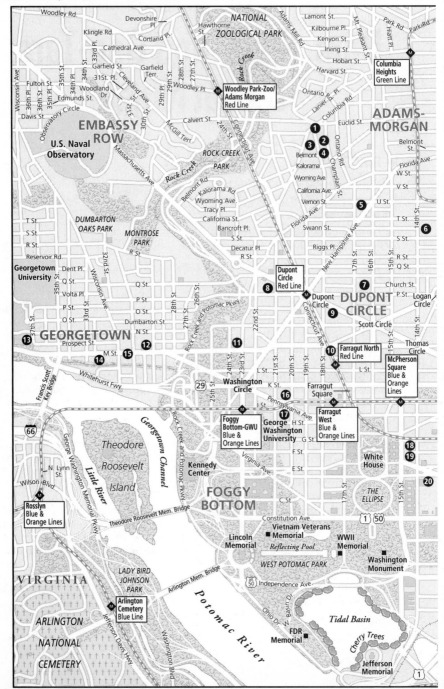

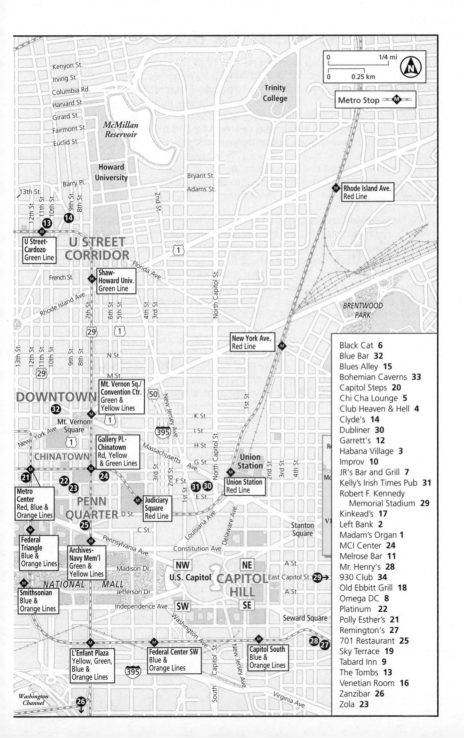

Black Cat **6**
Blue Bar **32**
Blues Alley **15**
Bohemian Caverns **33**
Capitol Steps **20**
Chi Cha Lounge **5**
Club Heaven & Hell **4**
Clyde's **14**
Dubliner **30**
Garrett's **12**
Habana Village **3**
Improv **10**
JR's Bar and Grill **7**
Kelly's Irish Times Pub **31**
Robert F. Kennedy
   Memorial Stadium **29**
Kinkead's **17**
Left Bank **2**
Madam's Organ **1**
MCI Center **24**
Melrose Bar **11**
Mr. Henry's **28**
930 Club **34**
Old Ebbitt Grill **18**
Omega DC **8**
Platinum **22**
Polly Esther's **21**
Remington's **27**
701 Restaurant **25**
Sky Terrace **19**
Tabard Inn **9**
The Tombs **13**
Venetian Room **16**
Zanzibar **26**
Zola **23**

Focusing on the Music: The Best Jazz Clubs

D.C.'s premier jazz club is **Blues Alley** (1073 Wisconsin Ave. NW, in the alley south of M Street; ☎ 202-337-4141; www.bluesalley.com) in Georgetown. All the top touring artists come here. Dizzy Gillespie, Charlie Byrd, Stanley Turrentine, Ahmad Jamal, and Ramsey Lewis cut live albums at the club. Blues Alley bills itself as a jazz supper club and serves Creole cuisine, steak, and seafood from 6 p.m. and lighter fare after 10 p.m. Reservations are recommended, and the best way to get the best seat is to book an early dinner. This place isn't cheap. In addition to your food and drink costs, you pay an $11.25 cover plus an additional ticket charge that varies according to the popularity of the musicians. Shows start at 8 and 10 p.m. most nights.

The **Bohemian Caverns** (2001 11th St. NW at U Street; ☎ 202-299-0801; www.bohemiancaverns.com) is a renovation and expansion of the Crystal Caverns, which showcased such jazz greats as Duke Ellington, Pearl Bailey, Miles Davis, John Coltrane, Ella Fitzgerald, and Billie Holiday from the '20s into the '60s. A full-service restaurant resides within this multi-storied jazz club. Call ahead for information on performances, which aren't scheduled every night. The club maintains a business-casual dress code. Cover is usually $5 to $15.

If you're looking for a romantic spot to share jazz with someone special, settle into the **Blue Bar** downtown in the Henley Park Hotel (926 Massachusetts Ave. NW, west of 9th Street; ☎ 202-638-5200). A small band plays traditional jazz here from 7 p.m. Thursday, Friday, and Saturday nights. The bar is softly lighted and is comprised of a collection of cubiclelike spaces that enable you and your companion to feel a sense of privacy while you listen to the music. The bar has no cover charge.

Friday nights on Capitol Hill, upstairs at **Mr. Henry's** (601 Pennsylvania Ave. SE at 6th Street; ☎ 202-546-8412) is the place for jazz. This comfortable, popular restaurant is known as a gathering plays for gays and lesbians, but it attracts lots of straight men and women for the music, the food, and the laid-back atmosphere. You pay an $8 cover to enter the room where the music plays.

Mainstream jazz is performed downtown without a cover charge at **701 Restaurant** (701 Pennsylvania Ave. NW at 7th Street; ☎ 202-393-0701) and **Kinkead's** restaurant (2000 Pennsylvania Ave. NW, between 20th and 21st streets; ☎ 202-296-7700). The music plays from 6:30 to 10:30 p.m. Sunday through Thursday at 701 and 7 to 11 p.m. Friday and Saturday. At Kinkead's, it's 6:30 to 10 p.m. Tuesday through Sunday.

Turning Up the Volume: Rock and Pop Venues

Many rockers believe the **930 Club**'s (815 V St. NW at Vermont Avenue; ☎ 202-393-0930; www.930.com.) state-of-the-art sound system makes it the best place to hear pop music. It's sure not the seats — there aren't any!

Sheryl Crow, Smashing Pumpkins, R.E.M., Red Hot Chili Peppers, Ice-T, Alanis Morissette, Shawn Colvin — and Tony Bennett! — have played here. The cover charge depends on the act. Call or check the Web site to find out when performances are scheduled. The club's only open when someone's playing, and you're wise to get advance tickets for big-name acts. Tickets are available through **tickets.com** (☎ 800-955-5566 or ☎ 703-218-6500; www.tickets.com) and the 9:30 Club box office, which is open Monday through Friday from noon to 7 p.m. and until 11 p.m. on show nights; Saturday from 6 to 11 p.m. on show nights; and Sunday from 6 to 10:30 p.m. on show nights. The 930 is in the U Street Corridor, an up-and-coming entertainment district. But the club's corner is still a pretty skuzzy looking place. Stick with the crowd on your way to and from the nearby U Street/Cardozo Metrorail Station. Don't go wandering down any dark side streets.

The coolest felines purr at the **Black Cat** (1831 14th St. NW between S and T streets; ☎ 202-667-7960). You don't pay a cover charge in the Red Room bar, which has pool tables, pinball machines, a jukebox with an eclectic selection of music, and a laid-back atmosphere. The ground floor Backstage hosts poetry readings and films. The menu at the smoke-free Food for Thought Cafe satisfies vegans, vegetarians, and carnivores alike. It's upstairs where things can get hopping, in the concert room, which showcases underground/alternative performers and has a dance floor that holds 400. Cover in the concert room depends on the act. Cherry Poppin' Daddies, Foo Fighters, Korn, Squirrel Nut Zippers — and Pete Seeger — are among those who have appeared here.

The big-big-big stars — the kind that can draw tens of thousands to a single concert — stop at the big-big-big venues. When Simon and Garfunkel brought their reunion tour to town in late 2003, for example, they set up shop at **MCI Center** (601 F St. NW at 6th Street; ☎ 202-628-3200; www.mcicenter.com). MCI also is where Bruce Springsteen and his fellow political-activist performers finished their ill-fated Vote for Change tour on the eve of the 2004 election. Normally MCI Center is where you find the Washington Wizards National Basketball Association team and the Washington Capitals, D.C.'s entry in the National Hockey League.

When MCI's 20,000-plus concert seats aren't enough, superstars take their acts to **Robert F. Kennedy Memorial Stadium** (East Capitol Street at 22nd Street; ☎ 202-547-9077; www.dcsec.com/rfk_stadium), which can accommodate 55,000 or more. The Rolling Stones rocked RFK, as do some giant music festivals. As a sports stadium, RFK is home to the D.C.

United Major League Soccer club and was slated to host the Washington Nationals (formerly Montreal Expos) Major League Baseball team in the spring of 2005. New baseball and soccer stadiums supposedly are in D.C.'s future, so some wonder what RFK's future will look like.

Shaking Your Groove Thing: Dance Clubs

Do you wanna dance? If so, see the preceding section of this chapter for details about the **930 Club** and the **Black Cat,** where rockers go dance as well as to listen to top-name performers. Then consider these other venues, where dancing's the thing and the music is as — or more — likely to be recorded as live.

As you may expect, **Club Heaven & Hell** (2327 18th St. NW at Columbia Road; ☎ **202-667-4355**) welcomes both angels and devils. Check your wings and pitchforks at this Adams-Morgan door. Here, it's Heaven that sizzles. It's a loud dancehall on the upper level (of course) that features different styles of music on different nights, sometimes live, sometimes DJ-generated. On weekends, the pearly gates don't close until 3 a.m. (2 a.m. Sunday through Thursday). Hell, downstairs, is a dark bar with a juke box and pool table.

Another Adams-Morgan nightspot, **Madam's Organ** (2461 18th St. NW, south of Columbia Road; ☎ **202-667-5370;** www.madamsorgan.com) — the owner likes puns — was named one of the 25 best bars in America by *Playboy* magazine in 2000. Madam's has a varied musical menu, with shows starting between 9 and 10 p.m. On Monday, it's funky jazz, Tuesday Delta blues, Wednesday bluegrass (with local TV news anchor Doug McKelway sometimes sitting in on banjo), Thursday R&B and blues, and Friday and Saturday "flaming hot blues." Sometimes you encounter smooth jazz, reggae, salsa, meringue, and/or a magician. You can eat sandwiches, snacks, and "soul food" here. Redheads get half price on Rolling Rock. The second floor bar is called "Big Daddy's Love Lounge & Pick-Up Joint." The place describes itself as a "blues bar and soul food restaurant where the beautiful people go to get ugly." If you want noise, body heat, and dancing, Madam's is the spot for you. Or you can go outside on the roof deck to cool off — or order something from the tiki bar! Madam's is open Sunday through Thursday from 5 p.m. to 2 a.m. and Friday and Saturday from 5 p.m. to 3 a.m. Cover usually is between $3 and $7.

Platinum (915 F St. NW, between 9th and 10th streets; ☎ **202-393-3555;** www.platinumclubdc.com) is a downtown upscale club with three dance floors on which the young and the beautiful usually move to mainstream music. Platinum has a VIP lounge with memberships for sale. The VIP lounge also takes table reservations and requires "proper attire." It's open 10 p.m. to 3 a.m. Thursday through Saturday, and 9 p.m. to 2:30 a.m. on Sunday, usually with a $10 to $15 cover. College students get in free before 11 p.m. Thursdays, while "ladies" are free until 11 p.m. Fridays.

Polly Esther's (605 12th St. NW, between F and G streets; ☎ 202-737-1970) three dance levels often showcase different themes — '70s music on floor, '80s on another. It has many bars and much noise. Thursday is College Night, featuring hip-hop and top-40 music with no cover and 18-year-olds welcome. Friday's $15 cover gives you access to an open bar all night, while DJs spin '70s and '80s music on one floor and current songs on another. Saturday all three floors hop with different music styles. Cover is $10. Polly is open Thursday from 9 p.m. to 2 a.m. and until 3 a.m. Friday and Saturday when you must be 21 to enter this downtown spot. Dress is "casual but neat."

If you'd like a view with your dancing, salsa on down to **Zanzibar** (700 Water St. SW, between 7th and 8th streets; ☎ 202-554-9100; www.ejzdesign.com/zan). Actually, you'd best take a cab. This large, popular dance club comes with picture windows that look out onto the boats tied up in the Washington Channel. You can cool down on outdoor decks during nice weather. Inside, year-round, the club sports multiple rooms, bars, and dance floors on several levels. A fair number of tables and comfortable seating are situated around the place. On the bottom floor, a restaurant becomes a nightclub with a stage at 10 p.m. Zanzibar offers live and recorded music of various genres, especially jazz, salsa, and R & B. This club draws an international, integrated clientele — especially Latin Americans, folks of Latin American heritage, and folks who like to dance to Latin music. Zanzibar is open Sunday from 5 to 8 p.m., Tuesday through Thursday from 5 p.m. to 1 a.m., Friday from 5 p.m. to 3 a.m., and Saturday from 9 p.m. to 4 a.m. Cover is $10 most nights.

Hanging Out: D.C.'s Best Bars

After a rough day of sightseeing, kicking back with your favorite aperitif can be therapeutic.

If you want to mix a little romance with your relaxation, consider the **Blue Bar,** described in the jazz section earlier in this chapter, or the **Venetian Room,** described in the next section, "Going International: Latin, Irish, and Italian Hot Spots." For cheek-to-cheek dancing — maybe with dinner first — try the **Melrose Bar** in the Park Hyatt Hotel (24th Street NW at M Street; ☎ 202-789-1234), where a dance band plays from 7 to 11 p.m. on Saturdays.

The well-worn comfort of the **Tabard Inn** (1739 N St. NW, between 17th and 18th streets; ☎ 202-833-2668) near Dupont Circle makes it a perfect spot for a drink all year round. It's even better in the winter, when you can cozy up to the fireplace. Every Sunday, live jazz plays from 7:30 to 10:30 p.m. The **Old Ebbitt Grill** (675 15th St. NW, between F and G streets; ☎ 202-347-4800) has the feel of an old-fashioned men's club, and as the evening wears on, that feeling grows. This downtown tavern is big enough and has multiple bars, so you ought to be able to find a spot that satisfies you. You have lots of choices in the nibbles department as well.

The lounge at **Zola** (800 F St. NW; ☎ 202-654-0999), with floor-to-ceiling windows looking at the street action in the Penn Quarter arts and entertainment district downtown, was named 2004's "Hottest Restaurant Bar Scene" by readers of both *The Washington Post's* Sunday magazine and the Restaurant Association of Metropolitan Washington's website. Zola prints an innovative cocktail and wine list and has become a popular after-work gathering spot.

Enjoy a panoramic view of Washington with your cocktail at the **Sky Terrace** atop the Hotel Washington (151 15th St. NW at Pennsylvania Avenue; ☎ 202-638-5900). Between May and October, weather willing, this outdoor restaurant is a wonderful vantage point for watching the sun set over the city or the lights come on at D.C.'s landmarks.

For a beer with some atmosphere, drop on a longtime Georgetown hangout. **Clyde's** (3236 M St. NW, between Wisconsin Avenue and Potomac Street; ☎ 202-333-9180) has helped to define eating and drinking in Georgetown since 1963. A 1996 renovation replaced much of its old-time-tavern feeling with the appearance of your typical, late-20th century, family-friendly theme bar (airplane models dangling from the ceiling in one room, for example). But it's still a comfortable spot for a beer and a burger — or bar munchies or a full meal. Clyde's is open Monday through Thursday from 11:30 a.m. until midnight, Friday 11:30 a.m. to 1 a.m., Saturday 10 a.m. to 1 a.m., and Sunday 9 a.m. until midnight.

If you prefer that worn, college-bar mystique, stroll east on M Street for about two blocks to **Garrett's** (3003 M St. NW at 30th Street; ☎ 202-333-8282; www.garrettsdc.com) where the street-level bar will remind you of some place you drank and dug the juke box in your past — except that this juke box is linked to the Internet and has a near-limitless selection of songs. The last time I was here, Dylan was spitting out "Rainy Day Woman" like it was 1966. Upstairs you find two more bars, a golf game, and a nice little restaurant. It's open daily 11:30 a.m. to 2 a.m.

Georgetown's main college bar is **The Tombs** (1226 36th St. NW at Prospect Street; ☎ 202-337-6668), which occupies the basement of a mid-19th-century house at the edge of the Georgetown University campus. Students, faculty, and other residents of the neighborhood frequent this comfortable, attractive pub, which once counted a young Bill Clinton among its regulars. The food is unusually good for a college hangout, because the excellent 1789 Restaurant occupies the rest of this house, and chef Ris Lacoste watches over the cooking down here as well. The Tombs is open Monday through Thursday from 11:30 a.m. to 2 a.m., Friday from 11:30 a.m. to 3 a.m., Saturday from 11 a.m. to 3 a.m., and Sunday from 9:30 a.m. to 2 a.m.

Hot and tired from a wild night of Adams-Morgan revelry? Take a break for a drink and some nibbles at **Left Bank** (2424 18th St. NW, between Belmont and Columbia roads; ☎ 202-464-2100), an impossible-to-categorize spot from the imagination of entertainment entrepreneur

Sahir Erozan. In nice weather, you can hang out at one of Left Bank's sidewalk tables or just inside the floor-to-ceiling window/doors Sahir swings open when it's warm outside. Inside are several different seating areas, from booths to communal breakfast-bar-like tables to picnic tables to a sushi bar and a regular bar (if a bar made from poured concrete can be termed "regular"). Left Bank opens at 7 a.m. for breakfast, with international magazines and newspapers served along with eggs and pastries. It closes at 2 a.m. (3 a.m. weekends). The morning's mobile breakfast carts become cocktail carts at night. The menu features small plates, sandwiches, and entrees, none of which exceeds $15. Had enough alcoholic beverages for the night? Try a peach-mango-raspberry smoothie for five bucks.

Going International: Latin, Irish, and Italian Hot Spots

Want to add a little international flavor to your Washington nightlife? If your tastes run to dancing and things Latin, you'll enjoy **Zanzibar,** described earlier in this chapter. If you need Latin dancing lessons, check when they're being offered at **Habana Village** (1834 Columbia Rd. NW, between Biltmore Street and Belmont Road; ☎ 202-462-6310), an Adams-Morgan nightspot where salsa and merangue are big Wednesday through Saturday from 6:30 p.m. to 3 a.m. The **Chi Cha Lounge** (1624 U St. NW, between 16th and 17th streets; ☎ 202-234-8400) entertains with Latin drinks, Latin music, and *tapas.* Oh, and also water pipes — but for smoking tobacco only. Chi Cha has a $15 tab minimum and is open Sunday through Thursday from 5:30 p.m. to 1:30 a.m. and Friday and Saturday from 5:30 p.m. to 2:30 a.m.

The Irish have been influential in American politics for a long time, so it stands to reason that America's capital would have its share of Irish pubs. On Capitol Hill, side-by-side competition occurs between the **Dubliner** (520 N. Capitol St. NW, at F Street; ☎ 202-638-6900) and **Kelly's Irish Times Pub** (14 F St. NW, between North Capitol Street and New Jersey Avenue; ☎ 202-543-5433). Both spots parcel out Irish beer, Irish food, and live Irish music. Both offer sidewalk tables in nice weather You find lots of Capitol Hill denizens here — congressional staffers, journalists, lobbyists, and the occasional legislator. The Times also attracts 20-somethings to a pop juke box in the basement and is open Sunday through Thursday from 11 a.m. to 1:30 a.m. and Friday and Saturday until 2:30 a.m. The Dubliner is open daily from 11 a.m. until the crowd thins out after midnight, and in the morning for breakfast: Monday through Friday from 7 to 10 a.m. and Saturday and Sunday from 7:30 to 10:30 a.m.

To combine your international explorations with romance, slip into the **Venetian Room** (2019 Pennsylvania Ave. NW, between 20th and 21st streets; ☎ 202-828-2600) in the Hotel Lombardy downtown. The ambience here is dark and lush. You sink into deep banquettes and chairs. As your eyes adjust to the candlelight, you admire the deep-colored velvets and silks. Between 5:30 and 9:30 p.m., you can nibble on delicious *spuntino,* Italian and Italian-influenced snacks, at $4 to $6 per plate. The Venetian Room is open daily for drinks from 4:30 p.m. till midnight.

Laughing the Night Away: Comedy Clubs

The best comedy in Washington is homegrown. **The Capitol Steps** (www. capsteps.com) did, in fact, blossom on the Capitol steps. Congressional staffers with talent saw the humor around them and turned it into an enduring musical act. I'm talking about songs like "It's a Whole Newt World," "Send in the Clones," "Don't Cry for Me, Judge Scalia," "Enron-Ron-Ron," "Papa's Got a Brand New Baghdad," and, following the 2004 election, "Hang Down Your Head, Tom Daschle." They've been doing this act since the early '80s ("The Wreck of the Walter Fritz Mondale," "Dutch, the Magic Reagan"). Now, they have a regular gig every Friday and Saturday at 7:30 p.m. in the amphitheater of the (don't you love irony?) Ronald Reagan Building, 1300 Pennsylvania Ave. NW, between 13th and 14th streets. You can purchase the $34 tickets from TicketMaster (☎ **800-551-7328** or 202-432-7328; www.ticketmaster.com), at the D.C. Visitor Information Center in the Reagan Building, or at the door after 6 p.m. on the night of the performance.

Headliners on the national comedy club circuit (and subheadliners, too, if the truth be known) perform at **The Improv** (1140 Connecticut Ave. NW, between L and M streets; ☎ **202-296-7008;** www.dcimprov.com). Ellen DeGeneres, Jerry Seinfeld, and Robin Williams have performed here. So have a whole bunch of people I've never heard of, supposedly with Comedy Central credentials. Drinks and light meals are available. Show times are Tuesday through Thursday at 8:30 p.m., Friday and Saturday at 8 and 10:30 p.m., and Sunday at 8 p.m. The cover varies with the lineup. You can make reservations in person at the box office, by phone, or from the Web site. You must be 18 to enter.

Stepping Out: The Gay and Lesbian Scene

Gays' full participation in the Washington community is reflected in the city's nightlife. As you may expect, Dupont Circle has the most gay-oriented night spots. But some of the best-known gay-focused spots are on Capitol Hill and downtown. And some attract a substantial straight clientele as well.

Among the most popular is **JR's Bar and Grill** (1519 17th St. NW, between P and Q streets. Dupont Circle Metro; ☎ 202-328-0090), which was named Washington's best gay bar by voters in *The Washington Post's* online readers poll in 2003. The bar draws upscale gay men and has big-screen TV and pool tables. JR's is open Sunday through Thursday from 4 p.m. to 2 a.m. and Friday and Saturday from 2 p.m. to 3 a.m.

Also attracting gay men in Dupont Circle is **Omega DC** (2122 P St. NW between 21st and 22nd streets; ☎ 202-223-4917), which scatters parties over two floors with several rooms that contain a piano bar, a cigar/martini bar, two more bars, a pool table, and a 60-inch video screen. The Monday drag show starts at 10:30 p.m. Omega DC is open Sunday from 7 p.m. to 2 a.m., Monday through Thursday from 4 p.m. to 2 a.m., Friday from 4 p.m. to 3 a.m., and Saturday from 8 p.m. to 2 a.m.

Capitol Hill boasts **Remington's** (639 Pennsylvania Ave. SE between 6th and 7th streets; ☎ 202-543-3113; www.remingtonswdc.com), a country-western bar that offers Western dance lessons and attracts mostly gay men. It's open Monday through Thursday from 9 p.m. to 2 a.m., Friday from 4 p.m. to 3 a.m., Saturday from 8 p.m. to 3 a.m., and Sunday from 5 p.m. to 2 a.m. (except during the summer when it doesn't open until 6:30 p.m.). Also on Capitol Hill, **Mr. Henry's** (601 Pennsylvania Ave. SE at 6th Street; ☎ 202-546-8412) lures a mixed gay/straight clientele for meals, and for jazz Friday nights on the second floor. It's open Sunday through Thursday from 11:15 a.m. until midnight and Friday and Saturday until 1 a.m.

Part VI
The Part of Tens

The 5th Wave   By Rich Tennant

"That? That's Schedule LVES-1. We've never had to use it. But, if anyone actually discovers how to grow money on trees, Uncle Sam's got a form to get his fair share of the leaves."

In this part . . .

Ah, tradition. The Part of Tens is to *For Dummies* books what monument hopping is to Washington — essential. In this part, I list the top ten views in D.C. and the top ten reasons to (gulp) drive around the city.

Chapter 17

Top Ten D.C. Views

. . . .

In This Chapter

▶ Discovering great places to see D.C. in all its spendor
▶ Climbing to high spots that overlook the city
▶ Rooftop dining and riverside walking
▶ Finding scenic spots for panorama photos

. . . .

S ooner or later, even the most jaded visitor succumbs to Washington's
beauty. During your visit, I hope you find time to admire Washington's
pretty face from one or more of the following sites. And don't forget to
put the film in your camera.

Washington Monument

It's pretty widely agreed that the best view of Washington comes from
the top of the **Washington Monument** (between Constitution Avenue NW,
Independence Avenue SW, and 15th and 17th streets; ☎ **202-426-6841;**
www.nps.gov/wash; advance tickets 800-967-2283 or reservations.
nps.gov). You take the fast elevator to the top, wander from window to
window to get a panoramic view and then ride down more slowly so that
you can gander at the monument's interior. Unfortunately, it's been
closed a couple times in recent years — first for a monumental face life
and then in fall 2004 for one of D.C.'s ubiquitous security upgrades. It
was scheduled to reopen in spring 2005. Call or check the Web site to
see whether it's open during your visit. When business is normal, the
elevator runs daily 9 a.m. to 4:45 p.m. See the monument's listing in
Chapter 11 for details on getting tickets.

Old Post Office Pavilion

Ride the elevator in the tower of the **Old Post Office Pavilion**
(Pennsylvania Avenue NW at 11th Street; ☎ **202-606-8691;** www.nps.
gov/opot). From the observation deck, 270 feet above the street,
you can see a view of downtown and beyond that many people think
is second only to the vista from the Washington Monument (see preceding section).

Top Washington, D.C. Views

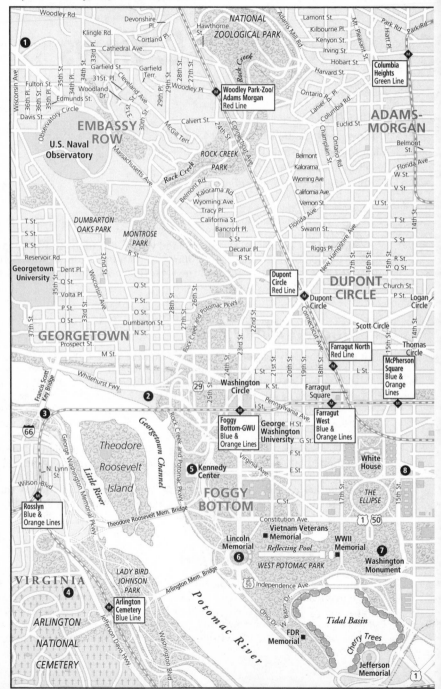

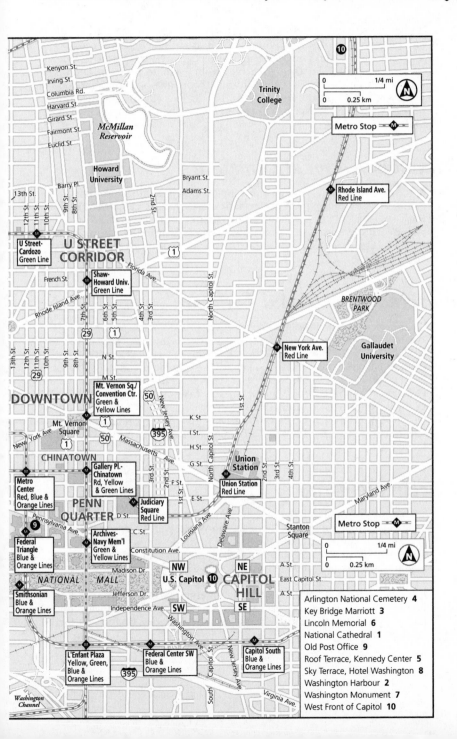

Arlington National Cemetery **4**
Key Bridge Marriott **3**
Lincoln Memorial **6**
National Cathedral **1**
Old Post Office **9**
Roof Terrace, Kennedy Center **5**
Sky Terrace, Hotel Washington **8**
Washington Harbour **2**
Washington Monument **7**
West Front of Capitol **10**

While you're here, take a look at the interior workings of the tower clock and bells and visit the ninth-floor exhibit room. The bells are rung on federal holidays and on special occasions declared by Congress. The tower is open Monday through Friday from 9 a.m. to 4:45 p.m. and until 7:45 p.m. from the first weekend in June through Labor Day. Year-round hours on weekends and holidays are 10 a.m. to 5:45 p.m. Because the observation deck is exposed to the elements, the tower may close in bad weather.

Arlington National Cemetery

If you don't own one, I suggest picking up a disposable panoramic camera before touring **Arlington National Cemetery** (☎ 703-607-8000; www.arlingtoncemetery.org). You can get some great shots of Washington from the Arlington House lawn (a Tourmobile stop) or from Pierre L'Enfant's grave below the house. (For more on Arlington, see Chapter 11.)

Washington National Cathedral

Washington's highest points above sea level are the towers of the Washington National Cathedral (Massachusetts and Wisconsin avenues NW; ☎ 202-537-6200; www.cathedral.org/cathedral), so the views from those spots are among the best in the city. Unfortunately, tourists can't go all the way to the top. But the view from the **Pilgrim Observation Gallery** is still pretty cool. One way to partake of that view is to have tea in the gallery. (See Chapter 10 for information on making reservations.) Or you can visit on your own from 10 a.m. to 5 p.m. Monday through Saturday or 1 to 4 p.m. Sunday. (See the Cathedral's listing in Chapter 11 for details.)

Lincoln Memorial

Take a break from reading the Gettysburg Address on the wall and gaze at the Reflecting Pool, the Mall, the World War II Memorial, the Washington Monument, and the Capitol from the steps of the **Lincoln Memorial** (23rd Street NW, between Constitution and Independence avenues, on the National Mall; ☎ 202-426-6841; www.nps.gov/linc). Then walk around to the back of Lincoln's place for a view across the Potomac River of Arlington National Cemetery and the eternal flame marking John F. Kennedy's grave. The Lincoln Memorial is always open, and the view is particularly impressive after dark. See Chapter 11 for more details.

Roof Terrace of the Kennedy Center

You don't need orchestra seats to visit the **Kennedy Center** (2700 F St. NW, between New Hampshire Avenue and Rock Creek Parkway; ☎ **202-416-8340;** www.kennedy-center.org). In fact, one of the best shows in town plays night and day, and it's free. Although you may want to dine in the **Roof Terrace Restaurant** (reservations ☎ **202-416-8555**) or the **KC Cafe** (no reservations), which also is located on the roof terrace level, you can feast on the view from the promenade *outside* the restaurants without spending a cent. Circle the promenade once for a 360-degree vista. The center is open daily from 10 a.m. until 30 minutes after the last performance. See Chapter 15 for more details.

Key Bridge Marriott Hotel

Visitors and locals have been flocking to the top floor of the **Key Bridge Marriott** (1401 Lee Highway, Arlington, Virginia, just across the Key Bridge from Georgetown; ☎ **703-524-6400**) since it opened more than 40 years ago. Although the hotel's restaurant has gone through more lives than a cat, the outstanding vista has endured. Diners at **JW's View Steakhouse** look out across the Potomac River to Georgetown and the rest of Washington's skyline. The steakhouse is open Monday through Saturday from 5 to 9 p.m. and Sunday from 9 a.m. to 2 p.m. for brunch.

Sky Terrace

Come to this open-air rooftop restaurant for the view, not the food. If you do eat at the **Sky Terrace** (in the Hotel Washington, 151 15th St. NW at Pennsylvania Avenue; ☎ **202-638-5900**), pick something simple, like a sandwich. Or just have a drink. You're here for the bird's-eye view of the White House in the next block and the rest of Washington further into the distance. Arrive by 5:30 p.m. if you want to beat out the locals and other tourists for a seat. The Sky Terrace is open daily 11:30 to 1 a.m. late April to mid-October.

Washington Harbour

Walk along the **riverfront promenade** at Washington Harbour, below K Street at Thomas Jefferson Street in Georgetown, and gaze across the Potomac toward Virginia. Dead ahead is Theodore Roosevelt Island. To the left, you can make out the Watergate and, beyond it, the Kennedy Center. To the right, Key Bridge connects Georgetown with Arlington, Virginia. If you're so moved, grab an outdoor seat at one of the harbour's restaurants and have a sip or a snack.

West Front of Capitol

One of the many victims of increased D.C. security is the marvelous view from the steps and terrace on the West Front of the Capitol. It's one of the best places to watch the sun set over the Washington Monument, Lincoln Memorial, and Potomac River. Seeing Washington's marble landmarks bathed in golden light, with purple and pink streaking the sky over the Potomac, is an awesome sight. The view at others times of the day and after dark ain't to shabby either. Now you can catch of glimpse of that view when you take a Capitol tour. Or you can walk across the West Lawn to the base of the steps and check out a lower-level perspective. (See the Capitol's listing in Chapter 11 for touring information.)

Chapter 18

If You Must Drive: Ten D.C. Roadside Attractions

know: If you've read any other chapter in this book, then you've seen my repeated warnings that you should not drive in Washington. This chapter, though, goes contrary to that advice because I'm actually giving you ten reasons *to* drive. I'll just call this chapter — as members of Congress do in the *Congressional Record* — a revision and extension of my remarks. If you happen to have a car, you can find some sights that are worth driving to. I'm not really advocating that you drive *in* central D.C. but encouraging you to use your car to reach sights and attractions that are mostly outside the District.

National Arboretum

The best time to visit the **National Arboretum** (3501 New York Ave. NE, between Bladensberg Road and South Dakota Avenue; ☎ **202-245-2726;** www.usna.usda.gov) is from late April into late May, when the azaleas are in full riot and crabapples, dogwoods, peonies, roses, and irises also bloom. If you can't make it during that timeframe, though, don't worry: The National Arboretum always has something to see, such as magnolias in early spring and holly berries in winter. Some manmade items will grab your attention as well, such as 22 sandstone columns that were removed from the East Portico of the Capitol during a renovation and now stand like an ancient ruin in the arboretum.

This 446-acre site is a research and educational facility of the Agricultural Department's Research Service. Stop at the Administration Building to pick up a map and guide and to find out what's blooming.

If the azaleas are in flower, you *have* to drive Azalea Road. You won't believe the cascade of colors! Pack a picnic.

From downtown D.C., go northeast on New York Avenue all the way to the arboretum's entrance (to the right). Watch carefully for the sign after you cross the big Bladensberg Road intersection. Returning to downtown is trickier because of traffic patterns. I suggest using the R Street exit from the arboretum, which is near the Administration Building. Turn left on Bladensburg and then right on Maryland Avenue, which carries you right to the Capitol. Watch out for the jog around Stanton Park Square at 6th and C streets. Arboretum grounds are open daily (except December 25) from 8 a.m. to 5 p.m.

Clara Barton National Historic Site

Hard as it is to believe, when **Clara Barton**'s last home (5801 Oxford Rd., Glen Echo, Maryland, southwest of Macarthur Boulevard; ☎ **301-492-6245;** www.nps.gov/clba) became part of the National Park Service in 1975, it was the first National Historic Site dedicated to the accomplishments of a woman. The founder of the American Red Cross lived here from February 28, 1897, until she died in her bedroom on April 12, 1912, at the age of 90. Until she resigned as Red Cross president in 1904, her residence was also the Red Cross headquarters and a warehouse for disaster supplies.

To reach the site, go west on M Street out of Georgetown and then turn left on Canal Road, which becomes Clara Barton Parkway. Then follow the signs to the Clara Barton National Historic Site. The interior of the house is shown by guided tour daily on the hour, with the first tour at 10 a.m. and the last tour at 4 p.m. (closed Thanksgiving, December 25, and January 1). Admission is free.

Don't leave Washington before 9:30 a.m., when a portion of Canal Road is inbound only. Conversely, don't drive into town between 3:30 and 6:30 p.m., when the road is one-way out.

Glen Echo Park

Glen Echo Park (7300 MacArthur Blvd., Glen Echo, Maryland, at Oxford Road; ☎ **301-492-6229,** recorded information 301-320-2330; www.nps.gov/glec) is a very strange place, located essentially next door to the Clara Barton House. Glen Echo is an abandoned amusement park with a marvelous working carousel and a bunch of sod-roofed Mongolian *yurts* (large, wooden-framed tents lined with felt) that house arts programs.

Glen Echo was a functioning amusement park, served by trolleys, from around 1900 until 1968, when slow business forced the park to close down. But some architecture remains, and the park's history lives on in

Ten D.C. Roadside Attractions

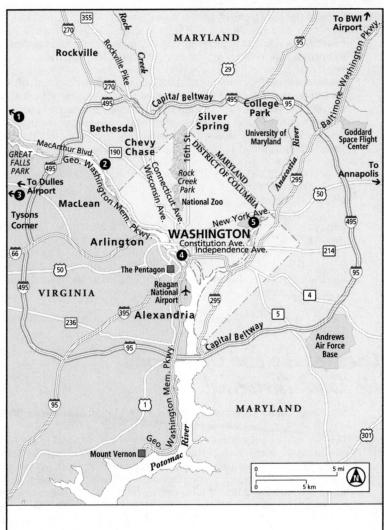

Chesapeake & Ohio
   Canal National Historical Park **1**
Clara Barton National Historic Site **2**
Glen Echo Park **2**
National Arboretum **5**
Theodore Roosevelt Island **4**
Wolf Trap **3**

the carousel — with 40 horses, 4 rabbits, 4 ostriches, a giraffe, a deer, a lion, a tiger, 2 circus chariots, more than 1,000 lights, and lots of mirrors — and the dances still held in the ballroom. Other facilities here house quite a few arts programs, many for children, plus puppet shows and other performances. You also can picnic at the park.

Restoration of the amusement park remnants is an ongoing project, conducted by the National Park Service and a few local groups inspired by the project. When I walk around this place — especially in winter when no one's here — I feel like an archeologist exploring some reasonably well-preserved ruin: You see the remains of the swimming pool over here, the abandoned bumper car pavilion over there. . . .

To get to Glen Echo Park, follow the directions to the Clara Barton House. You can't miss it: It's the abandoned amusement park with the stone tower and the yurts!

The park grounds and parking lot are open all the time. The carousel operates, May through June, Wednesday and Thursday from 10 a.m. to 2 p.m. and Saturday and Sunday from noon to 6 p.m.; July through August, Wednesday through Friday 10 a.m. to 2 p.m. and Saturday and Sunday noon to 6 p.m.; and September, Saturday and Sunday noon to 6 p.m. Tickets are 75 cents.

Call or explore the Web site for details on the many other activities.

Chesapeake and Ohio Canal National Historical Park

The **C&O Canal National Historical Park** (11710 MacArthur Blvd., Potomac, Maryland, at the end of the road; ☎ **301-767-3714;** www.nps.gov/choh) actually stretches along the old canal from Georgetown to Cumberland, Maryland. In this chapter, I'm talking about the section of the park at the Great Falls of the Potomac in Maryland. My family comes here regularly to picnic, stroll the boardwalk out to the falls, and hike along the canal and into the bordering hills. The setting is beautiful. You can brush up on your history at the visitor center in the old Great Falls Tavern, which served canal boat passengers. You can bring a picnic or buy simple foods at the park refreshment stand. Usually, you can take a 70-minute ride on a replica of a canal boat. *Note:* Unfortunately, the boat was taken out of service for repairs during 2004. Call to check whether the boat is back to plying the water during your visit.

To get to Great Falls, follow the directions to the Clara Barton House (see the section "Clara Barton National Historic Site," earlier in this chapter), but stay on the Clara Barton Parkway until it ends at McArthur Boulevard. Follow McArthur into the park.

The park is open daily during daylight hours, and the visitor center operates daily from 9 a.m. to 4:45 p.m. Admission is $5 per vehicle for a three-day pass.

Great Falls Park

Directly across the Potomac River from the C&O Canal Park's Great Falls area is Virginia's **Great Falls Park** (9200 Old Dominion Dr., McLean, Virginia, at Georgetown Pike; ☎ **703-285-2965;** www.nps.gov/grfa). You see the same falls from the opposite side, can picnic and hike, and can check out some additional history at Virginia's park. A substantial visitor center offers history and nature exhibits. Before he presided over the successful launch of a new nation, George Washington presided over a failed attempt to build a canal on this side of the Potomac. Remnants are visible.

Go west on M Street out of Georgetown, left on Canal Road, left over Chain Bridge, right on Virginia Route 123 (Chain Bridge Road), and then right on Virginia Route 193 (Georgetown Pike). Turn right at Old Dominion Drive at the sign to the park.

The park is open daily, except December 25, from 7 a.m. until dark. From mid-April to mid-October, the visitor center is open from 10 a.m. to 5 p.m. weekdays and 10 a.m. to 6 p.m. weekends. The rest of the year, it's open daily from 10 a.m. to 4 p.m. Admission is $5 per vehicle for a three-day pass.

Wolf Trap

The name says it all here: **Wolf Trap Farm Park for the Performing Arts** (1551 Trap Rd., Vienna, Virginia, off the Wolf Trap exit from the Dulles Toll Road; ☎ **703-255-1800;** www.nps.gov/wotr). At the Filene Center — a roofed, open-air theater with outdoor lawn seating as well — big-name artists perform before audiences of up to 7,000 from May through September. The **Meadow Pavilion** and the **Theatre in the Woods** host workshops in theater and other arts and crafts. Performances are held throughout the year in the **Barns of Wolf Trap,** a 352-seat indoor theater built in two restored 18th-century barns.

The word eclectic was created to describe Wolf Trap's performance schedule: the National Symphony Orchestra, the Wolf Trap Opera, pop, rock, country, folk, Broadway musicals, operettas, and lots of stuff for kids and for aging Boomers. It's becoming a summer tradition for my sister and her husband to come for a visit that includes a trip to Wolf Trap for some '50s/'60s/'70s group that's still keeping the candle burning — the Kingston Trio, the Smothers Brothers, the Doobie Brothers. Susan and I have seen Peter, Paul, and Mary here several times. We used to take Julie here for kids festivals. Most recently, she thought it would be fun to come for the Mikado. (She was right!) Wolf Trap has a restaurant (reservations are strongly advised) and lots of space for picnicking — and holding festivals — on the 117 acres of farm and forest land. Call or visit the Web site to find out which performances might appeal to you.

Drive west on Constitution Avenue to westbound I-66. Watch for signs to Virginia Route 267 local exits (the Dulles Toll Road). After you're on 267, watch for signs to Wolf Trap. (*Don't* get on the toll-free Dulles Access Highway, which is restricted to airport traffic.) Admission to the park is free. Fees for performances vary.

Theodore Roosevelt Island

This little island in the middle of the Potomac River is a memorial to the 26th president's history as an outdoorsman and advocate of conservation. **Theodore Roosevelt Island Park** (George Washington Memorial Parkway; ☎ 703-289-2500; www.nps.gov/this) contains 91 acres of woods, 2½ miles of trails, and a memorial plaza with an outsized statue of Roosevelt. It's a pleasant respite that's actually inside the city limits.

Drive west on Constitution Avenue and continue straight across the Theodore Roosevelt Memorial Bridge to the George Washington Memorial Parkway (northbound). The Roosevelt Island parking lot is to your right immediately after you enter the parkway. *Don't miss it!* The only entrance is from the northbound lanes. The park is open daily from sunrise to sunset, and admission is free.

George Washington Memorial Parkway

You can explore numerous interesting places along the **George Washington Memorial Parkway** (☎ 703-289-2500; www.nps.gov/gwmp; e-mail: gwnp_superintendent@nps.gov; mailing address: George Washington Memorial Parkway Headquarters, Turkey Run Park, McLean, VA 22101), which runs along the west bank of the Potomac River from I-495 northwest of D.C. to Mount Vernon. Julie and I spent one pleasant weekend driving along the road and stopping at places we'd never visited. Write, phone, or e-mail parkway headquarters before your visit to ask for a map/brochure to be mailed to you. Otherwise, get it at parkway headquarters in Turkey Run Park, near the north end of the beltway, between 7:45 a.m. and 4:15 p.m. Monday through Friday or from outdoor boxes along the parkway at Turkey Run, Mount Vernon, Marine Corps Memorial, Netherlands Carillon, and Fort Marcy. (You also can ask whether parkway brochures are available at other National Park Service sites you visit in the Washington area.)

Turkey Run is 700 acres of forest and hiking trails. Other parkway highlights include

- **Dyke Marsh:** This 380 acres of tidal marsh, floodplain, and swamp forest comprises the largest remaining freshwater tidal wetlands in the Washington Metropolitan area and attracts birdwatchers.

- **Fort Hunt:** Batteries here guarded the river approach to Washington from 1898 to 1918.

- **Fort Marcy:** The earthenwork remnant is just one example of the many forts that surrounded Washington during the Civil War.

- **Netherlands Carillon:** The 50-bell, 127-foot tall carillon was given by the Dutch to express gratitude to the United States after World War II. The bells strike the hour daily from 10 a.m. to 6 p.m. Carillonneurs present concerts Saturdays and national holidays from 2 to 4 p.m. in May and September and 6 to 8 p.m. in June, July, and August. During concerts, visitors are welcome to go up in the tower to watch the carillonneur perform. Automated concerts occur caily at noon and 6 p.m. On May 5, Dutch Independence Day, you hear The Netherlands' National Anthem. On July 4, by act of Congress, the largest bell tolls 13 times at 2 p.m. Patriotic songs are played at 9:04 a.m. September 2, the moment the Japanese armistice ended World War II. At 6 p.m. New Year's Eve, you can toast to Auld Lang Syne (a bit early, don't you think?)

- **Marine Corps Memorial:** This oversized sculpture of the famous World War II photograph, by Joe Rosenthal, shows Marines raising the U.S. flag during the battle for Iwo Jima.

- **Gravelly Point:** This is a popular spot for watching airplanes take off and land at National Airport. If you have a boat, put it in the Potomac here and view Washington's landmarks from the water.

The parkway also provides access to Arlington National Cemetery (see Chapter 11 for details), Mount Vernon (see Chapter 14), and Theodore Roosevelt Island (see earlier in this chapter). At Alexandria, the parkway runs through the city as Washington Street.

From D.C., drive west on Constitution Avenue and continue straight across the Theodore Roosevelt Memorial Bridge to the George Washington Memorial Parkway (northbound). Or drive west on Independence Avenue; as you pass the Lincoln Memorial, watch closely for signs to the Arlington Memorial Bridge. After you cross the bridge, turn right out of the traffic circle and then exit left to continue southbound or go straight to go northbound. The southbound route also is marked to National Airport.

 Do not sight-see along the parkway during rush hour. This road is a major commuter artery on weekdays. Drive here on the weekend or from mid-morning until mid-afternoon during the week. Also note: Some spots are accessible only from the northbound or southbound lanes.

Rock Creek Park

This marvelous urban park (☎ **202-895-6070;** www.nps.gov/rocr; e-mail: ROCR_superintendent@nps.gov; mailing address: 3545 Williamsburg Lane NW, Washington, DC 20008) winds its way from the Potomac River near the Kennedy Center all the way up to D.C.'s most northern tip. Write, phone, or e-mail the park headquarters before your visit to request a map/brochure. In the park, you can find information desks and activities at the following locations:

- ✔ The **Nature Center** (5200 Glover Rd. NW, south of Military Road; www.nps.gov/rocr/naturecenter) is open Wednesday through Sunday from 9 a.m. to 5 p.m. and is closed Thanksgiving, December 25, January 1, and July 4. The Nature Center features exhibits on plants, animals, and habitats in the park. It's the starting point for guided and self-guided nature walks. The hands-on Discovery room appeals to youngsters, as does the **planeterium**'s kid-oriented shows on Wednesdays at 4 p.m. Other planeterium presentations occur Saturdays at 4 p.m. and Sundays at 1 and 4 p.m. Restrooms and vending machines are available.

- ✔ **Peirce Barn** (Tilden Street at Beach Drive; ☎ **202-282-0927;** www.nps.gov/rocr/piercemill) is open weekends from noon to 4 p.m. (For you sharp-eyed readers, yes, pierce is spelled differently in the Web site address than in the site's name.) Programs here tell about nearby Peirce Mill, an early 19th-century water-powered grist mill that is closed for repairs.

- ✔ The **Park Police Station** (Beach Drive, south of the Military Road overpass) is open daily from 7 a.m. to 4 p.m.

You can also ask for the Rock Creek Park brochure and map at other National Park Service sites in the Washington area.

The park offers a wide range of outdoor activities, such as hiking, horseback riding, bicycling, picnicking, golf, tennis, and boating. The Nature Center, Planetarium, and Peirce Barn conduct numerous programs for children. The 4,000-seat **Carter Barron Amphitheatre** (16th Street and Colorado Avenue NW; ☎ **202-426-0486;** www.nps.gov/rocr/cbarron) hosts numerous outdoor performances, both paid and free, including free summer concerts by the National Symphony Orchestra and free plays by the Shakespeare Theatre.

To enter the park from central D.C., drive northwest on Virginia Avenue to Rock Creek Parkway and turn right.

Rock Creek Parkway and Beach Drive are major commuter routes during workday rush hours. South of Connecticut Avenue, the parkway is one-way south from 6:30 a.m. to 9 a.m. Monday through Friday and one-way north from 3:30 p.m. to 6 p.m. those days. On weekends and holidays,

Rock Creek Park Area

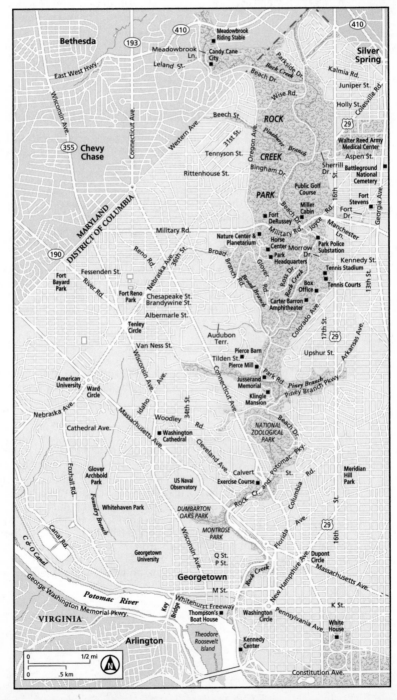

portions of Beach Drive are clogged with a different kind of traffic — bicyclists, roller bladers, walkers, and runners. The drive is closed to motor vehicles from Broad Branch Road to Military Road, from Picnic Grove 10 to Wise Road, and from West Beach Drive to the D.C.-Maryland border from 7 a.m. to 7 p.m. on holidays and from 7 a.m. Saturday until 7 p.m. Sunday on weekends.

Mount Vernon, Alexandria, and Annapolis

The tenth part in this Part of Tens actually is comprised of three places that I discuss in detail in Chapter 14. I'm mentioning them here because they're prime destinations for drives.

To drive to **Alexandria** (see Chapter 14), go west on Independence Avenue. As you pass the Lincoln Memorial, watch closely for signs to Arlington Memorial Bridge. After you cross the bridge, turn right out of the traffic circle and then exit left almost immediately, following signs to National Airport. After the parkway becomes Washington Street in Alexandria, turn left on King Street, which goes all the way to the water-front. To preserve normal blood pressure, I suggest parking in a lot or garage rather than hunting for at-a-premium street parking. Assuming that you're from out of town, you can get **free 24-hour parking** permits at the **Ramsay House Visitors Center** (221 King St., east of Fairfax Street; ☎ **703-838-4200;** www.funside.com).

Don't drive the parkway during rush hour.

To drive to **Mount Vernon** (see Chapter 14), follow the preceding directions for Alexandria, but keep going straight. The parkway ends in George's front yard.

To drive to **Annapolis** (see Chapter 14), go east on New York Avenue, which is U.S. 50, and follow 50 all the way. As you approach Annapolis, take Exit 24, Rowe Boulevard. Continue about 1 mile, hang a right at the governor's mansion, and go halfway around Church Circle. Take a right at the Maryland Inn (Duke of Gloucester Street) and follow signs to Main Street, City Dock, and the Historic District. Tune your radio to **1620 AM** as you approach the city for warnings about **parking** during special events. On-street parking is 50 cents an hour from 10 a.m. to 7:30 p.m. daily with a two-hour max. Smart drivers park in garages or at the Navy-Marine Corps Stadium (Rowe Boulevard and Taylor Avenue), where downtown shuttles run from 6:30 a.m. to 7 p.m. on weekdays October through May and from 10 a.m. to 6 p.m. on weekends as well the rest of the year.

Appendix

Quick Concierge

Fast Facts

AAA

The most centrally located AAA office is at 701 15th St. NW, between G and H streets (☎ 202-331-3000). For emergency road service, call ☎ 800-222-4357 or 703-222-5000.

American Express

An American Express Travel Service office is located downtown at 1150 Connecticut Ave. NW, between L and M streets (☎ 202-457-1300). Open Monday through Friday, 9 a.m. to 5:30 p.m.

Area Codes

If you're calling a D.C. number from outside D.C., dial **202**. If you're in D.C. and calling D.C., no area code is needed. Dial **703** for suburban Virginia. For most close-in Maryland suburbs, dial **301**. Annapolis is **410**.

ATMs

It's hard to walk a block in D.C. without encountering an ATM. They're located in or near hotels, restaurants, attractions, and Metro stations. Most, if not all, banks have them. For specific locations, call Cirrus (☎ 800-424-7787) or Plus (☎ 800-843-7587), depending upon which network is listed on your ATM card, or consult www.visa.com or www.master card.com.

Baby Sitters

Many hotels will secure a bonded sitter for your brood. Ask the concierge or at the front desk. White House Nannies (☎ 301-652-8088; www.whitehouse nannies.com) sends sitters to hotels on short notice.

Business Hours

D.C. banks tend to be open from 9 a.m. to 3 p.m. Monday through Friday, with many branches staying open till 5 p.m. Friday and some opening on Saturday morning. It's really impossible to talk about typical hours for stores anymore. Most will open by 10 a.m. and not close before 5 p.m. Monday through Friday Many are open into the evening and on Saturday, and some open Sunday afternoon. You'll tend to find more stores open at night in areas with substantial night life, such as Georgetown.

Camera Repair

If your shutter won't shut, head to Pro Photo, 1902 I St. NW (☎ 202-223-1292), or Penn Camera Exchange, 915 E St. NW (☎ 202-347-5777) and 1015 18th St. NW (☎ 202-785-7366).

Congress

Call the Capitol switchboard to locate a senator (☎ 202-224-3121) or member of the House (☎ 202-225-3121).

Convention Center

The new Washington Convention Center (☎ 800-368-9000 or 202-249-3000) occupies the area between N, K, 7th, and 9th streets NW.

Credit Cards

If your card is lost or stolen, call American Express (☎ 800-221-7282), MasterCard (☎ 800-307-7309), or Visa (☎ 800-847-2911). To obtain the phone number for other cards, call the toll-free information operator at ☎ 800-555-1212.

Dentists

In a dental emergency, call the District of Columbia Dental Society Referral Service at ☎ 202-547-7615.

Doctors

Ask your hotel's concierge or the front desk for the name of a physician who treats hotel guests. Or try the physicians referral services at George Washington University Hospital (☎ 888-449-3627), Washington Hospital Center (☎ 202-877-3627), or Georgetown University Hospital (☎ 202-342-2400).

Emergencies

For police, fire, and ambulance, call ☎ 911. The 24-hour poison control hotline is ☎ 202-625-3333. To contact the police when it's not an emergency, dial ☎ 202-727-1010.

Hospitals

For life-threatening emergencies, call ☎ 911. For emergency-room treatment, contact one of the following hospitals: Children's National Medical Center (111 Michigan Ave. NW, at 1st Street, about 2.5 miles due north of the Capitol;☎ 202-884-5000); George Washington University

Hospital, 900 23rd St. NW, at I Street Downtown (☎ 202-715-4911); Georgetown University Hospital, 3800 Reservoir Rd. NW, at 38th Street in Georgetown(☎ 202-784-2119); or Sibley Hospital, 5255 Loughboro Rd. NW, between MacArthur Boulevard and Dalecarla Parkway in Upper Northwest (☎ 202-537-4080). If you have a car, an emergency is not the time to drive in D.C. In life-threatening circumstances, call 911 for an ambulance. Otherwise, I suggest you take a taxi.

Hotlines

For help with a wide range of problems, call the Answers Please information and referral service (☎ 202-463-6211) or the D.C. Mental Health Department Access Help Line (☎ 202-561-7000). Other hotlines include the House of Ruth Domestic Violence Hotline (☎ 202-347-2777), the Alcohol and Drug Referral Network (☎ 888-304-9797), the D.C. Rape Crisis Center (☎ 202-333-7273), and the Poison Control Center (☎ 800-222-1222).

Information

For tourist information, contact the Washington, D.C. Convention and Tourism Corp., 1212 New York Ave. NW (☎ 800-422-8644; www.washington.org). For D.C. telephone directory information, dial ☎ 411; for telephone numbers outside the Washington area, dial the area code plus 555-1212. See the "Where to Get More Information" section later in this chapter.

Internet Access and Cybercafes

Check your e-mail at Kramerbooks & Afterwords Café (1517 Connecticut Ave. NW, just above Dupont Circle; ☎ 202-387-1400) or at any D.C. public library: Martin Luther King, Jr. Library (901 G St. NW, at 9th Street Downtown; ☎ 202-727-0321); West End Branch (1101 24th St. NW, at L

Street; ☎ 202-724-8707); **Georgetown Branch** (3260 R St. NW, at Wisconsin Avenue; ☎ 202-282-0220); and **Southeast Branch** (403 7th St. SE, at D Street on Capitol Hill, ☎ 202-698-3377). Call for hours, which vary.

Liquor Laws

You must be 21 to drink in D.C. Restaurants and bars can serve alcohol Sunday through Thursday from 9 a.m. to 2 a.m. and Friday and Saturday from 9 a.m. to 3 a.m. Retail stores can sell beer, wine, and liquor from 9 a.m. to 10 p.m. Monday through Saturday. Beer and wine can be sold Sunday as well.

Maps

Free city maps are available at many hotels and tourist sites and at the Washington Visitor Information Center, on the ground floor of the Ronald Reagan International Trade Center Building, 1300 Pennsylvania Ave. NW, between 13th and 14th streets (☎ **866-324-7386** or 202-328-4748; www.dcvisit.com).

Pharmacies

CVS pharmacies abound in Washington. It seems like you can find one on every corner. To locate the nearest one to you, call ☎ **888-607-4287** or click the Store Finder link at www.cvs.com. CVS 24-hour pharmacies are located at 2200 M St. NW, west of 22nd Street downtown (☎ **202-296-9876**); 4555 Wisconsin Ave. NW, between Albemarle and Brandywine streets in Upper Northwest (☎ **202-537-1587**); and on the western side of Dupont Circle (☎ **202-785-1466**). Rite Aid is another 24-hour pharmacy, at 1815 Connecticut Ave. NW, 2½ long blocks north of the Dupont Circle Metro's Q Street exit (☎ **202-332-1718**; www.riteaid.com).

Police

In case of emergency, dial ☎ **911**. To locate the nearest police station or for non-emergency business, call ☎ **202-727-1010**.

Post Office

For the nearest Post Office, ask at your hotel's front desk or call ☎ **800-275-8777**. For Zip code information, call the same number.

Radio Stations

Some of Washington's top AM radio stations are WABS, 780, Christian; WMAL, 630, news/talk/entertainment; WOL, 1450, urban talk; WPGC, 1580, gospel; WTEM, 980, sports; WTOP, 1500, news; WYCB, 1340, gospel. Among the top FM stations are WAMU, 88.5, NPR; WARW, 94.7, classic rock; WASH, 97.1, soft rock; WBIG, 100.3, oldies; WCSP, 90.1, C-SPAN; WETA, 90.9, NPR; WGMS, 103.5, classical; WHFS, 99.1, rock; WJFK, 106.7, talk; WJZW, 105.9, smooth jazz; WKYS, 93.9, urban hits; WMMJ, 102.3, urban adult contemporary; WMZQ, 98.7, country; WPFW, 89.3, Pacifica; WPGC-FM, 95.5, hip-hop/go-go/ R & B; and WWDC, 101.1, alternative rock.

Restrooms

One of the great things about being a tourist in Washington is that you're never far from clean, safe, and free restrooms — a particular benefit when you're traveling with young children. You can find them in all the government buildings, all the Smithsonian museums, the major monuments, and the larger food courts. One place you won't find them easily is inside the Metrorail system. In a truly extreme emergency, ask a Metrorail station attendant to let you use the station facility. Most stations have restrooms that are supposed to be available to the public on request, but Metrorail resists wide use.

Safety

Especially with heightened security around federal facilities these days, the major tourist areas and Metrorail are quite safe for walking and sightseeing. At night, use the buddy system and stick to the well-lighted, heavily trafficked, main commercial blocks. If Metrorail's service has stopped for the day and you're still out, take a taxi. Know your destination before you set out. Hold your kids' hands on city streets and sidewalks, on all Metro escalators, and on Metro platforms. Lock your hotel room door, car doors, and trunk. Don't leave luggage or other items visible in your car when you leave it. Lock valuables in a safe deposit box (if not in your room, at the front desk). Keep a tight hold on your pocketbook and camera. Hold onto your purse in a restaurant. Carry your cash and credit cards in a front pocket or a concealed money pouch. Leave the family jewels at home; what you do bring, don't flash.

Smoking

Most restaurants have smoking and non-smoking sections. State your preference when you reserve or when you meet the host or hostess. For a list of completely smokefree restaurants, visit www.smoke freedc.org.

Taxes

Sales tax on merchandise is 5.75 percent in D.C., 5 percent in Maryland, and 4.5 percent in Virginia. The restaurant taxes are 10 percent in D.C., 5 percent in Maryland, and 4.5 percent in Virginia. The hotel sales taxes are 14.5 percent in D.C., 5 percent (plus another 5 to 7 percent local or city tax) in Maryland, and about 10 percent in Virginia.

Taxis

D.C. taxis don't have meters. You're charged according to the zones you travel through — $5.50 within one zone, $7.60 for two, and so on. See Chapter 4 for a more detailed explanation of this complicated fare system. Washington cabs usually are easy to hail on the street. When I need to order a cab, I call **Diamond** (☎ **202-387-6200,** 202-797-5916, 202-797-5915, or, for airport service, 202-387-2600).

Time Zone

Washington is in the eastern time zone. For the correct time, dial ☎ **202-844-2525.**

Transit Info

For Metrorail (subway) and Metrobus information, call ☎ **202-637-7000** or visit the Metro Web site, www.wmata.com.

Weather

For the D.C. weather forecast, call ☎ **202-936-1212,** listen to WTOP 1500 am "on the 8s" (8 after the hour, 18 after, and so on), watch the Weather Channel, or surf over to www.weather.com.

Toll-Free Numbers and Web Sites

Airlines

Aer Lingus
☎ 800-474-7424
www.aerlingus.com

Aeroflot
☎ 888-86-4949
www.aeroflot.com

Air Canada
☎ 888-247-2262
www.aircanada.ca

Air Canada Jazz
☎ 888-247-2262
www.flyjazz.ca

Air France
☎ 800-237-2747
www.airfrance.com

Air Jamaica
☎ 800-523-5585
www.airjamaica.com

AirTran
☎ 800-247-8726
www.airtran.com

Alaska Airlines
☎ 800-252-7522
www.Alaskaair.com

Alitalia
☎ 800-223-5730
www.alitalia.it

American Airlines
☎ 800-433-7300
www.aa.com

America West Airlines
☎ 800-235-9292
www.americawest.com

ANA
☎ 800-235-9262
www.fly-ana.com

ATA
☎ 800-225-2995
www.ata.com

Austrian Airlines
☎ 800-843-0002
www.aua.com

BMI
☎ 800-788-0555
www.flybmi.com

British Airways
☎ 800-247-9297
www.british-airways.com

BWIA
☎ 800-538-2942
www.bwee.com

Continental Airlines
☎ 800-525-0280
www.continental.com

Delta Air Lines
☎ 800-221-1212
www.delta.com

Ethiopian Airlines
☎ 800-445-2733
www.flyethiopian.com

Frontier Airlines
☎ 800-432-1359
www.flyfrontier.com

Hooters Air
☎ 888-359-4668
www.hootersair.com

Icelandair
☎ 800-223-5500
www.icelandair.com

Independence Air
800-359-3594
www.flyi.com

Jet Blue
☎ 800-538-2583
www.jetblue.com

KLM Royal Dutch Airlines
☎ 800-374-7747
www.klm.com/nl_en

Korean Air
☎ 800-438-5000
www.koreanair.com

Lloyd Aereo Boliviano
☎703-572-6532
www.labairlines.com/index_eng.
asp

Lufthansa
☎ 800-645-3880
www.lufthansa.com

Midwest
☎ 800-452-2022
www.midwestairlines.com

Northwest Airlines
☎ 800-225-2525
www.nwa.com

SAS
☎ 800-221-2350
www.scandinavian.net

Saudi Arabian Airlines
☎ 800-472-8342
www.saudiairlines.com

Southwest Airlines
☎ 800-435-9792
www.southwest.com

Spirit
☎ 800-772-7117
www.spiritair.com

TACA
☎ 800-535-8780
www.taca.com

Ted
☎ 800-225-5833
www.flyted.com

United Airlines
☎ 800-864-8331
www.ual.com

US Airways
☎ 800-428-4322
www.usairways.com

USA 3000
☎ 800-872-3000
www.usa3000airlines.com

Virgin-Atlantic
☎ 800-862-8621
www.virgin-atlantic.com

Major hotel and motel chains

Best Western International
☎ 800-780-7234
www.bestwestern.com

Comfort Inns
☎ 800-228-5150
www.hotelchoice.com

Courtyard by Marriott
☎ 800-321-2211
www.courtyard.com

Days Inn
☎ 800-325-2525
www.daysinn.com

Doubletree Hotels
☎ 800-222-8733
www.doubletree.com

Econo Lodge
☎ 877-553-2666
www.hotelchoice.com

Fairfield Inn by Marriott
☎ 800-228-2800
www.fairfieldinn.com

Four Seasons Hotels and Resorts
☎ 800-819-5053
www.fourseasons.com

Hampton Inn
☎ 800-426-7866
www.hampton-inn.com

Hilton Hotels
☎ 800-HILTONS (445-8667)
www.hilton.com

Holiday Inn
☎ 800-HOLIDAY (465-4329)
www.holiday-inn.com

Howard Johnson
☎ 800-654-2000
www.hojo.com

Hyatt Hotels and Resorts
☎ 800-228-9000
www.hyatt.com

Inter-Continental
☎ 888-567-8725
www.interconti.com

Marriott Hotels
☎ 800-228-9290
www.marriott.com

Motel 6
☎ 800-466-8356
www.motel6.com

Quality Inns and Resorts
☎ 800-228-5151
www.hotelchoice.com

Radisson Hotels International
☎ 800-333-3333
www.radisson.com

Ramada Inn
☎ 800-272-6232
www.ramada.com

Red Roof Inn
☎ 800-843-7663
www.redroof.com

Renaissance Hotels and Resorts
☎ 800-228-9290
www.renaissancehotels.com

Residence Inn by Marriott
☎ 800-331-3131
www.residenceinn.com

Ritz-Carlton
☎ 800-241-3333
www.ritzcarlton.com

Sheraton Hotels and Resorts
☎ 800-325-3535
www.sheraton.com

Super 8
☎ 800-800-8000
www.super8.com

Travelodge
☎ 800-255-3050
www.travelodge.com

Westin Hotels
☎ 800-937-8461
www.westin.com

Wyndham
☎ 800-822-4200
www.wyndham.com

Major car-rental agencies

Alamo
☎ 800-327-9633
www.goalamo.com

Avis
☎ 800-831-1212
www.avis.com

Budget
☎ 800-527-0700
www.budgetrentacar.com

Dollar
☎ 800-800-4000
www.dollarcar.com

Enterprise
☎ 800-325-8007
www.pickenterprise.com

Hertz
☎ 800-654-3131
www.hertz.com

National
☎ 800-CAR-RENT (227-7368)
www.nationalcar.com

Thrifty
☎ 800-367-2277
www.thrifty.com

Where to Get More Information

If I haven't packed enough information into this book for you, you can consult the following resources for additional details.

Tourist information offices

✔ Call or write the **Washington, D.C., Convention and Tourism Corp**. (1212 New York Ave. NW; ☎ 800-422-8644; www.washington.org) and ask for a free copy of the *Washington, D.C., Visitors Guide,* which contains information about visitor services, hotels, restaurants, sights, transportation, and tours. The organization's Web site contains lots of info and updates you on events.

✔ Visit the Washington, D.C. Web site at www.dcvisit.com. Another site stuffed with current information for visitors to Washington, this one's produced by the **D.C. Chamber of Commerce.** Useful links take you to information on transportation providers, attractions, reservation services, and the like.

Newspapers and magazines

✔ You can find *The Washington Post* online at www.washingtonpost.com. The Web site provides up-to-the-minute news, weather, visitor information, restaurant reviews, and online discussions of various subjects. About halfway down the right side of the home page, click Visitors Guide for voluminous information about attractions, lodging, and nightspots, as well as restaurant reviews. The Entertainment Guide, about halfway down the left side of the home page, contains additional information of use to tourists.

✔ For another informed perspective on all those things visitors like to know about a city, visit the Web site of *Washingtonian,* D.C.'s leading local magazine (www.washingtonian.com). At the upper left of the home page are links to reviews of restaurants, entertainment venues, and other useful topics. Check out *Washingtonian's* lists of D.C.'s 100 best restaurants and the 100 best places to get an inexpensive meal. You can also access a museum guide and "What's Happening," which is a monthly tip sheet to what's going on at museums and theaters.

Other sources of information

✔ Go to the Web site www.nps.gov/parks.html to access the **National Park Service Guide.** You can find detailed information about all National Park Service sites, as well as individual listings for sites in the Washington area by name (Washington Monument, Lincoln Memorial). You can also find Washington's sites grouped in listings for National Capital Parks Central, National Capital Parks East, and National Mall.

✔ If you're looking for information about **National and Dulles airports**, go to the Web site www.metwashairports.com. It contains everything you want to know about flight schedules, flight status, ground transportation, terminal maps, and airport facilities.

✔ Visit the **Smithsonian Institution Web** site at www.si.edu to plan your visits to the Smithsonian museums — or to take a tour without setting foot in D.C. This Web site contains links to all the museums' Web sites, basic information about directions, hours, and facilities, and lots of online exhibits.

✔ At the **Washington Metropolitan Area Transit Authority** Web site (www.wmata.com), you can find timetables, maps, fare schedules, and more information useful to riders of Washington's **buses** and **subway.**

✔ I particularly like the online **map of the area around each Metrorail station** that you can find at stationmasters.com. Click System Map on the left side of the home page and then click the station you're interested in.

Index

See also separate Accommodations and Restaurant indexes at the end of this index.

General Index

• A •

AAA office, 309
AARP, 60
Above and Beyond Tours, 66
Abraham Lincoln's Birthday, 27
Access-Able Travel Source, 62
accessibility issues, 62–64
accommodations. *See also*
    Accommodations Index
  Alexandria, Virginia, 257
  best, 10–11
  cost of, 3, 38, 108
  gay-friendly, 66
  hotel and motel chains, 314–315
  with kitchen, 40, 58–59
  by location, 125
  map of, 102–103
  Metrorail service and, 53
  by price, 124–125
  rate, finding best, 101, 104–105
  restaurants in, 127
  room, reserving best, 106–107
Acela Express, 53
Adams-Morgan neighborhood
  description of, 83
  nightlife, 284
  restaurants, 130, 131
  shopping, 39, 235–236
Aielli, Fabrizio (chef-owner), 163
airfare, 50–52

airlines
  contact information, 312–314
  security issues, 74–76
  serving Baltimore-Washington
    International Airport, 50
  serving Ronald Reagan
    Washington National
    Airport, 48
  serving Washington Dulles
    International Airport, 49
Airport Car Service, 45
airports
  Baltimore-Washington
    International Airport, 49–50
  Ronald Reagan Washington
    National, 47–48, 75
  Washington-Dulles International,
    48–49
  Web sites, 46, 317
A.L. Goodies General Store, 262
Alexandria Archaeology
    Museum, 254
Alexandria, Virginia
  accommodations, 257
  attractions, 252–253
  driving to, 308
  history of, 17
  map of, 250
  Old Town, 249
  restaurants, 255–257
  shopping, 254–255
  tours, 251–252
  transportation to, 249, 251

Accommodations Index

BUSINESS, CAREERS & PERSONAL FINANCE

0-7645-5307-0

0-7645-5331-3 *†

Also available:
- ✔Accounting For Dummies †
  0-7645-5314-3
- ✔Business Plans Kit For Dummies †
  0-7645-5365-8
- ✔Cover Letters For Dummies
  0-7645-5224-4
- ✔Frugal Living For Dummies
  0-7645-5403-4
- ✔Leadership For Dummies
  0-7645-5176-0
- ✔Managing For Dummies
  0-7645-1771-6

- ✔Marketing For Dummies
  0-7645-5600-2
- ✔Personal Finance For Dummies *
  0-7645-2590-5
- ✔Project Management
  For Dummies
  0-7645-5283-X
- ✔Resumes For Dummies †
  0-7645-5471-9
- ✔Selling For Dummies
  0-7645-5363-1
- ✔Small Business Kit For Dummies *†
  0-7645-5093-4

HOME & BUSINESS COMPUTER BASICS

0-7645-4074-2

0-7645-3758-X

Also available:
- ✔ACT! 6 For Dummies
  0-7645-2645-6
- ✔iLife '04 All-in-One Desk Reference
  For Dummies
  0-7645-7347-0
- ✔iPAQ For Dummies
  0-7645-6769-1
- ✔Mac OS X Panther Timesaving
  Techniques For Dummies
  0-7645-5812-9
- ✔Macs For Dummies
  0-7645-5656-8
- ✔Microsoft Money 2004 For Dummies
  0-7645-4195-1

- ✔Office 2003 All-in-One Desk
  Reference For Dummies
  0-7645-3883-7
- ✔Outlook 2003 For Dummies
  0-7645-3759-8
- ✔PCs For Dummies
  0-7645-4074-2
- ✔TiVo For Dummies
  0-7645-6923-6
- ✔Upgrading and Fixing PCs
  For Dummies
  0-7645-1665-5
- ✔Windows XP Timesaving
  Techniques For Dummies
  0-7645-3748-2

FOOD, HOME, GARDEN, HOBBIES, MUSIC & PETS

0-7645-5295-3

0-7645-5232-5

Also available:
- ✔Bass Guitar For Dummies
  0-7645-2487-9
- ✔Diabetes Cookbook For Dummies
  0-7645-5230-9
- ✔Gardening For Dummies *
  0-7645-5130-2
- ✔Guitar For Dummies
  0-7645-5106-X
- ✔Holiday Decorating For Dummies
  0-7645-2570-0
- ✔Home Improvement All-in-One
  For Dummies
  0-7645-5680-0

- ✔Knitting For Dummies
  0-7645-5395-X
- ✔Piano For Dummies
  0-7645-5105-1
- ✔Puppies For Dummies
  0-7645-5255-4
- ✔Scrapbooking For Dummies
  0-7645-7208-3
- ✔Senior Dogs For Dummies
  0-7645-5818-8
- ✔Singing For Dummies
  0-7645-2475-5
- ✔30-Minute Meals For Dummies
  0-7645-2589-1

INTERNET & DIGITAL MEDIA

0-7645-1664-7

0-7645-6924-4

Also available:
- ✔2005 Online Shopping Directory
  For Dummies
  0-7645-7495-7
- ✔CD & DVD Recording For Dummies
  0-7645-5956-7
- ✔eBay For Dummies
  0-7645-5654-1
- ✔Fighting Spam For Dummies
  0-7645-5965-6
- ✔Genealogy Online For Dummies
  0-7645-5964-8
- ✔Google For Dummies
  0-7645-4420-9

- ✔Home Recording For Musicians
  For Dummies
  0-7645-1634-5
- ✔The Internet For Dummies
  0-7645-4173-0
- ✔iPod & iTunes For Dummies
  0-7645-7772-7
- ✔Preventing Identity Theft
  For Dummies
  0-7645-7336-5
- ✔Pro Tools All-in-One Desk
  Reference For Dummies
  0-7645-5714-9
- ✔Roxio Easy Media Creator
  For Dummies
  0-7645-7131-1

* Separate Canadian edition also available

† Separate U.K. edition also available

Available wherever books are sold. For more information or to order direct: U.S. customers
visit www.dummies.com or call 1-877-762-2974.
U.K. customers visit www.wileyeurope.com or call 0800 243407. Canadian customers visit
www.wiley.ca or call 1-800-567-4797.

SPORTS, FITNESS, PARENTING, RELIGION & SPIRITUALITY

0-7645-5146-9

0-7645-5418-2

Also available:

- Adoption For Dummies
  0-7645-5488-3
- Basketball For Dummies
  0-7645-5248-1
- The Bible For Dummies
  0-7645-5296-1
- Buddhism For Dummies
  0-7645-5359-3
- Catholicism For Dummies
  0-7645-5391-7
- Hockey For Dummies
  0-7645-5228-7

- Judaism For Dummies
  0-7645-5299-6
- Martial Arts For Dummies
  0-7645-5358-5
- Pilates For Dummies
  0-7645-5397-6
- Religion For Dummies
  0-7645-5264-3
- Teaching Kids to Read
  For Dummies
  0-7645-4043-2
- Weight Training For Dummies
  0-7645-5168-X
- Yoga For Dummies
  0-7645-5117-5

TRAVEL

0-7645-5438-7

0-7645-5453-0

Also available:

- Alaska For Dummies
  0-7645-1761-9
- Arizona For Dummies
  0-7645-6938-4
- Cancún and the Yucatán
  For Dummies
  0-7645-2437-2
- Cruise Vacations For Dummies
  0-7645-6941-4
- Europe For Dummies
  0-7645-5456-5
- Ireland For Dummies
  0-7645-5455-7

- Las Vegas For Dummies
  0-7645-5448-4
- London For Dummies
  0-7645-4277-X
- New York City For Dummies
  0-7645-6945-7
- Paris For Dummies
  0-7645-5494-8
- RV Vacations For Dummies
  0-7645-5443-3
- Walt Disney World & Orlando
  For Dummies
  0-7645-6943-0

GRAPHICS, DESIGN & WEB DEVELOPMENT

0-7645-4345-8

0-7645-5589-8

Also available:

- Adobe Acrobat 6 PDF
  For Dummies
  0-7645-3760-1
- Building a Web Site For Dummies
  0-7645-7144-3
- Dreamweaver MX 2004
  For Dummies
  0-7645-4342-3
- FrontPage 2003 For Dummies
  0-7645-3882-9
- HTML 4 For Dummies
  0-7645-1995-6
- Illustrator CS For Dummies
  0-7645-4084-X

- Macromedia Flash MX 2004
  For Dummies
  0-7645-4358-X
- Photoshop 7 All-in-One Desk
  Reference For Dummies
  0-7645-1667-1
- Photoshop CS Timesaving
  Techniques For Dummies
  0-7645-6782-9
- PHP 5 For Dummies
  0-7645-4166-8
- PowerPoint 2003 For Dummies
  0-7645-3908-6
- QuarkXPress 6 For Dummies
  0-7645-2593-X

NETWORKING, SECURITY, PROGRAMMING & DATABASES

0-7645-6852-3

0-7645-5784-X

Also available:

- A+ Certification For Dummies
  0-7645-4187-0
- Access 2003 All-in-One Desk
  Reference For Dummies
  0-7645-3988-4
- Beginning Programming
  For Dummies
  0-7645-4997-9
- C For Dummies
  0-7645-7068-4
- Firewalls For Dummies
  0-7645-4048-3
- Home Networking For Dummies
  0-7645-42796

- Network Security For Dummies
  0-7645-1679-5
- Networking For Dummies
  0-7645-1677-9
- TCP/IP For Dummies
  0-7645-1760-0
- VBA For Dummies
  0-7645-3989-2
- Wireless All In-One Desk Reference
  For Dummies
  0-7645-7496-5
- Wireless Home Networking
  For Dummies
  0-7645-3910-8

HEALTH & SELF-HELP

0-7645-6820-5 *†   0-7645-2566-2

Also available:
- Alzheimer's For Dummies
  0-7645-3899-3
- Asthma For Dummies
  0-7645-4233-8
- Controlling Cholesterol For Dummies
  0-7645-5440-9
- Depression For Dummies
  0-7645-3900-0
- Dieting For Dummies
  0-7645-4149-8
- Fertility For Dummies
  0-7645-2549-2

- Fibromyalgia For Dummies
  0-7645-5441-7
- Improving Your Memory For Dummies
  0-7645-5435-2
- Pregnancy For Dummies †
  0-7645-4483-7
- Quitting Smoking For Dummies
  0-7645-2629-4
- Relationships For Dummies
  0-7645-5384-4
- Thyroid For Dummies
  0-7645-5385-2

EDUCATION, HISTORY, REFERENCE & TEST PREPARATION

0-7645-5194-9   0-7645-4186-2

Also available:
- Algebra For Dummies
  0-7645-5325-9
- British History For Dummies
  0-7645-7021-8
- Calculus For Dummies
  0-7645-2498-4
- English Grammar For Dummies
  0-7645-5322-4
- Forensics For Dummies
  0-7645-5580-4
- The GMAT For Dummies
  0-7645-5251-1
- Inglés Para Dummies
  0-7645-5427-1

- Italian For Dummies
  0-7645-5196-5
- Latin For Dummies
  0-7645-5431-X
- Lewis & Clark For Dummies
  0-7645-2545-X
- Research Papers For Dummies
  0-7645-5426-3
- The SAT I For Dummies
  0-7645-7193-1
- Science Fair Projects For Dummies
  0-7645-5460-3
- U.S. History For Dummies
  0-7645-5249-X

Get smart @ dummies.com®

- Find a full list of Dummies titles
- Look into loads of FREE on-site articles
- Sign up for FREE eTips e-mailed to you weekly
- See what other products carry the Dummies name
- Shop directly from the Dummies bookstore
- Enter to win new prizes every month!

---

* Separate Canadian edition also available
† Separate U.K. edition also available

Available wherever books are sold. For more information or to order direct: U.S. customers visit www.dummies.com or call 1-877-762-2974.
U.K. customers visit www.wileyeurope.com or call 0800 243407. Canadian customers visit www.wiley.ca or call 1-800-567-4797.